The New
GOOD OLD INDEX

The New
GOOD OLD INDEX

William D. Goodrich

Gasogene Press, Ltd.
Dubuque, Iowa

Copyright © 1987, 1994 by William D. Goodrich. All rights reserved

ISBN 0-938501-20-8

No part of this publication may be reproduced, stored in a retrieval system, or transmitted, in any form or by any means, electronic, mechanical, photocopying, recording, or otherwise, without the prior written permission of the author and publisher.

Printed in the United States of America

10 9 8 7 6 5 4 3 2 1

For Mary

Author's Preface

I began work on *Good Old Index* many years ago because Jay Finley Christ's *Irregular Guide* was no longer available, and I needed an expanded reference keyed to the Doubleday single volume edition.

The format of this *New Good Old Index* is quite similar to that of Dr. Christ and his universal story title abbreviations have been retained and are listed following the subject summary. Most names, objects, places, and so forth, may be found in alphabetical order. Separate sections are included for Holmes, Watson, and 221B. An analysis of the general subject contents page that follows will give an idea of the organization. An effort has been made to cross reference but, when in doubt, an item has been included at several different points. Thus, Colonel Sir James Damery will be found alphabetically under Damery, but also under Names, both given name and surname, as well as under the categories of Knighthood and Army personnel.

Dr. Christ's *Guide* provided the basis for *New Good Old Index*. The *Encyclopedias* of Park and Tracy provided much help. Other Sherlockians whose published lists I have used as check points include Dakin, Ewing & Patrick, Dettman & Bedford, Redmond, and, of course, Edgar W. Smith.

William D. Goodrich

Introduction

This is, in a special way, an important book; a book that is needed; a book that will be hailed as an indispensible tool. If the reader has examined the contents of this volume in a cursory manner, he will wonder why I use such praise and exhibit such enthusiasm to introduce it. That is elementary!

Christopher Morley speaking of the large body of scholarly writing which has been done and published and avidly read about Mr. Sherlock Holmes and his world paraphrased Winston Churchill and said, "Never has so much been written by so many for so few." And it remains so some forty years later. There are some twenty-five, more or less, periodicals including at least five of superior professional quality, devoted to the study of The Great Detective. Each year a dozen or so books are published and plays, films, TV and radio shows continue to be produced and all relating to some aspect of Holmes. I do not include the many facile and contrived pastiches that well up each year.

Holmesian scholars have a two volume bibliography, an atlas, several in-depth commentaries, books of quotations, an almanac and an encyclopaedia. There are some seven published chronologies, a biography of Holmes, of Watson and of Moriarty . . . and much more. But until now there has not been such a reference as this. And what is it? Perhaps one could call this a concordance or a compendium although Bill Goodrich dubbed it *Good Old Index*. The title matters not, it is what we want.

*□ *Introduction*

Let me demonstrate how the book works: being humble I decided to look up my name 'John.' The first Johns were "John the butler," "John the coachman," "John Bull," and "John o'Groats." I proved that the index worked but I didn't pursue the personal nomenclatural exercise further. However, I should add that also included in each reference is information as to the Holmesian story in which the word appeared and a page number. This page number is keyed to the well-used *Complete Sherlock Holmes* published by Doubleday.

Twenty years ago, I staged an exhibition "The One Hundred Basic Sherlockian Books," which included books and pamphlets that I thought should be in every Holmesian's library. Later I issued this list as an ephemeral publication for friends with the title "The Basic Holmesian Library." Since then I have revised the list a number of times as there have been new publications or revisions of older works that must be included. In the case of the Goodrich book, it will go into the next version of my list as *the* concordance.

This much needed reference work is going to be on the desk of every Sherlockian scholar. It will be essential to essayists, biographers, crossword puzzle devisers, speechmakers, and even, one fears, to pastiche perpetrators.

Bill Goodrich is typical of the true Sherlockian. He is a businessman, a husband, a father, a house-holder, a taxpayer, a book collector, and withal he appears quite sane. But more so he has imagination and energy and is creative in his reading and in his research. He saw a real need, a void in fact, in the specialized world of Holmesian studies. He fills this need most satisfactorily with this book.

John Bennett Shaw, BSI
Santa Fe, New Mexico
1987

Primary Subject Contents

Ailments, illnesses
Alcoholic beverages
Aliases used
Aliases taken by
Animals
Animal imagery
Army personnel, units

Baker Street, 221B
    Furnishings
    Meals
    Rooms
    Watson in residence
    Weather
Beards, whiskers, moustaches
Business firms

Cabs, carriages, carts
Churches
Cities
Clients
Clothing
Clubs
Coins and currency

Counties, English
Criminals

Death, manner of
Detectives
Doctors

Food

Geographical locations

Holmes, Sherlock
    Disguises
    Dress
    Habits
    Knowledge
    Manner
    Methods
    Physical appearance
    Quotations
    Rewards
    Smoking
    Writings
Hotels

Jewels

Knighthood

Lamps and lanterns
Literary references
London bridges
London districts
London streets

Names, personal—Given
Names, personal—Surnames
Newspapers
Newspaper headlines

Peerage
Poisons
Police forces
Profanity

Railway journeys
Railway stations
Reported cases referred to
Residences and occupants
Rivers
Royalty

Scenes of investigations
Schools
Scotland Yard
Seasons of cases
Servants
Ships and boats
Sports and games
States, U.S.

Telegrams
Tobacco
Trees

Unreported cases

Vehicles

Watson, John H.
    Marriage
    Medical knowledge and practice
    Quotations
    Writings
Weapons

Christ Case Codes

ABBE	Abbey Grange	HOUN	Hound of the Baskervilles
BERY	Beryl Coronet		
BLAC	Black Peter	IDEN	A Case of Identity
BLAN	Blanched Soldier	ILLU	Illustrious Client
BLUE	Blue Carbuncle	LADY	Disappearance of Lady Frances Carfax
BOSC	Boscombe Valley Mystery		
BRUC	Bruce-Partington Plans	LAST	His Last Bow
		LION	Lion's Mane
CARD	Cardboard Box	MAZA	Mazarin Stone
CHAS	Charles Augustus Milverton	MISS	Missing Three-Quarter
COPP	Copper Beeches	MUSG	Musgrave Ritual
CREE	Creeping Man	NAVA	Naval Treaty
CROO	Crooked Man	NOBL	Noble Bachelor
DANC	Dancing Men	NORW	Norwood Builder
DEVI	Devil's Foot	PRIO	Priory School
DYIN	Dying Detective	REDC	Red Circle
EMPT	Empty House	REDH	Red-Headed League
ENGR	Engineer's Thumb	REIG	Reigate Squires
FINA	Final Problem	RESI	Resident Patient
FIVE	Five Orange Pips	RETI	Retired Colourman
GLOR	Gloria Scott	SCAN	A Scandal in Bohemia
GREE	Greek Interpreter		
GOLD	Golden Pince-Nez	SECO	Second Stain

SHOS	Shoscombe Old Place
SIGN	Sign of Four
SILV	Silver Blaze
SIXN	Six Napoleons
SOLI	Solitary Cyclist
SPEC	Speckled Band
STOC	Stock-broker's Clerk
STUD	A Study in Scarlet
SUSS	Sussex Vampire
THOR	Thor Bridge
3GAB	Three Gables
3GAR	Three Garridebs
3STU	Three Students
TWIS	Man with Twisted Lip
VALL	Valley of Fear
VEIL	Veiled Lodger
WIST	Wisteria Lodge
YELL	Yellow Face

The New
GOOD OLD INDEX

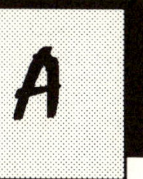

Abbas Parva	Veil	1096
Abbey, The (Westminster Abbey)	Seco	655
Abbey Grange	Abbe	636
Abbey School	Blan	1007
Abbey's accounts	Gold	608
Abbots	RedH	182
Abel White	Sign	145
Aberdeen (Scotland)	Nobl	295
Aberdeen Shipping Co.	Twis	234
Aberdonian accent	Vall	773
Abergavenny murder	Prio	539
Abernetty family	SixN	584
Abrahams, old (client)	Lady	943
Acetones	Copp	322
Achmet (merchant)	Sign	140
Acid	Stud	18
	Sign	109
	RedH	183
	Blue	249
	Engr	275
	Empt	493
	Illu	998
	Maza	1012

Acid (cont'd)
    carbolic | Card | 892
    hydrochloric | Iden | 198
    prussic | Veil | 1102
Acton, old (victim) | Reig | 398
Acushla | Vall | 823
Adair, Hilda | Empt | 483
Adair, Hon. Ronald | Empt | 483
Adams (culprit) | Gree | 437
Addleton tragedy | Gold | 607
Adelaide (Australia) | Abbe | 639
  | Lady | 947
Adelaide-Southampton | Abbe | 645
Adler, Irene "The Woman" | Scan | 161
  | Iden | 191
  | Blue | 245
  | Last | 979
    the late | Scan | 161
Admiralty | Glor | 385
  | Bruc | 916
  | Last | 973
    Lord of the | Prio | 539
A.D.P. pipe | Silv | 341
Adventuress | Scan | 165
Afghan campaign | Empt | 494
Afghan war, second | Stud | 15
Afghanistan | Stud | 17
  | Stud | 24
  | Sign | 99
  | Bosc | 202
  | Nobl | 287
  | Musg | 386
  | Reig | 398
  | Croo | 421
  | Nava | 464
Africa | Glor | 384
  | Soli | 527

Africa (cont'd)	Devi	961
	Devi	969
	Devi	970
	Blan	1000
	Veil	1097
Africa, Central	Devi	970
Africa, North	Veil	1097
Africa, South (*which see*)		
Africa, West	Devi	969
Agar, Dr. Moore	Chas	577
Agate	Sign	151
Agatha (housemaid)	Chas	577
Agony column	Sign	95
	Sign	131
	RedH	177
	Blue	249
	Engr	276
	Nobl	288
	Copp	316
	Gree	442
	Nava	457
	Soli	527
	Vall	770
	RedC	904
	Bruc	928
	Lady	948
	3Gar	1047
Agra (India)	Sign	145
Agra treasure	Sign	105
Ague	Sign	144
Ailments and diseases		
ague	Sign	144
aneurism	Stud	77
apoplexy (*see also* stroke)	Glor	377
	Croo	422

Ailments and diseases (cont'd)

asthmatic symptoms	Sign	133
	Norw	497
	3Gar	1026
black Formosa corruption	Dyin	934
brain fever	Copp	331
	Musg	389
	Croo	415
	Nava	447
	Houn	759
	Card	894
catalepsy	Resi	425
cataract	Empt	483
cold, summer	Stoc	363
consumption	Fina	478
	Miss	635
	Houn	762
Coram's	Gold	608
cough, workhouse	Sign	133
diabetes	Bosc	215
diphtheria	Glor	374
dropsy	Shos	1104
drug addiction	Twis	230
dyspnoea	Houn	677
enteric fever (*see* typhoid)	Stud	15
erysipelas	Illu	994
exhaustion	Prio	536
eyes, weak	Iden	194
	Gold	612
fainting (*which see*)		
gout	Miss	624
heart, weakness of	Stud	78
	Sign	103
	Glor	376
	Resi	426
	Houn	676

Ailments and diseases, heart, weakness | Lion | 1084
of (cont'd) | Shos | 1104
icthyosis | Blan | 1012
insanity (*see* mental illness) | Seco | 658
  | Devi | 957
  | Thor | 1067
jaundice | Glor | 383
leprosy, suspected | Blan | 1010
lumbago, suspected | Cree | 1074
meningitis, spinal, suspected | Suss | 1039
mental illness (*see* insanity) | Suss | 1040
  | Cree | 1074
nervous exhaustion | Bosc | 208
pneumonia | 3Gab | 1025
pseudo-leprosy | Blan | 1012
quinsy | Iden | 194
rheumatic fever | Lion | 1094
rheumatism   (Pref) | Last | 869
  | Lady | 942
rickets | Dyin | 937
St. Vitus's dance | Stoc | 362
Shlessinger sham | Lady | 944
scorbutic symptoms | Illu | 989
senility | Lady | 952
spinal meningitis, suspected | Suss | 1039
spine, twisted | Suss | 1037
spleen, enlarged | Sign | 102
stroke (*see also* apoplexy) | Glor | 379
Tapanuli fever | Dyin | 934
tetanus | Sign | 113
tropical diseases | Dyin | 934
typhoid (*see also* enteric fever) | Stud | 34
  | Vall | 793
yellow fever | Yell | 353
  | Houn | 681
Ainstree, Dr. | Dyin | 934
Airedale | Lion | 1090

Airgun   Fina   470
                              Empt   493
                              Maza   1014
Airplane   Last   970
Akbar, Dost   Sign   98
Albemarle Mansion   Wist   871
Albert chain   Stud   30
                              RedH   177
                              Iden   197
Albert Dock   Five   229
                              Card   897
Albert Hall   Reti   1116
Alcoholic beverages   Maza   1014
  beer   Scan   168
                              Scan   169
                              Blue   251
                              Soli   532
    half and half   Scan   168
  brandy   Sign   140
                              Five   220
                              Blue   255
                              Spec   262
                              Engr   275
                              Engr   276
                              Glor   376
                              Reig   407
                              Gree   445
                              Nava   466
                              Empt   485
                              Prio   539
                              Blac   562
                              3Stu   597
                              Seco   661
                              Houn   757
                              Houn   758
                              Vall   774

Alcoholic beverages, brandy (cont'd)

	Wist	871
	Lion	1092
and ammonia	Gree	445
and soda	Wist	871
and water	Engr	275
	Engr	276
curacao	Bruc	925
gin	Stud	80
	Twis	230
four of gin hot	Stud	34
liquor	Vall	834
rum	Blac	562
spirits	Houn	739
	Vall	826
whisky	Stud	42
	Stud	46
	Sign	132
	Sign	145
	Scan	162
	RedH	189
	Nobl	294
	Blac	562
	Vall	821
	Vall	831
	Vall	837
	Vall	843
	Vall	845
	Vall	854
	Vall	862
whisky peg	Sign	145
wine	Stud	16
	Nobl	296
	Abbe	639
	Houn	674
	Houn	736
	Houn	755

Alcoholic beverages, wine (cont'd)

	Cree	1079
	Shos	1108
ancient bottles	Nobl	296
Beaune	Sign	89
champagne	Vall	829
chianti	Sign	101
claret	Card	894
	Dyin	941
claret importer	Iden	196
comet vintage	Stoc	369
Montrachet	Veil	1098
port	Sign	135
	Glor	375
	Cree	1076
sherry (2)	Nobl	296
	Glor	383
Tokay	Sign	101
	Last	974
white	Sign	134

Aldersgate (station) — RedH 184

Aldershot — Copp 322; Croo 412

Aldgate station — Bruc 915

Aldridge — Card 897

Alexandria (Egypt) — Gold 615; 3Gar 1048

Alexis (Nihilist) — Gold 620

Algar (Liverpool police) — Card 897

Algeria — Maza 1016

Aliases (used by)

Altamont (Holmes)	Last	973
Angel, Hosmer (Windibank)	Iden	192
Barton, Dr. Hill (Watson)	Illu	995
Basil, Captain (Holmes)	Blac	559
Beddoes (Evans)	Glor	377
Black Jack of Ballarat (Turner)	Bosc	216
Blessington (Sutton)	Resi	425

Aliases (used by) (cont'd)

Boone, Hugh (St.Clair)	Twis	235
Burnett, Miss (Durando)	Wist	882
Coram, Professor (Sergius)	Gold	608
Cornelius (Oldacre)	Norw	505
Derbyshire, William (Straker)	Silv	342
Douglas, John (Edwards)	Vall	774
Escott (Holmes)	Chas	576
Evans, Carrie & Mr. (Norlett)	Shos	1105
Evans, Killer (Winter)	3Gar	1051
Ferguson (Becher)	Engr	281
Fournaye, Henri (Lucas)	Seco	659
Garrideb, John (Winter)	3Gar	1045
Hargrave (Baldwin)	Vall	803
Harris (Holmes)	Stoc	369
Henderson (Murillo)	Wist	896
Holmes, Sherlock (Stapleton)	Houn	697
Lucas (Lopez)	Wist	882
McMurdo (Edwards)	Vall	817
Montalva (Murillo)	Wist	887
Morecroft (Winter)	3Gar	1051
Morris, William (Archie)	RedH	182
Pierrot (Oberstein)	Bruc	928
Pinner (Beddington)	Stoc	365
	Stoc	366
Porlock, Fred (unknown)	Vall	769
Price (Watson)	Stoc	369
Robinson, John (Ryder)	Blue	254
Ross, Duncan (Archie)	RedH	178
Rulli (Lopez)	Wist	887
Shlessinger, Rev. (Peters)	Lady	944
Shlessinger, Mrs. (Fraser)	Lady	947
Sigerson (Holmes)	Empt	488
Spaulding (Clay)	RedH	178
Stapleton, Jack (Baskerville)	Houn	678
Stark, Colonel Lysander (Fritz)	Engr	277
Trevor (Armitage)	Glor	374

Aliases (used by) (cont'd)
    Vandeleur (Baskerville) — Houn — 753
    Von Kramm, Count (King of Bohemia) — Scan — 164
    Waldron (Prescott) — 3Gar — 1052
    Wilson, Steve (Edwards) — Vall — 858

Aliases taken by (aliases used)
    Archie (Morris, Ross) — RedH — 182
    Armitage, James (Trevor) — Glor — 374
    Baldwin, Ted (Hargrave) — Vall — 803
    Baskerville, Rodger
        (Holmes) — Houn — 678
        (Stapleton) — Houn — 697
        (Vandeleur) — Houn — 753
    Becher, Dr. (Ferguson) — Engr — 286
    Beddington (Pinner) — Stoc — 373
    Beddington (Pycroft) — Stoc — 373
    Clay, John (Spaulding) — RedH — 178
    Durando, Signnora (Burnet) — Wist — 885
    Edwards, Birdy
        (Douglas) — Vall — 774
        (McMurdo) — Vall — 817
        (Wilson) — Vall — 858
    Evans (Beddoes) — Glor — 382
    Frasier, Annie (Shlessinger) — Lady — 947
    Fritz (Stark) — Engr — 283
    Holmes, Sherlock
        (Altamont) — Last — 973
        (Basil) — Blac — 559
        (Escott) — Chas — 576
        (Harris) — Stoc — 369
        (Sigerson) — Empt — 488
    King of Bohemia (Von Kramm) — Scan — 164
    Lopez
        (Lucas) — Wist — 882
        (Rulli) — Wist — 887
    Lucas, Eduardo (Fournaye) — Seco — 659

Aliases taken by (aliases used) (cont'd)
   Murillo, Don Juan

(Henderson)	Wist	876
(Montalva)	Wist	887
Norlett, Mr. & Mrs. (Evans)	Shos	1111
Oberstein, Hugo (Pierrot)	Bruc	928
Oldacre, Jonas (Cornelius)	Norw	505
Peters, Holy (Shlessinger)	Lady	947
Prescott, Rodger (Waldron)	3Gar	1052
Ryder, James (Robinson)	Blue	254
Sergius (Coram)	Gold	619
Straker, John (Derbyshire)	Silv	342
St. Clair, Neville (Boone)	Twis	235
Sutton (Blessington)	Resi	434
Turner (Black Jack of Ballarat)	Bosc	216

   Watson, John H.

(Barton)	Illu	995
(Price)	Stoc	369
Windibank, James (Angel)	Iden	192

   Winter, James

(Evans)	3Gar	1051
(Garrideb)	3Gar	1045
(Morecroft)	3Gar	1045
Alice (maid)	Nobl	293
Alicia **(cutter)**	Thor	1054
Alienist	Cree	1074
Alison's rooms	Sign	106
Alkaloids	Stud	17
	Sign	113
Allahabad	Veil	1098
Allan Brothers' (land agents)	Wist	873
Allan Water	Vall	837
Allardyce's (butcher)	Blac	559
Allegro (theater)	Nobl	290
Allen, Mrs. (housekeeper)	Vall	781
Alley, yew	Houn	677
Almanac, Whitaker's	Vall	772

Almondy odor	Veil	1102
Almoner	Houn	734
Alpha Inn	Blue	251
Alpine-stock	Fina	479
Altamont	Last	973
Alton	Houn	692
Aluminum crutch	Musg	387
Aluminum pencil case	Silv	341
Amalgam	Engr	285
Amateur Mendicant Society	Five	218
Amati (violin)	Stud	27
Amazon River	Thor	1060
Amber		
fly in	Yell	351
pipe mouthpiece	Yell	351
	Prio	545
Amberley, Josiah	Reti	1113
Ambuscade	Nava	467
	Empt	491
	Danc	524
	Blac	585
	SixN	592
	Houn	755
	Wist	880
	Bruc	930
	3Gar	1053
American accent	Houn	700
	3Gar	1045
American backgrounds	Stud	52
	Five	219
	Nobl	289
	Yell	353
	Danc	523
	Houn	688
	Vall	780
American-British union	Nobl	300
American business principle	Vall	777

American cities (*see* Cities, U.S.)		
American Civil War	Five	226
	Resi	424
	Card	889
American clothing	Houn	685
	Vall	810
American contraction ("Abe")	Danc	523
American Encyclopaedia	Five	225
American Exchange	Stud	30
American slang	Stud	77
	Nobl	293
	Danc	524
	Houn	685
	Houn	693
	Vall	816
	Last	975
	Last	976
	3Gar	1046
	3Gar	1051
American states (*see* States, U.S.)		
Ames (butler)	Vall	781
Amethyst	Iden	191
Ammonia	Gree	445
Amoy River	Blue	249
Amputees		
Amberley, Josiah	Reti	1114
Cushing, Mary	Card	900
Fairbairn, Alec	Card	900
Hatherley, Victor	Engr	275
news-vendor	Illu	993
Prosper, Francis	Bery	310
Small, Jonathan	Sign	110
tradesman	Sign	102
Amsterdam	Maza	1020
Anarchist	SixN	588
Anatomy, study of	Stud	22
	Five	225

Anatomy, study of (cont'd)

	Houn	672
	3Gar	1048
	Cree	1072
Anchor (tatoo)	Stud	26
Anchor, Blue (pub)	Reti	1116
Ancient British barrow	Gold	607
Ancient Order of Freemen	Vall	833
Andaman Islands	Sign	95
Anderson (soldier)	Blan	1009
Anderson (constable)	Lion	1085
Anderson murders	Houn	754
Andover	Iden	196
Andrews (Scowrer)	Vall	848
Anerley Arms (inn)	Norw	500
Aneurism	Stud	77
Angel Gabriel	Veil	1107
Angel Moroni	Stud	57
Angel, Hosmer	Iden	192
Anglo American union	Nobl	300
Anglo-Indian Club	Empt	494
Anglo-Saxon race	Stud	58
Animal (*see also* Animal Imagery)		
baboon	Spec	260
badger	Sign	117
bear	Stud	72
grizzly	Stud	52
bearskin hearthrug	Prio	539
beasts	Stud	74
big game	Maza	1015
heavy game	Empt	494
bighorn sheep	Stud	72
birds	Sign	117
	Spec	271
	Copp	324
	Soli	533
	Blac	565

Animal (see also Animal Imagery),
  birds (cont'd)

aviary	Bruc	926
	Illu	992
	Norw	503
bittern	Houn	708
British Birds	Empt	485
buzzard	Stud	52
canary	Croo	416
	Blac	559
cock	Wist	879
cormorant	Veil	1095
curlew	Prio	546
	Houn	738
ducks	Glor	374
goose	Blue	245
geese	Blue	251
grouse, brace	Sign	134
ostrich feather	Silv	342
owl	Stud	69
partridge	Veil	1098
petrel, stormy	Reig	406
	Nava	448
pheasant	Nobl	296
hen	Glor	374
in preserve	Thor	1063
months	Musg	388
pigeon	Last	976
plover	Prio	546
raven	Houn	708
	Houn	745
sea birds	Lion	1090
swan	Abbe	645
whippoorwill	Stud	69
woodcock	Blue	250
	Nobl	296
bison	Stud	55
bullock	Stud	60

Animal (*see also* Animal Imagery)
 (cont'd)
  cat | | Yell | 357
  | | Norw | 503
  | | Chas | 578
  | | Last | 974
  cattle | | Stud | 60
  | | Prio | 548
  | | Houn | 699
    bullocks | | Stud | 60
    cows | | Stud | 60
  | | Prio | 548
  | | Houn | 699
  cheetah | | Spec | 260
  circus animals | | Veil | 1096
  coyote | | Stud | 52
  creatures hunted by Watson | | Sign | 138
  crocodile | | Sign | 145
    crocodile-skin hand-bag | | Danc | 520
  Cyanea Capillata (jellyfish) | | Lion | 1093
  deer's heads | | Abbe | 639
  dog | | Sign | 116
  | | Sign | 121
  | | Blue | 253
  | | Silv | 344
  | | Reig | 404
  | | Chas | 577
  | | Miss | 631
  | | Abbe | 640
    attacks owner | | Copp | 331
  | | Cree | 1072
    faithful nature | | Lion | 1089
    in night time | | Silv | 347
    native | | Sign | 145
    poisoned | | Stud | 49
  | | Suss | 1043

Animal (see also Animal Imagery), dog (cont'd)

use in detection, contemplated monograph on	Cree	1071
used by Holmes	Stud	49
	Sign	119
	Miss	633
	Shos	1109
airedale	Lion	1090
beagle	Miss	633
bloodhound	Houn	757
	Vall	852
	Cree	1071
bull pup	Stud	19
bull terrier	Glor	374
draghound	Miss	633
foxhound	Miss	633
hound	Sign	112
	Houn	674
	3Gab	1032
lurcher	Sign	117
mastiff	Copp	326
	Houn	671
	Houn	757
Newfoundland	Sign	138
	Cree	1081
sheep dog	Houn	679
sleuth-hound	Cree	1071
spaniel	Sign	117
	Houn	671
	Suss	1039
	Shos	1103
	Shos	1107
terrier	Stud	48
	Houn	671
Airedale	Lion	1090
bull terrier	Glor	374

18 ◻ Good Old Index

Animal (*see also* Animal Imagery), dog (cont'd)

wolfhound	Cree	1072
Carlo (mastiff)	Copp	326
Carlo (spaniel)	Suss	1039
Hound of the Baskervilles		
1647	Houn	673
1888	Houn	757
Pompey	Miss	633
Roy	Cree	1072
Shoscombe spaniels	Shos	1103
Toby	Sign	115
fish	Glor	374
tattoo of	RedH	177
dace	Shos	1108
deep-sea fishes	Scan	165
eel	Shos	1108
herring	Sign	112
jack (pike)	Shos	1108
pike	Houn	752
	Shos	1108
shark	Sign	127
trout	Shos	1107
in the milk	Nobl	294
fox	Houn	745
game, big	Maza	1015
heavy	Empt	494
gila	Suss	1034
grizzly bear	Stud	52
Heavy Game of the Western Himalayas	Empt	494
horse	Stud	32
	Stud	55
	Stud	65
	Stud	68
	Stud	73
	Sign	145

Animal (*see also* **Animal Imagery**), horse (cont'd)		Gree	441
		Danc	521
		Soli	534
		Prio	552
		Gold	608
		Gold	613
		Houn	675
		Houn	679
		Houn	701
		Houn	754
		Vall	851
	beauties, pair of	Scan	163
	chestnuts	Chas	573
	grays	Miss	631
		Shos	1109
	roan	Stud	60
	groomed by Holmes	Scan	168
	cab-horse	Stud	79
		Sign	99
		Scan	169
		Stoc	364
		Houn	697
		Lady	953
	carriage-horse	Scan	163
		Engr	279
		Chas	573
		Miss	631
	with brougham	Fina	474
	with dog-cart	Twis	233
	with landau	Scan	169
	with trap	Twis	240
	with van	Fina	473
	with wagonette	Houn	700
	cavalry horse	Blan	1009
	mare	Houn	674
		Houn	697

Animal (see also Animal Imagery),
  horse (cont'd)

mule		Stud	59
		Stud	68
mustang		Stud	60
pack-horse at Maiwand		Stud	15
Poncho		Stud	60
pony, lost in Grimpen Mire		Houn	707
racehorse			
	Bayard	Silv	337
	Desborough	Silv	347
	Iris	Silv	347
	Negro, The	Silv	347
	Norberton's at Grand National	Shos	1102
	Pugilist	Silv	347
	Rasper	Silv	347
	Shoscombe Prince	Shos	1103
	Shoscome Prince's half-brother	Shos	1104
	Silver Blaze	Silv	335
	Somomy (Isonomy)	Silv	336
trotter		Vall	784
ichneumon (mongoose)		Croo	421
insect			
bees		Seco	650
		Last	978
		Lion	1083
beetle		Sign	117
bug hunter (Garrideb)		3Gar	1054
butterflies and moths		3Gar	1048
	collection	Houn	758
	Cyclopides	Houn	709
	lepidoptera	Houn	711
	Vandeleur moth	Houn	762
centipedes		Sign	146
cockroaches		Copp	319
flies and bluebottles		Blac	561

Animal (*see also* Animal Imagery),
   insect (cont'd)

mosquitoes	Sign	144
scorpions	Sign	146
various insects	Copp	324
jackal	Sign	145
kid	Wist	879
lamb	Wist	879
langur (monkey)	Cree	1082
leech, red	Gold	607
lion	Devi	961
	Maza	1016
Sahara King	Veil	1097
mongoose	Croo	421
mouse	Copp	324
	Illu	988
mule	Stud	59
	Stud	68
oysters	Sign	134
	Dyin	936
pig	Blac	559
	Vall	773
rabbit		
in warren	Bosc	205
stuffed	Sign	115
presumed	Norw	510
rabbit-skin cap	Sign	105
rat, giant, of Sumatra	Suss	1034
red leech	Gold	607
seal	Blac	560
sealskin pouch	Silv	341
serpents, in the Zoo	Chas	572
sheep	Stud	60
	Silv	346
bighorn	Stud	72
moor	Prio	546
slowworm	Sign	117

Animal (*see also* **Animal Imagery**)
(cont'd)
  snake
      cobra

	Croo	421

      serpents, in the Zoo   Chas   572
      swamp adder   Spec   272
      viper   Dyin   941
                                       Suss   1034
      wiper   Sign   116
  stags' heads   Houn   702
  stoat   Sign   117
                                       Croo   416
  tiger   Empt   492
     man-eating   Empt   494
     cub   Sign   99
                                       Iden   201
     tiger skin rug   Sign   100
                                       Abbe   640
  tortoise-shell snuff box   Gree   437
  venomous lizard, or gila   Suss   1034
  weasel   Sign   115
                                       Croo   416
  whale   Blac   560
  worm, remarkable, unknown to   Thor   1055
     science

Animal footmarks   Stud   73
                                       Silv   344
                                       Croo   416
                                       Prio   548
                                       Houn   679

Animal imagery
  animal   Spec   258
                                       Glor   378
                                       Houn   725
                                       Houn   745
                                       Houn   748
     ass   Bruc   929

Animal imagery (cont'd)
bear	Vall	863
	RedC	912
beast	Bosc	217
	Five	218
	Reig	406
	Empt	488
	Blac	561
	Abbe	648
	Houn	701
	Houn	713
	Wist	878
	Card	898
	RedC	912
	Blan	1010
	Maza	1018
	Veil	1096
	Veil	1099
	Veil	1100
	Veil	1101
beastman	Illu	991
bat	Cree	1081
bird	Sign	112
	Twis	230
	Gree	444
	Nava	463
	Nava	467
	Danc	511
	Danc	520
	3Stu	602
	Abbe	644
	Houn	674
	Vall	774
	Bruc	929
	Last	979
	3Gar	1047
	3Gar	1052

Animal imagery, bird (cont'd)
    bird of prey

	Spec	264
	Reti	1119
bittern	Houn	708
chicken	Stud	29
	Resi	431
	Lady	943
	Lady	954
	3Gab	1025
cocks and hens	Stud	54
cock-and-bull story	Five	221
crow	Sign	112
	Shos	1108
dove	Silv	342
	Last	973
eagle	Seco	650
	Last	971
	Maza	1015
	Shos	1108
flamingo	Sign	121
goose, wild	RedH	186
	3Gar	1051
goose step	Sign	144
hawk	Stud	20
	Sign	94
	RedH	184
	Vall	824
	Devi	961
hens	Stud	54
jay	Danc	526
lark	Stud	36
ostrich	Engr	285
peacock	Sign	156
petrel, stormy	Reig	406
	Nava	448
pheasant	Musg	388
cock pheasant	3Gar	1047

Animal imagery, bird (cont'd)

plover's egg	Copp	318
raven	Nava	465
	Vall	826
	Illu	996
strange	RedH	184
vulture	Vall	835
	Blan	1002
	Shos	1111
buffalo	Stud	28
	Bosc	212
bull	Five	221
	Glor	382
	Blac	569
	Blan	1010
	3Gab	1023
boar	Veil	1100
calf	Copp	326
camel	Croo	420
caribou	Vall	813
cat	Sign	156
	Abbe	647
	Abbe	648
	Houn	737
	Houn	740
	Vall	798
	Wist	882
	Illu	988
	Illu	990
	Illu	998
feline	Vall	798
cow	Lion	1090
crab	Spec	266
creature	Engr	274
	Thor	1065
	Reti	1113

Animal imagery (cont'd)

deer		Reig	400
		Vall	852
		Wist	882
dog		Stud	75
		Stud	78
		Stud	81
		Stud	85
		Sign	99
		Sign	147
		RedH	186
		Bosc	212
		Silv	342
		Soli	535
		SixN	591
		Houn	705
		Houn	750
		Vall	818
		Vall	832
		Bruc	927
		Shos	1105
	bulldog	RedH	187
		Twis	235
		Blac	569
		Seco	659
		Houn	754
		Wist	871
		Card	895
	bloodhound	Stud	36
		Stud	76
		Sign	112
		Resi	429
		Vall	846
		Vall	865
	cur	Stud	80
		Vall	846

Animal imagery, dog (cont'd)

	foxhound	Stud	31
		Bruc	920
		Devi	963
	hell-hound	Sign	140
		Soli	534
	hound	Stud	31
		Stud	35
		Stud	80
		Sign	140
		Chas	581
	(2)	Abbe	648
		Vall	812
		Vall	822
		Vall	825
		Devi	926
		3Gab	1032
	hounds, old	Prio	543
	Irish setter	RedH	180
	Newfoundland	Sign	138
	retriever	Danc	520
	sleuthhound	RedH	185
	staghound	Stud	51
	terrier	Croo	420
eel		Vall	813
ferret		Stud	29
		Stud	85
		Bosc	207
		Norw	499
		Card	891
		Lady	948
fish		Sign	139
		Sign	158
		Stoc	369
		Fina	476
		Vall	810
		Illu	998

28 ◼ *Good Old Index*

Animal imagery, fish (cont'd)

		Blan	1007
		Shos	1104
gudgeon		Maza	1014
pike		Houn	750
		Houn	752
pilot fish		Vall	769
salmon		3Gab	1023
shark		Vall	769
		Maza	1014
fox		Nava	458
		Lady	943
		Devi	966
frog		Cree	1081
goat		Devi	969
		3Gar	1048
mountain		Houn	725
gudgeon		Maza	1014
herring		Sign	112
red herring		Prio	543
horse		Blue	252
		Engr	281
		Vall	859
cart horse		Wist	881
insect			
bee		Stud	59
		Sign	146
		Nobl	298
		Houn	715
		Vall	775
		Bruc	916
beetle		Stud	71
		Stoc	372
		Glor	382
		Prio	551
		Blac	561
		Houn	745
		Card	899

Animal imagery, insect (cont'd)

	butterfly	Houn	750
		Illu	990
		3Gab	1031
	fly	Bosc	208
		Five	228
		Nobl	294
		Glor	374
		Chas	580
		Vall	785
		Thor	1056
	glow-worm	Sign	118
	hornet	Stud	68
	insect	Houn	672
		Illu	988
	moth	Lady	950
		Illu	990
	spider	Sign	114
		Five	224
		Five	228
		Fina	471
		Norw	496
		Danc	517
		Vall	776
jackal		Blac	565
		Vall	769
kid		Empt	492
lamb		Abbe	639
		Card	898
		3Gab	1033
		Suss	1036
lion		Sign	148
		Silv	340
		Abbe	644
		Vall	769
		Lion	1093
		Reti	1119

Animal imagery (cont'd)

lioness			Houn	757
lobster			RedH	187
lynx			Stud	69
mare's nest			Sign	115
mole			Sign	107
			Bosc	212
			Twis	241
			Gold	607
monkey			Houn	693
			Cree	1083
	ape		Stud	29
			Norw	503
			SixN	592
			Devi	959
	baboon		Stud	36
			SixN	586
		chimpanzee	Croo	421
		gorilla	Vall	828
		simian	Stud	29
			SixN	586
mouse			Sign	149
			Nava	461
			Abbe	647
			Bruc	920
			Illu	988
			Blan	1002
octopus			Sign	90
ox			RedC	909
			Lion	1094
oyster			Sign	124
pig			Veil	1097
			Veil	1100
pike			Houn	750
			Houn	752
rabbit			Sign	113
			Sign	150

Animal imagery, rabbit (cont'd)

		RedH	178
		Five	223
		Norw	508
		Shos	1105
rat		Stud	22
		Stud	42
		Stud	43
		Iden	199
		Blue	253
		Glor	382
		Croo	420
		Norw	509
		Chas	575
		Vall	812
		Vall	848
		Shos	1111
reptile		Fina	472
salmon		3Gab	1023
seal		Gree	437
shark		Vall	769
		Maza	1014
sheep		Five	221
		Vall	843
		Vall	861
		Vall	863
shrimp		Blue	255
skunk		Vall	860
		Card	900
snake		Sign	155
		Five	223
		Vall	784
		Reti	1114
	cobra	Illu	988
		Lion	1093
	serpent	Chas	572
		Houn	731
	viper	Dyin	941

32 ◻ *Good Old Index*

Animal imagery, (cont'd)
    squirrel   Abbe   644
    tiger   Sign   148
                                                 Sign   150
                                                 Empt   491
                             (2)   Empt   492
                                                 Blac   565
                                                 SixN   592
                                                 Vall   829
                                                 Vall   832
                                                 Vall   834
                                                 Vall   846
                                                 Bruc   913
                                                 Dyin   934
                                                 Lady   946
                                                 Reti   1119
    wolf   Stud   35
                                                 Stud   57
                                                 SixN   592
                                                 Vall   813
                                                 3Gab   1033
                                                 Suss   1036
    worm   Bosc   217
                                                 Vall   774
        glow   Sign   118
    heraldic, ornamental, etc.
        Black Swan   Copp   322
        boars' heads   Houn   701
        The Bull   Wist   877
        dragon   Chas   578
        Eagle Commercial Hotel   Vall   803
        Eagle Ravine   Stud   68
        Fighting Cock   Prio   550
        Green Dragon   Shos   1103
        griffins   Shos   1108

Animal imagery, heraldic, ornamental, etc. (cont'd)

lion		
crouching	Seco	652
rampant	Vall	787
Red Bull	Prio	546
Sea Unicorn	Blac	560
White Eagle Tavern	Sign	122
White Hart	Stud	34
Aniseed	Miss	633
Anna	Gold	619
Annuity	3Gab	1028
Anstruther (doctor)	Bosc	202
Anthony (manservant)	Houn	764
Anthropological Journal	Card	896
Antimacassar	Card	891
Antonio (manservant)	Houn	764
Aortic aneurism	Stud	77
Aortic valve	Sign	100
Apaches, American	Nobl	298
Apaches, Parisian	Illu	989
Apoplexy	Glor	377
	Croo	422
stroke	Glor	379
Apple	SixN	586
ribston pippin	Blac	569
Appledore, Sir Charles	Prio	539
Appledore, Edith	Prio	539
Appledore Towers (house)	Chas	572
Aqua tofana (poison)	Stud	41
Arabian Nights	Nobl	296
	3Gar	1031
Arabs, street	Stud	42
Arc-and-compass breastpin	RedH	177
Arcadia mixture (tobacco)	Croo	411
Archaeologist	Devi	956
Archery	RedH	182

34 ◻ *Good Old Index*

Archie (alias)	RedH	189
Architectural styles		
Elizabethan	Prio	553
	Blan	1002
Georgian	3Gar	1048
	Thor	1063
Gothic	3Stu	598
Jacobean	Vall	779
	Wist	882
Palladian	Abbe	637
Queen Anne	Reig	403
Tudor	Soli	531
	Suss	1039
	Thor	1063
Victorian	Bruc	927
	Blan	1002
Architecture	RedH	182
Arctic Ocean	Blac	566
Argentine	Blac	562
Aristocrat of crime (Baron Gruner)	Illu	988
Arizona	Nobl	298
Arkansas River	3Gar	1046
Armitage (gentleman)	Spec	263
Armitage, James	Glor	381
Armitage, Percy	Spec	263
Armour	RedH	182
	Gree	440
Arms (*see* Coat-of-arms)		
Armstrong, Dr. Leslie	Miss	629
Army personnel, British (*see* Navy, Royal)		
Barclay, Colonel James	Croo	412
Brown, Lieutenant Bromley	Sign	152
Campbell, Sir Colin	Sign	151
Carruthers, Colonel	Wist	870
Damery, Colonel Sir James	Illu	985
De Merville, General	Illu	986

Army personnel, British (*see* Navy, Royal) (cont'd)

Devoy, Colour-sergeant	Croo	413
Dorking, Colonel	Chas	574
Emsworth, Colonel	Blan	1001
Emsworth, Lance-corporal Godfrey	Blan	1009
Freebody, Major	Five	222
Gordon, General	Resi	423
	Card	889
Greathed, Colonel	Sign	151
Hayter, Colonel	Reig	398
Holder, Sergeant John	Sign	144
Martin, Lieutenant	Glor	383
Moran, Colonel Sebastian (*which see*)		
Moriarty, Colonel	Fina	469
Morstan, Captain Arthur	Sign	94
Munro, Colonel Spence	Copp	318
Murphy, Major	Croo	413
Murray (orderly)	Stud	15
Neill, General	Croo	420
Prendergast, Major	Five	219
Ross, Colonel	Silv	336
Sholto, Major John	Sign	95
Stark, Colonel Lysander	Engr	277
Stoner, Major-General	Spec	260
Upwood, Colonel	Houn	761
Walter, Colonel Valentine	Bruc	917
Warburton, Colonel	Engr	274
Wardlaw, Colonel	Silv	347
Wilson	Sign	151
Wood, Corporal Henry	Croo	418

Army personnel, U.S.

Hood, General	Five	219
Jackson, General	Five	219
Lee, General R. E.	Five	219
Openshaw, Colonel Elias	Five	219

36 ◼ *Good Old Index*

Army, British, regiments
    Berkshires | Stud | 15
    Coldstream Guards | Nava | 455
    Fifth Northumberland Fusiliers | Stud | 15
    Imperial Yeomanry | Blan | 1000
    Middlesex Corps | Blan | 1000
    One hundred and seventeenth foot | Croo | 413
    Royal Artillery | Gree | 437
    Royal Marine Light Infantry | Stud | 25
    Royal Munsters | Croo | 412
    Third Buffs | Sign | 144

Army, Indian, regiments
    Bengal Artillery | Spec | 260
    First Bangalore Pioneers | Empt | 494
    Indian Army | Empt | 492
     | Thor | 1054
    Third Bengal Fusiliers | Sign | 146
    Thirty-fourth Bombay Infantry | Sign | 95

Army coach | Fina | 471
Army Medical Department | Stud | 15
Arnsworth Castle business | Scan | 173
Arrowheads | Devi | 961
Arrow poison | Stud | 80
 | Sign | 109
 | Suss | 1043
Arson | Norw | 497
Art | Sign | 101
 | Houn | 692
 | Houn | 749
 | Vall | 775
Artery, subclavian | Stud | 15
Arthur, Lord Saltire | Prio | 556
Artifical limb | Sign | 102
 | Sign | 110
 | Bery | 310
 | Illu | 993
 | Reti | 1114

Ashes, monograph upon	Stud	33
	Sign	91
	Bosc	214
Asphalt paving	Silv	344
	Gree	439
Assassination	Bruc	914
Assizes	Bosc	204
	Blue	248
	Danc	526
	Wist	887
	Thor	1056
Asteroid, The Dynamics of an	Vall	770
Aston, Birmingham	3Gar	1050
Astronomy	Stud	21
	Five	225
Asteroid, The Dynamics of an	Vall	770
astronomer, amateur	Houn	715
astronomers' personal equation	Musg	395
eclipses	Vall	775
obliquity of the ecliptic	Gree	435
Solar System	Stud	21
Atavism	Gree	435
	Houn	750
Athene, bust of	Chas	578
Athens (Greece)	Gree	440
Asthmatic symptoms	Sign	133
	Norw	497
	3Gab	1026
Atkinson brothers	Scan	161
Atlanta (Georgia)	Yell	353
Atlantic Ocean	Stud	23
	Stud	59
	Five	229
	Nobl	289
	Glor	383
Attenta pericolo	RedC	907
Attica (Greece)	RedH	182

38 ◘ Good Old Index

Atwood (ironworks owner)	Vall	836
Auckland (New Zealand)	Iden	193
Audley Court	Stud	32
August, most terrible	Last	970
Au revoir (*see also* Sherlock Holmes)	Last	974
Aurora (steam launch)	Sign	124
Australia	Bosc	203
	Glor	381
	Empt	483
	Prio	558
	Abbe	638
	Lady	947
Austrian stamp	Cree	1082
Automobiles		
Benz	Last	971
Ford	Last	974
Autumn cases (*see* Seasons)		
Aveling (schoolmaster)	Prio	547
Avenging Angels	Stud	63
Aviary	Norw	503
Ayrshires (stock)	Stoc	365
Azof, Sea of	Lady	948

B

Baboon	Spec	260
Backgammon	Five	220
Backwater, Lord	Nobl	288
	Silv	337
Baden	Lady	944
Badger	Sign	117
Bagatelle (card club)	Empt	484
	Empt	494
Bain, Sandy	Shos	1106
Baker, Henry	Blue	245
Baker, Mrs. Henry	Blue	245
Baker Street	Stud	19
	Sign	90
	Scan	161
	RedH	185
	Iden	190
	Bosc	211
	Five	218
	Twis	237
	Blue	249
	Spec	258
	Engr	274
	Nobl	287
	Bery	301
	Copp	317

Baker Street (cont'd)

	Yell	351
	Stoc	362
	Reig	398
	Croo	419
	Resi	424
	Gree	443
	Nava	448
	Fina	475
	Empt	488
	Norw	496
	Danc	512
	Soli	527
	Prio	538
	Blac	559
	Chas	582
	SixN	588
	3Stu	596
	Gold	607
	Miss	622
	Abbe	646
	Seco	650
	Houn	683
	Vall	815
	Wist	887
	Card	888
	Bruc	913
	Lady	947
	Illu	984
	Maza	1012
	Suss	1042
	3Gar	1051
	Cree	1071
	Shos	1103
	Reti	1114

Baker Street, 221B

across from Camden House	Empt	489
bath, Watson takes	Sign	125

Baker Street, 221B (cont'd)
   bearskin hearthrug

	Prio	539

   bedroom, Holmes's

	Stud	39
	Sign	129
	Scan	167
	Bery	311
	Yell	362
	Musg	386
	Chas	575
	Houn	690
	Dyin	932
	Maza	1012

      mantelpiece in

	Dyin	934

      second door from

	Maza	1015

      storage of papers in

	Musg	386

   bedroom, Watson's

	Stud	22
	SixN	585

     Watson comes down from

	Sign	125
	Five	227
	Spec	258
	Bery	312
	Norw	505
	Thor	1055

      mantelpiece in

	Spec	258

      overlooks back yard

	Thor	1055

   bell, electric

	Maza	1020

   bell, front door

	Stud	38
	Sign	126
	Scan	162
	Iden	192
	Five	218
	Nobl	291
	Bery	301
	Copp	318
	Norw	496
	Danc	512
	Houn	671

Baker Street, 221B, bell, front door
(cont'd)
    bell, servants

    blinds

        Holmes's shadow upon
        of Holmes's bedroom
    bookshelf (*see* Shelves)
    butter-dish
    books at
        American Encyclopaedia
        Bible (suggested)
        black-letter volumes

        Bradshaw

        casebook, Holmes's
    commonplace books (*see* Holmes:
        Commonplace books)
    Continental Gazetteer
    Crockford
    De Jure inter Gentes
    diary, Holmes's
    diary, Watson's
        journal
    Gazetteer

Thor	1059
Cree	1072
Stud	23
Scan	169
Five	227
Blue	257
Nava	465
SixN	591
Wist	875
Card	890
Maza	1015
Sign	129
Iden	192
Resi	422
Illu	993
Empt	489
Dyin	935
Musg	386
Five	225
Vall	772
Sign	89
RedH	185
Copp	322
Vall	772
Spec	259
Scan	163
Reti	1117
Stud	38
Blan	1007
Houn	726
Stud	76
Sign	127
Scan	163

Baker Street, 221B, books at (cont'd)
    indexes (*see* Holmes:
        Commonplace books)

Martydom of Man	Sign	97
medical directory	Houn	671
newspaper files in lumber-room	SixN	591

    reference works (*see* Holmes:
        Commonplace books)

telephone directory	3Gar	1045
Vie de Boheme (Murger)	Stud	40
Whitaker's Almanac	Vall	772
Watson's	Resi	423
medical treatise	Gold	607
novels	Bosc	209
	Croo	411
scrapbooks	Stud	41
boots (*see* Servants)	Card	890
bow window	Sign	97
	Spec	258
	Bery	301
	Nava	465
	Houn	670
	Maza	1013
boy in buttons	Iden	192
carpet	Empt	493
	Norw	505
	Blac	571
hearthrug	Houn	669
	RedC	904
bearskin rug	Prio	539
	Stud	49
	Blue	255
chairs	Scan	177
	Five	218
	Nobl	291
	Seco	657

Baker Street, 221B, chairs (cont'd)

    Holmes's

Bruc	916
Thor	1058
Stud	22
Sign	143
Scan	162
RedH	176
Iden	198
Blue	245
Engr	276
Bery	301
Glor	373
Musg	386
Nava	448
Empt	488
SixN	583
Gold	608
Bruc	915
Lady	942
Illu	995
Maza	1013
3Gab	1023
Cree	1071
Reti	1114

    Watson's

Sign	94
Scan	162
Glor	373
Musg	386
Empt	488
3Gab	1023
Cree	1071

    armchair

Stud	43
Iden	192
Bery	312
Gree	443
Nava	448
Danc	514
Abbe	647

Baker Street, 221B, chairs, armchair (cont'd)

velvet	Sign	89
basket chair	Blue	254
	Nobl	291
cane-backed chair	Lady	942
easy-chair	Nobl	287
	Bery	302
	RedC	906
straight chair	Sign	94
	Nava	465
	Norw	496
	Houn	669
wooden chair	Blue	244
chamber, for changing into disguise	Bery	311
charts on walls	Empt	493
	Maza	1012
chemical work at	Sign	109
	Sign	135
	Iden	198
	Copp	322
	Musg	386
	Nava	448
	Danc	511
	3Stu	596
	Dyin	932
	Maza	1012
clocks	Nobl	291
	Thor	1058
Holmes's bedroom	Dyin	935
Watson's bedroom	Spec	258
coal-scuttle	Musg	386
	Maza	1012
coffee pot, silver	Houn	669
couch (*see* settee, sofa)		
"couple of rooms"	Stud	20
criminal relics	Musg	386

Baker Street, 221B (cont'd)
    cupboard (*see also* sideboard)

    cushion
    desk
        Holmes'

        Watson's
    drawer
        revolver in

        paper in
    fanlight

    fire set to rooms
    fireplace (*see also* hearthrug,
        mantelpiece)

Five	228
Vall	773
Stud	49
Spec	259
Bery	313
Nava	448
Fina	480
Danc	511
Vall	772
Sign	92
Sign	98
Fina	472
Glor	374
Blue	250
Dyin	936
Illu	999
Fina	475
Stud	22
Scan	162
Iden	190
Five	218
Blue	245
Spec	258
Nobl	289
Bery	307
Copp	317
Glor	373
Musg	386
Resi	424
Chas	572
Gold	608
Abbe	647
Houn	676
Houn	761

Baker Street, 221B, fireplace (*see also* hearthrug, mantelpiece) (cont'd)	Wist	869
	RedC	904
	3Gab	1023
	Veil	1098
fire tongs	Copp	317
poker	Spec	265
	3Gab	1023
first mention of	Stud	19
gasogene	Scan	162
	Maza	1014
gramaphone	Maza	1021
hallway		
ground floor	Stud	38
	Scan	162
	RedH	186
	Bery	312
	Norw	496
	Gold	608
	Illu	993
	Thor	1055
passage, first, floor	Stud	39
	Scan	164
	Iden	198
American second	Five	218
	Yell	351
	Dyin	936
landing	Nobl	297
hearthrug	Houn	669
	RedC	904
bearskin	Prio	539
hook	Five	218
key		
to Holmes's bedroom	Dyin	934
to sitting room	Stud	38
	Iden	199
to street door	Stud	40
	Scan	173

Baker Street, 221B (cont'd)
    landing

	Nobl	297
landlady	Stud	40
	Stud	42
Mrs. Hudson	Sign	126
	Blue	250
	Spec	258
	Nava	465
	Empt	488
	Danc	517
	Blac	568
	Seco	656
	Vall	865
	Wist	871
	Dyin	932
	Lady	947
	Last	974
	Maza	1022
	3Gar	1045
	Lion	1083
Mrs. Turner	Scan	170
letterbox	Vall	865
lighting	Yell	362
candles	Resi	425
	Abbe	636
gas	Copp	317
	Dyin	935
lamps	Five	218
	Chas	572
	Houn	683
lamp in hall	Gold	608
spirit lamp	Gold	613
lumber room upstairs	SixN	591
location of/route to	Empt	489
	Gold	608

maids (*see* Servants)

Baker Street, 221B (cont'd)
    mantelpiece

Sign	89
Iden	200
Blue	255
Engr	276
Nobl	288
Musg	386
Resi	425
Seco	654
Veil	1102

        in Holmes's bedroom   Dyin   934
        in Watson's bedroom   Spec   258
    meals at
        breakfast

Stud	23
Stud	42
Sign	125
Sign	130
Sign	131
Scan	173
Five	227
Spec	265
Engr	276
Bery	312
Copp	317
Resi	433
Nava	465
Norw	496
Norw	505
Blac	559
Blac	568
Seco	659
Houn	669
Houn	685
Vall	769
RedC	904
Bruc	913

50 ◘ *Good Old Index*

Baker Street, 221B, meals at, breakfast (cont'd)	Bruc	928
	Thor	1055
Scotchwoman	Nava	465
lunch	Chas	582
	Wist	869
dinner	Stud	37
	Sign	134
	Scan	170
	Blue	250
	Blue	257
	Nobl	296
	Chas	577
	Sixn	591
	Abbe	647
	Bruc	929
	Lady	948
	Maza	1022
	Veil	1098
mirror above fireplace	Bery	311
number, 221B, given	Stud	19
	Stud	37
	Sign	131
	Blue	249
	Nava	457
page (*see* Servants)		
passage (*see* Hallway)		
pavement, outside	Iden	192
Persian slipper	Musg	386
	Nava	448
	Empt	493
	Illu	994
pictures	Resi	423
	Card	889
	Dyin	354
pipe rack	Iden	196
	Blue	244

Baker Street, 221B (cont'd)
   pistol practice, indoor   Musg   386
                                              Dyin   932
   plane tree, in back yard   Thor   1055
   portmanteau   Stud   51
   rack (coat)   RedH   186
   rental   Stud   20
                                              Dyin   932
   rugs (*see* Carpets)
   safe   SixN   595
   salver   Seco   656
   salver, brass   Sign   93
   second room on first floor   RedH   176
                                              Blac   569
   servants   Stud   38
      cook, new   Thor   1055
      maid   Stud   40
                                              Five   227
                                              Bruc   914
      page   Sign   93
                                              Iden   192
                                              Nobl   291
                                              Yell   351
                                              Gree   444
                                              Nava   448
                                              Wist   475
                                              Shos   1103
      Billy   Vall   770
                                              Maza   1012
                                              Thor   1057
      boots   Card   890
      boy in buttons   Iden   192
   settee (*see also* sofa)   RedH   176
                                              Seco   651
                                              Houn   670
                                              Illu   989
   seventeen steps   Scan   162

Baker Street, 221B (cont'd)
    shelves

Sign	127
Scan	163
Five	225
Empt	493
Card	889
Veil	1095

        beside mantelpiece

Nobl	288

        Watson's medical shelf

Houn	671

    sideboard

Iden	199
Five	228
Blue	250
Nobl	295
Bery	311
Veil	1098

    sitting room

Stud	20
Sign	132
Scan	162
Iden	192
Blue	250
Engr	276
Bery	301
Chas	581
Gold	608
Houn	683
Bruc	913
Dyin	932
Lady	948
Maza	1012

    sofa (*see also* settee)

Stud	36
Sign	128
Blue	244
Engr	276
Musg	386
Resi	422
SixN	591
Gold	613

Baker Street, 221B, sofa (*see also* settee) (cont'd)

	Card	888
	Bruc	915
	Maza	1013
	Cree	1075
spirit case	Scan	162
stairs	Stud	25
	Sign	93
	Scan	162
	Iden	192
	Five	227
	Blue	257
	Nobl	297
	Bery	301
	Copp	322
	Yell	352
	Gree	443
	Norw	496
	Danc	512
	Blac	568
	Chas	573
	SixN	591
	SixN	593
	Gold	608
	Abbe	647
	Seco	656
	Houn	671
	Vall	865
	Wist	870
	Dyin	938
	Illu	999
	Maza	1015
	Thor	1058
	Cree	1072
seventeen steps	Scan	162
starting point of tales	Empt	489
stool	Musg	386
	Danc	511

Baker Street, 221B (cont'd)
   strong box, Holmes's
   table

	Blue	250
	Stud	23
	Sign	131
	Iden	196
	Five	227
	Blue	257
	Nobl	287
	Copp	317
	Yell	351
	Musg	386
	Resi	429
	Nava	465
	Fina	472
	Norw	505
	Danc	516
	Prio	539
	Chas	572
	SixN	585
	Gold	612
	Abbe	647
	Seco	659
	Houn	683
	Illu	994
	3Gab	1023
	Suss	1034
	3Gar	1045
	Reti	1113
deal-topped, chemical	Empt	493
in groundfloor hall	Thor	1055
in Holmes's bedroom	Dyin	935
mahogany	Nobl	296
side-table	Gree	442
	Nava	448
	Blac	568
	Maza	1016
tantalus	Scan	162

Baker Street, 221B (cont'd)
   telephone

   tray, card
   violin case, in corner

   waiting room

Watson
   living at

		Illu	984
		3Gar	1047
		Reti	1116
		Maza	1015
		Empt	493
		Maza	1012
	(?)	RedH	176
		Maza	1015
		Stud	20
		Sign	89
		Spec	258
		Nobl	287
		Bery	301
		Copp	317
		Silv	336
		Yell	351
		Glor	373
		Reig	398
		Resi	422
		Gree	435
		Norw	496
		Danc	511
		Soli	527
		Prio	538
		Blac	559
		Chas	572
		SixN	582
		Gold	607
		Miss	622
		Abbe	635
		Seco	655
		Houn	669
		Vall	769
		Wist	869
		Card	888

Baker Street, 221B, Watson, living at (cont'd)

	Bruc	913
	Lady	942
	Suss	1033
	3Gar	1044
	Thor	1055
	Shos	1102
	Reti	1114
not living at	Scan	161
	RedH	176
	Iden	190
	Bosc	202
	Five	218
	Twis	229
	Blue	244
	Engr	274
	Stoc	362
	Musg	386
	Croo	411
	Nava	448
	Fina	469
	Empt	483
	Dyin	932
	Last	980
	Illu	984
	Blan	1000
	Maza	1012
	3Gab	1023
	Cree	1071
	Lion	1083
	Veil	1095
probably living at	3Stu	596
	RedC	901
	Devi	955
returns to	Norw	496

Baker Street, 221B (cont'd)
   weather at
      bleak and windy

	Nobl	301
	Empt	490
	Wist	869
clear	Blue	251
	Bery	301
	Danc	512
	Houn	690
cold	Blue	245
	Chas	572
	Gold	613
	Abbe	635
equinoctial gales	Five	218
fog	Stud	27
	Sign	93
	Sign	98
	Copp	317
	Danc	512
	Abbe	630
	Bruc	913
	Dyin	932
yellow	Sign	93
	Copp	317
	Bruc	913
frosty	Abbe	635
gloomy	Miss	622
hot	Card	888
rain	Stud	80
	Sign	98
	Five	218
	Nobl	287
	Resi	422
	Gold	607
snow	Bery	301
sunny	Five	227
	Bery	301

Baker Street, 221B, weather at, sunny (cont'd)

	Danc	512
	Card	888
	Illu	993
wild November night	Gold	607
wild October morning	Thor	1055
windy	Five	218
	Nobl	287
	Resi	424
	Empt	490
	Chas	575
	Gold	607
	Wist	869
	Thor	1055
windows	Stud	20
	Sign	93
	Scan	163
	Iden	192
	Blue	245
	Spec	258
	Bery	301
	Resi	422
	Danc	512
	Gold	607
	Abbe	648
	Seco	656
	Houn	670
	Card	888
	Bruc	913
	Dyin	935
	Blan	1000
	Maza	1013
	Thor	1055
facing East (?)	Danc	512
facing West (?)	Card	888
blinds of	Sign	129
	Iden	192
	Resi	422

Baker Street, 221B, windows, blinds of (cont'd)	Dyin	935
	Illu	993
bow	Sign	97
	Spec	258
	Bery	301
	Nava	465
	Houn	670
	Maza	1013
fanlight	Blue	250
	Dyin	936
	Illu	999
yard, back	Thor	1055
Baker Street Irregulars	Stud	42
	Sign	126
	Croo	419
	Lady	948
Baker Street Station	Bery	301
Baldwin, Ted	Vall	813
Baldwin (card club)	Empt	484
Ballarat (Australia)	Sign	107
	Bosc	214
Ballarat Gang	Bosc	216
Balloon	Sign	122
Balmoral, Duchess of	Nobl	290
Balmoral, Duke of	Nobl	288
	Silv	347
Balmoral, Lord	Empt	484
Balzac (Honore de)	Iden	197
Bang (drug)	Sign	147
Bangor (Wales)	Prio	539
Bank of England	Danc	520
	3Gar	1054
Bank of France	RedH	187
Bannister (servant)	3Stu	597
Barberton (South Africa)	Lady	947
Barcarole	Maza	1019
Barcelona (Spain)	Wist	885

Barclay, Colonel James	Croo	412
Barclay, Nancy	Croo	413
Barclay Square (*see also* Berkeley)	Bruc	917
Bardle, Inspector	Lion	1090
Barelli, Augusto	RedC	911
Barges	Sign	138
Bari (Italy)	RedC	911
Baritsu	Empt	486
Bark (ship)	Five	218
	Five	228
	Glor	380
Barker, Cecil James	Vall	781
Barker (detective)	Reti	1118
Barking Level	Sign	138
Barnes, Josiah	Shos	1104
Barney (argument)	Blan	1002
Barnicot, Dr.	SixN	583
Bar of Gold (opium den)	Twis	230
Barometer	Sign	116
	Bosc	207
	Reig	399
Baron	Reig	398
	Prio	539
	Last	971
	Illu	985
	Maza	1016
Baronet	Abbe	643
	Houn	685
	Shos	1110
Barouche (carriage)	Shos	1109
Barraud (watch)	Stud	30
Barrett, Constable	Seco	655
Barrister(*see also* Lawyer, Solicitor)	Houn	736
	Illu	995
	Thor	1065
Barrow	Gold	607
	Houn	714

Barrymore, Eliza	Houn	676
Barrymore, John	Houn	676
Barton, Dr. Hill	Illu	995
Barton, Inspector	Twis	236
Barton's Crossing	Vall	815
Bart's (hospital)	Stud	16
Baryta	Iden	198
Basil, Captain	Blac	559
Baskerville Hall	Houn	674
Baskerville		
brother of Charles	Houn	681
Beryl	Houn	709
Sir Charles	Houn	673
Elizabeth	Houn	676
Sir Henry	Houn	677
Hugo, c. 1640	Houn	673
Hugo, 1742	Houn	676
John	Houn	676
Rear-Admiral	Houn	749
Rodger	Houn	676
	Houn	681
Sir William	Houn	749
Baskervilles, curse of the	Houn	673
Baskervilles, Hound of the		
1647	Houn	673
1888	Houn	757
Basle (Switzerland)	Fina	476
***Bass Rock* (steamship)**	Abbe	646
Bates, Marlow	Thor	1057
Bath-chair	Gold	609
Bath sponge	Twis	242
Bathing-cot	Lion	1087
Bathsheba	Croo	422
Battery, artillery	Sign	146
	Croo	420
Battery, electrical	Dyin	934
Baxter, Richard	Bosc	217

Baxter, Edith	Silv	337
Bay, the (Bay of Biscay)	Glor	383
Bay of Bengal	Sign	127
Bayard (horse)	Silv	337
Baynes, Inspector	Wist	871
Bay window	Chas	578
	3Gar	1048
Bayswater bus	Miss	627
Beacons of the future, schools	Nava	456
Beagle	Miss	633
Bear	Stud	72
grizzly	Stud	52
Bearskin hearthrug	Prio	539
Beards and whiskers		
Akbar (black)	Sign	149
apocryphal, robber's	Abbe	639
Baker (brown, grizzled)	Blue	250
Bellamy, T. (red)	Lion	1087
Brackenstall (black)	Abbe	640
Breckenridge	Blue	252
Cairns	Blac	569
Cantlemere (black)	Maza	1021
Carey (black)	Blac	561
commissionaire	Stud	26
Coram (white)	Gold	615
country doctor	Danc	519
Dodd	Blan	1000
Drebber (black)	Stud	29
Eccles (gray)	Wist	870
Emsworth, Colonel (gray)	Blan	1002
false		
Carruthers (dark)	Soli	529
Holmes		
gray	Sign	133
	Scan	167
white	Empt	485
	Chas	575

Beards and whiskers, false (cont'd)

Peters	Lady	944
Pinner, A. (black)	Stoc	365
Stapleton (black)	Houn	690
Windibank (black)	Iden	197
Ferguson (chinchilla)	Engr	281
Ferrier (brown)	Stud	53
Fowler	Copp	325
Frankland (gray)	Houn	736
Garrideb, N.	3Gar	1048
Gregory	Silv	340
Gregson (flaxen)	Stud	28
Green (black)	Lady	944
Harraway	Vall	835
Heidegger	Prio	548
Holdernesse (red)	Prio	543
Holmes (as Altamont)	Last	975
Hope	Stud	78
Kemp	Gree	441
Kent	Blan	1005
Khan	Sign	147
Lancaster (white)	Blac	569
Lawler (grizzled)	Vall	848
Lucca (black)	RedC	903
McGinty (black)	Vall	826
Melas (black)	Gree	445
Menzies	Vall	850
Prescott	3Gar	1052
Sandeford (grizzled)	SixN	593
Selden	Houn	725
Singh	Sign	147
Slaney (black)	Danc	524
Small (black)	Sign	139
spectator in court	Vall	846
Staunton's father-in-law (grizzled)	Miss	623
Sterndale (golden)	Devi	961
Toller (grizzled)	Copp	324

Beards and whiskers (cont'd)
    Tregennis, M.
    Trevelyan
    Turner
    Walter, Valentine (light)
    Williamson (gray)
    Wood (gray)
Beauchamp Arriance (woods)
Beaune
Becher, Dr.
Beckenham
Bed clamped to floor
Beddington
Beddoes
Bedford
Beech (tree)

Beecher, Henry Ward

Beer (*see* alcohol)
Beeswax
Beeswing
Beetle on a card, like a
Beggar
Beige dress

Belfast (Ireland)
Belgian masters
Belgium
Belgrade (Serbia)
Bell rope, dummy
    as evidence

Devi	963	
Resi	424	
Bosc	215	
Bruc	921	
Soli	535	
Croo	418	
Devi	961	
Sign	89	
Engr	286	
Gree	443	
Spec	270	
Stoc	373	
Glor	377	
Blan	1001	
Sign	119	
Bosc	212	
Copp	319	
Musg	393	
Vall	779	
Resi	423	
Card	889	
Dyin	941	
Abbe	641	
Blac	561	
Twis	235	
Sign	94	
Copp	325	
Card	890	
Houn	692	
Last	972	
Seco	666	
Spec	267	
Iden	192	
Spec	267	

Bell rope, dummy, as evidence (cont'd)	Nava	451
	Abbe	641
Belladona	Dyin	941
Bellamy, Maud	Lion	1086
Bellamy, Tom	Lion	1087
Bellamy, William	Lion	1087
Belle dame sansa merci	3Gab	1031
Bellinger, Lord	Seco	650
Belliver Tor	Houn	738
Belminster, Duke of	Seco	656
Belmont Place	Sign	123
Benares metal-work	Sign	142
Bender, Mr. (pioneer)	Stud	54
Bengal, Bay of	Sign	127
Bengal Artillery	Spec	260
Benito Canyon	Vall	792
Bennett, Trevor (Jack)	Cree	1072
Bentinck Street	Fina	473
Bentley's private hotel	Miss	623
Benz (automobile)	Last	971
Beppo (murderer)	SixN	588
Berkeley Square (*see also* Barclay)	Illu	991
Berkshire	Spec	259
	Engr	278
	Veil	1097
	Shos	1106
Berkshire Constabulary	Veil	1098
Berkshires (regiment)	Stud	15
Berlin (Germany)	Last	971
Bermondsey	Stoc	369
Bermuda Dockyard	Bosc	210
Bernstone, Mrs. (housekeeper)	Sign	107
Bertillon (Alphonse)	Nava	460
	Houn	672
Beryl	Sign	151
	Scan	164
	Bery	303

Beryl Coronet	Bery	303
Betting	Blue	253
	Silv	336
	Empt	484
	Miss	628
	Shos	1102
Betting book	Silv	339
Beverley, Baron (Holdernesse)	Prio	539
Bhurtee (India)	Croo	420
Bible	Sign	140
	Iden	195
	Blue	255
	Glor	382
	Croo	415
	Croo	422
	Houn	675
	Vall	772
Biblical Quotations/Allusions		
There is nothing new under the sun. (H)	Stud	29
"and there is no new thing under the sun." **ECCL 1:9**		
the schemer falls into the pit which he digs for another (H)	Spec	272
"He that diggeth a pit shall fall into it," **ECCL 10:8**		
"Whoso diggeth a pit shall fall therein" **PROV 26:27**		
You see, but you do not observe. (H)	Scan	162
"Seeing many things but thou observest not," **ISAI 42:20**		

Biblical Quotations/Allusions (cont'd)

We can but possess our souls in patience. (H)	3Gar	1053
We can only possess our souls in patience. (H)	Wist	876
Possess our souls in patience. (H)	Vall	809
	Lady	948

> *"in your patience possess ye your souls,"*
> **LUKE 21:19**

Sufficient for tomorrow is the evil thereof. (H)	Houn	748

> *"Sufficient unto the day is the evil thereof"*
> **MATH 6:34**

I can't make bricks without clay (H)	Copp	322

> *"Ye shall no more give the people straw to make brick."*
> **EXOD 5:7**

And so I say again that we have much to hope from the flowers. (H)	Nava	456

> *"And yet I say unto you, that even Solomon in all his glory was not arrayed like one of these."*
> **MATH 6:28–29**

I dropped ash all over the space in front . . . (H)	Gold	621

> *"Now David had commanded his servants to bring ashes, and those they strewed throughout all the temple . . ."*
> **BEL & DRAGON 14**

Biblical Quotations/Allusions (cont'd)

Things must be done decently and in order. (H) "*Let all thing be done decently and in order.*" **1COR 14:40**	Reti	1119
This fellow has clearly proven a broken reed. (H) "*Lo, thou trustest in the staff of this broken reed, on Egypt.*" **ISAI 36:6**	3Gab	1029
What would it profit a woman . . . if her own ruin must immediately follow. (H) "*For what shall it profit a man . . . and lose his own soul.*" **MARK 8:36**	Chas	573
The wages of sin, Watson, (H) "*For the wages of sin is death*" **ROM 6:23**	Illu	998
He will guard it as the apple of his eye. (H) "*he led him about, . . . he kept him as the apple of his eye.*" **DEUT 32:10**	Silv	345
the powers that be (Mycroft) "*the powers that be are ordained by God.*" **ROM 13:1**	Bruc	916

Biblical Quotations/Allusions (cont'd)

Then there came a time of trouble (Anna)	Gold	619

"*Which I have reserved against the time of trouble.*"
        JOB 38:23
    "*but in the time of their trouble*"
        JERE 2:27
    "*a refuge for the oppressed, a refuge in times of trouble*"
        PSAL 9:9
    "*for in the time of trouble he shall hide me*"
        PSAL 27:5		

You shall smart for this! (Stangerson)	Stud	66
"*He that is surety for a stranger shall smart for it.*" **PROV 11:15**		
The hand of the Lord shall be heavy upon you. (Drebber)	Stud	66
"*For day and night thy hand was heavy upon me.*" **PSAL 32:4**		
They have perished, and by my hand (Hope)	Stud	78
"*. . . the heavens are the work of thy hands. They shall perish, but thou shalt endure.*" **PSAL 102:25–6**		

Biblical Quotations/Allusions (cont'd)

I knew that my sin had found me out. (Gilchrist)   3Stu   606
> "... *and be sure your sin will find you out.*"
> **NUMB 32:23**

I'll see that you reap! (Baldwin)   Vall   825
> "*Whatsoever a man soweth, that shall he also reap.*"
> **GALA 6:7**

Coals of fire (C. Smith)   Dyin   939
> "*For thou shalt heap coals of fire upon his head,*"
> **PROV 25:22**

Providence, which would not forever punish the innocent beyond the third or fourth generation. (Sir Hugo B.)   Houn   675
> "*visiting the iniquity of the fathers upon children unto the third and fourth generation.*"
> **EXOD 20:5**

Roylott bends the poker at 221B   Spec   265
> "*That which is crooked cannot be made straight*"
> **ECCL 1:15**
> "*And the crooked shall be made straight.*"
> **ISAI 40:4**
> "*and the crooked shall be made straight.*"
> **LUKE 3:5**

Biblical Quotations/Allusions, Roylott
bends the poker at 221B (cont'd)
 "*I will make . . . crooked things
 straight.*"
 ISAI 42:16

   the small affair of Uriah and   Croo   422
      Bathsheba (H)
      2SAM 11–12

Bicycle	Five	219
	Soli	527
	Prio	541
	Prio	547
	Miss	631
	Vall	790
Biddle (murderer)	Resi	434
Big Ben	Lady	953
Bigamy	Bosc	210
Bigamy suspected	Yell	359
Bighorn sheep	Stud	72
Bijou villa	Scan	168
Bill (helper)	Blue	253
Bill, as clue	Nobl	296
	Silv	350
Billiard cue	Miss	624
Billiard-marker	Gree	437
Billiard room	Glor	376
	Musg	389
	Abbe	638
	Houn	703
Billiards	Danc	511
Billy (page)	Vall	770
	Maza	1012
	Thor	1057
Bi-metallic question	Bruc	914
Binomial theorem	Fina	470

Birchmoor (estate)	Nobl	289
Bird (*see* animals)		
Bird, Simon	Vall	849
Bird's-eye (tobacco)	Sign	91
Birlstone	Vall	779
Birlstone Manor House	Vall	774
Birlstone railway smash	Vall	782
Birlstone Ridge	Vall	808
Birmingham	Stoc	363
	Glor	375
	3Gab	1023
	3Gar	1050
Bishopgate jewelcase	Sign	113
Bishops, bench of	Illu	996
Bisulphate of baryta	Iden	198
Bittern	Houn	708
Bizarre, Holmes's love of the	RedH	176
Black Formosa corruption	Dyin	934
Black Gorgiano	RedC	909
Black Jack of Ballarat	Bosc	216
Black-letter editions	Sign	89
	RedH	185
Black pearl of the Borgias	SixN	594
Black Peter	Blac	560
Black Sea	Glor	381
Black sheep	Houn	681
Black Steve (Dixie)	3Gab	1026
Black Swan Hotel	Copp	322
Black Tor	Houn	736
Blackfeet Indians	Stud	52
Blackheath	Norw	499
	Miss	623
	Suss	1036
Blackheath Station	Reti	1116
Blackmail	Scan	165
	Bosc	216
	Glor	379

Blackmail (cont'd)	Reig	409
	Blac	570
	Chas	572
	Seco	664
	Houn	695
	Houn	730
	Vall	826
	Vall	836
	Vall	864
	RedC	912
	3 Gab	1032
Blackmail, suspected	Yell	359
Blacksmith	Spec	260
	Prio	551
farrier	Houn	681
Blackwall	Sign	138
Blackwater, Earl of	Prio	540
Blackwell, Lady Eva	Chas	573
Blair Island (Andamans)	Sign	152
Blaker (foreman)	Vall	835
Blandford Street	Empt	489
Blasting powder	Vall	852
Bleat, unmitigated	RedC	904
Blessington	Resi	425
Blondin (Charles)	Sign	118
Blood, tests for	Stud	18
	Nava	448
Blood, writing in	Stud	31
Bloodhound	Houn	757
	Vall	852
	Cree	1071
Bloodstains	Stud	18
	Stud	26
	Stud	30
	Stud	47
	Sign	119
	Bosc	203

74 ◼ *Good Old Index*

Bloodstains (cont'd)	Twis	235
	Engr	274
	Bery	315
	Silv	338
	Reig	414
	Norw	498
	Norw	506
	Danc	519
	Soli	535
	Prio	548
	Blac	561
	SixN	581
	SixN	586
	SixN	592
	Gold	609
	Abbe	639
	Abbe	644
	Seco	659
	Houn	744
	Vall	782
	Card	900
	RedC	909
	Bruc	927
	Illu	993
	Suss	1035
	3Gar	1053
	Lion	1084
	Veil	1100
	Norw	506
Bloomsbury	Blue	251
	RedC	910
Blotting paper	Twis	238
	Miss	625
Blount (student)	Lion	1090
Blue (athlete)	3Stu	600
	Miss	633
	Lion	1083

Blue Anchor (pub)	Reti	1116
Blue carbuncle	Blue	248
Blue ribbon	Card	898
Blue-tinted glasses	Sign	117
Blymer estate	Maza	1017
Board schools	Nava	456
Boarder, undesireable	Stud	44
	RedC	901
	Veil	1096
Boarding establishment (school)	Sign	94
Boarding house (*see also* Hotel, Inn)	Danc	512
	Vall	797
Mme. Charpentier's	Stud	43
Mrs. Merrilow's	Veil	1095
Mrs. Warren's	RedC	901
Boat chase	Sign	137
Boat, row	Card	900
Boat, tug	Sign	138
Boats (*see* Ships)		
Boats, fishing	Lion	1083
Bob (Ferrier?)	Stud	54
Boccaccio (Giovanni)	Stud	30
Bodkin	Stud	18
Boer War	Blan	1000
South African War	3Gar	1044
Boers	Blan	1009
Bog	Houn	707
Bogus laundry affair	Card	897
Bohemia	Scan	163
	Cree	1079
Bohemia, King of	Scan	165
	Iden	191
	Iden	198
	Copp	317
	Last	979
Bohemian	Scan	161
	Engr	274

76 ◼ *Good Old Index*

Bohemian (cont'd)	Musg	386
	3Gar	1048
	Cree	1078
"Bolted" (telegraph message)	Reti	1117
Bombay (India)	Stud	15
Bond Street		
Kennington	Sign	122
Westminster	Silv	342
	Houn	692
Bones, human	Shos	1106
"Book of Life, The"	Stud	23
Bonnet, daintiest thing under a	Scan	168
Books (*see* Literary references & allusions)		
Boone, Hugh	Twis	235
Bootlaces, as clue	Yell	352
Boots (*see* Clothing)		
Bordeaux (France)	Iden	195
Borgias, black pearl of the	SixN	594
Borough, The (Southwark)	Houn	697
Boscombe Pool	Bosc	203
Boscombe Valley	Bosc	202
Boswell (James)	Scan	164
Bouguereau (A.W.)	Sign	101
Boulevard assassin	Gold	607
Bouquet	Nobl	292
Bovington's (pawnshop)	Lady	948
Bowling-alley	Soli	535
Bow Street	Twis	241
Bow window	Bery	301
	Gree	437
	Maza	1013
	3Gab	1028
Bowery (New York)	RedC	911
Box, deed	Reti	1113
Box, tin (*see* Tin Box)		

Boxer	Stud	22
	Sign	102
	Sign	106
	Five	225
	Yell	351
	Glor	374
	Soli	532
	Last	972
	Maza	1014
	3Gar	1023
	Shos	1103
Boxer cartridges	Musg	386
Boxer's ears	Glor	375
"Boys, the"	Vall	831
Bracelets (*see* handcuffs)	Sign	144
Brackenstall, Sir Eustace	Abbe	637
Brackenstall, Lady	Abbe	637
Bradford	Stud	18
Bradley's (tobacconist)	Houn	740
Bradshaw (railway guide)	Copp	322
	Vall	772
Bradstreet, Inspector	Twis	241
	Blue	248
	Engr	284
Brag and bounce	Stud	25
Brain-fever	Copp	331
	Musg	389
	Croo	415
	Nava	447
	Houn	759
	Card	894
Brambletye Hotel	Blac	567
Brand	Vall	784
Brandy (*see* Alcohol)		
Brass box	Five	220
Brazil (Brazils)	Sign	141
	Thor	1057

78 ◻ *Good Old Index*

Breckenridge (poultry dealer)   Blue   251
Brewer, Sam   Shos   1102
Briarbrae (house)   Nava   447
Brickfall and Amberley   Reti   1113
Bricks (toys)   Twis   234
Bride   Scan   169
    Iden   195
    Nobl   290

Bridges (*see* London)
Brig (ship)   Glor   385
Brilliant (gem)   Iden   191
    Lady   948

Brinvilliers, Marchioness de   Stud   41
Briony Lodge   Scan   167
Bristol   Bosc   205
Britannia personnified (Martha)   Last   974
Britannica, Encyclopaedia   RedH   181
British Birds   Empt   485
British Broken Hills (stock)   Stoc   365
British Law   Stud   22
    Resi   434
    Danc   525
    Houn   714
    Vall   812
    Vall   814
    Wist   885
    Devi   968
    Last   975
    Illu   999
British Medical Journal   Stoc   362
    Blan   1011
British Museum   Blue   251
    Musg   387
    Houn   762
    Wist   879
    RedC   905

Brixton	Stud	26
	Sign	121
	Blue	253
	Nava	452
	Blac	568
	RedC	904
	Lady	949
	3Gar	1054
Brixton, Lower	Gree	444
	SixN	583
Brixton, South	Veil	1095
Brixton bus	RedC	904
Brixton Road	Stud	26
	Blue	253
	Lady	953
Brixton Workhouse Infirmary	Lady	952
Broadmoor (asylum)	Reti	1120
Broads, The (marshland)	Glor	374
Broad Street	Sign	123
Broderick and Nelson's (lumberyard)	Sign	122
Broken heart	Stud	78
	Chas	580
	Wist	885
	Bruc	921
Broken reed	3Gab	1029
Brooklyn (New York)	RedC	911
Brooks (villain)	Bruc	914
Brook Street	Resi	425
Brotherhood, The	Gold	620
Brougham	Stud	84
	Scan	163
	Resi	424
	Resi	431
	Fina	474
	Miss	631
	Illu	993
	Illu	999

Brown, Lieutenant Bromley	Sign	152
Brown, Josiah	SixN	590
Brown, Sam	Sign	143
Brown, Silas	Silv	337
Browner, James	Card	893
Browner, Mary	Card	893
Bruce-Partington submarine	Bruc	916
Bruce Pinkerton Prize	Resi	425
Bruises	Stud	17
	Spec	263
Brunton, Richard	Musg	388
Brush, gum	RedC	901
Brussels (Belgium)	Stoc	366
	Fina	476
Buckboard	3Gar	1050
Buda	Devi	968
Buda-Pesth (Hungary)	Gree	446
Buddha	Sign	142
	Veil	1097
Buddhism of Ceylon	Sign	134
Budget (British Government)	Bruc	916
Buffalo (New York)	Last	978
Buffelsspruit (South Africa)	Blan	1009
Bull, The (inn)	Wist	877
Bull-dog's head pin	Stud	30
Bull pup	Stud	19
Bull Ring (Birmingham)	3Gab	1023
Bull terrier	Glor	374
Bull's eye lantern	Sign	117
Bullock	Stud	60
Bunsen lamp	Stud	17
	Sign	109
	Nava	448
Burberry (coat)	Lion	1084
Burglar alarm	Illu	991
Burglary kit	Chas	577
Burglars, habits of	Abbe	646

Burnet, Miss	Wist	882
Burnwell, Sir George	Bery	304
Bus	Nava	458
	Miss	627
	RedC	904
	RedC	905
Bushman	Houn	768
Bushmen of Africa	Sign	127
Business Firms, British		
accountant	RedH	182
advertising agency	Blue	249
antique dealers		
Christie's	Illu	995
	3Gar	1048
Sotheby's	Illu	995
	3Gar	1048
art dealers		
Harding Bros.	SixN	585
Morse Hudson	SixN	583
banks		
Bank of England	Danc	520
	3Gar	1054
Capital and Counties	Twis	234
	Prio	554
	Bruc	916
City and Suburban	RedH	185
Cox & Co.	Thor	1054
Dawson and Neligan	Blac	566
Holder & Stevenson	Bery	302
Post Office Bank	3Gab	1027
Silvester's	Lady	943
barristers (*see also* Lawyers, Solicitors)	Houn	736
	Illu	995
Cummings, Joyce	Thor	1065
Norton, Godfrey	Scan	168
bars (*see* Public Houses)		

Business Firms, British (cont'd)
   bicycle makers
      Openshaw   Five   219
      Rudge-Whitworth   Vall   791
   bird-stuffer
      Sherman   Sign   115
   blacksmith   Spec   260
       Prio   551
     farrier   Houn   681
   boarding houses (*see also* Hotels, Inns)   Danc   512
       Vall   797
      Charpentier   Stud   43
      Merrilow   Veil   1095
      Warren   RedC   901
   boat yard
      Paul's Wharf   Twis   232
   boatmen   Sign   124
      Bellamy, Tom   Lion   1087
      Jacobson   Sign   135
      Smith, Mordecai   Sign   123
   bootmakers   Houn   688
      Latimer's   Lady   942
   brewer   Twis   233
   butcher
      Allardyce   Blac   559
   cabaret   Lady   946
   cab yard
      Shipley's Yard   Houn   697
   carriage-maker
      McFarlane's   RedH   185
   circuses   Stud   39
      Ronder   Veil   1097
      Sanger   Veil   1097
      Wombwell   Veil   1097
   collier
      Theophilus Johnson   Houn   692

Business Firms, British (cont'd)
- colourman
  - Brickfall & Amberley — Reti — 1113
- cutlery maker
  - Weiss & Co. — Silv — 342
- dog dealers
  - Ross and Mangles — Houn — 762
  - Sherman — Sign — 115
- electrical apparatus
  - Swan and Edison — Houn — 702
- electricians
  - Midland Electrical Company — Soli — 529
  - Morton & Kennedy — Soli — 538
- employment agency
  - Westaway's agency for governesses — Copp — 318
- factories
  - artificial kneecaps — RedH — 182
  - artistic materials — Reti — 1113
  - Brickfall and Amberley — Reti — 1113
  - Gelder & Co. — SixN — 588
  - Morton and Waylight — RedC — 905
  - Openshaw's — Five — 219
- financial agent
  - Pinner, A. — Stoc — 365
- general store
  - Dorak — Cree — 1078
- grocer
  - Francis Prosper — Bery — 310
- gunmakers
  - Straubenzee — Maza — 1014
  - Von Herder — Empt — 493
- hardware
  - Franco-Midland Hardware Company — Stoc — 365
- hatter
  - Underwood, John, and Sons — Stud — 43
- hay dealer — Silv — 342

Business Firms, British (cont'd)
    hop merchant
        Munro, Grant   Yell   353
    hotels (*see also* Boarding
        houses, Inns)
        Anerley Arms   Norw   500
        Bentley's Private   Miss   623
        Carlton   Gree   436
        Charing Cross   Bruc   931
        Claridge's   Last   978
                                            Thor   1056
        Cosmopolitan   Blue   248
        Dacre   SixN   594
        Grand   Illu   993
        greater London hotels   Stud   78
                                            Card   894
                                            Cree   1075
        Grosvenor   Fina   478
        Halliday's Private   Stud   46
        Langham   Sign   94
                                            Scan   166
                                            Lady   947
        Mexborough Private   Houn   763
        Northumberland   Houn   685
        Northumberland Avenue   Nobl   296
            hotels   Gree   438
        private hotels   Stud   15
                                            Miss   623
                                            Houn   763
            Birmingham   Stoc   367
            Brambletye Hotel   Blac   567
            Eagle Commercial (Tunbridge   Vall   803
                Wells)
            Hereford Arms (Ross)   Bosc   207
            Plymouth   Devi   962
            Railway Arms (Little   Reti   1118
                Purlington)

Business Firms, British, hotels (*see also* Boarding houses, Inns), private hotels (cont'd)

Westville Arms (Birlstone)	Vall	785
St. Pancras	Iden	195
House agents	Soli	531
Allan Bros.	Wist	873
Holloway and Steele	3Gar	1051
hydraulic engineers		
Hatherley, V.	Engr	274
Hayling, J.	Engr	284
Venner & Matheson	Engr	276
inns (*see also* Hotels, Boarding Houses, Public Houses)		
Alpha (London)	Blue	251
Black Swan (Winchester)	Copp	322
Blue Anchor	Reti	1116
Bull (Esher)	Wist	877
Chequers		
Lamberley	Suss	1039
Camford	Cree	1076
Crown (Stoke Moran)	Spec	263
"Dangling Prussian"	Last	980
Fighting Cock (Hallamshire)	Prio	552
Green Dragon (Shoscombe)	Shos	1103
Red Bull (Hallamshire)	Prio	546
unnamned	Spec	265
	Yell	353
	Nava	466
	Danc	521
	Prio	544
	Gold	613
	Miss	630
	Houn	705
	Blan	1006
	Thor	1069

Business Firms, British (cont'd)
  iron-master
    Harrison   Nava   457
  jeweler
    Gross & Hankey   Scan   168
  lawyers (*see* Barristers, Solicitors)   Five   220
    Fordham   Five   220
  map dealer
    Stamford's   Houn   683
  market
    Covent Garden   Blue   252
  milliner
    Lesurier   Silv   342
  moneylender
    Sam Brewer   Shos   1102
  newsagent   Silv   336
  newspaper shop   RedH   185
  opium den
    Bar of Gold   Twis   230
  outfitter
    Marx and Co.   Wist   878
  pawnbrokers
    Bovington's   Lady   948
    Wilson, Jabez   RedH   178
  plumbers   Scan   170
                           Iden   193
                           Blue   248
                           Nava   467
                           Chas   576
  poultry distributor
    Breckenridge   Blue   251
    Oakshott   Blue   253
  press syndicate
    Central Press Syndicate   SixN   585
  public houses (*see* Inns and Taverns)   Sign   121
                           Copp   330
                           Soli   532

Business Firms, British, public houses (*see* Inns and Taverns) (cont'd)

alehouse	Blac	561
	Shos	1107
Alpha Inn	Sign	136
Criterion (restaurant)	Blue	251
gin shops	Stud	16
	Stud	80
	Twis	230
Holborn Bar	3Gab	1023
Ivy Plant	Seco	661
White Eagle	Sign	122
White Hart	Stud	34
restaurants		
Cafe Royal	Illu	993
Claridge's	Last	978
Criterion	Stud	16
Goldini's	Bruc	925
Holborn	Stud	16
Marcini's	Houn	766
Simpson's	Dyin	941
	Illu	998
Vegetarian	RedH	185
shipping agents		
Sumner	Blac	567
shipping companies		
Aberdeen Shipping Company	Twis	234
Adelaide-Southampton Company	Abbe	645
Cunard Line	Illu	994
Guion Steamship Company	Stud	30
Liverpool, Dublin and London Steam Packet Company	Card	897
shoemaker	Stud	39
Latimer's	Lady	942
slop shop	Twis	230
solicitors (*see also* Lawyers, Barristers)	Reig	408
	Soli	527
	Houn	692
McFarlane, John Hector	Norw	497

Business Firms, British, solicitors (*see also* Lawyers, Barristers) (cont'd)

Morris (imposter)	RedH	182
Morrison, Morrison & Dodd	Suss	1034
Sutro	3Gab	1025
Whyte, William	Stud	38

stables

King's Pyland	Silv	336
Mapleton	Silv	336
Shipley's Yard (cab yard)	Houn	697
Shoscombe Stables	Shos	1103

stationers (4) 3Stu 603

stockbrokers

Coxon & Woodhouse	Stoc	364
Dodd, James M.	Blan	1000
Mawson & Williams	Stoc	364

surgical instruments

Weiss & Co.	Silv	342

tailor

Hyam's	Norw	503

taverns (*see* Public Houses)

tea brokers

Ferguson and Muirhead	Suss	1034

theatres

Albert Hall	Reti	1116
Allegro	Nobl	290
Covent Garden	RedC	913
Day's Music Hall (Birmingham)	Stoc	368
Haymarket	Reti	1115
Imperial	Soli	527
Lyceum	Sign	95
St. James's Hall	RedH	184
Woolwich	Bruc	916

timber yards

Broderick and Nelson's	Sign	122
Oldacre	Norw	498

Business Firms, British (cont'd)
    tobacconists

	Vall	807
Bradley's	Houn	740
Mortimer's	RedH	185
tradesman, harmles	Sign	102
travel agent		
Cook's	Lady	944
turkish bath	Lady	942
	Illu	984
typewritists		
Lyons, Laura	Houn	731
Sutherland, Mary	Iden	192
undertaker		
Stimson and Co.	Lady	952
watchmaker		
Barraud's	Stud	30
wax works		
Tussaud, Madame	Maza	1019
wine dealers		
Vamberry	Musg	387
Westhouse & Marbank	Iden	196

Business Firms, Continental

banks		
Bank of France	RedH	187
Credit Lyonnaise	Vall	777
	Lady	943
	Maza	1018
Deutsche Bank	Vall	777
gunmakers		
Von Herder	Empt	493
hotels		
Dulong (Lyons)	Reig	398
du Louvre (Paris)	Bruc	931
Englischer Hof		
Meiringen	Fina	477
Baden	Lady	944

Business Firms, Continental, hotels
(cont'd)

Escurial (Madrid)	Wist	887
National (Lausanne)	Lady	943

lawyers

Barelli (Posilippo)	RedC	911

pencil maker

Johann Faber	3Stu	599

press syndicate

Reuters	Fina	469

restaurant

in Strasbourg	Fina	477

tobacconists

Ionides (Alexandria)	Gold	615

wax works

Meunier of Grenoble	Empt	489
Tavernier	Maza	1016

Business Firms, North America
boarding houses

MacNamara, Widow	Vall	830
Shafter's	Vall	818

bootmaker

Meyer (Toronto)	Houn	760

coal companies

Lee	Vall	836
Max Linder & Co.	Vall	836
Rae & Sturmash	Vall	834
Archie Swindon	Vall	836
Todman	Vall	836
Walker Brothers	Vall	836
West Gilmerton General Mining Company	Vall	836
West Section Coaling Company	Vall	836

detective agency

Pinkerton	Vall	854
	RedC	908

Business Firms, North America
  (cont'd)
  dry goods store
      Morris   Vall   841
  fruit importers
      Castalotte and Zamba   RedC   911
  gunmakers
      Pennsylvania Small Arms Co.   Vall   785
      Smith & Wesson   Vall   861
  ironworks
      Atwood   Vall   836
      General   Vall   836
      Iron Dike Co.   Vall   851
      Manson   Vall   836
      Shuman   Vall   836
      Van Deher   Vall   836
  lawyers
      Garrideb, John (imposter)   3Gar   1045
      Hebron, John   Yell   353
      Reilly   Vall   843
  outfitter
      Neal   Vall   811
  newspaper
      Vermissa Herald   Vall   837
  railroads   Vall   815
      Canadian Pacific Railway   Blac   562
      State & Merton County   Vall   836
  saloon
      Joint, The   Danc   525
      Lake Saloon   Vall   828
      Union House   Vall   818
Butlers (*see also* Servants)   Nobl   290
                                               Reig   399
                                               Prio   543
                                               Wist   882
                                               Bruc   921
                                               Illu   996

Butlers (*see also* Servants) (cont'd)
    Ames   Vall   781
    Anthony   Houn   764
    Bannister   3Stu   597
    Barrymore, John   Houn   676
    Brunton, Richard   Musg   386
    Hudson   Glor   378
    Jacobs   Seco   665
    John   Miss   630
    khitmutgar   Sign   100
    native butler   Spec   260
    Ralph   Blan   1002
    Rao, Lal   Sign   120
    Staples   Dyin   936
    Stephens   Shos   1104
Butter, parsley sunk into   SixN   585
Butterfly net   Houn   706
Butterfly collectors
    Garrideb   3Gar   1048
    Stapleton   Houn   706
Buzzard   Stud   52

C

Cab (*see also* carriage, cart, etc.)	(2)	Stud	32
	(2)	Stud	34
		Stud	46
		Stud	51
		Stud	79
		Stud	83
		Sign	115
		Sign	135
		Sign	141
		Scan	169
		RedH	186
		RedH	189
		Bosc	202
		Bosc	210
		Twis	236
		Spec	265
		Engr	286
		Nobl	299
		Bery	304
		Gree	444
		Nava	457
		Fina	473
		Danc	525
		Blac	572

94 ■ *Good Old Index*

Cab, (*see also* carriage, cart, etc.)
  (cont'd)

	SixN	585
	SixN	588
	Gold	608
	Miss	628
	Miss	629
	Abbe	636
	Abbe	646
	Houn	682
	Houn	696
	Houn	697
	Vall	776
	Wist	883
	Card	890
	Card	894
	Card	900
	RedC	905
	Bruc	920
	Dyin	936
	Dyin	941
(3)	Lady	949
	Lady	954
	Illu	988
	Illu	991
	Maza	1015
	Maza	1021
	3Gab	1031
	Reti	1119
four-wheeler	Stud	32
	Stud	40
	Sign	98
	Sign	99
	Iden	195
	Blue	254
	Stoc	363
	Gree	444
	Nava	454
	Norw	501

Cab (*see also* carriage, carts, etc.), four-wheeler (cont'd)		Prio	543
		Blac	563
		SixN	591
		RedC	908
growler (four-wheeler)		Stud	84
hansom		Stud	16
		Stud	27
		Stud	79
		Sign	127
		Scan	168
	(2)	RedH	186
		Iden	195
		Iden	198
		Twis	230
		Engr	276
		Croo	412
		Gree	443
		Nava	453
		Nava	465
	(2)	Fina	474
		Empt	488
		Norw	501
		Danc	514
		Chas	577
		Houn	690
		Lady	942
		Lady	953
		Illu	993
		Cree	1076
		Veil	1098
Cab stand		Fina	484
Cabaret		Lady	946
Cabinet (government)		Nava	454
		Seco	652
		Bruc	925

Cabinet minister, involved in case	Nava	454
	Prio	539
	Seco	652
Cabinet, photo (*see also* photographs)	Scan	171
Cablegrams (*see also* telegrams)	Five	229
	Soli	536
	Vall	865
Cabul (Afghanistan)	Empt	494
Cadet branch of family	Nobl	288
	Musg	388
Cafe noir	Musg	389
Cafe Royal	Illu	993
Cairns, Patrick	Blac	569
Cairo (Egypt)	3Gab	1030
Calcutta (India)	Sign	154
	Spec	260
Calendar of crime, Holmes a walking	Stud	18
Calhoun, Captain James	Five	228
California	Stud	60
	Nobl	289
	Vall	780
Callosities, inferences from	Glor	375
Caltrop (heraldry)	Nobl	288
Cam (river)	Miss	633
Camberwell	Stud	41
	Sign	121
	Iden	196
	Five	218
	Vall	775
	Lady	943
Camberwell, Lower	Sign	115
Camberwell poisoning case	Five	218
Camberwell Road	Stud	43
Cambridge	Miss	622
Cambridge (University)	Nava	447
	Gold	609
	Miss	622

Cambridgeshire	Miss	631
Camden House	Empt	489
Cameos, Vatican	Houn	677
Camera	RedH	178
	SixN	586
Camford	Cree	1072
Camford (University)	Cree	1072
Campden House Road	SixN	586
Campden Mansions	Bruc	925
Canada	Houn	681
	Bruc	914
Canadian Pacific Railway	Blac	562
Candahar (Afghanistan)	Stud	15
Canary	Croo	416
Canary-trainer, notorious	Blac	559
Candle	Stud	28
	Sign	116
	Spec	271
	Engr	283
	Silv	341
	Yell	355
	Yell	360
	Yell	362
	Musg	389
	Resi	425
	Nava	467
	Empt	492
	Danc	519
	Blac	565
	Abbe	636
	Abbe	641
	Houn	703
	Houn	716
	Houn	721
	Houn	725
	Houn	750
	Vall	782

48 ◼ *Good Old Index*

Candle (cont'd)		Vall	805
		Wist	877
		RedC	907
	(4)	Devi	957
		3Gar	1053
as evidence		Resi	425
		Vall	782
as signal		Houn	721
		RedC	907
outdoors		Houn	725
red wax		Stud	28
Cannibal		Sign	128
		Sign	152
		Wist	887
Cannon Street (Station)		Twis	233
Canoe		Sign	153
Can-opener		Last	975
Canteen		Croo	421
Canterbury		Fina	476
Cantlemere, Lord		Maza	1013
Cantonment		Croo	429
Canula		Cree	1073
Cap (percussion)		Scan	170
Cape Town (South Africa)		Vall	865
		Blan	1001
Cape Verdes (islands)		Glor	384
Capital & Counties Bank		Twis	234
		Prio	554
		Bruc	916
Caravan, circus		Veil	1097
Carbolic (acid)		Card	892
Carbolized bandages		Engr	275
Carbonari		Stud	41
		RedC	911
Carboys		Sign	109
Carbuncle		Blue	248

Cardboard boxes		Sign	95
		Card	890
Card case, Russian leather		Stud	30
Cardinal Tosca		Blac	559
Cards, playing		Sign	152
		RedH	188
		Bery	304
		Empt	484
		Soli	537
		3Stu	601
		3Stu	603
		Houn	733
		Devi	957
Carere, Mlle.		Houn	761
Carey, Captain Peter		Blac	559
Carey, Miss		Blac	560
Carey, Mrs.		Blac	563
Carfax, Lady Frances		Lady	943
Carina (singer)		Reti	1116
Carlo (mastiff)		Copp	326
Carlo (spaniel)		Suss	1039
Carlsbad (Germany)		Scan	163
Carlton Club		Gree	436
		Illu	984
Carlton House Terrace		Prio	539
Carlton Terrace		Last	973
Carlyle (Thomas)		Stud	21
		Sign	121
Carnaway, Jim		Vall	835
Carolinas		Five	226
Carotid artery		Gold	610
		Cree	1081
Carpet-bag politicians		Five	221
Carpet bags		Stoc	373
		SixN	593
Carriage (*see also* cab, cart, etc.)	(2)	Bosc	207
		Engr	279

Carriage (*see also* cab, cart, etc.)
(cont'd)

	Nobl	293
	Gree	438
	Gree	444
	Danc	517
	Blac	563
	Chas	573
	Abbe	636
	Wist	884
	Devi	957
	Devi	959
	Blan	1007
	3Gab	1024
	Suss	1039
	Shos	1104
	Reti	1118
barouche	Shos	1107
brougham	Stud	84
	Scan	163
	Resi	424
	Resi	431
	Fina	474
	Miss	631
	Illu	993
	Illu	999
drag	Silv	347
gig	Houn	678
landau	Scan	168
	Silv	340
Carriage-building depot	RedH	185
Carriage side-lights	Scan	171
Carritons (house)	Suss	1035
Carruthers, Bob	Soli	528
Carruthers, Colonel	Wist	870
Carson City (Utah Territory)	Stud	68
Carstairs (Scotland)	Empt	483
Carston, Earl of (Holdernesse)	Prio	539
Carston Castle	Prio	539

Cart		Stud	55
		Twis	240
		Engr	286
		Soli	533
	dog-cart	Twis	232
		Spec	259
		Copp	321
		Glor	377
		Musg	393
		Danc	518
		Soli	533
		Soli	534
		Prio	552
		Houn	730
		Vall	785
		Devi	962
	trap	Bosc	205
		Twis	240
		Spec	265
		Copp	330
		Reig	403
		Soli	529
		Prio	552
		Gold	613
		Houn	751
		Wist	872
		Blan	1006
		Thor	1069
	van	Yell	354
		Fina	473
		Lady	949
	wagon	Stud	55
		Bosc	216
	wagonette	Houn	700
		Houn	754
Carter (Scowrer)		Vall	858
Cartwright (murderer)		Resi	434

Cartwright (boy)	Houn	691
Case-book (*see* Holmes, Sherlock)		
Cassel-Felstein	Scan	165
Castalotte, Tito	RedC	911
Castalotte and Zamba	RedC	911
Castor oil	Sign	105
Cat	Yell	357
	Norw	503
	Chas	578
	Last	974
Catalepsy	Resi	425
Cataract	Empt	483
Cataract knife	Silv	338
Cathedral (Winchester Cathedral)	Copp	323
Catholic (*see* Roman Catholic Church)		
Catholic emblem	SixN	590
Cat-o'-nine tails	Lion	1091
Cats' eyes	Sign	151
Cattle	Stud	60
	Prio	548
bullocks	Stud	60
cattle tracks	Prio	548
cows	Stud	60
	Prio	548
	Houn	699
Catullus (poet)	Empt	485
Caulfield Gardens	Bruc	925
Cauliflower ears	Glor	375
Caunter (student)	Prio	540
Cavalier	Musg	397
	Houn	749
Cavendish (club)	Empt	484
Cavendish (tobacco)	Silv	341
Cavendish Square	Resi	425
	Empt	489
Cawnpore (India)	Sign	146

C.B. (Companion of the Bath)	Empt	494
C.C.H. (Charing Cross Hospital)	Houn	669
Cedars, The (house)	Twis	233
Celt	Houn	700
Celtic power	Sign	90
Celtic soul	Musg	396
Celts (implements)	Devi	961
Central Africa	Devi	970
Central America	Houn	681
	Wist	884
Central Press Syndicate	SixN	585
Ceramics	Illu	987
Cesspool, Great London	Stud	15
Ceylon, Buddhism of	Sign	134
Chairman of Committees	Houn	749
Chaldean language	Devi	955
Chalk, billiard	Danc	511
Chalk, figures written in	Danc	513
Chalk, on shoes	Five	219
Chalk cliffs	Last	971
	Lion	1083
Chalk downs	Vall	779
Chalk marks (billiards)	Gree	437
Chalk-pits	Five	222
	Veil	1101
Chain and weakest link	Vall	770
Champagne	Vall	829
Chancellery	Seco	653
Chancellor, Last, of Germany	Last	971
Chandos, Sir Charles	Vall	786
Channel (English)	Last	973
	Lion	1083
Chaparral bushes	Stud	52
Chapel	Glor	374
	Shos	1104
Chaplet	Sign	102
Charasiab (Afghanistan)	Empt	494

Charcoal, suffocation from burning | Gree | 445
Charing Cross | Twis | 240
 | Gree | 438
 | Thor | 1054
Charing Cross Hospital | Houn | 670
 | Illu | 993
Charing Cross Hotel | Bruc | 931
Charing Cross Post Office | Houn | 685
 | Wist | 870
   Telegraph Office | Abbe | 636
Charing Cross Station | Scan | 174
 | Empt | 494
 | Gold | 608
 | Abbe | 636
 | Seco | 659
 | Illu | 993
Charlatanism | Sign | 93
Charles I (King) | Stud | 38
 | Musg | 396
 | Vall | 807
Charles II (King) | Musg | 397
Charles Street | Nava | 451
Charlington | Soli | 526
Charlington Hall | Soli | 528
Charlington Heath | Soli | 528
Charpentier, Alice | Stud | 44
Charpentier, Arthur | Stud | 42
Charpentier, Madame | Stud | 41
Charpentier's Boarding Establishment | Stud | 43
Chart of house | Nava | 451
 | Gold | 610
Charters, early English | 3Stu | 596
Charwoman | Nava | 453
Charybdis, Scylla and | Resi | 422
Chatham | Gold | 608
Chatham Road | Gold | 617

Chauffeur	Last	974
Check-book	Prio	554
Check-book, Waton's	Danc	511
Check, forged	Maza	1018
Checkers (draughts)	Five	220
Cheese	Stud	24
	Blan	1004
	Suss	1039
Cheeseman's (house)	Suss	1035
Cheetah	Spec	260
Chemical analysis	Sign	135
	Nava	448
	Empt	488
Chemical laboratory		
Bart's	Stud	17
Bartholomew Sholto's	Sign	109
Chemistry (*see* Holmes, Sherlock)		
Chequers (inn)	Suss	1039
	Cree	1076
Chess	Reti	1113
Chesterfield	Twis	242
	Prio	546
Chesterfield High Road	Prio	546
Chesterton	Miss	632
Chestnut hair	Stud	64
	Copp	320
Chestnut trees	Yell	351
	Wist	877
Chianti (wine)	Stud	101
Chicago	Danc	523
	Vall	793
	Last	978
	3Gar	1046
Chicago Central (police precinct)	Vall	831
Chillian Wallah (India)	Sign	147
Chiltern Grange	Soli	528
Chin China Coaster	Glor	382

China	RedH	177
	Blue	249
Chinese coin	RedH	177
Chinese dynasties	Illu	995
Chinese pottery	Illu	987
Chinese sailors	Glor	381
Chinese tea trade	Glor	381
Chiselhurst Station	Abbe	637
Chiswick	SixN	590
Chloroform	Lady	953
	Last	977
	3Gab	1029
Chokey (jail)	Sign	155
Chopin (Frederic)	Stud	36
Chorus of groans, cries and bleatings (agony column)	RedC	904
Chosen Valley (Utah)	Stud	63
Chowdar, Lal	Sign	103
Christian	Stud	64
	Houn	723
Christian Cross	Sign	147
Christie's (auction rooms)	Illu	995
	3Gar	1048
Christmas	Blue	244
	Spec	260
Chronicle (newspaper; *see also Daily Chronicle*)	Iden	190
	Silv	336
	Card	890
Chubb lock (key)	Scan	168
	Gold	614
Church clock chiming	Nava	467
	Blac	565
	Bruc	929
Big Ben	Lady	953
Palace, South Kensington	Sign	117

Churches
    chapels

	Glor	374
	Croo	413
	Shos	1104

    East Anglian   Danc   517
    Kensington, great church   Bruc   929
    St. George's   Nobl   289
    St. Monica's   Scan   168
    St. Paul's   Sign   137

	RedH	182
	Iden	195

    St. Saviour's
    Watt Street chapel   Croo   413
    Westminster Abbey   Seco   655
    Winchester Cathedral   Copp   323

Church Row   Chas   577
Church Street
    Kensington   Empt   485
    Stepney   SixN   588

C.I.D. (*see also* Scotland Yard)

	Vall	775
	Maza	1015
	3Gar	1054

Cigar (*see also* Holmes and Watson)
    ashes as clue

	Bosc	214
	Houn	680

    evidence from   Resi   432
    Havana   Resi   432
    Indian   Bosc   213

	Spec	261
	Resi	432

    kept in coal scuttle   Musg   386
    Trichinopoly   Stud   32

	Sign	91

Cigarette (*see* Holmes and Watson)
Cigarette, identification from   Houn   739
Cigarette-end as clue   RedC   904
Cigarettes, handmade   Houn   672
Cigarettes, solution derived from   Gold   621

Ciphers and codes

	Glor	379
	Musg	392
	Danc	511
	Seco	653
	Vall	770
	Vall	855
	RedC	907
Circus	Stud	39
	Veil	1097

Cities, towns, villages—Great Britain (*see also* London-districts and environs)

Aberdeen	Twis	234
	Nobl	295
	Vall	773
Abergavenny	Prio	539
Aldershot	Copp	322
	Croo	412
Alton	Houn	692
Andover	Iden	196
Aston	3Gar	1050
Bangor	Prio	539
Bedford	Blan	1001
Birmingham	Stoc	363
	Glor	375
	3Gab	1023
	3Gar	1050
Bradford	Stud	18
Bristol	Bosc	205
Cambridge	Nava	447
	Miss	622
	Gold	609
Canterbury	Fina	476
Chatham	Gold	608
Chesterfield	Twis	242
	Prio	546
Chesterton	Miss	632

Cities, towns, villages—Great Britain (see also London-districts and environs) (cont'd)

Chiselhurst	Abbe	637
Clapham Junction	Silv	330
Coventry	Five	219
	Soli	529
Crewe	Spec	260
Croydon	Card	890
Darlington	Scan	173
Derby	Vall	806
Doncaster	SixN	586
Dundee	Five	222
	Blac	560
Eastbourne	Wist	869
Edinburgh	Sign	94
Eton	RedH	186
	Empt	494
Exeter	Silv	336
Falmouth	Glor	380
Fareham	Five	222
Farnham	Soli	527
Fordingbridge	Glor	379
Forest Row	Blac	560
Frinton	Reti	1117
Gloucester	Houn	692
Gravesend	Sign	123
	Five	229
	Twis	238
Guildford	Wist	887
Harwich	Last	974
Helston	Devi	959
Hereford	Bosc	209
Histon	Miss	632
Horsham	Five	218
	Suss	1035
Leatherhead	Spec	259

110 ◼ *Good Old Index*

Cities, towns, villages—Great Britain (*see also* London-districts and environs) (cont'd)

Leeds	Houn	687
Leicester	Vall	806
Lewes	Lion	1086
Liverpool	Stud	30
	Prio	541
	Vall	806
	Card	893
	Illu	994
	Maza	1020
Margate	Seco	657
	Veil	1101
New Brighton	Card	900
Newcastle	Houn	692
Newhaven	Fina	476
Newmarket	Shos	1102
North Walsham	Danc	517
Norwich	Danc	517
Nottingham	Vall	806
Oxford	RedH	186
	Empt	494
	Miss	623
Pershore	Sign	144
Petersfield	Nobl	289
Plymouth	Silv	342
	Houn	717
	Devi	961
Portsmouth	Stud	15
	Nava	456
	Last	973
Reading	Bosc	202
	Spec	263
	Engr	278
	Silv	336
	SixN	590

**Cities, towns, villages—Great Britain
(see also London-districts and
environs)** (cont'd)

Redruth	Devi	958
Reigate	Reig	398
Ripley	Nava	466
Ross	Bosc	203
Rosythe	Last	973
St. Ives	Devi	959
Southampton	Copp	324
	Copp	332
	Abbe	646
	Houn	681
	Vall	806
	Blan	1001
Swindon	Bosc	207
Tarleton	Musg	387
Tavistock	Silv	337
Tunbridge Wells	Blac	571
	Vall	779
Uppingham	Gold	609
Wallington	Card	894
Walsall	Copp	332
Waterbeach	Miss	632
Wilton	Spec	267
Winchester	Copp	319
	Silv	347
	Thor	1056
Windsor	Bruc	931
Woking	Nava	447
York	Houn	753

**Cities, towns, villages—Great
Britain—fictitious**

Abbas Parva	Veil	1096
Addleton	Gold	607
Birlstone	Vall	779
Camford	Cree	1072

Cities, towns, villages—Great Britain—fictitious (cont'd)

Charlington	Soli	526
Coombe Tracey	Houn	729
Crane Water	Spec	263
Crendall	Shos	1104
Donnithorpe	Glor	374
Eyford	Engr	278
Fernworthy	Houn	715
Foulmire	Houn	684
Fulworth	Lion	1083
Grimpen	Houn	671
Hurlstone	Musg	388
Kings Pyland	Silv	336
Lamberley	Suss	1035
Little Purlington	Reti	1117
Mackleton	Prio	539
Mapleton	Silv	336
Marsham	Abbe	636
Moosmoor	Reti	1117
Oakington	Miss	632
Riding Thorp	Danc	512
Shoscombe	Shos	1107
Stoke Moran	Spec	257
Tredannick Wollas	Devi	957
Trumpington	Miss	634
Tuxbury	Blan	1000

Cities, towns, villages—Irish

Belfast	Card	890
Dublin	Card	896
Skibbareen	Last	978
Waterford	Card	896

Cities, towns, villages—European

Amsterdam (Holland)	Maza	1020
Athens (Greece)	Gree	440
Baden (Germany)	Lady	944
Barcelona (Spain)	Wist	885

Cities, towns, villages—European
(cont'd)

Bari (Italy)	RedC	911
Basle (Switzerland)	Fina	476
Belgrade (Serbia)	Seco	666
Berlin (Germany)	Last	971
Bordeaux (France)	Iden	195
Brussels (Belgium)	Stoc	366
	Fina	476
Buda	Devi	968
Buda-Pesth (Austria-Hungary)	Gree	446
Carlsbad (Bohemia)	Scan	163
Copenhagen (Denmark)	Stud	44
Davos Platz (Switzerland)	Fina	478
Dieppe (France)	Fina	476
Florence (Italy)	Empt	487
Flushing (Holland)	Last	972
Frankfort (Germany)	Stud	18
Geneva (Switzerland)	Fina	469
	Fina	477
Grodno (Russia)	Houn	754
Grenoble (France)	Empt	489
Hague, The (Holland)	Iden	196
Heidelberg (Germany)	3Gar	1048
Interlaken (Switzerland)	Fina	477
Lausanne (Switzerland)	Lady	942
Leuk (Switzerland)	Fina	477
Liege (Belgium)	Stud	38
Lucerne (Switzerland)	Fina	478
	3Gab	1027
Lyons (France)	Reig	398
Madrid (Spain)	Seco	666
	Wist	885
Malplaquet (France)	Reig	403
Marengo (Italy)	Abbe	644
Marseilles (France)	Iden	192
Meiringen (Switzerland)	Fina	477

Cities, towns, villages—European (cont'd)

Milan (Italy)	3Gab	1027
Montpellier (France)	Stud	18
	Empt	488
	Lady	943
Munich (Germany)	Nobl	293
Naples (Italy)	SixN	590
	RedC	911
Narbonne (France)	Fina	469
Nimes (France)	Fina	469
Oporto (Portugal)	Resi	434
Paris (France)	Stud	76
	Nobl	299
	Stoc	367
	Nava	447
	Fina	475
	Seco	658
	Wist	885
Posilippo (Italy)	RedC	911
Prague (Bohemia)	Scan	165
	Illu	985
	Cree	1073
Rome (Italy)	Stoc	367
	Wist	885
	3Gab	1025
Rosenlaui (Switzerland)	Fina	478
Rotterdam (Holland)	Bosc	214
	Last	976
San Remo (Italy)	Stoc	366
Seville (Spain)	Stud	62
Sparta (Greece)	Houn	739
Strasbourg (Germany)	Fina	476
Syracuse (Sicily)	3Gar	1048
Utrecht (Holland)	Stud	29
Venice (Italy)	Sign	104

Cities, towns, villages—European (cont'd)

Warsaw (Russian Poland)	Scan	165
Waterloo (Belgium)	Abbe	644

Cities, towns, villages—European—fictitious

Eglow	Scan	163
Eglonitz	Scan	163
Egria	Scan	163

Cities, towns, villages—U.S.

Atlanta	Yell	353
Brooklyn	RedC	911
	Last	978
Carson City	Stud	68
Chicago	Danc	523
	Vall	793
	Last	978
	3Gar	1046
Cleveland	Stud	26
Detroit	Vall	821
Fort Dodge (Kansas)	3Gar	1046
Lebanon	RedH	178
Nauvoo (Illinois)	Stud	57
New Orleans	Stud	18
New York	Stud	30
	Danc	523
	Abbe	647
	Houn	761
	Vall	836
	RedC	908
	Last	976
Palmyra (New York)	Stud	57
Philadelphia	Copp	321
	Vall	836
St. Augustine	Five	223
St. Louis	Stud	60
	Sign	90

Cities, towns, villages—U.S. (cont'd)

Salt Lake City	Stud	59
San Francisco	Nobl	289
Savannah	Five	228
Topeka	3Gar	1046
Washington (D.C.)	Vall	864

Cities, towns, villages—U.S.—fictitious

Barton's Crossing	Vall	815
Gilmerton	Vall	850
Helmdale	Vall	815
Hobson's Patch	Vall	818
Ironhill	Vall	849
Moorville (Kansas)	3Gar	1045
Stagville	Vall	815
Stake Royal	Vall	850
Stylestown	Vall	857
Vermissa	Vall	811

Cities, towns, villages—other

Adelaide (Australia)	Abbe	639
	Lady	947
Agra (India)	Sign	145
Alexandria (Egypt)	Gold	615
	3Gar	1048
Allahabad (India)	Veil	1098
Auckland (New Zealand)	Iden	193
Ballarat (Australia)	Sign	107
	Bosc	214
Bangalore (India)	Empt	494
Barberton (South Africa)	Lady	947
Benares (India)	Sign	142
Bombay (India)	Stud	15
	Sign	95
Broken Hill (Australia)	Stoc	365
Cabul (Afghanistan)	Empt	494
Cairo (Egypt)	3Gab	1030

Cities, towns, villages—other (cont'd)

Calcutta (India)	Sign	154
	Spec	260
Candahar (Afghanistan)	Stud	15
Capetown (South Africa)	Vall	865
	Blan	1001
Cawnpore (India)	Sign	146
Charasiab (Afghanistan)	Empt	494
Chilian Wallah (India)	Sign	147
Darjeeling (India)	Croo	420
Delhi (India)	Sign	151
Halifax (Canada)	Copp	318
Havana (Cuba)	Resi	432
Hope Town (Andaman Islands)	Sign	152
Jiddah (Arabia)	Sign	155
Johannesburg (South Africa)	Soli	528
Khartoum (Sudan)	Empt	488
Kimberley (South Africa)	Soli	536
Lhassa (Tibet)	Empt	488
Lucknow (India)	Sign	146
Madras (India)	Sign	152
Maiwand (Afghanistan)	Stud	15
Manaos (Brazil)	Thor	1060
Mecca (Arabia)	Empt	488
Melbourne (Australia)	Bosc	216
Muttra (India)	Sign	145
Nara (Japan)	Illu	997
Odessa (Russia)	Stud	84
	Scan	161
Peking (China)	Illu	995
Pernambuco (Brazil)	3Gab	1031
Peshawar (India)	Stud	15
Pondicherry (India)	Sign	102
	Five	220
Pretoria (South Africa)	Blan	1001
Riga (Russia)	Sign	90
St. Petersburg (Russia)	Stud	76

118 ◻ *Good Old Index*

Cities, towns, villages—other (cont'd)
    Sao Paulo (Brazil) — Blac 562
    Shahgunge (India) — Sign 146
    Singapore — Sign 155
    Sydney (Australia) — Glor 385
    Toronto (Canada) — Houn 760
    Trichinopoly (India) — Stud 32
        Sign 91
    Trincomalee (Ceylon) — Scan 161
    Victoria (Australia) — Bosc 208

Cities, towns, villages-other-fictitious
    Bhurtee (India) — Croo 420
    Buffelsspruit (South Africa) — Blan 1009

City (of London) The — Sign 137
    RedH 178
    Iden 198
    Five 227
    Twis 230
    Twis 234
    Bery 302
    Yell 356
    Stoc 364
    SixN 588

City and Suburban Bank — RedH 185
City police — Stoc 373
Civil War, American — Five 226
    Resi 424
    Vall 853
    Card 889

Civil War, English (Great Rebellion) — Musg 397
    Houn 674
    Vall 807

Civil War, Irish — Last 972
Clapham Junction — Silv 350
    Gree 442
    Nava 456

Clarendon, Lord — Houn 674

Claret	Iden	196
	Card	894
	Dyin	941
Claridge's Hotel	Last	978
	Thor	1056
Clay, John	RedH	186
Clay, as a clue	3Gar	597
Clayton, John	Houn	697
Cleft Tor	Houn	723
Clergyman		
unfrocked	Soli	536
pompous	Reti	1118
as a disguise		
Peters	Lady	947
Holmes	Scan	170
	Fina	474
Wilson	Glor	383
Clergymen	Scan	169
	Blac	560
	Vall	811
Desmond, James	Houn	695
Elman, J.G.	Reti	1117
Parker	Danc	512
Roundhay	Devi	956
Stone, Joshua	Wist	876
Whitney, Elias	Twis	229
Clergymen, directory of (Crockford)	Reti	1117
Cleveland (Ohio)	Stud	26
Client, illustrious	Bery	303
	Illu	985
Clients in recorded cases		
Amberley, Josiah	Reti	1113
Barclay, Mrs. Nancy	Croo	419
Baskerville, Sir Henry	Houn	681
Bennett, Trevor	Cree	1072
Blackwell, Lady Eva	Chas	573
Bohemia, King of	Scan	165

Clients in recorded cases (cont'd)

British Government	Seco	650
	Bruc	915
	Last	978
	Maza	1013
Cubitt, Hilton	Danc	512
Damery, Sir James (agent)	Illu	984
Dodd, James M.	Blan	1000
Eccles, John Scott	Wist	870
Ferguson, Robert	Suss	1034
Forrester, Inspector	Reig	400
Garrideb, Nathan	3Gar	1045
Gibson, J. Neil	Thor	1056
Gregson, Inspector Tobias	Stud	26
Hatherley, Victor	Engr	274
Holder, Alexander	Bery	302
Holdernesse, Duke of	Prio	539
Hopkins, Inspector Stanley	Blac	559
	Gold	608
	Abbe	636
Hunter, Violet	Copp	318
Huxtable, Dr. Thorneycroft	Prio	538
Lestrade, Inspector G.	Stud	26
	Bosc	204
	SixN	582
	Card	890
Maberley, Mary	3Gab	1024
MacDonald, Inspector	Vall	773
Mason, John	Shos	1103
McFarlane, John Hector	Norw	497
Melas, Mr.	Gree	438
Morstan, Mary	Sign	93
Mortimer, Dr. James	Houn	671
Munro, Grant	Yell	353
Musgrave, Reginald	Musg	388
Openshaw, John	Five	219
Overton, Cyril	Miss	622

Clients in recorded cases (cont'd)
    Phelps, Percy | Nava | 447
    Pycroft, Hall | Stoc | 364
    Ronder, Eugenia | Veil | 1095
    Ross, Colonel | Silv | 336
    Roundhay, Mr. | Devi | 956
    St. Clair, Mrs. Neville | Twis | 237
    St. Simon, Lord Robert | Nobl | 291
    Smith, Violet | Soli | 527
    Soames, Hilton | 3Stu | 596
    Stoner, Helen | Spec | 259
    Sutherland, Mary | Iden | 192
    Trevelyan, Dr. Percy | Resi | 425
    Trevor, Victor | Glor | 374
    Warren, Mrs. | RedC | 901
    Wilson, Jabez | RedH | 176

Clipper (ship)	Glor	381
Clocks, chiming	Blac	565
Big Ben	Lady	953
Kensington church	Bruc	929
Palace, South London	Sign	117
Woking	Nava	467
Clothing		
apron	Stud	53
	Nava	451
	Houn	748
	Card	891
blouse	Lady	946
boa	RedC	904
fur	Iden	192
bonnet	Nobl	290
	Yell	355
	3Gar	1052
Scotch	Blue	250
boots	Stud	30
	Sign	117
	Bosc	211

Clothing, boots (cont'd)

	Twis	235
	Twis	240
	Bery	311
	Bery	315
	Silv	345
	Stoc	364
	Glor	376
	Musg	391
	Nava	453
	Abbe	648
	Houn	683
	Houn	688
	Houn	690
	Houn	693
	Houn	721
	Houn	739
	Houn	755
	Vall	797
	Vall	810
	RedC	906
	3Gar	1045
ammunition	Gree	437
dress	Wist	871
elastic sided	Iden	197
	Bery	311
fur	Scan	164
patent leather	Stud	29
	Houn	693
resoled	Nava	460
shooting	Bosc	213
square toed	Stud	32
	Bosc	212
	Silv	345
woman's	Iden	196
braces	Stoc	371

Clothing (cont'd)

cap	Blac	569
	Houn	745
	Shos	1102
cloth	Engr	274
	Silv	337
	Soli	529
	Blac	565
country	Last	974
cricket	Prio	546
lady's	Card	893
leather	Twis	235
mob	Lady	946
peaked	Twis	241
rabbitskin	Sign	105
soft	Vall	804
velvet, black smoking	Vall	832
	Dyin	937
Holmes's	Bosc	202
cloth	Houn	740
ear-flapped	Silv	335
cassock, black (priest)	Fina	475
cloak	Sign	98
	Scan	164
	Bosc	213
	Copp	329
	Nava	461
	Nava	467
	Fina	474
Holmes's, long gray	Bosc	202
coat	Scan	169
	Twis	236
	Twis	240
	Stoc	371
	Glor	382
	Resi	432
	Gree	437

Clothing, coat (cont'd)

	Nava	466
	Prio	549
	Houn	710
	Vall	778
	Vall	809
	RedC	905
	Dyin	932
	Dyin	941
	Lady	942
	Illu	984
	Blan	1005
	Blan	1007
	3Gar	1045
	Lion	1092
plaid	Bosc	206
seedy	Bery	311
tweed	Shos	1102
with astrakhan	Sign	105
	Scan	164
dustcoat	Bosc	207
	Last	974
frock coat	Stud	29
	RedH	177
	RedH	186
	Iden	197
	Blue	250
	Spec	264
	Nobl	291
	Nobl	297
	Bery	301
	Silv	340
	Resi	425
	Houn	671
	Vall	848
	Illu	985
	Cree	1076

Clothing, coat, frock coat (cont'd)

	Holmes's	Empt	486
		Norw	502
		Houn	690
	greatcoat	RedH	177
		Chas	577
		RedC	908
	mackintosh	Silv	338
	overcoat	Five	224
		Silv	338
		Empt	491
		Houn	701
		Vall	804
		Vall	840
		Bruc	916
		Bruc	925
		Maza	1021
		3Gar	1053
		Cree	1080
	astrakhan	Chas	573
	Burberry	Lion	1084
	Holmes's	Stud	27
		Nobl	296
		3Stu	598
		Gold	608
		Abbe	636
		Cree	1080
	summer	Norw	497
	velvet collar	RedH	177
	yellow	Vall	810
ulster		Scan	173
		Nobl	290
	Holmes's	Stud	39
		Blue	251
	waterproof	Five	218
		Gold	608
		Houn	738

Clothing, coat, waterproof (cont'd)

Holmes's	Bosc	212
	Houn	738
Watson's	Houn	730
collar	Stud	29
	Prio	539
	Houn	741
cords, leather	Soli	534
cravat	Nobl	295
	Bery	311
	Silv	338
	RedC	908
	Bruc	929
Holmes's	Stud	39
	Blue	251
	Gold	608
black satin	Illu	985
cuff	Stud	29
note written on	Nava	452
	Houn	682
cummerbund	Sign	149
dress	Spec	258
	Engr	280
	Copp	320
	Copp	328
	Danc	519
beige	Sign	94
court	Chas	582
dinner	Thor	1056
sequin-covered dinner	Abbe	637
mouseline de soie with pink chiffon	Twis	237
rich material	Engr	280
silk	Silv	342
wedding, of watered silk	Nobl	295
with plush at neck and sleeves	Iden	196
frock	Stud	53
	Yell	361

Clothing (cont'd)
    dress-clothes   Chas   577
    dressing-gown   Spec   262
                                       Spec   272
                                       Musg   389
                                       Reig   400
                                       Gree   440
                                       Danc   515
                                       Danc   519
                                       Abbe   637
                                       Vall   782
                                       Vall   792
                                       Cree   1080
        flannel   SixN   585
        Holmes's   Engr   276
                                       Bery   301
                                       Resi   431
                                       Nava   448
                                       Fina   472
                                       Houn   683
                                       Vall   778
                                       Card   890
                                       Lady   953
                                       Maza   1013
                                       Maza   1018
        blue   Twis   240
        mouse   Empt   494
                                       Bruc   920
        purple   Blue   244
    frock   Stud   53
                                       Yell   361
    gaiters   Iden   197
                                       Spec   264
                                       Nobl   291
                                       Bery   301
                                       Silv   337
                                       Silv   340

128 ◘ *Good Old Index*

Clothing, gaiters (cont'd)

	Soli	534
	Soli	535
	Vall	785
spats	Wist	870
	Illu	985
galoshes	Gold	608
gloves	Sign	94
	Iden	192
	Iden	196
	Iden	199
	Spec	259
	Nobl	291
	Yell	361
	Soli	527
	3Stu	606
	Seco	656
	Card	894
kid	RedC	909
	Illu	985
leather	Blan	1007
gown	Gree	440
handerkerchief	Sign	117
	Sign	136
	Iden	195
	Engr	274
	Bery	302
	Copp	325
	Soli	535
	Abbe	638
	Vall	877
	Devi	967
	Lion	1086
bandana	Sign	132
red silk	Gree	437
hat	Stud	45
	Stud	46
	Sign	98

Clothing, hat (cont'd)

	Scan	170
	RedH	184
	Bosc	203
	Twis	235
	Bery	308
	Copp	329
	Silv	340
	Resi	429
	Gree	437
	Fina	475
	Norw	504
	Blac	559
	Chas	582
	Abbe	645
	Seco	666
	Houn	683
	Houn	690
	Houn	707
	Houn	717
	Vall	799
	Vall	840
	Wist	880
	Card	894
	Dyin	932
	Devi	959
	Blan	1007
	Maza	1016
billycock	Blue	245
bowler	Blan	1005
broad-brimmed	Scan	164
	Iden	192
	Bruc	929
curly-brimmed	Nobl	291
felt	Vall	824
hard felt	Blue	244
opera	Empt	491
Panama	Danc	524

Clothing, hat (cont'd)
   Scotch bonnet   Blue   250
   shiny   RedH   186
     Bery   301
     Card   894
   soft   Vall   849
   sombrero   Stud   61
   straw   Houn   706
     Reti   1114
    with red feather   Iden   196
   top hat   Stud   29
     RedH   177
     Iden   199
     Spec   264
     Stoc   364
     Miss   626
     Illu   985
    Holmes's   Chas   577
    Watson's with stethescope   Scan   162
   turban   Sign   100
     Sign   149
    with white feather   Sign   94
   wideawake   Yell   352
  jacket   Sign   121
     Iden   196
     Spec   259
     Glor   376
   Eton   Prio   540
   frogged   Twis   241
   Norfolk   Blac   565
   pea   Sign   130
     Sign   132
     RedH   186
     Nobl   295
     Vall   828
   reefer   Vall   804
   smoking   Vall   804

Clothing (cont'd)
    knickerbockers   Blac   565
    leggings, leather   Bosc   207
    mantle   Yell   355
                                     Chas   580
                                     Seco   662
    muff   Iden   195
    muffler, shepherd's check   Musg   395
    neckcloth   Stud   51
    necktie (*see* tie)   Resi   425
                                     Soli   531
                                     Miss   626
                                     Maza   1015
    night clothes   Danc   519
                                     Gold   610
                                     Vall   782
    night-dress   Stud   47
                                     Spec   262
                                     Resi   431
    night shirt   Prio   549
                                     Abbe   635
    petticoats   Vall   830
    sash   Sign   100
    scarf   Sign   133
    shawl   Sign   149
                                     Spec   261
                                     Houn   722
                                     Thor   1056
                                     Shos   1109
        gray   Stud   53
        paisley   Nava   452
    shirt   Twis   236
                                     Bery   306
                                     Glor   376
                                     Prio   539
                                     Prio   541
                                     SixN   592

Clothing, shirt (cont'd)

              dress
      shirt-cuff, note on

              shoes

                    canvas
                    jumping
                    patent leather
                    rubber-soled
                    satin
                    square-toed
                    tennis

                    varnished
             skirt
            slippers

                    carpet
                    list
                    patent leather
                    red Turkish
             socks

                    stockings
             spats

Houn	716
Houn	745
Empt	491
Nava	452
Houn	682
Stud	53
Stud	56
Spec	271
Prio	549
Reti	1114
Lion	1084
3Stu	606
Nobl	291
Chas	577
Nobl	295
Resi	430
Chas	577
Devi	968
Illu	985
Seco	657
Blue	254
Musg	391
Abbe	647
Vall	797
Vall	782
Nava	453
Stoc	363
Spec	272
Stud	56
Twis	235
Prio	541
Vall	810
3Gar	1045
Sign	117
Wist	870
Illu	985

Clothing, spats (cont'd)

gaiters	Iden	197
	Spec	264
	Nobl	291
	Bery	301
	Silv	337
	Silv	340
	Soli	534
	Soli	535
	Vall	785
stockings	Sign	117
stole	Vall	832
	Vall	837
suit	Sign	113
	Copp	325
	Yell	352
	Stoc	364
	Musg	391
	Soli	529
	3Stu	600
	Houn	706
	Vall	804
	3Gab	1023
flannel	Danc	524
tweed	Scan	167
	Silv	337
	Soli	535
	Blac	559
	Houn	685
	Houn	740
	Vall	785
tweed, gray	Vall	810
tweed, heather	Engr	274
dress clothes	Chas	577
surplice	Soli	535

Clothing (cont'd)

tie	Scan	169
	Scan	170
	3Gab	1023
trousers	Stud	29
	Scan	170
	RedH	177
	Bery	301
	Bery	306
	Resi	425
	Nava	466
	Prio	540
	SixN	592
	Abbe	638
	Houn	671
	Houn	716
	Houn	754
	Blan	1007
	3Gar	1047
	Lion	1084
dungaree	Glor	376
Harris tweed	Iden	197
knickerbockers	Blac	565
leather cords	Soli	534
tunic, velveteen	Stud	56
underclothes	Vall	810
uniform	Stud	22
	Card	893
veil	Spec	258
	Nobl	295
	Chas	580
	Veil	1096
vest	Vall	826
waistcoat	Stud	29
	RedH	177
	Five	222
	Twis	240

Clothing, waitcoat (cont'd)	Nobl	291
	Silv	344
	Stoc	371
	Gree	437
	Soli	535
	Prio	543
	Vall	807
	Vall	837
	Vall	860
	Wist	871
Clubs (Members)		
Alpha Inn Goose (Baker)	Blue	251
Amateur Mendicant Society	Five	218
Anglo-Indian (Moran)	Empt	494
aristocratic (Arthur Holder)	Bery	304
Bagatelle		
(Adair)	Empt	484
(Moran)	Empt	494
Baldwin (Adair)	Empt	484
Carlton (Damery)	Illu	984
Cavendish (Adair)	Empt	484
Diogenes (Mycroft)	Gree	435
	Bruc	914
Hurlingham (Baron Gruner)	Illu	987
Nonpareil	Houn	761
Prince's Skating	RedC	904
Tankerville		
(Openshaw)	Five	219
(Moran)	Empt	494
Watson's	Houn	683
Clues to a man's calling	Stud	23
Coachman (*see also* servants)	Scan	168
	Reig	399
	Croo	413
	Gree	446
	Prio	551
	Miss	631

136 ◘ *Good Old Index*

Coachman (*see also* **servants**) (cont'd)	Houn	700
	Illu	999
	Cree	1081
	Shos	1109
Coal-scuttle	Musg	386
	Maza	1012
Coal-tar derivatives	Empt	488
Coats of arms (*see also* **Heraldic**	Nobl	287
Emblems)	Nobl	288
	Prio	542
	Chas	574
	Abbe	636
	Houn	702
	Illu	990
	Illu	999
	Shos	1110
Cobb, John	Bosc	205
Cobbler's wax	RedH	180
Coburg branch of bank	RedH	185
Coburg (Saxe-Coburg) Square	RedH	178
Cobwebs	Gold	619
Cocaine (*see also* **poison**)	Sign	89
	Sign	158
	Scan	161
	Five	225
	Twis	232
	Yell	351
	Miss	622
	Dyin	934
possible allusions	Devi	955
	Cree	1071
Cock, as a sacrifice	Wist	879
Cockneys	Stoc	364
Cocoanut matting	Sign	108
	Gold	611
Coffee	Stud	23
	Sign	125

Coffee (cont'd)

Scan	173
RedH	185
Five	227
Spec	258
Bery	305
Bery	312
Reig	399
Nava	450
Nava	465
Nava	466
Blac	559
SixN	585
Gold	613
Houn	669
Houn	683
Houn	731
Houn	755
Wist	884
Bruc	925
Illu	989

cafe noire

Coffee pot, as mirror

Musg	389
Houn	699

Coffin

Lady	949
Shos	1110

Coiner

Engr	285
Vall	828
Shos	1102

Coins, ancient

3Gar	1048

Coins and Currency

   coins, Great Britain

      bob

Sign	126

      penny

Sign	156
RedH	186
Twis	236
Twis	243
Blue	251
Miss	627

Coins and Currency, coins, Great
 Britain, penny (cont'd)

	Seco	654
	Seco	662
	Vall	807
copper	Scan	171
	Twis	243
	Twis	244
	Danc	513
half-penny	Twis	236
	Houn	687
farthing	Bery	305
half-crown	Scan	163
	Twis	233
	Engr	285
	Nobl	296
	Silv	344
	Dyin	935
	Dyin	941
florin	Sign	123
	Croo	418
quid	Maza	1019
shilling	Stud	42
	Sign	123
	Sign	126
	Sign	127
	Sign	136
	Sign	144
	Iden	195
	Blue	250
	Nobl	296
	Bery	316
	Resi	426
	Blac	571
	SixN	589
	SixN	592
	Miss	624
	Houn	691
	Houn	692

Coins and Currency, coins, Great
    Britain, shilling (cont'd)

sixpence		Wist	875
		RedC	902
		Stud	15
		Sign	95
		Sign	126
		Thor	1064
threepence		Resi	426
twopence		Scan	168
		Iden	193
silver		Sign	126
		Twis	243
sovereign		Scan	169
		RedH	181
	(2)	Blue	253
		Silv	341
		Gree	441
		Prio	550
		Prio	551
		Lady	953
half-sovereign		Stud	34
		Stud	36
		Sign	129
		Scan	169
	(2)	Blac	569
		Houn	697
guinea		Sign	93
		Sign	127
		Scan	163
		Engr	277
		Silv	342
		Resi	426
		Miss	630
		Houn	697
half-guinea		Scan	168
tanner		Sign	126
coins		Musg	387
dollars (?)		Twis	243

Coins and Currency, coins, Great
Britain (cont'd)

dollar		Vall	828
		Vall	835
		Card	898
dime		Houn	863
		Vall	842
		Vall	863
cent		3Gar	1046
gold		Stud	68
coins, other			
Chinese		RedH	177
moidore		Sign	148
Napoleon		RedH	187
rupee		Sign	143
		Sign	149
		Croo	418
Syracusan		3Gar	1048
currency, Great Britain			
5 pounds	(2)	Blue	252
		Stoc	366
		Miss	627
		Houn	691
10 pounds		Sign	143
		Silv	340
		Empt	484
		SixN	593
		Miss	627
		Vall	770
		RedC	902
50 pounds		Danc	520
100 pounds		Stoc	366
		3Gar	1054
1000 pounds		Bery	303
currency, U.S.			
$1		Vall	860
$20		Vall	858

Coins and Currency, currency, U.S.
(cont'd)

dollars		Stud	68
		Stud	76
		Houn	688
		Vall	812
		Vall	813
		Vall	842
		Vall	863
		Last	976
	(2)	3Gar	1046
Coke		Sign	123
Cold Harbour Lane		Sign	99
Coldstream Guards		Nava	455
Colin, Sir (Campbell)		Sign	151
Collectors' mania		Illu	995
		3Gar	1048
College of St. Luke's		3Stu	596
College of Surgeons, Museum of the		Houn	699
Colonies, Under-Secretary for the		Nobl	288
Colonna, Prince and Princess of		SixN	594
Colorado River		Stud	52
Coloured glasses		Empt	485
Colourman		Reti	1113
Colours			
"our own"		Wist	874
racing		Silv	347
scarlet thread of murder		Stud	36
Colour-sergeant		Croo	413
		Vall	853
Columbine's New Fangled Banner		Stud	35
Comet vintage		Stoc	369
Commercial Road		Cree	1078
Commissionaire		Stud	25
		Blue	245
		Nava	450

142 ◼ *Good Old Index*

Commonplace books (*see* Holmes, Sherlock)		
Commons, House of (*see also* Parliament)	Houn	749
Compass	Stud	54
	Glor	384
	Musg	394
Compasses (drawing)	Engr	285
Company, The (East India)	Sign	148
Comparative anatomy	Houn	678
	Cree	1072
Comparative pathology	Houn	671
Compliments of the season	Blue	244
Compositors	Sign	91
	Copp	317
	Vall	839
Conduit Street	Empt	494
Condyle	Shos	1106
Confectioner's man	Nobl	296
Conk-Singleton forgery case	SixN	596
Conqueror (steam packet)	Card	893
Conquistadors	3Gab	1031
Conservative (Party)	Nava	447
	Wist	870
Constable (*see* Police)		
Consumption	Fina	478
	Miss	635
	Houn	762
Continent, The	Fina	470
Continental express	Fina	474
Continental Gazetteer	Scan	163
Convict	Houn	701
"Cooee!"	Bosc	205
Cook, Constable	Five	227
Cook (*see* servants)		
Cook's (tourist agency)	Lady	944

Coolies	Sign	145
	Dyin	939
Coombe Tracey	Houn	729
Copenhagen (Denmark)	Stud	44
Copernican Theory	Stud	21
Copper (metal)	Shos	1102
Copper (penny)	Scan	171
	Twis	243
	Twis	244
	Danc	513
Copper Beeches (house)	Copp	319
Coptic monasteries	Gold	615
Coptic Patriarchs	Reti	1114
Coram, Professor	Gold	608
Cork	Silv	342
	Gold	612
Cork-cutters	Sign	91
Corkscrew	Abbe	641
Cormac, Tiger	Vall	834
Cormorant	Veil	1095
Cornelius, Mr.	Norw	505
Cornish Horror	Devi	955
Cornish language	Devi	955
Cornwall	RedH	186
	Blac	566
	Devi	955
Coroner's jury	Bosc	204
	Seco	658
	Houn	677
	Thor	1056
Coronet	Bery	303
	Shos	1110
Corot (Jean Baptiste)	Sign	101
Corporation Street (Birmingham)	Stoc	366
Cosmopolitan, Hotel	Blue	248

Cost of living

Costa Rica

Coster
Cottonwoods
Councillor
Count Von Kramm
Count Grafenstein
Count Sylvius
Counterfeiters

Counterfoil
Countersign
Countess

Counties, English
   Bedfordshire
   Berkshire

   Cambridgeshire
   Cornwall

   Devonshire

   Essex

   Hallamshire
   Hampshire

   Herefordshire

Iden	193
Copp	319
Blac	562
Houn	761
RedH	179
Sign	127
Vall	826
Scan	164
Last	979
Maza	1014
Engr	285
Vall	828
3Gar	1053
Miss	626
Stud	70
Blue	248
Chas	580
Blan	1007
Spec	259
Engr	278
Veil	1097
Shos	1106
Miss	631
RedH	186
Blac	566
Devi	955
Silv	340
Houn	671
Last	974
Reti	1117
Prio	539
Spec	259
Copp	319
Glor	378
Thor	1055
Bosc	203

Counties, English (cont'd)
    Kent

	Sign	145
	Twis	233
	Fina	476
	Gold	608
	Abbe	636
	Vall	779
	Lion	1093
Lancashire	Prio	539
Middlesex	Twis	237
	Yell	353
Norfolk	Glor	374
	Danc	512
Northumberland	Nava	457
Surrey	Sign	99
	Sign	137
	Twis	237
	Spec	257
	Reig	398
	Nava	465
	Soli	527
	Wist	871
Sussex	Five	219
	Musg	388
	Blac	560
	Vall	778
	Suss	1035
	Lion	1083
Westmoreland	Houn	695
Worcestershire	Sign	144
Yorkshire	Houn	762
County Monaghan (Ireland)	Vall	821
"Country of the Saints, The"	Stud	52
Coupe-de-maitre	Fina	476
Court-martial, private	3Stu	604
Court of Queen's Bench	Houn	736
Covent Garden Market	Blue	251

146 ◘ *Good Old Index*

Covent Garden Theatre	RedC	913
Coventry	Five	219
	Soli	529
Coventry, Sergeant	Thor	1062
Cow	Stud	60
	Prio	548
	Houn	699
Cowper (Mormon)	Stud	73
Cox & Co. (bank)	Thor	1054
Coxon (stockbroker)	Stoc	364
Coxon & Woodhouse	Stoc	364
Coyote	Stud	52
C.P.R. (Canadian Pacific Railway)	Blac	562
Crabbe (victim)	Vall	857
Cracksman	Stoc	373
Crane Water (house)	Spec	263
Cranial characteristics	Blue	247
	Houn	672
Craven Street	Houn	763
Credit Lyonnais	Vall	777
	Lady	943
	Maza	1018
Cremona violins	Stud	27
Crendall	Shos	1104
Creole	Seco	659
Creosote	Sign	112
Crewe	Spec	260
Cricket	Nava	447
	3Stu	600
Crimean War	Glor	381
	Croo	412
	Gold	609
	Lady	948
	Blan	1001
Criminal syndicate	Fina	474

Criminals

Adams	Gree	437
Akbar, Dost	Sign	98
Amberley, Josiah	Reti	1113
Anna	Gold	619
Archie	RedH	189
Armitage, James (Trevor)	Glor	381
Baldwin, Ted	Vall	813
Baskerville, Rodger	Houn	678
Beddington No. 1	Stoc	365
Beddington No. 2	Stoc	373
Beppo	SixN	588
Biddle	Reti	434
Brooks	Bruc	914
Browner, Jim	Card	893
Cairns, Patrick	Blac	569
Calhoun, Captain James	Five	228
Carruthers, Robert	Soli	528
Carruthers, Colonel	Wist	870
Cartwright	Resi	434
Clay, John	RedH	186
Cunninghams, father and son	Reig	399
Dixie, Steve	3Gab	1023
Dowson, Baron	Maza	1016
Evans (Beddoes)	Glor	377
Evans, Killer	3Gar	1051
Ferguson, Jack	Suss	1037
Ferguson, Mr.	Engr	281
Fournaye, Mme. Henri	Seco	658
Fraser, Annie	Lady	947
Gorgiano, Giuseppe	RedC	908
Gruner, Baron Adelbert	Illu	985
Hayes, Reuben	Prio	550
Hayward	Resi	434
Hope, Jefferson	Stud	51
Howells, Rachel	Musg	389
Hudson	Glor	377

Criminals (cont'd)

Huret	Gold	607
Kemp, Wilson	Gree	446
Khan, Abdullah	Sign	98
Kirwan, William	Reig	399
Latimer, Harold	Gree	438
Lefevre	Stud	18
Leonardo	Veil	1097
Lopez	Wist	886
Lucas, Eduardo	Seco	654
Mason	Stud	18
Mathews	Empt	494
McGinty, Bodymaster	Vall	797
Merridew	Empt	494
Merton, Sam	Maza	1014
Milverton, Charles Augustus	Chas	572
Moffat	Resi	434
Moran, Colonel Sebastian (*which see*)		
Morgan	Empt	494
Moriarty, Professor (*which see*)		
Muller	Stud	18
Murillo, Don Juan	Wist	884
Neligan, Senior	Blac	566
Oldacre, Jonas	Norw	497
Palmer, Dr.	Spec	270
Parker	Empt	490
Peace, Charlie	Illu	987
Peters, Henry	Lady	947
Pinner, Arthur	Stoc	365
Pinner, Harry	Stoc	366
Porlock, Fred	Vall	769
Prescott, Rodger	3Gar	1052
Pritchard, Dr.	Spec	270
Randalls, The	Abbe	637
Ronder, Eugenia	Veil	1095
Ross, Duncan (Archie)	RedH	178
Roylott, Dr. Grimesby	Spec	258

Criminals (cont'd)

Samson	Stud	18
Selden	Houn	701
Sergius	Gold	619
Sholto, Major John	Sign	95
Singh, Mahomet	Sign	98
Slaney, Abe	Danc	521
Small, Jonathan	Sign	98
Smith, Culverton	Dyin	935
Stark, Colonel Lysander	Engr	277
Staunton, Arthur H.	Miss	623
Staunton, Henry	Miss	623
Sterndale, Dr. Leon	Devi	961
Stevens, Bert	Norw	504
Stockdale, Barney	3Gab	1024
Straker, John	Silv	336
Sutton	Resi	434
Sylvius, Count Negretto	Maza	1014
Tonga	Sign	140
Tregennis, Mortimer	Devi	956
Turner, John	Bosc	203
Upwood, Colonel	Houn	761
Van Seddar	Maza	1020
Venucci, Pietro	SixN	590
Von Bischoff	Stud	18
Wainwright	Illu	987
Walter, Colonel Valentine	Bruc	917
Wild, Jonathan	Vall	777
Wilder, James	Prio	540
Williamson	Soli	531
Wilson	Blac	559
Windibank, James	Iden	192
Winter, James	3Gar	1051
Winter, Kitty	Illu	989
Woodhouse	Bruc	913
Woodley, Jack	Soli	528
Criterion Bar	Stud	16

150 ■ *Good Old Index*

Cro-Magnon (early man)	3Gar	1048
Crocker, Captain Jack	Abbe	646
Crockford (clerical directory)	Reti	1117
Crocodile	Sign	145
Crocodile-skin hand-bag	Danc	520
Crocuses	Spec	264
	Empt	484
Crooksbury Hill	Soli	529
Croquet lawn	Devi	963
Crosby (banker)	Gold	607
Cross, stone	Devi	956
Cross Street (Croydon)	Card	890
Crowder, William	Bosc	203
Crow Hill (mine)	Vall	849
Crown Derby tea set	3Gab	1027
Crown, greatest subject of	Prio	540
Crown Inn	Spec	263
Crown Diamond	Maza	1013
Crown of the Stuarts	Musg	397
Croydon	Card	890
Cruet-stand	SixN	589
Crusade, first	Vall	779
Crutch, aluminum	Musg	387
Crypt, family	Shos	1104
Crystal Palace	Yell	356
Cubitt, Hilton	Danc	512
Cubitt, Elsie	Danc	512
Cuffs and sleeves, inferences from	RedH	177
	Iden	197
Cummings, Joyce	Thor	1065
Cunard (steamship line)	Illu	994
Cunningham	Reig	399
Cunningham, Alec	Reig	399
Cunning fiend (Holmes)	Empt	492
Curacao (liqueur)	Bruc	925
Curare	Suss	1042

Curlew	Prio	546
	Houn	738
Curling tongs	Seco	657
Currency (*see* Coins and Currency)		
Curry	Silv	337
	Nava	465
Curzon Square	Wist	887
Curzon Street	Shos	1102
Cusack, Catherine	Blue	248
Cushing, Mary	Card	893
Cushing, Sarah	Card	893
Cushing, Susan	Card	890
Cutter	Thor	1054
Cutthroats, one of the greatest (Pietro Venucci)	SixN	590
Cuvier (Baron)	Five	225
Cyanea capillata	Lion	1093
Cyclopides	Houn	709

D

Dacre Hotel	SixN	594
Daily Chronicle	Card	890
Chronicle	Iden	190
	Silv	336
Daily Gazette	RedC	902
Daily Herald	Vall	840
Daily News	Stud	41
	Gree	442
Daily Telegraph	Stud	41
	Copp	316
	Norw	497
	Seco	658
	Bruc	928
Telegraph	Silv	336
D'Albert, Countess	Chas	580
Damery, Colonel Sir James	Illu	984
Dane	Twis	234
"Dangling Prussian, The" (hypothetical inn)	Last	980
Danite Band	Stud	63
Danseuse	Nobl	290
Danton (Georges Jacques)	Vall	848
Dantzig (Germany)	Nava	447

154 ◼ *Good Old Index*

Darbies (derbies; *see also* handcuffs)	RedH	189
	Card	897
Darjeeling (India)	Croo	420
Dark lantern (*see also* lamp, lantern)	Sign	106
	Sign	117
	RedH	187
	Spec	271
	Empt	492
	Chas	577
	SixN	592
	Wist	878
	Bruc	925
	Shos	1110
bull's eye	Sign	117
pocket	Sign	99
	Wist	878
reflector	Vall	775
Darlington substitution scandal	Scan	173
Dartmoor	Silv	335
	Houn	671
Dartmoor (prison)	Sign	140
Princetown	Houn	684
Darwin (Charles) and music	Stud	37
Darwinian theory	Stud	41
Data, theorizing without	Stud	27
	Scan	163
	Spec	272
	Copp	321
	Vall	779
	Wist	876
Daubensee (lake, Switzerland)	Fina	477
Davenport, J.	Gree	443
David (biblical)	Croo	415
Davos Platz (Switzerland)	Fina	478
Dawson (banker)	Blac	566
Dawson (groom)	Silv	344
Dawson (planter)	Sign	145

Dawson & Neligan	Blac	566
Day's Music Hall (Birmingham)	Stoc	368
D.D. (Doctor of Divinity)	Twis	229
De Brinvillers, Marchioness	Stud	41
De Capus, Hugo	Vall	779
De Croy, Philippe	Stud	38
De Jure inter Gentes	Stud	38
De Merville, General	Illu	986
De Merville, Violet	Illu	986
De Quincey (Thomas)	Twis	229
De Reszkes (opera singers)	Houn	766
Deacon, Inner	Vall	853
Dear me, Mr. Holmes, Dear me.	Vall	865
Death, face and posture in	Stud	29
	Sign	109
	Musg	395
	Croo	415
	Resi	431
	Blac	561
	Miss	634
	Abbe	640
	Houn	679
	Houn	745
	RedC	909
	Devi	959
	Devi	963
	Lion	1084
Death, manner of		
accident?	Five	222
	Blac	570
alcoholism	Sign	92
apoplexy	Glor	379
	Croo	422
Asiatic fever	Dyin	936
at sea	Resi	434
	Blac	570

Death, manner of (cont'd)
   bludgeoning with
      club

	Prio	548
	Card	900
	Veil	1100
life-preserver	Bruc	930
poker	Stoc	373
	Abbe	637
stone	Bosc	203
unknown instrument	Wist	874
wooden leg	Sign	155
broken heart	Stud	74
	Spec	262
	Chas	580
	Bruc	921
consumption	Miss	635
dart, poisoned	Sign	109
diseases (*see* Ailments)		
drowning	Five	221
	Five	227
	Resi	434
	Blac	570
	Vall	865
	Veil	1101
explosion	Glor	384
fall from cliff	Five	222
	Empt	486
	Houn	744
gas	Gree	445
	Reti	1120
hanging	Resi	433
heart (*see* Ailments)		
horse's kick	Silv	350
lion's mane	Lion	1084
mire?	Houn	760
pneumonia	3Gar	1025

Death, manner of (cont'd)
   poison

	Stud	18
	Gold	621
	Dyin	939
	Devi	957
	Devi	963
senility	Lady	952
snake bite	Spec	272
shooting	Sign	139
	Reig	399
	Empt	484
	Danc	517
	Chas	581
	Vall	779
	3Gar	1052
	Thor	1056
stabbing	Stud	47
	Gree	446
	Blac	561
	SixN	586
	Gold	610
	Seco	655
	RedC	909
suffocation	Musg	395
	Reti	1120
suicide, presumed	Five	221
	Five	222
	Five	227
throat cut	Glor	385
tuberculosis	Miss	635
unknown	Wist	887
Death certificate	Yell	353
	Lady	950
	Lady	952
Debutante	Chas	573
Decameron (Boccaccio)	Stud	30

Deduction, Science of	Stud	23
	Sign	89
Deep Dene House	Norw	498
Deer's heads	Abbe	639
Delhi (India)	Sign	151
Dennis, Sally	Stud	39
Dennis, Tom	Stud	39
Deptford Reach	Sign	138
Derbies (darbies; *see also* handcuffs)	RedH	189
	Card	897
Derby	Vall	806
Derby, The (race)	Shos	1103
Derbyshire Mrs.	Silv	342
Derbyshire, William	Silv	342
Desborough (horse)	Silv	339
Descent from the general to the particular	Lady	943
Desmond, James	Houn	695
Despatch—box (*see* dispatch—box)	Seco	664
Detectives (*see also* Police)		
consulting		
Holmes, Sherlock	Stud	24
	Sign	90
	SixN	589
	Houn	695
continental		
Dubugue (Paris)	Nava	447
Le Brun (Paris)	Illu	989
Le Villard, Francois (Paris)	Sign	90
Von Waldbaum (Dantzig)	Nava	447
private	Stud	24
	Sign	130
	Gold	620
	Wist	870
Barker	Reti	1118
Edwards, Birdy (Pinkerton)	Vall	855
Leverton (Pinkerton)	RedC	908

Detectives (*see also* Police) (cont'd)
provincial

	Bosc	204
	Five	223
	Engr	284
	Devi	963
Algar (Liverpool)	Card	897
Bardle (Sussex)	Lion	1090
Baynes (Surrey)	Wist	871
Edmunds (Berkshire)	Veil	1098
Forrester (Surrey)	Reig	400
Martin (Norfolk)	Danc	517
Mason, White (Sussex)	Vall	778
Scotland Yard (C.I.D.)	Stud	77
	Sign	135
	Sign	141
	RedH	188
	Twis	234
	Bery	302
(?)	Empt	485
	Danc	517
	Illu	998
	3Gab	1029
Barton	Twis	236
Bradstreet	Twis	241
	Blue	248
	Engr	284
Brown, Sam	Sign	143
Forbes	Nava	453
Gregory	Silv	337
Gregson, Tobias	Stud	26
	Sign	90
	Gree	444
	Wist	871
	RedC	908
Hill	SixN	590
Hopkins, Stanley	Blac	559
	Gold	608

Detectives (see also Police), Scotland Yard (C.I.D.), Hopkins, Stanley (cont'd)
    Jones, Athelney
    Jones, Peter
    Lanner
    Lestrade, G.

	Miss	622
	Abbe	636
	Sign	90
	RedH	186
	Resi	431
	Stud	22
	Sign	90
	Bosc	204
	Nobl	288
	Empt	491
	Norw	498
	Chas	581
	SixN	582
	Seco	658
	Houn	752
	Card	890
	Bruc	916
	Lady	948
	3Gar	1051
MacDonald	Vall	773
MacKinnon	Reti	1119
Merivale	Shos	1102
Montgomery	Card	898
Morton	Dyin	936
Patterson	Fina	480
Youghal	Maza	1015

U.S.
    Hargreave, Wilson (New York City)
    Marvin (Chicago, Vermissa)

Detectives, qualities required by

	Danc	523
	Vall	831
	Stud	24
	Stud	40
	Sign	91
	Reig	409
	Houn	750

Detectives, qualities required by (cont'd)	Vall	807
	Wist	884
Detroit (Michigan)	Vall	821
Deutsche Bank	Vall	777
Devil	Blue	249
	Spec	264
	Glor	377
	Houn	684
	Wist	883
	Devi	963
Evil One	Chas	573
Father of Evil	Houn	681
Satan	Devi	963
Devil's-foot root	Devi	968
Devine (sculptor)	SixN	584
Devine, Marie	Lady	943
Devon County Chronicle	Houn	676
Devonshire	Silv	340
	Houn	671
Devonshire, Duchess of	Iden	192
Devoy, Nancy	Croo	413
Devoy, Colour-sergeant	Croo	413
Diabetes	Bosc	215
Diadem	Bery	310
	Musg	397
Diamond	Sign	151
	Blue	248
	Chas	574
	Chas	582
	Vall	860
	Card	893
	Lady	943
	Maza	1013
brilliant	Iden	191
	Lady	948
Diamond, Great Mogul	Sign	151
Diamond-polishers, hands of	Sign	91

Diamond Hill (South Africa)	Blan	1001
Diary		
Baron Gruner	Illu	990
Holmes (*see also*	Blan	1007
Holmes—Commonplace Books)		
Watson	Houn	726
journal	Stud	76
Dictionary	Vall	772
Dieppe (France)	Fina	476
Digger Indians	Sign	127
Dingle, The (house)	Wist	876
Diogenes Club	Gree	435
	Bruc	914
Diphtheria	Glor	374
Diplomas	Gold	616
Directory, clerical (Crockford)	Reti	1117
Directory, Hotel	Houn	691
	3Gab	1027
Directory, medical	Houn	671
Discs of metal	Musg	387
Disease (*see* Ailments)		
Disjecta membra	Blue	251
Dispatch—box (*see* Watson—dispatch cases and despatch—box)	Thor	1054
Dissecting rooms	Stud	17
District messenger	Illu	996
office	Houn	691
express messenger	SixN	592
messenger	SixN	585
	Bruc	925
Divan, eastern	Twis	240
Divorce	Houn	742
	Devi	968
Dixie, Steve	3Gab	1023
Dixon, Jeremy	Miss	632
Dixon, Mrs. (housekeeper)	Soli	528
Dobney, Susan	Lady	943

Doctors

	Copp	332
	Croo	414
	Danc	518
	Card	894
	Devi	963
(2)	Illu	998
	Blan	1010
Agar, Moore	Devi	955
Ainstree	Dyin	934
Anstruther	Bosc	202
Armstrong, Leslie	Miss	629
Barnicot	SixN	583
Barton, Hill	Illu	995
Becher	Engr	286
Bennett, Trevor	Cree	1081
Ernest, Ray	Reti	1113
Farquhar	Stoc	362
Ferrier	Nava	454
Fisher, Penrose	Dyin	933
Fordham	Glor	379
Horsom	Lady	952
Jackson	Croo	412
Kent	Blan	1008
Meek, Sir Jasper	Dyin	933
Mortimer, James	Houn	669
Oakshott, Sir Leslie	Illu	993
Palmer (William)	Spec	270
Pritchard (Edward)	Spec	270
Richards	Devi	957
Roylott, Grimesby	Spec	258
Saunders, Sir James	Blan	1010
Somerton	Sign	152
Starr, Lysander (sic)	3Gar	1047
Sterndale, Leon	Devi	961
Trevelyan, Percy	Resi	425
Verner	Norw	496
Watson, John H. (*which see*)		

164 ◻ *Good Old Index*

Doctors (cont'd)
   Willows — Bosc — 208
   Wood — Vall — 781
Doctors' Commons — Spec — 265
Doctors' Quarter (of London) — Blue — 251
Dodd, James M. — Blan — 1000
Dog (*see* Animal)
Dog-cart (*see also* cab, cart, etc.) — Twis — 232
   Spec — 259
   Copp — 321
   Glor — 377
   Musg — 393
   Danc — 518
   Soli — 533
   Soli — 534
   Prio — 552
   Houn — 730
   Vall — 785
   Devi — 962
Dog-grate — Wist — 873
Dog-lash (whip) — Spec — 272
   Wist — 883
Dogs, Isle of — Sign — 138
Dolichocephalic skull — Houn — 672
Dolores (maid) — Suss — 1037
Dolsky of Odessa — Stud — 84
Don Juan — Musg — 389
Doncaster — SixN — 586
Donnithorpe — Glor — 374
Dorak, A. — Cree — 1078
Doran, Aloysius — Nobl — 289
Doran, Hatty — Nobl — 289
Dorking, Colonel — Chas — 574
Doss house — Illu — 987
Double-barrelled tiger cub — Sign — 99
Douglas, Ivy — Vall — 774
   Vall — 865

Douglas, John		Vall	774
Dovercourt, Earl of		Chas	573
Downing (constable)		Wist	880
Downing Street		Nava	459
Downs (uplands)		Seco	650
		Vall	779
	(Pref)	Last	869
		Last	978
		Lion	1083
Downs, The (anchorage)		Sign	136
Dowson, Baron		Maza	1016
Drag (carriage)		Silv	347
Draghound		Miss	633
Drains and typhoid		Stud	34
Draper Gardens		Stoc	364
Draughts (game)		Five	220
Drawbridge		Vall	780
Drebber (Mormon elder)		Stud	26
Drebber, Enoch J.		Stud	26
Dresser (surgeon's assistant)		Stud	16
Dressing gown (*see* Clothing)			
Drills		Chas	578
Dropsy		Shos	1104
Drugs, in case		Stud	20
		Twis	230
		Devi	964
		Cree	1082
	bang	Sign	147
	belladona	Dyin	941
	cocaine	Sign	89
		Sign	158
		Scan	161
		Five	225
		Twis	232
		Yell	351
		Miss	622
		Dyin	934

166 ◘ *Good Old Index*

Drugs, in case (cont'd)		
morphine (morphia)	Sign	89
	Illu	993
	Illu	998
	Cree	1081
	Lion	1092
opium	Sign	147
	Twis	229
	Silv	338
	Wist	884
Dublin (Ireland)	Card	896
Dubugue (detective)	Nava	447
Duchess	Nobl	290
	Prio	540
Duchess of Devonshire fashion	Iden	192
Duck shooting	Glor	374
Duke	Nobl	288
	Silv	347
	Prio	539
	Seco	656
	3Gab	1031
royal duke	RedH	186
Duke of York's steps	Last	974
Du Louvre, Hotel	Bruc	931
Dumb-bell, as clue	Vall	790
Dunbar, Grace	Thor	1056
Duncan Street	Stud	39
Dundas separation case	Iden	191
Dundee (Scotland)	Five	222
	Blac	560
Dunlop tire	Prio	547
Dunn, Josiah H.	Vall	849
Dupin (C. Auguste)	Stud	24
Durando, Signora	Wist	885
Durando, Victor	Wist	885

Dyspnoea	Houn	677
Dutch language	Blan	1009
Dynamics of an Asteroid, The	Vall	770

E

Eagle Commercial (hotel)	Vall	803
Eagle Ravine (canyon)	Stud	68
Earl	Empt	483
	Prio	539
	Chas	573
	Lady	943
Early English charters	3Stu	596
Ears		
bitten	Lady	947
boxers'	Glor	375
deductions from	Card	896
jagged	Lady	947
monograph upon	Card	896
pierced	RedH	183
	Card	892
variations among	Card	896
East Anglia	Danc	517
East End, of London	Blac	559
	Blac	571
	Dyin	938
East London	Five	225
East Ham	Vall	806
East Indies	Resi	432
East London (*see also* East End)	Five	225
East Ruston (parish, Norfolk)	Danc	521

East wind coming, an	Last	980
Eastbourne	Wist	869
Eastern railway line (South Africa)	Blan	1009
Ecarte (card game)	Houn	731
Eccles, John Scott	Wist	869
Echo (newspaper)	Stud	86
	Blue	249
Eckermann (author)	Wist	887
Ecliptic	Gree	435
Eclipses	Vall	775
Economic conditions	RedH	178
	Spec	265
Edgeware Road	Scan	168
	3Gar	1047
Edinburgh (Scotland)	Sign	94
Edmonton Street	Wist	887
Edmunds (Berkshire constabulary)	Veil	1098
Edwards, Birdy	Vall	855
Effigy, burning of	Houn	715
	Houn	736
Egan (Scowrer)	Vall	857
Eggspoon	Stud	23
Eglow	Scan	163
Eglonitz	Scan	163
Egria (Bohemia)	Scan	163
Egypt	Gold	615
	Last	973
Egyptian letters	Stud	57
Elders, principal Morman	Stud	59
Electric bell	Blue	257
	Prio	557
	Maza	1020
Electric lights	Chas	578
	3Stu	599
	Last	972

Electric lights (cont'd)		
pink	Dyin	936
	3Gab	1031
to be installed	Houn	702
Electric-blue dress	Copp	320
Electrical engineer	Soli	528
Electro-telegraph	Stud	64
Elementary	Iden	197
	Croo	412
	Houn	670
	Blan	1006
Eley's No. 2 (cartridges)	Spec	265
Elimination of the impossible	Sign	92
	Sign	111
	Bery	315
	Soli	529
	Bruc	926
	Blan	1011
Elise	Engr	283
Elizabethan knight	Houn	703
Elm	Yell	351
	Musg	392
	Abbe	637
	Vall	787
Elman, J.C.	Reti	1117
Elrige's farm	Danc	521
Embankment, The	Five	227
Embassy		
French	Nava	450
German	Last	972
Russian	Nava	450
	Gold	621
Embezzlement	Glor	381
Emerald	Sign	151
	Scan	175
	Bruc	931
Eminent Order of Freemen	Vall	817

Emsworth, Colonel	Blan	1001
Emsworth, Godfrey	Blan	1001
Emsworth, Mrs.	Blan	1001
Encyclopaedia		
American	Five	225
Britannica	RedH	181
Endell Street	Blue	252
Endowment House (Salt Lake City)	Stud	74
Engineer, electrical	Soli	528
Engineer, hydraulic	Engr	276
England, home and beauty, for	Bruc	928
England saved from scandal	Nava	447
	Seco	650
	Bruc	916
Englischer Hof (inn)		
Baden	Lady	944
Meiringen	Fina	477
English charters, early	3Stu	596
English Law (*see* British Law)		
Entailed estate	Prio	557
	Houn	695
Enteric fever	Stud	15
Environment and heredity,	Gree	435
Holmes's views on	Fina	470
Equinoctial gales	Five	218
Ernest, Dr. Ray	Reti	1113
Erysipelas	Illu	994
Escott (Holmes's disguise)	Chas	576
Esher	Wist	871
Esmeralda (ship)	Sign	141
Esquimau	Houn	686
Essex	Last	974
	Reti	1117
Estate	Prio	557
	Houn	695
Estimates (Parliamentary)	Bruc	916
Ether, injected	Lady	953

Etherege, Mrs.	Iden	192
Eton	RedH	186
	Empt	494
Euclid, 5th proposition of	Stud	23
	Sign	90
Eustace, Lord	Nobl	290
Euston station	Stud	41
	Prio	543
	Blan	1007
Evans (Beddoes)	Glor	382
Evans (policeman)	Vall	853
Evans (Norlett)	Shos	1111
Evans, Carrie	Shos	1105
Evans, "Killer"	3Gar	1051
Evening News	Blue	249
Evening Standard (see also Standard)	Stoc	372
Evil, Father of	Houn	681
Evil One	Chas	573
Excelsior and Busy Bee (motto)	Cree	1076
Executor	Houn	681
Exeter	Silv	336
Express messenger	SixN	592
district messenger	Illu	996
messenger	SixN	585
	Bruc	925
Cartwright	Houn	691
Eyeglasses (*see* spectacles)		
Eyford	Engr	278

F

Faber, Johann	3Stu	599
Fainting		
Barclay, Nancy	Croo	414
Baskerville, Sir Henry	Houn	757
Brackenstall, Lady	Abbe	639
Doran, Hatty	Nobl	298
Emsworth, Godfrey	Blan	1009
Emsworth, Mrs.	Blan	1012
Gruner's footman	Illu	998
Harker, Horace	SixN	586
Hatherley, Victor	Engr	275
Holder, Mary	Bery	306
Holmes, feigned	Reig	403
	Dyin	940
Horner, John	Blue	249
Huxtable, Thorneycroft	Prio	539
Lady on Brixton bus	RedC	904
Murdoch, Ian	Lion	1092
Patrick, Elsie	Danc	513
Porter, Mrs.	Devi	959
Small, Jonathan	Sign	145
Stapleton, Beryl	Houn	758
Trevor, Senior	Glor	375

Fainting (cont'd)
   Walter, Valentine
   Watson
Fainting, feigned

Fairbairn, Alec
Fairbank (house)
Fair sex
Fairy tales

Falder, Lady Beatrice
Falder, Sir Denis
Falder, Sir James
Falder, Sir William
Falmouth
False alarm, of fire

False teeth
Family Herald (magazine)
Fancy, the
Fanlight

   at 221B

Fareham
Farintosh, Mrs. (client)
Farnham
Farquhar, Mr. (physician)
Farrier
  blacksmith

Farrington Street
Fate(s)

Bruc	929
Empt	485
Reig	403
Seco	661
Dyin	940
Card	899
Bery	308
Seco	657
Houn	676
Suss	1034
Shos	1103
Shos	1110
Shos	1103
Shos	1110
Glor	380
Scan	172
Norn	508
Iden	191
Thor	1055
Sign	106
Empt	489
SixN	591
Blue	250
Dyin	936
Illu	999
Five	222
Spec	259
Soli	527
Stoc	362
Houn	681
Spec	260
Prio	551
RedH	187
Reig	400
Vall	788

Father of Evil	Houn	681
Felony		
commuted	Blue	257
compounded	3Gab	1033
concealed	Bosc	217
	Spec	258
	Abbe	649
	Seco	663
	Devi	970
	Suss	1044
condoned	Prio	557
Femur	Shos	1106
Fen	Glor	374
Fenchurch Street	Iden	196
Ferguson (Becher)	Engr	281
Ferguson (secretary)	Thor	1057
Ferguson, Captain	3Gab	1026
Ferguson, Jack	Suss	1037
Ferguson, Mrs.	Suss	1040
Ferguson, Robert	Suss	1034
Ferguson & Muirhead	Suss	1034
Feringhee	Sign	148
Fernworthy	Houn	715
Ferrers Documents	Prio	539
Ferrier, Dr.	Nava	454
Ferrier, John	Stud	57
Ferrier, Lucy	Stud	57
Fetish	Wist	887
Ffolliott, Sir George	Wist	876
Fiddle (*see also* **Holmes—violin**)	Stud	22
Field glasses	Silv	336
Fifth Northumberland Fusiliers	Stud	15
Fighting Cock Inn	Prio	552
Fingerprints	Sign	95
	Twis	239
	Norw	506
	Card	891

178 ◼ *Good Old Index*

Fingerprints (cont'd)
  sought | 3Stu | 599
   | RedC | 903
  suggested | 3Gab | 1030
Finns | Five | 229
Fir (tree) | Nava | 466
   | Houn | 700
  scotch fir | Yell | 354
Firbank Villas | Lady | 952
Fire alarm, false | Scan | 172
   | Norw | 508
Fire brigade | Vall | 780
Fire engines | Engr | 286
   | Norw | 498
First Bangalore Pioneers | Empt | 494
First brain of Europe | Vall | 771
First cab or second | Fina | 474
First case, Holmes's | Glor | 374
First-class carriage | Houn | 699
   | Houn | 754
First folio, Shakespeare | 3Gab | 1027
Fisher, Penrose | Dyin | 933
Fishing | Glor | 374
   | Musg | 394
   | Shos | 1109
Fishing-rod | Musg | 394
   | Shos | 1106
Fishmonger | Nobl | 287
Five shilling reply | Wist | 875
Flagstaff | Glor | 378
   | Vall | 840
Flaubert, Gustave | RedH | 190
Fleet Street | RedH | 178
   | Resi | 424
Flint arrows | Devi | 960
Flint instruments | 3Gar | 1048

Floor plan	Nava	451
	Gold	610
Florence (Italy)	Empt	487
Florida	Five	219
	Five	226
Florin	Croo	418
Flowers		
crocus	Spec	264
	Empt	484
geranium bed	3Gab	1029
gorse	Soli	530
	Soli	533
	Prio	548
	Wist	886
hart's tongue fern	Houn	700
heather	Nava	449
	Prio	550
	Thor	1069
honeysuckle	Yell	354
mare's tail	Houn	709
moss rose	Nava	456
orchid	Houn	709
rhododendron	Nava	466
rose-bush	Engr	284
sulphur rose	Houn	733
wistaria	Cree	1076
Flowers, Lord	Seco	666
Flushing (Holland)	Last	972
Fly-paper	Glor	379
Fog	Stud	27
	Sign	93
	Sign	98
	Copp	317
	Abbe	636
	Houn	727
	Houn	755
	Houn	761

120 ◼ *Good Old Index*

Fog (cont'd)

	RedC	905
	RedC	907
	Bruc	913
	Bruc	915
	Bruc	925
	Dyin	932
	Suss	1039
Folkestone Court	Houn	764
Food		
apple	SixN	586
bacon	Engr	276
beef	Scan	169
	Bery	311
biscuits	Prio	539
	Dyin	941
bread	Stud	24
	Stud	68
	Five	228
	Bery	311
	Prio	551
	Norw	723
	Houn	739
buckwheat cakes	Stud	54
butter, parsley sunk into	SixN	585
cheese	Stud	24
chicken, curried	Nava	465
cocoa	Prio	547
cocoanuts	Sign	155
cutlets	Gold	617
eggs	Stud	23
	Sign	125
	Engr	276
	Nava	465
	Vall	800
	Thor	1055
	Reti	1116

Food (cont'd)
goose	Blue	245
goose liver	Nobl	296
grouse	Sign	134
ham	Sign	125
	Nava	465
meat	Stud	68
	Houn	723
raw	Sign	156
salt	Glor	377
milk	Stud	49
	Prio	539
mutton, curried	Silv	338
nuts	Glor	375
orange	Five	228
	Reig	405
oysters	Sign	134
	Dyin	936
parsley, sunk into butter	SixN	585
partridge	Veil	1098
pate de foie gras pie	Nobl	296
peas	3Stu	603
peaches	Houn	739
pheasant	Nobl	296
pheasant months	Musg	388
plum pudding	SixN	594
rice	Sign	152
salt meat	Glor	377
sandwich	RedH	185
	Bery	311
	Nava	466
	Seco	657
sugar	Shos	1104
sweet potatoes	Sign	155
toast	Stud	23
	Scan	173

Food, toast (cont'd)

    tongue
    trout
    vegetables
    woodcock

    yams

Food, drugged

Foolscap

Footman (*see* Servants)
Footsteps (footprints)

Vall	800
Reti	1116
Houn	739
Shos	1109
Twis	240
Blue	250
Nobl	296
Sign	155
Silv	338
Nava	465
Wist	884
SixN	586
Houn	685
Vall	773
Stud	84
Sign	112
Bosc	212
Engr	286
Bery	315
Silv	343
Silv	344
Musg	391
Croo	416
Resi	428
Nava	461
Danc	520
Prio	545
Prio	548
Chas	582
SixN	585
Houn	677
Vall	782
Wist	877
RedC	909
Lion	1085

Footsteps (footprints) (cont'd)

on carpet	Norw	504
	Gold	621
none	Reig	408
	Gold	611
	Devi	961
of a hound	Houn	679
one way	Fina	479
monograph promised	Sign	91
Forbes (detective)	Nava	453
Forceps	Twis	244
Ford (automobile)	Last	974
Fordham (lawyer)	Five	220
Fordham, Dr.	Glor	379
Fordingbridge	Glor	379
Foreign Office	Nava	447
	Empt	488
Foresight, evidence of	Blue	247
Forest Row	Blac	560
Forgers	Vall	828
	Shos	1102
Beddington	Stoc	373
Clay	RedH	186
Evans and Prescott	3Gar	1052
Lynch	Suss	1034
Stamford	Soli	527
Staunton	Miss	623
Forgery case	Stud	24
Forgery case, Conk-Singleton	SixN	596
Foreign office	Nava	460
Formosa corruption, black	Dyin	934
Forrester, Inspector	Reig	400
Forrester, Mrs. Cecil	Sign	94
Fort Dodge (Kansas)	3Gar	1046
Fortescue Scholarship	3Stu	596
Forton Old Hall	Wist	876
Fossil bones	3Gar	1048

184 ▫ *Good Old Index*

Foulest antecedents	Gree	446
Foulmire	Houn	684
Four-in-hand	Last	971
Four-wheeler (*see* Cab)		
Fournaye, Henri	Seco	659
Fournaye, Mme. Henri	Seco	658
Fourth smartest man in London (John Clay)	RedH	184
Fowler (fiancé)	Copp	331
Foxhound	Miss	633
Fox hunting	Vall	787
France (*see also* French)	Iden	193
	Stoc	366
	Fina	469
	Empt	488
	Prio	540
	SixN	583
	Gold	607
	Lady	946
	Last	972
French embassy	Nava	450
France, Bank of	RedH	187
Franco-Midland Hardware Co.	Stoc	365
Franco-Prussian War	Nobl	295
Frankfort (Germany)	Stud	18
Frankland	Houn	678
Frankland vs. Morland	Houn	736
Frankland vs. Regina	Houn	736
Franz Josef (emperor)	Last	977
Fraser (tutor)	Houn	762
Fraser, Annie	Lady	947
Fraser, Mary	Abbe	639
Fratton	Last	976
Freebody, Major	Five	222
Freemasons		
Barker	Reti	1116
Drebber, Enoch J.	Stud	30

Freemasons (cont'd)		
McFarlane, John Hector	Norw	497
Wilson, Jabez	RedH	177
Freemen, Ancient Order of	Vall	833
Free trade	Houn	686
French		
embassy	Nava	450
foreign office	Nava	460
gold	RedH	187
Government	Fina	469
music	RedH	184
President	Gold	607
quotations	Stud	42
	Sign	104
	Sign	114
	RedH	190
	Iden	197
	Bosc	213
school of art	Sign	101
will	Sign	90
window	Croo	414
	Norw	500
	Abbe	638
Fresno Street	Twis	234
Friesland (steamship)	Norw	496
Frinton	Reti	1117
Fritz	Engr	283
Frosted glass	Engr	280
Frou-frou (of skirts)	Seco	657
Fulham Road	Houn	762
Fuller's earth	Engr	278
Fulworth	Lion	1083
Furies	Last	972
Furnace	Shos	1106
Furniture van	Nobl	286

Furniture warehouse
Furze bushes

Five 218
Silv 338
Gree 441

G

Gables, The (house)		Lion	1083
Gaboriau (Emile)		Stud	25
Gabriel, Angel		Veil	1100
Gaelic (race)		Houn	700
Gales, equinoctial		Five	218
Gallows		Danc	517
		Prio	558
halter		Sign	121
Gamekeeper (*see also* Servants)		Bosc	203
		Musg	389
		Vall	785
		Thor	1056
Ganges River (India)		Sign	144
Gaol (jail)			
chokey		Sign	155
pass needed		Bosc	209
		Thor	1062
pass not needed		Twis	241
Garcia, Aloysius		Wist	870
Garcia, Beryl		Houn	761
Gardener (*see also* Servants)		Glor	378
		Musg	388
		Chas	582
		Gold	609

Garrideb, Alexander Hamilton	3Gar	1046
Garrideb, Howard	3Gar	1050
Garridbeb, John	3Gar	1045
Garrideb, Nathan	3Gar	1045
Garroter	Empt	490
Gas to conceal clue	Reti	1120
Gas turned up as signal	Dyin	940
Gas flare for light	Blue	252
Gasfitters' ball	Iden	193
Gaslights in houses	Bery	306
	Resi	429
	Gree	439
	Bruc	929
	Lady	950
at 221B	Copp	317
	Dyin	935
Gaslights in streets	Sign	98
	Sign	116
	Sign	137
	Scan	171
	RedH	187
	Blue	245
	Blue	253
	Resi	430
	Empt	488
	SixN	587
	SixN	591
	Miss	631
	Seco	662
	RedC	907
	Vall	819
Gasogene	Scan	162
	Maza	1014
Gazetteer	Sign	127
	Scan	163
Gelatin	Dyin	937
Gelder & Co.	SixN	588

Gemmi Pass (Switzerland)	Fina	477
Geneva (Switzerland)	Fina	477
Genii	Nobl	296
Genius loci	Vall	803
Geographical locales of cases (*see* Scenes of Investigations)		
George II (King)	Vall	807
George III (King)	Nobl	299
Georgia	Five	226
	Five	228
Georgian house	3Gar	1048
	Thor	1063
Geranium beds	3Gab	1029
Germ cultures	Dyin	937
German		
murder not done by a	Stud	33
books	Engr	280
embassy	Last	972
language	Scan	163
	Last	979
mechanic	Empt	493
music	RedH	184
Ocean	Danc	517
quotations	Sign	115
	Sign	158
Vehmgericht	Stud	41
	Stud	62
war (Pref.)	Last	869
Germany	Vall	848
	Cree	1073
Gesellschaft	Scan	163
Ghazis, murderous	Stud	15
Ghosts, none need apply	Suss	1034
Giant rat of Sumatra	Suss	1034
Gibson, Maria	Thor	1060
Gibson, J. Neil	Thor	1055

140 ◘ *Good Old Index*

Gig	Houn	678
Gila	Suss	1034
Gilchrist (student)	3Stu	600
Gilchrist, Sir Jabez	3Stu	600
Gilmerton (USA)	Vall	850
Gilmerton mountains	Vall	815
Gin	Stud	80
	Twis	230
four of gin hot	Stud	34
Gladstone bag	Twis	240
Glass cutter	Chas	577
Glass, frosted	Engr	280
Glasses (*see* Spectacles)		
Glasshouse Street	Illu	993
Globe	Vall	775
Globe (newspaper)	Blue	249
	Prio	539
Gloria Scott (ship)	Glor	380
Gloucester	Houn	692
Gloucester Road	Bruc	925
Gloucester Road Station	Bruc	926
Gloves, as a clue	3Stu	606
	Blan	1007
Glue, as a clue	Shos	1102
Godno (Russia)	Houn	754
Godolphin Street	Seco	655
Goethe (Johann)	Sign	115
	Sign	157
Goggle eyes	Wist	878
Gold, French	RedH	187
Gold, King (J. Neil Gibson)	Thor	1055
Gold shares	Soli	530
Goldini's restaurant	Bruc	925
Golf	Gree	435
	Blac	568

Good Old Index	Suss	1034
Goodge Street	Blue	245
Goodwins (shoals)	Five	229
Goose	Blue	245
	Blue	251
Gordon, General (Charles George)	Resi	423
	Card	889
Gordon Square	Nobl	299
Gorgiano, Giuseppe	RedC	908
Gorot, Charles	Nava	450
Gorse	Soli	530
	Soli	533
	Prio	548
	Wist	886
Gossip, as source of information	Soli	532
	Reti	1116
Gout	Gold	624
Governesses (*see also* Servants)		
Burnett	Wist	882
Dobney	Lady	943
Dunbar, Grace	Thor	1056
Hunter, Violet	Copp	318
Morstan, Mary	Sign	95
Smith, Violet	Soli	528
Gower (Scowrer)	Vall	838
Goyal	Houn	675
Grace of God (there but for the, goes Sherlock Holmes)	Bosc	217
Gracious Lady, a certain	Bruc	931
Grafenstein, Count von und zu	Last	979
Graham and McFarlane	Norw	498
Gramophone	Maza	1021
Grand Duke	Scan	165
Grand Hotel	Illu	993
Grand National (steeplechase)	Shos	1102

Gravesend   Sign   123
                                        Five   229
                                        Twis   238
Gray's Inn Road   Miss   628
Great Alkali Plain   Stud   52
Great George Street   Bruc   925
Great Mogul (diamond)   Sign   151
Great mutiny   Sign   145
Great Orme Street   RedC   905
Great Peter Street Post Office   Sign   125
Great Rebellion (*see also* Civil War, Houn   674
    English)
Great Salt Lake   Stud   59
Greathed, Colonel (E.H.)   Sign   151
Greek e   Sign   96
                                        Reig   408
                                        Vall   769
Greek examination   3Stu   596
Greek legation   Gree   442
Green, Admiral   Lady   948
Green, Hon. Philip   Lady   946
Green Dragon (inn)   Shos   1104
Greenhouse   Chas   577
Green peas, landlady babbles of   3Stu   603
Green room   Twis   243
Greenwich   Sign   124
                                        Engr   276
Gregory, Inspector   Silv   337
Gregson, Tobias   Stud   26
                                        Sign   90
                                        Gree   444
                                        Wist   871
                                        RedC   908
Grenoble (France)   Empt   489
Gresham Buildings   Norw   498
Greuze, Jean Baptiste   Vall   775
Greyminster, Duke of   Blan   1007

Grice Patersons	Five	218
Griffin	Shos	1110
Griggs, Jimmy	Veil	1097
Grimm's fairy tale	Suss	1034
Grimpen (parish)	Houn	671
Grimpen (village)	Houn	694
Grimpen Mire	Houn	707
Grit, in a sensitive instrument	Scan	161
Groom (*see* servants)		
Gross & Hankey (jewelers)	Scan	168
Grosvenor buildings (Aston)	3Gar	1050
Grosvenor Hotel	Fina	478
Grosvenor Mansions	Nobl	288
Grosvenor mixture (tobacco)	Yell	352
Grosvenor Square	3Gab	1031
Grosvenor Square furniture van	Nobl	288
Grouse	Sign	134
Growler (cab)	Stud	84
Gruner, Baron Adelbert	Illu	985
Guaiacum (blood) test	Stud	18
Guessing, effects of	Sign	93
Guild of St. George	Croo	413
Guildford Assizes	Wist	887
Guion Steamship Company	Stud	30
Guitar	Wist	878
Gum	Houn	687
Gum brush	RedC	901
Gunroom	Musg	389
	Abbe	638
	Shos	1111
Gypsies	RedH	183
	Spec	260
	Silv	338
	Prio	546
	Houn	677
	Houn	730

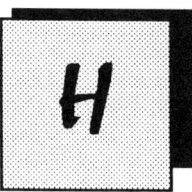

Haemoglobin	Stud	17
Hafiz	Iden	201
Hague, The (Holland)	Iden	196
Haines-Johnson (auctioneer)	3Gab	1027
Hair, woman's, cut	Copp	320
Hairpin	Seco	657
Hair-trigger	Musg	386
Hales Lodge (house)	Vall	781
Hales, William	Vall	850
Half moon (*see* Moon)		
Half Moon Street	Illu	995
Halifax (Nova Scotia)	Copp	318
Hallamshire	Prio	539
Halle's concert	Stud	34
Halliday's Private Hotel	Stud	46
Halt-on-demand railroad station	Shos	1107
Hammer, stone	Sign	109
Hammer and nails	Vall	783
Hammerford Will case	Illu	984
Hammersmith	Seco	655
Hammersmith Bridge	SixN	591
Hammersmith Wonder, Vigor, the	Suss	1034
Hampshire	Spec	259
	Copp	319

Good Old Index

Hampshire (cont'd)	Glor	378
	Thor	1055
Hampstead	Stoc	365
	Chas	572
	Vall	781
Hampstead Heath	Chas	577
	RedC	905
Handbag, crocodile	Danc	520
Handcuffs	Stud	51
	Sign	140
	Danc	524
	Blac	569
	SixN	592
	Dyin	941
	Maza	1021
bracelets	Sign	144
darbies	Card	897
derbies	RedH	189
Hands, form of trade and	Sign	91
	RedH	177
	Iden	192
	Copp	317
	Soli	527
	Cree	1080
Handwriting, clues from	Sign	96
	Scan	163
	Twis	238
	Reig	408
	Nava	448
	Norw	501
	Vall	769
	Wist	874
	Card	891
	RedC	903
Hanged man	Stoc	371
	Resi	431
Hanover Square	Nobl	289

Hansom cab (*see* cab)		
Harden, John Vincent	Soli	527
Harding	SixN	593
Harding Brothers	SixN	585
Hardy (plumber)	Iden	193
Hardy, Sir Charles	Seco	666
Hardy, Sir John	Empt	484
Hare, John	Scan	170
Hargrave (alias)	Vall	803
Hargreave, Wilson	Danc	523
Harker, Horace	SixN	583
Harley Street	Blue	251
	Resi	430
	Devi	955
	Shos	1103
Harmonium	Engr	280
	Blac	561
Harold, Mrs. (victim)	Maza	1017
Harpoon	Blac	561
Harraway (Scowrer)	Vall	835
Harringby, Lord	Wist	876
Harris (Holmes's alias)	Stoc	369
Harrison, Annie	Nava	449
Harrison, Joseph	Nava	449
Harrow	Spec	260
	3Gab	1023
Harrow Weald case	3Gab	1024
Hart's-tongue ferns	Houn	700
Harvey (stableboy)	Shos	1106
Harvey's (house)	Suss	1035
Harwich	Last	974
Hat, as a clue	Blue	244
Hatherley, Victor	Engr	274
Hatherley Farm	Bosc	203
Haunted crypt	Shos	1104
Havana cigar	Resi	432

148 ◻ Good Old Index

Haven, The (house)	Lion	1087
	Reti	1114
Hayes, Reuben.	Prio	550
Hayes, Mrs.	Prio	556
Hayling, Jeremiah	Engr	284
Haymarket Theatre	Reti	1115
Hayter, Colonel	Reig	398
Hayward (murderer)	Resi	434
Hazel (tree)	Wist	879
Headlines (*see* Newspapers)		
Hearse	Lady	953
Heart, weak (*see* Ailments)		
Heather	Nava	449
	Prio	550
	Thor	1069
Heavy Game of the Western Himalayas	Empt	494
(Moran)		
Hebron, Effie	Yell	353
Hebron, John	Yell	361
Hebron, Lucy	Yell	361
Hebrew Rabbi	Scan	165
Heidegger	Prio	541
Heidelberg (early man)	3Gar	1048
Height		
and length of stride	Stud	33
	Sign	121
	Bosc	214
and level of eyes	Stud	33
and reach	Abbe	644
importance of	3Stu	602
Heinrich	Last	979
"Hell, London"	Illu	989
Hell-hound	Sign	140
	Soli	534
	Houn	681
Helmdale (U.S.A.)	Vall	815
Helston	Devi	959

Henderson (alias)	Wist	876
Henrietta Street	Stud	34
Herald (newspaper)	Vall	837
Heraldic emblems (*see also* Coat of Arms)	Soli	530
	Seco	652
	Houn	701
	Vall	787
	Illu	990
	Shos	1108
Hercules	Scan	164
	Resi	427
Herder, Von (airgun maker)	Empt	493
Heredity	Gree	435
	Fina	470
	Empt	494
Hereford	Bosc	209
Hereford Arms	Bosc	207
Herefordshire	Bosc	203
Herling, Baron Von	Last	971
Hieroglyphics	Sign	98
	Danc	511
	Miss	625
Higgins (Scowrer)	Vall	834
High Barrow (parish)	Houn	671
High Gable (house)	Wist	876
High Holborn	Wist	878
High Lodge (house)	Houn	692
High Street		
Kensington	SixN	588
Winchester	Copp	323
High Street Station	SixN	585
High Tor	Houn	684
Hill, Inspector	SixN	590
Himalayas	Empt	494
	Cree	1082
Hindoo	Sign	100
Hippocratic smile	Sign	112

Histon	Miss	632
Hive, emblem	Stud	59
Hobbs, Fairdale	RedC	901
Hobbies (*see also* **Sherlock Holmes**)		
astronomy (Frankland)	Houn	715
ceramics (Baron Gruner)	Illu	997
chess (Josiah Amberley)	Reti	1113
detection (Mycroft)	Gree	436
nervous diseases (Percy Trevelyan)	Resi	425
Oriental diseases (Culverton Smith)	Dyin	937
photography		
(Vincent Spaulding)	RedH	178
(Jephro Rucastle)	Copp	327
Hobson's Patch (USA)	Vall	818
Hoffman "Barcarole"	Maza	1019
Holborn	Blue	251
Holborn, The (restaurant)	Stud	16
Holborn Bar	3Gab	1023
Holder, Alexander	Bery	302
Holder, Arthur	Bery	304
Holder, John	Sign	144
Holder, Mary	Bery	304
Holder & Stevenson (bank)	Bery	302
Holdernesse, Duke of	Prio	539
Holdernesse, Duchess of	Prio	540
Holdernesse Hall	Prio	539
Holdhurst, Lord	Nava	447
Holland	Last	976
	Maza	1020
Holland, reigning family of	Scan	161
	Iden	191
Holland Grove	Stud	34
Hollis (spy)	Last	976
Holloway and Steele (house-agent)	3Gar	1051
Holly-bush	Shos	1109
Holly, Sir Edward	Glor	375

Holmes, Mycroft
    abilities of | Gree | 436
     | Bruc | 914
    age of | Gree | 435
    at 221B | Gree | 443
     | Bruc | 916
    British Government, was the | Bruc | 914
    cab driver, as | Fina | 474
    Canada, expert on | Bruc | 914
    description of | Gree | 436
     | Bruc | 916
    Diogenes Club, and | Gree | 435
    first appearance | Gree | 435
    Jupiter, compared with | Bruc | 915
    lodgings of | Gree | 436
     | Bruc | 914
    refuge, used by Sherlock as | Empt | 487
    salary of | Bruc | 914
    smoking of | Gree | 443
    snuff taking of | Gree | 437
    source of most interesting cases | Gree | 442
    unique position of | Bruc | 914

Holmes, Sherlock
    absence from London excites criminals | Lady | 943
    abstraction, power of | Houn | 683
     | Houn | 692
    active for twenty-three years | Veil | 1095
    activity on the scent | Devi | 963
    actor, would have made an | Stud | 18
     | Sign | 133
     | Scan | 170
     | Maza | 1016
    accuracy a speciality | Reig | 404
    acuteness less than Mycroft's | Gree | 435
    admiration, warmed by | Vall | 776
    admiration and applause, love of | SixN | 594
    advertisements of (*see* Newspapers)

Holmes, Sherlock (cont'd)

advice refused by police	Bosc	213
	Wist	881
affianced	Chas	575
afternoon walk	Nobl	287
	Yell	351
	Blac	565
age, middle-	Bosc	204
age, sixty	Last	975
agency, refers to himself as	Copp	317
	Suss	1034
agent, first criminal in Europe	Empt	483
agent, uses an	Sign	130
	Wist	883
	Illu	987
agony columns (*see* Agony Column)		
aim of career	Fina	470
alias		
Harris	Stoc	369
Escott	Chas	576
Sigerson	Empt	488
Captain Basil	Blac	559
Altamont	Last	973
alpine-stock	Fina	479
amateur sport, opinion on	Miss	623
amateur of crime	Blac	560
	Dyin	937
ambuscade laid by	Nava	467
	Empt	491
	Blac	565
	SixN	592
	Houn	755
	Bruc	930
	3Gar	1053
American experiences	Last	978
Americans, liking for	Nobl	299
amnesty, asks for	Silv	350

Holmes, Sherlock (cont'd)
    ancestry of   Gree   435
    anticipation of cases   Bery   301
                                                  Danc   512
                                                  SixN   583
                                                  Houn   680
    apologizes to Watson   Sign   93
                                                  Empt   485
    apology to: from
        Armstrong   Miss   635
        Cantlemere   Maza   1022
        Lestrade   Norw   509
        Ross, Colonel   Silv   348
    applause   Norw   496
        averse to   Devi   954
        love of   SixN   594
    appreciation of nature, none   Resi   423
    archives of (*see* Commonplace Books)   Reti   1122
    art, basis of   Thor   1070
    art, ideas about   Houn   692
    art for art's sake   Copp   316
                                                RedC   907
                                                Reti   1115
    art's sake, lives for his   Blac   559
    art of deduction   Reig   407
                                                Abbe   636
    art of detection an impersonal thing   Copp   317
    artist (dramatist)   Empt   489
                                                Dyin   941
    artist, impersonal job of the true   Vall   773
    aspect on chase   Bruc   929
    assurance of power   Devi   967
    astronomy   Stud   21
                                                Musg   395
                                                Gree   435
                                                Houn   713

Holmes, Sherlock (cont'd)
    attacked

	Reig	405
	Nava	467
	Fina	473
	Illu	993
	3Gar	1053
attitude when listening	Spec	261
automaton, as an	Sign	96
avocations of	RedH	185
axioms of	Iden	194
	Bruc	926
	Illu	994
battle-signals of	Gold	618
beard of	Last	975
beaten by a woman	Scan	175
beaten four times	Five	219
beats corpses	Stud	17
bees	Seco	650
	Last	978
	Lion	1083
benefactor of the race	RedH	190
berates a duke	Prio	557
Bertillon		
admires	Nava	460
compared with	Houn	672
best and wisest man, as	Fina	480
betting	Stud	36
	Blue	252
	Silv	348
	SixN	591
bicycle, uses	Miss	631
bicycle tires, knowledge of	Prio	547
bigamy, suspects	Bosc	210
	Yell	359
billiards, knowledge of	Danc	511
bitten by dog	Glor	374

Holmes, Sherlock (cont'd)

black-letter editions of	Sign	89
	RedH	185
blank day	Miss	632
blank mind, approaches case with	Card	895
blind as a mole	Twis	241
blood, tests for	Stud	18
	Nava	448
bluff, calls a	Devi	967
bluffs	Thor	1059
Boheman		
habits of	Engr	274
soul of	Scan	161
bones, feels it in his	Nava	504
books of (*see* Baker Street 221B)		
Boswell, lost without his	Scan	164
box received by	Dyin	940
box to think in, considered	Houn	684
boxing	Sign	106
	Five	225
	Yell	351
	Glor	374
	Soli	532
	Empt	494
brain		
always governs heart	Lion	1088
without a heart	Gree	435
cubic capacity, theory of	Blue	247
do not overfill	Stud	21
like a crowded box-room	Lion	1090
like an empty attic	Stud	21
must be at work	Sign	90
	Miss	622
	Devi	960
razor-like	Norw	500
	Vall	778
throws out of action	Bruc	929

Holmes, Sherlock (cont'd)
brain-attic	Five	225
bribe refused by	Prio	555
	3Gar	1054
British Treasury behind	Seco	654
brother first mentioned	Gree	435
brutality of speech	Dyin	935
BSI's used	Stud	42
	Stud	51
	Sign	126
	Croo	419
burglar, acts as	Gree	445
	Chas	577
	Bruc	927
	Illu	997
	Reti	1120
business		
to be inquisitive	Devi	962
to examine lady's hand	Soli	527
to follow continental crime	Illu	985
to know things	Blan	1008
to see justice done	Croo	419
to uphold law	Shos	1111
bust of, in wax	Empt	489
	Maza	1013
Busybody, Mr., called	Spec	264
	Soli	537
	Maza	1016
cab, suspect escapes from	Stud	40
	Houn	690
cabdriver, calls upon	Stud	51
	Houn	697
cabinet, awaits findings of	Bruc	925
cabinet minister, interviewed by	Nava	459
	Prio	544
	Seco	651
	Last	978

Holmes, Sherlock (cont'd)
    calculating machine, as   Sign   96
    calendar of crime, walking   Stud   18
    callers, various   Stud   22
    calling, reveals to Watson   Stud   24
    calls a bluff   Devi   967
    calm does not deceive Watson   Danc   516
    calm is dangerous to   Miss   622
    cane of   Spec   271
         Thor   1064
    canine tooth knocked out   Empt   494
    card, of   Stud   35
         Croo   419
         Nava   449
         Soli   538
         Miss   629
         Abbe   645
         Card   895
         Bruc   922
         Lady   947
         Illu   988
         Blan   1008
         3Gab   1031
         Cree   1076
    Carlyle
        not known to   Stud   21
        referred to by   Sign   121
    carols like a lark   Stud   36
    carte blanche given to   Scan   166
         Bery   311
    casebook of (*see* commonplace books)   Spec   259
    cases, none commonplace   Spec   257
    cases to overlap, would not permit   Houn   761
    cattle tracks, deceived   Prio   551
    celebrated by Watson   Sign   90
         Houn   706

Holmes, Sherlock (cont'd)

Chaldean roots in ancient Cornish language	Devi	955
Chapel, bitten on way to	Glor	374
character, according to		
Stamford	Stud	16
Watson	Stud	21
	Five	225
charters, early English, researches in	3Stu	596
check	Prio	558
	Last	980
checkmated	Houn	698
chemical experiments of	Stud	17
	Sign	130
	Iden	198
	Copp	322
	Glor	377
	Nava	448
	3Stu	596
	Dyin	932
	Devi	965
chemistry, knowledge of "profound"	Stud	22
Chicago crooks, knowledge of	Danc	523
children, study of	Copp	330
chivalrous opponent, as	Dyin	932
cigar case of	Scan	162
	Silv	336
	Card	890
cigarette box of	Empt	486
cigarette case of	Bosc	207
	Fina	479
	Norw	497
ciphers and codes, solves	Glor	379
	Musg	397
	Danc	511
	Seco	653
	Vall	770

Holmes, Sherlock, ciphers and codes, solves (cont'd)

circumstantial evidence, on

city life preferred by

client
    identity of concealed

    may confide in Watson

    model
    stratagem seen by

    unhurried by
    unwelcome at first

clothing (*see* dress of)
cocaine, use of

    (?)
    drug use suspected
    second dose
Cocksure, Mr., called
codes (*see* ciphers)
cold-bloodedness

	Vall	855
	RedC	907
	Bosc	204
	Nobl	294
	Resi	423
	Scan	164
	Suss	1036
	Scan	164
	RedH	176
	Spec	258
	Chas	573
	Cree	1072
	Veil	1099
	Sign	96
	Suss	1036
	Reti	1120
	Blan	1000
	Soli	527
	RedC	901
	Sign	89
	Sign	158
	Scan	161
	Five	225
	Twis	232
	Yell	351
	Stoc	364
	Miss	622
	Dyin	934
(?)	Cree	1071
	Stud	20
	Sign	92
	Blue	253
	Stud	17

Holmes, Sherlock (cont'd)

cold trails, on		Silv	344
		Prio	543
		Blac	563
colleague after his own heart		Houn	680
college career of		Glor	374
		Musg	387
commends local police		Reig	402
		Wist	874
		Wist	879
commonplace books (*see also* notebooks)		Engr	284
		Musg	386
		Miss	623
		Veil	1096
archives		Reti	1122
case-book		Spec	259
		Houn	761
		Suss	1034
diary		Blan	1007
index		Scan	165
		Iden	196
		Five	218
		Empt	494
		Houn	761
		RedC	901
		RedC	904
		Bruc	913
		Suss	1034
		Cree	1071
Good Old Index		Suss	1034
reference book		Nobl	288
		Empt	493
		Prio	539
		Vall	772
		Vall	776
		Bruc	913

Holmes, Sherlock, commonplace books
(*see also* notebooks) (cont'd)

scrap book	Empt	493
	3Stu	596
	RedC	901
	RedC	904
commonplace cases, none	Spec	257
commonplace, effort to escape	RedH	190
commonplace, life is, without cases	Wist	870
common sense, his art is	Blan	1011
commutes a felony	Blue	257
complimented by Moriarty	Fina	472
compliments please him	Reig	399
composer, as	RedH	185
compounds a felony	Maza	1018
	3Gab	1033
conceals a crime	Bosc	217
	Blue	257
	Spec	273
	Prio	558
	Chas	582
	Abbe	649
	Seco	663
	Devi	970
	3Gab	1033
	Suss	1043
conceit denied by	Copp	317
	Gree	435
conceit of	Stud	25
concentrated atmosphere, desired for thought	Houn	684
concentration erases past	Houn	761
conclusion reached too soon	Yell	359
	Nava	456
confession	Bosc	215
confidences are awkward	Vall	799
confides in Mycroft only	Empt	487

Holmes, Sherlock (cont'd)

congenial case	Norw	502
connoisseur of		
crime	Vall	807
painting	Houn	692
constitution		
curious	Sign	127
iron	Reig	398
iron, weakened	Devi	955
wiry	Illu	994
consulting detective	Stud	24
	Sign	90
consulting expert	SixN	589
consulting practice	Houn	695
contempt for bully	Spec	265
	Silv	345
continental	Sign	90
practice of	Fina	470
conversationalist	Sign	134
correspondence, variety of	Nobl	287
	Dyin	941
courage of, admired by Watson	Fina	473
court of appeal, last	Five	219
courtesy of	Iden	192
	Dyin	932
lack of	Scan	175
	Chas	573
	Houn	752
	Thor	1058
crime in city, reflects upon	Fina	471
crime in country, reflects upon	Copp	323
criminal expert	Norw	496
criminal, fortunate that he was not a	Chas	577
	Bruc	913
criminal, he would have made a	Sign	112
	Gree	445
criminal, puts self in place of	Musg	395

Holmes, Sherlock (cont'd)
criminal world knows him well	Sign	133
	Fina	471
	Soli	536
criminals, knowledge of	Illu	985
criticizes Watson	Copp	317
	Soli	531
	Lady	946
criticizes Watson's writings	Sign	90
	Copp	317
	Wist	869
crocuses, talks of	Spec	264
crowning glory of career	Seco	659
culprit described as fish	Houn	750
	Houn	752
	Maza	1014
cunning fiend, called a	Empt	492
danger		
attracted to	3Gab	1032
effects of	Fina	472
in real	Reig	405
	Fina	472
	Empt	491
	Illu	993
	Maza	1014
understates	Maza	1014
dangerous companion	Fina	477
dangerous course the only one	Chas	576
dark, power to see in	Chas	578
Darwin and music	Stud	37
day-dreams	Silv	341
day or night, offers to go	Copp	321
death of, reported	Fina	480
deceit of, impossible	Stud	23
deceived at first	Copp	330
	Yell	359

Holmes, Sherlock, deceived at first (cont'd)

by cattle tracks	Prio	551
by clothing	Houn	744
by good story	Abbe	642
deceives		
Culverton Smith	Dyin	940
Lestrade	Seco	661
Stanley Hopkins	Abbe	650
declines case without all facts	Seco	652
	Thor	1058
declines to help Lestrade	Chas	582
Deduction, Art of	Five	225
deductions, twenty-three	Reig	408
deep waters	Spec	263
	Reig	401
	Shos	1106
defeated temporarily	Abbe	642
	Lady	952
defect in character of	Houn	754
delerium of	Dyin	936
delicacy of touch	Stud	20
depreciates his own work	Musg	388
depressed by failure	Five	228
	Danc	517
details		
insists upon	RedC	902
of a thousand cases	Stud	24
devil, referred to as	Devi	968
	Maza	1021
diary of (*see also* commonplace books)	Blan	1007
diplomatic secrets of	Seco	651
disappearance of	Fina	479
discretion	Veil	1095

Holmes, Sherlock (cont'd)
  disguises
    difficulties of   Empt   485
    fools him   Stud   40
    he penetrates   Scan   165
  disguises of
    Altamont   Last   974
    accountant, Harris   Stoc   370
    book collector   Empt   485
    Captain Basil   Blac   559
    clergyman, simple   Scan   170
    fisherman   Shos   1107
    groom   Scan   167
    loafer   Bery   311
    master mariner   Sign   132
    opium addict   Twis   231
    plumber, Escott   Chas   575
    priest, Italian   Fina   474
    registration agent   Croo   418
    sailor   Sign   130
    Sigerson   Empt   488
    sporting man   Maza   1016
    theatre-goer   Chas   577
    tourist   Houn   740
    woman, old   Maza   1012
    workman   Chas   575
                                            Maza   1012
    workman, French   Lady   946
  distractions, resents   Soli   527
  distrusts Watson   Empt   488
  documents kept by   Musg   386
  dog
    bites   Glor   374
    borrowed   Sign   117
                                            Miss   633
                                            Shos   1108
    fails him   Sign   122

Holmes, Sherlock, dog (cont'd)

repelled by stick		Miss	631
shot		Copp	331
		Houn	757
used by		Stud	49
		Sign	119
		Miss	633
		Shos	1109
dog-cart, driven by		Twis	233
		Soli	534
door, smashed by		Sign	109
		Stoc	370
drama, love for		Silv	348
		Vall	774
dramatic captures by		Stud	51
		Sign	139
		Blac	569
		SixN	594
dramatic denouement by		Blue	257
		Nava	466
		Abbe	647
dramatic effects, cannot resist		Nava	466
		Empt	486
		Vall	809
		Maza	1022
dramatic introduction of		Devi	955
dramatic solution by		Lady	953
		Maza	1022
dramatic talents of		Sign	133
		Scan	170
		Maza	1022
dress of			
boots		Sign	117
		Twis	240
		Houn	739
		RedC	906

Holmes, Sherlock, dress of (cont'd)

cap, cloth	Bosc	202
	Houn	740
ear-flapped	Silv	335
cloak, long gray	Bosc	202
coat	Twis	240
	Vall	778
	Dyin	941
	Illu	984
frock	Norw	502
	Houn	690
frock, seedy	Empt	486
overcoat	Stud	27
	Nobl	296
	3Stu	598
	Gold	608
	Abbe	636
	Cree	1080
ulster	Stud	39
	Blue	251
waterproof	Bosc	212
	Houn	738
cravat	Stud	39
	Blue	251
	Gold	608
dress-clothes	Chas	577
dressing gown	Engr	276
	Bery	301
	Resi	431
	Nava	448
	Fina	472
	Houn	683
	Vall	778
	Card	890
	Lady	953
	Maza	1013
	Maza	1018

Holmes, Sherlock, dress of, dressing gown (cont'd)

	blue	Twis	240
	mouse	Empt	494
		Bruc	920
	purple	Blue	244
galoshes		Gold	608
handkerchief		Sign	117
hat		Bery	308
		Resi	429
		Blac	559
		Abbe	645
		Seco	666
		Wist	880
		Card	894
		Devi	959
		Blan	1007
	top hat	Chas	577
jacket		Sign	121
	pea jacket	Sign	132
		RedH	186
scarf		Sign	133
shoes		Spec	271
	tennis shoes	Chas	577
slippers		Blue	254
		Abbe	647
trousers		Nava	466
tweeds		Scan	167
		Houn	740
waistcoat		Twis	240
		Silv	344
		Vall	807
drinking		Sign	134
		Sign	135
		Scan	168
		Scan	169
		RedH	189

Holmes, Sherlock, drinking (cont'd)
	Blue	251
	Nobl	294
	Glor	375
	Reig	407
	Card	894
	Bruc	925
	Dyin	941
	Last	974
	Cree	1079
	Veil	1098
	Shos	1108
coffee	Gold	613
tea	Sign	97
	Bosc	207
	Bery	311
	Yell	360
	Nava	466
	Vall	799
drives trap or dog-cart	Twis	233
	Soli	534
drugs, uses (*see* cocaine, morphine)		
dual nature of	RedH	185
duck shooting	Glor	374
early cases of	Stud	22
	Spec	259
	Glor	374
	Musg	386
	Nava	458
	Houn	691
Eastbourne, lives near (Pref)	Last	869
eating habits		
diet	Yell	351
digesting cannot spare energy for	Norw	505
faculties refined by starving	Maza	1014
faints from inanition	Norw	505
food	Stud	24
	Sign	97

Holmes, Sherlock, eating habits, food (cont'd)

	Sign	134
	Scan	169
	Scan	173
	RedH	185
	Five	228
	Bery	311
	Yell	351
	Vall	800
	Dyin	940
food neglected	Scan	169
	Five	228
	Norw	505
	Seco	657
	Vall	771
	Dyin	941
	Maza	1012
eaves-dropper caught by	3Gab	1025
eclipse, temporary	Lady	954
economy of words	Blan	1007
education, continuing, of	RedC	907
egotism annoys Watson	Sign	90
	Copp	317
ejected from suspect's home	Lady	952
	Cree	1077
emotion and judgement, opinion on	Sign	96
emotion, capacity to hide	Scan	161
	Croo	419
encyclopedia of reference (*see also* commonplace books)	Prio	539
energy, comments on	Stud	20
	Musg	386
	Gree	436
	Soli	534
	Prio	547
engaged to be married	Chas	575
English, well of, defiled	Last	978

Holmes, Sherlock (cont'd)

escapes by flight	Fina	475
	Chas	581
escapes from Reichenbach	Empt	487
Europe rings with his name	Reig	398
exaggerations, characterizes Watson's tales as	Blan	1000
exceptions, never makes	Sign	90
exclusion, process of	Sign	92
	Sign	97
	Sign	111
	Bery	315
	Soli	529
	Bruc	926
	Blan	1006
	Blan	1011
exercise of	Yell	351
	Soli	532
	Blac	559
expenses of	RedH	189
facts before theories	Stud	27
	Scan	163
	Bosc	211
	Spec	272
	Seco	657
	Vall	779
	Wist	876
	Card	895
facts vs. instinct	Norw	503
	Abbe	642
failures of	Scan	175
	Five	229
	Engr	286
	Yell	351
	Yell	362
	Musg	387
	Gree	446

Holmes, Sherlock, failures of (cont'd)

	Soli	526
	Houn	690
	Wist	883
fame of	Blac	558
fame, philosophy of	Stud	25
	SixN	594
	Thor	1058
farm of his dreams	Cree	1080
fate, comments on	Bosc	217
	Veil	1101
favorite weapon, hunting crop	SixN	594
fees	Stud	24
	Scan	175
	RedH	189
	Iden	191
	Spec	259
	Bery	313
	Fina	470
	Prio	540
	Blac	559
disclaims	RedH	189
	RedC	907
on a fixed scale	Thor	1058
princely	Prio	540
felon in eyes of law	Chas	577
felony (*see also* Felony)		
aiding and abetting	Houn	728
commuted	Blue	257
compounded	Maza	1018
	3Gab	1033
condoned	Prio	557
fencing skill	Glor	374
	Illu	993
fiend, called	Empt	492
fifty men have reason to kill	Bruc	914
fifty murder cases investigated by	Chas	572
fifty-three cases handled by	Nava	458

Holmes, Sherlock (cont'd)
fights, involved in	Sign	106
	Nava	467
	Fina	470
	Empt	486
	Empt	494
	Soli	532
	Illu	993
final court of appeal	Musg	387
fingerprints, known by	Norw	506
firearms, knowledge of	Vall	785
first appearance of	Stud	17
first case	Glor	374
first mentioned	Stud	17
first name used		
by Mycroft	Gree	437
	Bruc	916
by old Sherman	Sign	117
first rule of investigation	Blac	567
fish, likens criminal to	Houn	750
	Houn	752
	Maza	1014
fishing,		
as a blind	Shos	1109
as a pleasure	Glor	374
five hundred cases handled by	Houn	693
flask of	Sign	140
	Nava	466
	Empt	485
flattery, susceptible to	Stud	34
	RedC	901
flees	Fina	475
	Chas	581
flowers, admiration of	Nava	455
fly out the window, if we could	Iden	191
fog threatens success of	Houn	756
follows without being seen	Devi	967

Holmes, Sherlock (cont'd)
  food (*see* Eating Habits)
  fool, calls self   Twis   240
  fooled
    by alias   Norw   505
    by plaster   Vall   814
    by disguise   Stud   40
  football, ignorance of   Miss   623
  foot in door   Lady   950
  footmarks, always present   Blac   562
  footprints
    monograph upon   Sign   91
    not visible   Gold   621
    use of   Stud   84
                                    Bosc   212
  forceps, uses   Blue   244
  forgets   Sign   112
                                    Scan   173
                                    Dyin   941
  foxhound, compared with   Stud   31
  fresh and trim after night out   Bery   312
  friends   Seco   657
    at college   Glor   374
                                    Musg   387
    few   Five   218
    none except Watson   Five   218
  friendship, not prone to   Vall   774
  frontal development of   Fina   472
  game for game's sake   Bruc   917
  genius defined by   Stud   31
  genius for detail   Sign   91
  ghosts, none need apply   Suss   1034
  gone for days at a time   Bery   312
  good luck aids him   Blac   571
  "Good old index"   Suss   1034
  grandmother of   Gree   435
  grasp of iron of   Last   977

Holmes, Sherlock (cont'd)
great heart of	3Gar	1053
guess work never used by	Sign	93
	Houn	687
gun in dressing-gown pocket	Fina	472
habits		
bohemian	Scan	161
	Engr	274
discloses methods	Reig	407
frugal	Prio	554
irregular	Seco	657
	Dyin	932
	Dyin	941
	Maza	1012
narrow and concentrated	Cree	1071
regular	Stud	20
several days in bed	3Gar	1044
simple	Yell	351
sits with back to window	Blan	1000
Spartan	Houn	739
untidy	Musg	386
	Dyin	932
when puzzled	Vall	769
when on a case	Stud	31
	Sign	130
habitually half-humorous	Devi	966
handcuffs, recommends to Yard	Stud	51
hand, injured	Nava	465
	Fina	470
handwriting, deduces age from	Reig	408
handwriting, precise	Empt	494
	Danc	521
hard day's work	Bery	316
hard, dry statement	Illu	991
harpoon, practices with	Blac	559
harshness foreign to his nature	Soli	527
head, not heart, rules	Illu	992

Holmes, Sherlock (cont'd)

health undermined	Reig	398
	Devi	955
height of	Stud	20
	3Stu	605
heredity, views on	Gree	435
	Empt	494
hideouts in London, five	Blac	559
hobbies		
crime detection	Sign	91
	Glor	376
	Houn	686
knowledge of London	RedH	185
music of middle ages	Bruc	913
opening safes	Chas	578
holidays aimless and unusual	Fina	470
honour, professional	Veil	1095
honours list, no interest in	Bruc	917
hours		
irregular	Maza	1012
strange	Dyin	932
housebreaking, commits	Gree	445
	Chas	577
	Bruc	927
	Reti	1120
humor, sense of (*see* Mannerisms—chuckles, laughs, smiles, etc.)		
hundreds of cases of	Soli	526
hunting crop of	RedH	186
	Iden	201
	SixN	594
hypothesis, working	Houn	670
	Devi	964
idiot, calls self	Stoc	372
	Vall	805

Holmes, Sherlock (cont'd)
  ignorance of
    generally | Stud | 21
    specifically | Bruc | 916
  illness, nervous prostration | Reig | 398
       | Dyin | 932
       | Devi | 955
  illness, pretended | Reig | 403
       | Resi | 430
       | Dyin | 932
  imagination, value of | Silv | 344
  impossible, elimination of | Sign | 92
       | Sign | 97
       | Sign | 111
       | Bery | 315
       | Soli | 529
       | Bruc | 926
       | Blan | 1006
       | Blan | 1011
  inaction, effects of | Sign | 90
       | Vall | 778
  index (*see also* Commonplace books) | Scan | 165
       | Iden | 196
       | Five | 218
       | Empt | 494
       | Houn | 761
       | RedC | 901
       | RedC | 904
       | Bruc | 913
       | Suss | 1034
       | Cree | 1071
    "Good old index" | Suss | 1034
  inhuman effect of | Sign | 96
       | Gree | 435
  injured | Nava | 465
       | Fina | 470
       | Empt | 487

228 ◼ *Good Old Index*

Holmes, Sherlock, injured (cont'd)

	Empt	494
	Soli	532
	Illu	993
instinct of	Bruc	925
	Suss	1043
sometimes false	Thor	1069
instinct vs. facts	Norw	503
	Abbe	642
interest		
extraordinary	Houn	680
in client's tale	Yell	358
primarily in story	Nobl	287
renewed, signs of	Abbe	639
international complication prevented	Fina	469
international peace preserved	Nava	460
	Seco	662
	Bruc	916
intuition	Stud	24
intuition of women, opinion on	Bosc	208
	Twis	239
	Lion	1088
iron nerves of	Illu	998
irregular hours of	Maza	1012
irregulars, we are the	Lady	949
jack-in-office, called	Spec	265
jack-knife	Musg	386
joke, practical	Maza	1022
judicial posture	RedH	176
juries, must satisfy	Norw	503
keepsakes	Scan	175
	Iden	191
knife		
jack	Musg	386
pen	Stud	49
	Dyin	934
pocket	3Gar	1053
knighthood refused by	3Gar	1044

Holmes, Sherlock (cont'd)
  knighthood, not interested in   Danc   917
  knowledge
    passion for exact   Stud   17
    still seeking   RedC   907
    vast store of   Lion   1090
  knowledge of (*see also* Writings)
    anatomy   Stud   16
       Stud   22
       Five   225
    ashes (tobacco)   Bosc   214
    astronomy   Stud   21
       Five   225
    bicycle tires   Prio   547
    billiards   Dyin   511
    botany   Stud   21
       Five   225
    brokers' failures   Blac   566
    chemistry   Stud   16
       Stud   22
       Five   225
    Chicago crooks   Danc   523
    crime   RedH   176
    crime records   Five   225
    criminals   Illu   985
    ears   Card   896
    firearms   Vall   785
    foreign cases   Stud   18
       Sign   90
       Houn   754
    geology   Stud   21
       Five   225
    history of crime   Stud   22
    law   Stud   22
       Five   225
       Copp   317
       Abbe   646

Holmes, Sherlock, knowledge of (*see also* Writings), law (cont'd)

	Wist	883
	Wist	886
	Last	975
literature	Stud	21
literature, sensational	Stud	22
	Five	225
London	Sign	121
	RedH	185
	Empt	489
London criminals	Fina	471
	Danc	523
newspapers	Houn	687
perfumes	Houn	765
philology	Devi	955
philosophy	Stud	21
	Five	225
politics	Stud	21
	Five	225
preexisting cases	Nobl	294
secret writings	Danc	522
sensational literature	Stud	22
	Five	225
soil	Five	219
wrestling	Empt	486
knows what there is to know	Maza	1013
last exploit intended	Seco	650
Latin quotations by	Stud	86
	RedH	177
	Blue	251
	Abbe	650
laurels, fresh leaves added to	Maza	1021
law		
breaks	Iden	201
	Gree	445
	Chas	577
	Bruc	927

Holmes, Sherlock, law, breaks (cont'd)	Illu	997
	Reti	1120
can't wait for	Lady	950
could not help with Moran	Empt	495
foremost champion of	Fina	480
Legion of Honour	Gold	607
lens, uses	Stud	31
	Sign	92
	Sign	98
	Sign	108
	Sign	112
	Scan	161
	RedH	187
	Iden	199
	Bosc	212
	Blue	244
	Spec	267
	Bery	310
	Resi	432
	Norw	506
	Blac	563
	Gold	607
	Gold	614
	Houn	670
	Vall	790
	Bruc	924
	Devi	963
	Thor	1064
	Lion	1091
	Shos	1110
liar trapped by	Vall	811
	3Gar	1047
	Thor	1059
lies, test of	3Gar	1047
life is pathetic and futile	Reti	1113
life, meaning of unknown	Card	901

Holmes, Sherlock (cont'd)

life with, effects on Watson	Stud	22
	Houn	731
	Cree	1071
limits of	Stud	21
lip injured	Soli	532
little things important	Iden	194
London criminals, thoughts on	Norw	496
	Bruc	913
London dull when quiet	Norw	496
lost without his Boswell	Scan	164
loved, never	Devi	970
love of bizarre	RedH	176
love, thoughts on	Sign	157
loyalty of	Seco	653
lunatic, calls himself	Vall	805
M's, fine collection of	Empt	494
machine, perfect reasoning, as	Scan	161
madness in his method	Reig	402
magic of his name	Sign	106
	Sign	117
magician, called	Bery	310
magnifying glass (*see* lens)		
magnum opus	Last	978
mail, caution in opening	Dyin	941
manner at work	Stud	31
	RedH	185
	Bosc	211
	Silv	343
	SixN	587
	Houn	754
	Wist	879
	Thor	1068
manner not effusive	Scan	162
mannerisms		
abrupt	Stud	50
	Gree	444

Holmes, Sherlock, mannerisms (cont'd)

absent-minded	Houn	682
absorbed	Sign	104
	Danc	516
	Vall	785
	Devi	960
	Suss	1034
	Thor	1068
absorbed in thought (*see* lost)		
abstract	Sign	104
	Iden	192
	Copp	322
	Chas	582
	Cree	1074
active	Prio	547
	Bruc	913
	Maza	1013
admiration	Last	975
affable	Croo	419
	Maza	1021
affectionate	Prio	558
agitated	Five	228
	Empt	490
	Thor	1069
alert	Empt	490
	Norw	502
	Prio	547
	Prio	553
	3Stu	600
	Abbe	641
	Houn	740
	Houn	749
	Devi	963
	Bruc	919
	Bruc	929
aloof	Reti	1117

Holmes, Sherlock, mannerisms (cont'd)

amazed	Prio	539
	Seco	655
	Houn	697
	Houn	756
	Vall	776
	Bruc	921
	Lady	951
amiable	Cree	1077
amused	Stud	40
	Stud	42
	Sign	133
	Resi	430
	Norw	507
	Danc	511
	Miss	623
	Houn	749
	Maza	1015
	Maza	1017
	Suss	1034
	Suss	1042
	Cree	1077
angry	Stud	25
	Chas	574
	Seco	661
	Dyin	933
animated	RedH	186
annoyed	Sign	135
	Yell	351
	Danc	517
	Chas	577
	SixN	588
	Abbe	639
	Lady	952
	Illu	992
	Lion	1090

Holmes, Sherlock, mannerisms (cont'd)

anxious		Stud	19
		Stud	42
		Norw	502
		Danc	517
		Danc	518
		Seco	660
		Houn	677
apathetic		Stud	27
appalled		Miss	634
approving		SixN	591
arid		Prio	554
ascetic		Empt	488
		Devi	960
asperity		Nava	457
		Empt	490
		Houn	672
		Vall	809
assured		Scan	198
		Empt	489
		Shos	1111
astonished		Glor	377
		Prio	556
		Seco	655
astute		RedH	185
		Reig	409
attentive		Danc	513
		Gold	617
		Card	894
austere		Empt	488
		Soli	531
		Houn	699
		Bruc	925
		Bruc	927
		Dyin	933
		3Gar	1044
avid		Prio	554

236 ◼ *Good Old Index*

Holmes, Sherlock, mannerisms (cont'd)

baffled		Chas	574
bewildered		Glor	380
bitter		Stud	36
		Stud	83
		Sign	104
		Stoc	363
		Norw	505
		Gold	610
		Seco	661
		Houn	690
		Houn	744
black reaction		Sign	89
bland		Stud	51
		RedH	189
		Blue	254
		Spec	264
		Prio	543
blank		Stoc	369
blunders		Silv	337
		Soli	534
		Soli	538
		Abbe	644
		Houn	690
		Lady	952
bored		Wist	870
bright		Stud	83
		Sign	97
		Sign	134
		Thor	1055
brilliant		Sign	134
brisk		Sign	94
		Nobl	297
		Wist	879
		Card	892
		Illu	987
		Thor	1057

Holmes, Sherlock, mannerisms (cont'd)

brooding	Silv	336
	Reti	1115
brusque	Stud	26
bumptious	Stud	25
calm	Stud	23
	Stud	26
	Bosc	213
	Five	227
	Norw	506
	Norw	508
	Danc	516
	Chas	578
capricious	Blac	559
careful	Sign	98
	SixN	586
	SixN	587
	Miss	625
	Abbe	640
careless	Blue	252
chafing	Bruc	913
chagrinned	Stud	40
	Stud	49
	Scan	174
	Blue	253
chattered	Stud	31
chatty	3Gab	1023
cheerful	Blue	254
	Spec	258
	Resi	425
	Nava	464
	Vall	799
	Vall	806
	Vall	808
	Card	894
	Lady	951

Holmes, Sherlock, mannerisms, cheerful (cont'd)
    chuckles

3Gab	1031
Thor	1055
Stud	18
Stud	30
Sign	91
Scan	162
RedH	178
Iden	197
Five	228
Twis	240
Spec	265
Silv	346
Glor	374
Croo	412
Danc	515
Soli	529
Prio	553
Blac	559
Blac	567
SixN	589
Gold	612
Miss	628
Vall	773
Vall	775
Wist	873
RedC	906
RedC	907
Bruc	914
Dyin	940
3Gab	1024
Suss	1033
Shos	1110
Reti	1118

    cleanliness, catlike   Houn   740
    clear   Silv   339
            Soli   534
            Houn   740

Holmes, Sherlock, mannerisms (cont'd)

cocksure	Norw	506
cold	Scan	161
	Scan	175
	Empt	488
	Norw	496
	Soli	535
	Prio	554
	SixN	595
	Seco	656
	Houn	740
	Illu	992
	Illu	994
	3Gab	1032
	Suss	1035
	Thor	1058
comic	Miss	630
composed	Croo	412
	Vall	774
	Bruc	929
concentration	Sign	94
	Iden	193
	Reig	401
	Nava	448
	Suss	1034
	Thor	1068
confident	Stud	48
confidential	Miss	628
contemplative	RedH	185
contemptuous	Bruc	913
cool	Sign	89
	Reig	405
	Prio	552
	Chas	581
	Lady	952
	Maza	1016
	3Gab	1023

Holmes, Sherlock, mannerisms, cool (cont'd)
 cordial

 courteous
 crestfallen
 crisp

 critical

 cunning
 curious

 curses
 curt

 cynical
 debonair

 decisive
 dejected

 deliberate
 delighted

Thor	1069
Shos	1111
Stud	17
RedH	176
Musg	388
Iden	192
Sign	92
Sign	108
Dyin	938
Sign	135
Stoc	369
Five	229
RedC	902
Suss	1039
Suss	1041
3Gar	1047
3Gar	1048
Fina	476
Stud	32
Reig	406
Devi	954
Vall	799
Maza	1019
Silv	343
Sign	130
Miss	630
Sign	89
Stud	17
Stud	18
Stud	19
Stud	48
Stud	49
Sign	112
Bery	313
Stoc	368
Danc	517
Prio	548

Holmes, Sherlock, mannerisms,
  delighted (cont'd)
    demure

    deprecating

    depressed

    derisive
    despondent

    detachment, power of

    determination
    didactic

    dignity
    direct
    disappointed

    disconsolate
    discrete

Devi	955
Devi	963
Bosc	211
Prio	555
Card	893
Norw	496
Vall	769
Five	228
Reig	398
Maza	1017
Danc	517
Soli	534
Bruc	929
Devi	955
Devi	961
Illu	987
Illu	994
Sign	90
Nava	467
Miss	633
Houn	752
Stud	49
Sign	123
Sign	128
Musg	394
Musg	395
Blac	567
SixN	588
Miss	625
Miss	632
Seco	661
Vall	771
Vall	773
Suss	1034
Stud	39
Scan	164
3Stu	596

242 ◘ *Good Old Index*

Holmes, Sherlock, mannerisms, discrete (cont'd)

		Miss	635
		Seco	653
		Veil	1095
disgusted		Sign	150
		Resi	430
		Chas	572
dismal		Sign	157
dismayed		Danc	517
distrait		Silv	349
		Gold	616
drawls		Nobl	296
dreamer		RedH	185
		Prio	547
		Houn	689
dry		Sign	114
		Scan	164
		Houn	748
		Illu	991
		Reti	1118
eager		Stud	18
		Sign	97
		Sign	138
		Scan	161
		Bosc	212
		Twis	238
		Engr	276
		Bery	310
		Musg	388
		Musg	391
		Empt	488
		Prio	545
		Prio	547
		Chas	594
		Abbe	636
		Seco	661
		Houn	690
		Houn	691

Holmes, Sherlock, mannerisms, eager (cont'd)

	Vall	778
	Vall	785
	Vall	800
	Wist	875
	Wist	879
	Card	892
	Card	893
	RedC	907
	Bruc	919
	Bruc	920
	Bruc	925
	Lady	953
	Devi	963
	Suss	1034
	Suss	1041
	Thor	1068
	Lion	1090
	Lion	1093
earnest	Sign	128
	Nobl	292
	Danc	514
	Danc	521
	Prio	551
	Prio	554
	3Stu	598
	Suss	1042
	Thor	1066
	Shos	1110
easy	Scan	198
	Blue	250
	Bery	302
eccentric	Dyin	932
egotistic	Sign	90
	Copp	317
eloquent	Illu	992
embarrassed	Twis	238
	Reig	404

Holmes, Sherlock, mannerisms (cont'd)

energetic	Stud	27
	RedH	185
enigmatic	Stud	19
	Norw	500
	3Stu	598
enthusiastic	Copp	330
ever-active	Lady	942
exaltation	Houn	749
excited	RedH	183
	Silv	341
	Stoc	370
	Stoc	372
	Reig	402
	Croo	419
	Nava	462
	Empt	490
	Empt	491
	Norw	506
	Danc	515
	Danc	516
	Seco	661
	Houn	769
	Card	893
	Bruc	924
	Devi	963
	Veil	1097
exclamation	Abbe	637
exhausted	Illu	998
exhilaration	Prio	547
expectant	Prio	547
	SixN	593
	Houn	749
	Bruc	916
exuberant	Fina	477
exultant	Stud	48
	Prio	548

Holmes, Sherlock, mannerisms, exultant (cont'd)	Houn	756
	Vall	771
fascinated	Houn	750
feline	Vall	798
feverish	Sign	130
	Houn	745
fidgeted	Empt	490
firm	Sign	108
	Lady	950
	Lady	951
flame-like	Cree	1071
flippant	Houn	682
formidable	Thor	1061
frank	Abbe	644
	Houn	747
	Houn	752
frantic	Stoc	370
frenzied	Seco	661
frivolous	Bruc	926
frugal	Prio	554
furious	Illu	992
furtive	Sign	112
galvanized	Twis	238
gay	Sign	135
genial	Sign	106
	Blue	250
	Engr	276
	Yell	352
gentle	Sign	96
	Bosc	215
	Abbe	645
	Dyin	932
glared	3Gar	1053
glee	Houn	686
	Vall	803
gloomy	Empt	488
	Danc	521

Holmes, Sherlock, mannerisms, gloomy (cont'd)

good-humored

good-natured
grave

grief
grim

Danc	526	
Prio	547	
Reig	403	
Nava	457	
Prio	550	
Blac	570	
3Stu	597	
Miss	623	
Wist	879	
Prio	550	
Stud	42	
Stud	43	
Bosc	215	
Spec	272	
Nobl	297	
Copp	321	
Copp	322	
Copp	323	
Copp	329	
Soli	530	
Soli	533	
Miss	633	
Houn	699	
Vall	808	
Vall	811	
Vall	814	
Card	892	
Bruc	922	
Lady	947	
Lady	948	
3Gar	1051	
Reti	1117	
Soli	534	
Spec	268	
Nava	465	
Devi	955	
Cree	1080	

Holmes, Sherlock, mannerisms (cont'd)

grins	Sign	126
	Five	225
	Twis	232
groans	Stud	31
	Sign	157
	Fina	476
	Prio	550
	Houn	744
	Bruc	913
	Dyin	939
growls	Sign	122
grunts	Reig	399
	Veil	1096
haggard	Sign	130
	Norw	502
	Danc	517
	Danc	518
	Devi	962
half-hearted	Gold	617
half-humorous (*see* humorous)		
happy	RedH	185
hard	Illu	991
harassed	Norw	505
hearty	Stud	83
	Twis	232
	Blue	253
	Spec	265
	Nobl	295
	Reig	407
	Resi	423
	Soli	532
	Chas	575
	3Stu	607
	Card	888
high-strung	Bruc	920

Holmes, Sherlock, mannerisms (cont'd)

hilarity	Sign	135
	Norw	506
	Bruc	925
homely	Iden	191
horror	Spec	272
	Glor	377
humorous	Norw	496
half-humorous	3Stu	603
	Lady	944
hurried	Prio	539
	Chas	582
	Shos	1110
ice-cold	Wist	883
impassive	Resi	429
	Houn	678
	Wist	879
	Lady	952
impatient	Stud	21
	Stud	35
	Stud	49
	Sign	112
	Scan	165
	Copp	322
	Yell	353
	Stoc	371
	Empt	490
	Danc	516
	Soli	533
	Prio	546
	3Stu	600
	Gold	611
	Houn	680
	Houn	755
	Houn	756
	Vall	769
	Bruc	913

Holmes, Sherlock, mannerisms, impatient (cont'd)

	Bruc	920
	Bruc	928
	Shos	1102
impenetrable	Sign	98
imperious	Dyin	933
imperturbable	Spec	264
	Silv	347
	Nava	460
	Thor	1059
incisive	Scan	167
	Houn	740
indefatigable	Yell	351
indiscreet	Houn	691
indulgent	Norw	510
inexorable	Empt	486
	Prio	544
inquisitive	Devi	962
inscrutable	Bery	311
	Miss	622
insistent	Maza	1021
intent (intense)	Stud	29
	Sign	98
	Twis	238
	Stoc	370
	Reig	401
	Croo	412
	Resi	429
	Nava	455
	Nava	458
	Nava	462
	Empt	490
	Prio	541
	Blac	564
	Chas	573
	Chas	579
	Chas	581
	SixN	587

Holmes, Sherlock, mannerisms, intent (intense) (cont'd)

	Gold	613
	Houn	676
	Houn	749
	Vall	778
	Vall	788
	Vall	789
	Card	893
	Bruc	919
	Bruc	920
	Dyin	938
	Devi	957
	Suss	1034
	Suss	1041
interested	Blac	566
	Gold	612
	Houn	670
	Houn	672
	Houn	679
	Houn	742
(2)	Vall	774
	Lady	947
	Devi	963
	Suss	1034
	Shos	1106
introspective	Scan	162
	RedH	184
	Blue	246
	Prio	547
ironic	Blac	562
	Houn	740
irregular	Dyin	932
irresolute	Stud	50
	Miss	633
irritated	Vall	773
	Lady	953
jaunty	Dyin	936
jealous	Houn	672

Holmes, Sherlock, mannerisms (cont'd)

	jesting	Vall	773
	joyful	Empt	489
		Houn	750
		Thor	1055
		Thor	1069
	judicial	RedH	176
		Houn	678
		Vall	786
	keen	Sign	107
		Sign	108
		Sign	130
		Scan	161
		Scan	167
		RedH	184
		RedH	185
		Spec	268
		Engr	276
		Copp	331
		Stoc	363
		Croo	412
		Resi	424
		Resi	429
		Empt	486
		Empt	488
		Empt	490
		Norw	501
		Blac	566
		SixN	583
		Gold	621
		Abbe	639
		Houn	679
		Houn	685
		Houn	696
		Houn	740
		Bruc	919

Holmes, Sherlock, mannerisms (cont'd)

kindly	Sign	93
	Sign	110
	Twis	242
	3Stu	605
	Last	980
laconic	Cree	1071
languid	Sign	89
	Sign	96
	Scan	165
	RedH	185
	Iden	196
	Norw	499
	Seco	661
	Houn	689
	3Gab	1023
	Thor	1059
laughs	Stud	19
	Stud	31
	Stud	35
	Stud	40
	Stud	86
	Sign	91
	Sign	106
	Sign	122
	Sign	125
	Scan	163
	Scan	165
	Scan	166
	Scan	167
	RedH	182
	RedH	186
	Iden	192
	Iden	195
	Iden	201
	Bosc	204
	Bosc	207

Holmes, Sherlock, mannerisms, laughs (cont'd)

	Bosc	208
	Bosc	211
	Twis	232
	Twis	238
	Twis	239
	Blue	245
	Blue	247
	Blue	253
	Blue	254
	Spec	258
	Spec	265
	Spec	271
	Engr	284
	Engr	287
	Nobl	288
	Nobl	294
	Nobl	295
	Nobl	296
	Nobl	297
	Bery	301
	Silv	345
	Silv	348
	Yell	361
	Stoc	363
	Reig	400
	Reig	407
	Reig	409
	Resi	423
	Gree	435
	Nava	456
	Fina	475
	Empt	489
	Empt	494
	Norw	506
	Norw	507
	Soli	530
	Soli	532

254 ◼ *Good Old Index*

Holmes, Sherlock, mannerisms, laughs (cont'd)

		Prio	550
		Prio	552
		Blac	567
		Chas	575
		Miss	623
		Miss	630
		Miss	633
		Seco	662
		Houn	683
		Houn	694
		Houn	697
		Houn	745
	(2)	Houn	750
		Vall	773
		Vall	787
		Vall	789
		Vall	809
		Vall	865
		Wist	870
		Wist	876
		Wist	879
		Card	888
		Card	895
		Bruc	914
		Devi	960
		Maza	1022
		Suss	1033
		3Gar	1054
hearty, noiseless		Blue	253
joke on self		Houn	697
rarely		Houn	750
seldom		Maza	1022
lazy		Stud	27
		Sign	157
		Bery	310
		Empt	494
leisurely		Norw	496

Holmes, Sherlock, mannerisms (cont'd)

lethargic	Musg	386
light	Sign	91
listless	Sign	143
	Seco	661
lively	3Gab	1026
loathing	Spec	272
lost (absorbed, sunk) in thought	Stud	50
	RedH	183
	Bosc	213
	Twis	233
	Spec	266
	Bery	308
	Silv	341
	Silv	343
	Yell	358
	Reig	401
	Resi	423
	Resi	431
	Nava	456
	Empt	488
	Blac	563
	Prio	551
	3Stu	603
	Gold	616
	Abbe	646
	Seco	654
	Houn	696
	Houn	748
	Vall	769
	Vall	797
	Bruc	928
	Devi	957
	Devi	959
	Illu	987
	3Gab	1028
	3Gab	1031

Holmes, Sherlock, mannerisms, lost (absorbed, sunk) in thought (cont'd)

	Suss	1034
	Suss	1038
	3Gar	1049
	Thor	1056
	Thor	1069
	Cree	1071
	Shos	1105
	Shos	1106
	Shos	1112
lucid	Dyin	938
luxurious	Sign	91
masterly	Sign	89
	Twis	232
	Soli	536
	Houn	754
	Bruc	926
	Dyin	932
	Reti	1120
meditative	Soli	530
melancholy	Danc	517
	Reti	1113
menacing	Silv	345
methodical	Sign	98
	Sign	108
mischievious	Musg	387
	Nava	466
	Miss	627
	Wist	869
	Lady	942
	Thor	1068
mocking	Devi	954
	Maza	1016
moody	Five	218
morose	Sign	130
	Seco	657
mortified	Chas	574
	Miss	631

Holmes, Sherlock, mannerisms (cont'd)

motionless	Twis	240
	Chas	575
mournful	Seco	653
moved	Five	227
muttered	Stud	36
	Stud	46
	Sign	99
	Sign	110
	Sign	112
	Sign	129
	Seco	664
	Bruc	919
	Lady	951
	Illu	993
negligent	Nava	462
nervous	Scan	162
	Five	228
	Miss	626
	Thor	1068
nettled	Danc	511
nonchalant	Stud	28
	Sign	89
	Spec	264
	Empt	486
observant	Vall	789
obtuse	Soli	538
offhand	Sign	112
	Yell	352
ominous	Sign	123
paced	Stud	49
	Sign	129
	Scan	161
	Bosc	202
	Five	227
	Copp	329
	Reig	402

Holmes, Sherlock, mannerisms, paced (cont'd)

	Nava	462
	Empt	490
	Danc	516
	Gold	615
	Seco	659
	Houn	671
	Bruc	913
	Lady	953
	Devi	960
	Thor	1068
pained	Bosc	213
passionate	Musg	386
	Houn	756
patient	Blac	564
	Seco	661
	Vall	809
	Lady	942
	3Gar	1053
peering	Houn	682
pensive	Stud	34
	Sign	97
	Sign	111
	Yell	352
perplexed	Spec	267
	3Gar	1050
perseverance	Prio	548
petulant	Stud	26
philosophic (*see* philosophizes)	Miss	630
	Reti	1113
phlegmatic	Devi	963
pity	Veil	1102
pleasant	Abbe	644
pleased	Stoc	369
poetic	RedH	185
polite	SixN	593
	RedC	901
	Maza	1021

Holmes, Sherlock, mannerisms (cont'd)

practical	SixN	595
	Bruc	926
prattled	Stud	27
precise	Scan	161
preoccupied	Reti	1117
professional	Danc	516
profound	Abbe	646
protest	Veil	1102
proud	Empt	489
	Norw	496
	SixN	594
	Suss	1035
punctual	Nava	465
purposeful	SixN	587
	Shos	1110
puzzled	Danc	516
	Prio	547
	3Stu	603
	Miss	622
	Abbe	642
	Seco	660
	3Gar	1049
queerly	Reig	402
querulous	Stud	25
	Bruc	913
quick	Scan	167
	Soli	534
	Miss	626
quiet	Stud	20
	Stud	37
	Sign	90
	Sign	113
	Sign	133
	Sign	139
	Sign	144
	Iden	199

Holmes, Sherlock, mannerisms, quiet (cont'd)

	Bosc	213
	Blue	255
	Spec	264
	Engr	276
	Engr	285
	Silv	348
	Reig	406
	Fina	473
	Danc	524
	Miss	629
	Vall	812
	Maza	1018
	Shos	1111
quivering	Empt	489
	Norw	497
rambled	Silv	336
raved	Five	223
ravenous	Nava	465
relentless	RedH	185
relieved	Stud	42
	3Gar	1053
reminiscent	Suss	1034
reproachful	Yell	351
reproving	Vall	812
reserved	SixN	594
resigned	Reig	399
	Soli	527
	3Stu	603
	Seco	661
	Houn	673
	RedC	901
resolute	Five	229
restless	Bruc	913
	Bruc	920
	Lady	953
	Thor	1068

Holmes, Sherlock, mannerisms (cont'd)

reticent	Stud	20
	Gree	435
	Houn	754
	Vall	806
reverent	Vall	785
reverie	Spec	268
	Nava	456
	Bruc	920
	Suss	1024
	Cree	1071
rigid	Empt	490
	3Stu	600
roared	Twis	238
rueful	Musg	386
ruffled	Norw	502
sarcastic	Stud	32
	Stud	45
	Sign	113
	Musg	387
	Empt	492
	Gold	611
	Houn	682
	Vall	770
	Vall	771
	Last	979
sardonic	Stud	25
	Stud	28
	Empt	488
	Vall	769
	Maza	1016
satisfied	Stud	28
	Sign	89
	Musg	387
	Norw	497
	Danc	516
	Danc	520

262 ◻ *Good Old Index*

Holmes, Sherlock, mannerisms, satisfied (cont'd)		SixN	590
		Abbe	644
		Houn	682
		Houn	686
		Houn	690
		Card	893
		RedC	904
		Bruc	916
		Bruc	925
		Veil	1096
		Shos	1110
	savage	Spec	272
	self-absorption	Nava	455
	self-confident	Stud	37
	self-contained	Suss	1035
	sententious	Stud	43
	serene	Blac	568
	serious	Houn	693
		Vall	790
		Vall	808
		Vall	865
		Shos	1106
	severe	RedH	187
		Soli	531
		Soli	533
		Prio	541
		3Gab	1026
		Reti	1114
	shaken	Five	228
		Houn	743
		3Gar	1053
	sharp	Stud	39
		Stud	40
		Stud	42
		Blue	251
		Fina	477
	short	Sign	150

Holmes, Sherlock, mannerisms (cont'd)

shouts		
shrugged	Stud	17
	Sign	114
	Sign	124
	Sign	139
	RedH	190
	Twis	233
	Twis	237
	Blue	251
	Silv	346
	Reig	399
	Resi	433
	Nava	462
	Nava	468
	Norw	496
	Chas	576
	SixN	587
	3Stu	596
	3Stu	603
	Miss	625
	Abbe	645
	Houn	681
	Houn	698
	Houn	746
	Houn	752
	Wist	881
	RedC	903
	Bruc	919
	Illu	991
	Maza	1016
	3Gab	1033
	Cree	1077
sighed	Sign	89
	Miss	630
silent	Sign	112
	Bosc	213
	Twis	240

Holmes, Sherlock, mannerisms, silent (cont'd)

	Spec	267
	Copp	317
	Silv	335
	Yell	358
	Nava	455
	Nava	458
	Empt	488
(2)	Empt	490
	Danc	511
	Danc	513
	Soli	529
	Chas	575
	Abbe	636
	Abbe	649
	Houn	696
	Bruc	920
	Bruc	924
	Bruc	929
	Devi	970
	Thor	1068
	Veil	1098
simple	Iden	191
sings	Stud	36
	Danc	516
slow	Sign	108
	Sign	110
	Lion	1090
slow-witted	Abbe	644
sluggish	Thor	1070
smiles	Stud	18
	Stud	19
	Stud	21
	Stud	26
	Stud	28
	Stud	31
	Stud	33
	Stud	42

Holmes, Sherlock, mannerisms, smiles (cont'd)

	Stud	51
	Stud	83
	Sign	89
	Sign	96
	Sign	128
	Sign	135
	Sign	139
	Sign	141
	Scan	170
	RedH	177
	RedH	185
	Spec	259
	Spec	265
	Nobl	287
	Nobl	294
	Nobl	301
	Bery	301
	Copp	321
	Silv	345
	Yell	353
	Stoc	363
	Musg	387
	Reig	399
	Reig	403
	Reig	408
	Croo	422
	Resi	430
(2)	Gree	437
	Fina	470
	Fina	472
	Fina	477
	Empt	485
	Empt	488
	Norw	496
	Norw	500
	Norw	505
	Norw	509

Holmes, Sherlock, mannerisms, smiles (cont'd)

	Norw	510
	Danc	521
	Danc	526
	Soli	527
	Soli	528
(2)	Prio	555
	Blac	568
	SixN	588
	SixN	593
(2)	3Stu	598
	Gold	610
	Gold	612
	Gold	616
	Miss	632
	Seco	652
	Seco	657
	Seco	666
	Houn	671
	Houn	698
	Vall	774
	Vall	776
	Vall	787
	Vall	798
	Wist	873
	Wist	875
	Wist	879
	Card	891
	RedC	904
	Bruc	917
	Bruc	925
	Lady	942
	Devi	960
	Devi	968
	Last	979
	Illu	985
	Illu	986
	Illu	989

Holmes, Sherlock, mannerisms, smiles (cont'd)

		Blan	1000
		Maza	1015
		Maza	1016
		Maza	1021
		Maza	1022
		3Gab	1028
		3Gab	1030
		Suss	1034
		Suss	1041
		Suss	1042
	(2)	3Gar	1045
		3Gar	1047
	(2)	Thor	1059
		Cree	1071
		Cree	1074
		Cree	1075
		Cree	1076
		Cree	1077
		Cree	1079
		Lion	1092
		Reti	1121
		Reti	1122
snarls		Seco	661
		Suss	1034
sneers		Thor	1061
sniffs		Stud	25
snorts		Bruc	913
solemn		Card	901
sombre		Twis	240
		Devi	954
soothing		Spec	258
		Bery	302
		Nava	466
		Wist	870
		Card	891
		RedC	902

Holmes, Sherlock, mannerisms,
  soothing (cont'd)
    spellbound
    staggered
    startled

    stern

    strategic
    strong
    suave

    subtle

    sunk in thought (*see* lost)
    surprised

Suss	1039
3Gar	1045
Copp	329
Scan	174
Sign	112
Scan	174
Spec	271
Blue	255
Bery	313
Empt	488
Danc	524
Card	892
Devi	967
Devi	969
Thor	1061
Shos	1110
Reti	1117
Sign	123
Soli	536
Iden	199
Nobl	291
3Stu	604
Dyin	935
Scan	167
Resi	424
Stud	38
Sign	112
Sign	124
Sign	128
Scan	174
Musg	393
Gree	443
Danc	517
Chas	578
Miss	623
Houn	694

Holmes, Sherlock, mannerisms,
surprised (cont'd)

	Houn	740
	Vall	785
	Card	893
	Card	896
	Bruc	929
	Last	975
	Cree	1075
sweetly	Blue	254
swift	Sign	112
	Scan	161
	Chas	581
sympathetic	Norw	488
	Norw	497
	Vall	806
	Veil	1101
taciturn	Nava	464
	Seco	657
taken aback	Blac	563
	Houn	697
tender	Musg	386
	Vall	810
	Bruc	926
tense	Fina	470
	Seco	660
	Wist	879
	Devi	963
	Maza	1018
	Thor	1068
thorough	Lion	1091
thoughtful	Sign	94
	Bosc	204
	Blue	249
	Reig	399
	Resi	432
	Gree	435
	Danc	514
	Soli	532

Holmes, Sherlock, mannerisms, thoughtful (cont'd)

Chas	582
Houn	693
Vall	769
Vall	786
Vall	791
Vall	798
Vall	802
Vall	865
Wist	869
Card	892
Bruc	920
Maza	1017
Suss	1036
3Gar	1050
Thor	1064
Veil	1098

tickled — Soli 532
tolerant — Reti 1122
triumphant

Stud	51
Silv	344
Stoc	372
SixN	594
3Stu	606
Houn	697
Lion	1093
Shos	1102

troubled — Sign 128
unconcerned — Houn 747
uneasy

Danc	517
SixN	593

unemotional — Gree 435
ungracious — 3Stu 596
unresponsive — Norw 497
unsociable — Glor 374
untidy

3Stu	596
Dyin	932

untiring — Yell 351

Holmes, Sherlock, mannerisms (cont'd)

	unwittingly	Reti	1118
	unworldly	Blac	559
	vacant	Stud	28
	vanity	Stud	34
		Sign	90
		Houn	672
	vexed	Houn	690
	vibrating	Seco	661
		Thor	1068
	vigorous	Prio	553
	violent	Vall	810
	voracious	Five	228
	weary	Sign	157
		Engr	276
		Soli	527
		Lady	942
		3Gab	1032
	whimsical	Norw	496
		Illu	986
		Cree	1071
	whispered	Twis	231
		Blue	254
		Spec	271
		Spec	272
		Fina	475
		Empt	489
		Chas	577
		Chas	578
		SixN	592
	(2)	Houn	743
		RedC	907
		Dyin	938
		Dyin	939
		Dyin	940
		Illu	993

Holmes, Sherlock, mannerisms,
 whispered (cont'd)
  whistled

	Suss	1043
	3Gar	1052
	Stud	31
	Scan	163
	Twis	232
	Blue	248
	Silv	344
	Resi	431
	Fina	474
	Empt	491
	Danc	516
	SixN	585
	Bruc	929
	3Gab	1029
wild	Stud	49
worn	Sign	130
	Five	228
	Houn	740
wriggled	RedH	178
yawned	Stud	45
	Scan	166
	RedH	190
	Nobl	289
	Reig	400
	Seco	661
	Houn	676
maps used by (*see* Ordnance)		
marriage, views on	Vall	801
marrying man, not a	Sign	157
	Chas	575
masked	Chas	577
master		
Watson refers to him as	Houn	736
Hopkins refers to him as	Blac	570
meddler, called	Spec	264
meditation, deep	Card	892

Holmes, Sherlock (cont'd)
    memory of

	Stud	21
	Five	225
	Suss	1035
methods of	Stud	23
	Stud	26
	Stud	31
	Stud	84
	Sign	91
	Sign	93
	Sign	110
	Sign	119
	Scan	162
	RedH	177
	Iden	197
	Bosc	204
	Bosc	211
	Bosc	214
	Five	225
	Blue	246
	Spec	259
	Nobl	300
	Bery	310
	Bery	315
	Copp	330
	Silv	343
	Yell	352
	Stoc	363
	Glor	375
	Musg	395
	Reig	407
	Croo	411
	Croo	412
	Croo	416
	Resi	423
	Resi	424
	Gree	437

Holmes, Sherlock, methods of (cont'd)

Gree	444
Nava	457
Nava	468
Fina	471
Norw	497
Norw	501
Danc	511
Prio	546
Prio	549
SixN	587
3Stu	599
3Stu	605
Gold	612
Abbe	641
Houn	670
Houn	686
Vall	771
Vall	787
Vall	801
Vall	803
Vall	806
Wist	870
Wist	881
Card	892
Card	895
RedC	903
Bruc	920
Lady	942
Devi	956
Devi	960
Devi	968
Blan	1000
Blan	1011
Suss	1038
Suss	1043
3Gar	1051
Thor	1069

Holmes, Sherlock, methods of (cont'd)

	Lion	1091
	Shos	1108
	Reti	1120
Watson exaggerates	Suss	1039
Watson attempts	Fina	479
	Empt	485
	Soli	531
	Houn	669
	Lady	944
metier of	Bosc	204
microscope used by (*see also* lens)	Shos	1102
mind (*see also* brain)	Scan	161
crowded boxroom	Lion	1090
like a racing engine	Wist	870
	Devi	960
theory of	Stud	21
	Five	225
minutiae, genius for	Sign	91
mistakes of	Copp	330
	Yell	359
referred to by self	Yell	351
	Thor	1069
modesty not a virtue	Gree	435
monographs (*see* Writings)		
Moriarty		
compliments Holmes	Fina	472
had met	Fina	472
had not met	Vall	776
visits Holmes	Fina	472
morphine, uses	Sign	89
motive, misses a	3Stu	607
much to learn	RedC	907
music and	Stud	22
	Stud	34
	Stud	36
	Stud	37
	RedH	185

276 ◘ *Good Old Index*

Holmes, Sherlock, music and (cont'd)

		Houn	766
		Bruc	913
		Reti	1116
music as a hobby		Bruc	913
music at strange hours		Dyin	932
music, gift for improvisation		Sign	129
Mycroft		Gree	436
	and Holmes	Fina	474
		Empt	487
		Bruc	914
name, effect of		Soli	536
		Dyin	937
name, kept out of cases		Stud	86
		Sign	90
		Nava	458
		Empt	493
		Norw	509
		Card	895
		Thor	1058
		Thor	1062
		Reti	1119
names, called			
	automaton	Sign	96
	burglar	Lady	951
	busybody	Spec	265
		Soli	537
		Maza	1016
	calculating machine	Sign	96
	Cocksure, Mr.	Blue	253
	cunning fiend	Empt	492
	Detective, Mr.	Miss	627
	devil	Devi	968
		Maza	1021
	fool	Twis	240
	gadabout	Silv	344
	idiot	Stoc	372
		Vall	805

Holmes, Sherlock, names, called (cont'd)

impudent fellow	Abbe	645
jack-in-office	Spec	265
magician	Bery	310
meddler	Spec	264
plain clothes copper	Soli	537
rogue	Sign	133
sorcerer	Seco	666
Theorist, Mr.	Sign	114
traitor, double	Last	979
wizard	Abbe	646
	Seco	666
	Blan	1000
	Reti	1116
natural explanation demanded	Houn	682
	Devi	958
	Suss	1034
nature, views on	Sign	121
	Resi	423
	Nava	458
	Wist	879
	Card	888
	Lion	1083
necromancer, likened to	Stud	23
nerves, strong	Fina	472
	Illu	998
newspapers, reads	Stud	41
	Sign	125
	Bosc	202
	Engr	276
	Bery	312
	Copp	322
	Silv	336
	Norw	496
	Norw	505
	Danc	517

Holmes, Sherlock, newspapers, reads (cont'd)

	SixN	591
	Seco	655
	Card	890
	Bruc	915

newspapers, uses

	Stud	37
	Sign	131
	Bosc	205
	Blue	244
	Blue	249
	Nobl	288
	Copp	316
	Nava	457
	SixN	591
	Houn	687
	RedC	904
	Bruc	928
	Lady	948
	3Gar	1047
	Thor	1055

Norbury, to be whispered when overconfident

Yell	362

Norway, trip proposed to
notebooks (*see also* Commonplace books)

Blac	572
Sign	95
Scan	167
Bosc	202
Nava	457
Fina	479
Fina	480
Norw	503
Soli	536
Prio	541
Prio	558
SixN	590
Miss	630
Wist	876
Wist	888
Lady	942

Holmes, Sherlock, notebooks (*see also* Commonplace books) (cont'd)	Illu	987
	Blan	1000
	Maza	1015
	3Gab	1031
	Cree	1076
note for Watson	Glor	373
	Musg	387
	Fina	469
	Fina	479
	Houn	730
	Cree	1071
note in cipher	Danc	512
notes	Nobl	294
	Houn	766
	Suss	1038
on old envelope	Reti	1113
on shirt cuff	Nava	452
	Houn	682
number of cases	Iden	191
	Spec	257
	Nava	458
	Fina	477
	Soli	526
	Chas	572
	Houn	693
object, to help justice	Vall	787
observation is trade	Iden	192
	Card	893
obvious, is not fooled by	Norw	501
odds, gives	SixN	591
old woman, fooled by	Stud	40
opium den, found in	Twis	231
opponent, went home in cart	Soli	533
opposite traits of	RedH	185
oratorical, for once	Illu	992

Holmes, Sherlock (cont'd)

ordnance maps, in use by	Engr	285
	Prio	545
	Houn	683
organization of, small	Lady	948
outpaces Watson	Soli	534
	Houn	757
outwits swindler, unreported case	Reig	398
overlapping cases not allowed	Houn	761
overlooks something	Sign	112
	Sign	136
	Lady	954
Paganini, discussed by	Card	894
palimpsests, works with	Gold	607
parentage of	Gree	435
patriotism appealed to	Seco	653
pays for information	Stud	36
	Scan	168
	Blue	253
	Bery	316
	Silv	344
	Houn	698
	Vall	770
pen of	Bosc	215
penknife of	Stud	49
	Dyin	934
perceptive faculties of	Stud	28
perfumes, knowledge of	Houn	765
personal equation, astronomers', and	Musg	395
Petrarch, reads	Bosc	207
philology, books on	Devi	955
philosophizes	Sign	121
	Sign	137
	Iden	190
	Iden	201
	Bosc	217
	Nava	455

Holmes, Sherlock, philosophizes (cont'd)	Card	901
	RedC	907
	Illu	998
	Thor	1068
	Cree	1082
	Veil	1101
	Reti	1113
photo enlarged by	Lion	1091
physical characteristics of		
appearance	Stud	20
	Bosc	211
arms		
folded	Spec	265
long	Five	218
	Last	975
	Veil	1101
long, thin	Prio	539
	Illu	984
nervous	Illu	984
sinewy	Sign	89
thin, sinewy	Empt	486
wiry	3Gar	1053
back		
long, thin	Danc	511
brows (eyebrows)		
black	Devi	960
bushy	Vall	773
clouded	Vall	771
	Vall	865
contracted	Devi	957
dark	Spec	268
	Danc	517
	Lady	953
drawn	Stud	46
	Sign	98
	Bosc	211
	Empt	488

Holmes, Sherlock, physical characteristics of, brows (eyebrows), drawn (cont'd)

	Prio	541
	Abbe	646
	Houn	696
	Wist	875
	Devi	960
furrowed	Danc	516
	Prio	541
	Cree	1071
heavy	Bruc	919
	Lady	953
knit	Bery	307
	Copp	322
	Silv	336
	Abbe	642
	Lady	953
raised	Stud	28
	Sign	109
	Seco	656
	Seco	660
	Houn	694
	Devi	962
	Maza	1015
	Shos	1103
ruffled	Prio	549
tufted	Bruc	919
twitched	Vall	773
cheeks		
flushed	Stud	34
	Iden	201
	Bosc	211
	Five	228
	Bery	312
	Reig	401
	Croo	412
	Prio	547

Holmes, Sherlock, physical
characteristics of, cheeks, flushed
(cont'd)

	SixN	594
	Gold	618
	Houn	778
sallow	Five	228
	Bery	312
thin	Croo	412
chin		
on breast	Bery	308
	Silv	336
	Stoc	371
	Reig	402
	Chas	575
on hands	Spec	263
	Silv	343
	Yell	358
	Prio	548
scratches	Spec	267
square and prominent	Stud	20
ears pricked up	Silv	341
	Danc	516
elbows on knees	Fina	470
eyebrows (*see* brows)		
eyelids		
drawn	Sign	104
drooping	Sign	96
puckered	RedH	184
eyes		
abstracted	Abbe	642
amused	Danc	511
	Houn	740
	Houn	749
beady	Sign	112
bright	Reig	401
	Norw	505
	SixN	593
	Wist	879
	Reti	1114

Holmes, Sherlock, physical
characteristics of, eyes (cont'd)

clear	3Gar	1053
cocked at problem	Yell	352
	Stoc	369
	Reig	399
color, gray	Houn	740
	Maza	1016
	3Gar	1044
	Thor	1064
	Reti	1114
dark shadows	Norw	505
darting	Prio	552
	Miss	626
deep set	Sign	112
	Danc	511
	Miss	622
	Abbe	641
dreamy	Sign	92
	RedH	185
	Thor	1059
eager	Houn	690
excited	Danc	515
far-away expression	Stud	29
	Thor	1068
fateful	Vall	866
fire	Twis	232
flashing	Stud	51
full of thought	Suss	1039
gleaming	Sign	112
	Sign	122
	Silv	341
	Musg	387
	Danc	511
	Danc	518
	Vall	773

Holmes, Sherlock, physical
characteristics of, eyes (cont'd)

glistening	Sign	94
	Vall	778
glittered	Stud	18
	Sign	104
	Bosc	211
	Houn	679
hard	3Gar	1053
heavy-lidded	Engr	276
inexorable	Danc	518
inscrutable	Miss	622
keen	Sign	133
	Bosc	208
	Soli	527
	Abbe	641
	Vall	789
	Wist	875
	Reti	1114
kindled	Croo	412
kindly	Scan	162
lackluster	Stud	26
	Sign	92
languid	RedH	185
lovingly	Suss	1034
mischievous	Musg	386
peering	Bosc	212
penetrating	Miss	626
points of steel	Maza	1017
questioning	Bruc	919
quick	RedH	177
	Fina	477
	Bruc	921
	Thor	1064
sharp and piercing	Stud	20

Holmes, Sherlock, physical
    characteristics of, eyes (cont'd)
        shine
            brightly

	RedH	184
at a crisis	Gold	618
in moonlight	Houn	756
shining	Norw	506
	Prio	547
	Gold	618
	Devi	963
sparkling	Scan	163
	Vall	800
steady	Maza	1016
triumph in	SixN	591
twinkle	Sign	129
	Twis	240
	Nobl	295
	Bery	312
	Nava	466
	Miss	627
	Wist	869
	Lady	942
	3Gar	1044
vacant	Stud	26
	Twis	240
	Danc	516
	Chas	582
	Devi	960
venomous	Dyin	933
when interested	Sign	98
	Houn	679

       face
           aquiline

	Sign	138
	Twis	240
	Empt	486
ascetic	Miss	622
austere	Bruc	927

Holmes, Sherlock, physical
characteristics of, face (cont'd)

clouded	Copp	330
cold	Lady	949
dark	Sign	128
darkened	Bosc	211
darkening	Prio	547
dead-white	Empt	486
expressive	Stud	42
flint	3Gar	1053
frown	Vall	771
gaunt	RedC	907
granite	Chas	573
gray	Lady	949
grim	Spec	268
	Nava	465
haggard	Dyin	938
	Devi	960
hollow-eyed	Lady	953
honest	Maza	1014
pale	Nava	465
	Fina	470
	Norw	505
	Miss	630
	Houn	756
	Lady	953
	Illu	994
	Illu	998
	Thor	1068
pale and drawn	Maza	1013
rigid	Seco	661
	Cree	1074
sharp, eager	Silv	336
tense	Seco	660
thin	Bery	310
troubled	Sign	128
worn	Fina	470

Holmes, Sherlock, physical
characteristics of (cont'd)

facial expression		Empt	486
		Vall	774
		Vall	778
		3Gar	1053
features			
	hawklike	Sign	94
	sharp	Empt	489
figure			
	athletic	Houn	743
	austere	Houn	699
	gaunt	Sign	128
		Bosc	202
		Last	975
		Reti	1114
	lean	Stud	20
		Vall	805
	long	Iden	198
		Maza	1013
	muscular	Sign	89
		Spec	265
		Bery	310
		Yell	351
		Blac	559
	saturnine	Maza	1012
	spare	Scan	161
		Empt	488
		Prio	547
	supple	Prio	547
	tall	Scan	161
		Bosc	202
		Empt	488
		Prio	547
		Houn	699

Holmes, Sherlock, physical	Houn	726
characteristics of, figure, tall (cont'd)	Vall	805
	Last	975
thin	Iden	198
	Empt	486
	Houn	726
	Houn	740
	Maza	1013
finger, shakes	Blac	563
fingers		
cold	Empt	489
drummed	Stud	49
	Thor	1068
long	Sign	89
	RedH	185
	Silv	337
	Yell	352
	Empt	489
	Danc	519
	RedC	902
	Lady	953
	Thor	1068
nervous	Sign	89
	Vall	773
nimble	Stud	29
quivering	Empt	491
strong	Bery	310
taps	Blue	257
	Empt	490
	Bruc	913
	Bruc	928
	Lady	953
thin	RedH	185
	Silv	337
	Yell	352
	Empt	489
	Danc	519

Holmes, Sherlock, physical
   characteristics of, fingers, thin

	Vall	773
	RedC	902
	Lady	953
	Thor	1068
twitched	Vall	773
white	Sign	89
fingertips together	Sign	89
	RedH	176
	Iden	192
	Iden	196
	Five	224
	Copp	318
	Fina	470
	Norw	499
	Houn	673
	Houn	678
	Vall	776
	Cree	1079
forehead		
contracted	Devi	960
wrinkled	Vall	789
hair, black	Danc	511
hands		
clapped	Stud	18
	Iden	197
	SixN	591
	Maza	1017
clapped to forehead	Cree	1080
clasped behind	Scan	161
	Five	228
clenched	Five	223
	Lady	952
in pockets	Sign	117
	Scan	167
	Iden	200
	Bery	301
	Copp	329

Holmes, Sherlock, physical
characteristics of, hands, in pockets
(cont'd)

	Stoc	371
	Reig	402
	Nava	462
	Chas	575
long	Sign	158
	Five	228
on knees	Sign	150
lips		
compressed	Bosc	211
gnawed	Stud	49
thin	Empt	488
tightened	Bruc	919
nails, bites	Stoc	369
	Bruc	913
neck, long sinewy	Bosc	211
nose		
hawklike	Stud	20
	RedH	184
long, thin	Sign	112
thin	Stud	20
nostrils quiver	Bruc	919
shins long, thin	Nava	448
shoulders square	Empt	489
voice		
high pitched	Stoc	362
	Card	892
sweet	Silv	344
vibrant	Lady	949
wrist, sinewy	Sign	89
picture galleries, visits	Houn	692
picture, uses as identification	SixN	588
	Seco	663
	Houn	753
pictures of	3Gar	1045
pistol, holds to man's head	Bery	316
	Danc	524
	Maza	1020

Holmes, Sherlock (cont'd)

pity and protest, gesture of	Veil	1102
plain clothes copper, called	Soli	537
plays the game	Vall	787
pocketbook of	Reig	404
	Danc	512
	Houn	752
	Devi	963
poison, dabbles in	Stud	18
poker, bends	Spec	265
police, called by	Sign	110
	Engr	284
	Stoc	373
	Musg	395
	Soli	536
	Lady	949
police, chaffs	Lion	1095
police, shares evidence with	Devi	965
police know Holmes very well	Lady	952
political news not known to	Bruc	913
pomp and ceremony, attitude toward	Norw	508
poor man, claims to be	Prio	558
Pope, cases taken at desire of	Blac	559
	Houn	677
portmanteau of	Stud	51
powers that are not human, possesses	Prio	556
	Abbe	646
powers of, well known	3Stu	596
practical joke, plays	Nava	466
	Maza	1022
practice, length of	Veil	1095
practice, three continents	Scan	191
praise, moved by	SixN	595
praises Watson	Houn	741
	Dyin	938
prayer of gratitude	Houn	757
precipitate, is never	Chas	576

Holmes, Sherlock (cont'd)
precision, fond of	Soli	527
prejudice, lack of	Reig	407
press, opinions of	SixN	590
princely offer to	Prio	540
	Wist	869
princely payments to landlady	Dyin	932
private judgment, right to	Abbe	647
probabilities, balances	Houn	687
problem, great perennial	Card	901
problems, effect of, upon	Sign	94
	Sign	98
profession, created his own	Sign	90
professional honour	Veil	1095
professions, others open to	Sign	106
	Scan	170
	Reti	1120
profile on window shade	Scan	161
	Empt	489
property left to Mycroft	Fina	480
provisional theory of	Yell	359
public cases, consulted in	Soli	526
publicity, aversion to	Norw	496
	Devi	954
qualities of a detective, opinions on	Sign	91
	Scan	174
questions methods	Bery	309
	3Stu	601
	Miss	625
	Houn	687
	Thor	1063
quotations (*see also* Biblical Quotations/Allusions and Literary references, Shakespearean Quotations/Allusions)		
Abandon the case	Vall	806
Account, A very remarkable	Sign	157

Holmes, Sherlock, quotations (*see also* Biblical Quotations/Allusions and Literary references, Shakespearean Quotations/Allusions) (cont'd)

Acting a part is to be it, The best way of successfully	Dyin	940
Active mind, One drawback of an	Thor	1069
Afghanistan, You have been in	Stud	18
Admirable	Prio	550
Air of London is the sweeter for my presense	Fina	477
Alias, It is always awkward doing business with an	Blue	254
Alternative, One should always look for a possible	Blac	567
And yet—and yet	SixN	587
	Thor	1057
	Thor	1069
	Reti	1116
Anonymously, I prefer to work	Thor	1058
Antidote to sorrow, work is the best	Empt	488
Art for art's sake	RedC	907
	Reti	1115
Art for it's own sake	Copp	316
Art in the blood . . .	Gree	435
Art's sake, lived for his	Blac	559
Ass, Write me down an	Bruc	929
Assistance too highly, He rates my	Sign	91
Attention, I am all	Gree	438
Attention, Is there any point to which you would wish to draw my	Silv	347
Au revoir	Stud	96
	Houn	689
	Vall	879
Bad business, I am afraid this is a	Yell	359

Holmes, Sherlock, quotations (*see also* Biblical Quotations/Allusions and Literary references, Shakespearean Quotations/Allusions) (cont'd)

Badly, You have done remarkably	Soli	531
Beautiful, beautiful	Stud	18
Before, It has all been done	Stud	29
	Vall	777
Before our time, We are	Vall	773
Bizarre a thing is the less mysterious, The more	RedH	183
Blackmail in it, There is	Yell	359
Blank mind, We approached the case with an absolutely	Card	895
Bleat, Watson, unmitigated bleat	RedC	904
Blind as a mole, I have been	Twis	241
Bluff, Watson, bluff	Thor	1059
Blushes, My	Vall	769
Book, Let me recommend this	Sign	97
Book made me positively ill, That	Stud	25
Booming, I am not in need of a	Thor	1058
Box-room, My mind is like a crowded	Lion	1090
Brain, I am a, rest mere appendix	Maza	1014
Brain originally like a little empty attic	Stud	21
Brain work without sufficient material is like racing an engine, To let the	Devi	960
Brains, What has become of my	Lady	953
Brainwork, I cannot live without	Sign	93
Bricks without clay, I cannot make	Copp	322
Burglary has always been an alternative profession	Reti	1120

Holmes, Sherlock, quotations (*see also* Biblical Quotations/Allusions and Literary references, Shakespearean Quotations/Allusions) (cont'd)

Business . . . , It is my	Blue	254
	Soli	527
	Devi	962
	Illu	985
Business to know things, It is my	Iden	192
	Blan	1008
Capital	Norw	508
	Vall	808
	Shos	1103
Case, We have got our	Abbe	644
Chain is stronger than its weakest link, No	Vall	770
Child's play, It was	Stud	33
Circles, Everything comes in	Vall	777
Circumstantial evidence		
tricky thing	Bosc	204
convincing	Nobl	294
Clear, I hope that I have made myself	Scan	176
Colleague after our own heart	Houn	680
Come at once if convenient—If inconvenient, come all the same	Cree	1071
Come, Watson	ubiq	
Commonplace	Stud	26
	RedH	183
	Iden	191
Complex mind, Criminals have that	Illu	987
Concentrated atmosphere helps . . . thought	Houn	684
Conductor of light, You are a	Houn	669
Consistency, We must look for	Thor	1065

Holmes, Sherlock, quotations (*see also* Biblical Quotations/Allusions and Literary references, Shakespearean Quotations/Allusions) (cont'd)

Court of appeal, I am the last ... and highest	Five	219
	Stud	90
Crime is commonplace	Sign	93
Criminal, It is fortunate for the community that I am not a	Bruc	913
Cruelly used, You have been	Spec	263
Danger is part of my trade	Fina	472
Data, Consider the	Sign	127
Data, Dangerous to reason from insufficient	Spec	272
Data, Capital mistake to theorize before	Scan	163
Data, Error to argue in front of your	Wist	876
Data, data, data	Copp	322
Data, Hardly any	Sign	92
Data, I have no	Copp	321
Data, I think that I have nearly all my	Nobl	294
Data, Let us consider our	Shos	1108
Data yet, No	Stud	27
Date being, The	Cree	1074
Dear me	ubiq	
Dear me, dear me	Miss	630
Deep waters	Spec	263
	Reig	401
	Shos	1106
Detail, I pay a good deal of attention to ...	Norw	509
Detection is an exact science	Sign	90
Devil, What in the name of the	Spec	264
Doctor does go wrong ... first of criminals	Spec	270

Holmes, Sherlock, quotations (*see also* Biblical Quotations/Allusions and Literary references, Shakespearean Quotations/Allusions) (cont'd)

Dull indeed, I am	Bruc	920
Dumps at times, I get in the	Stud	19
Education never ends	RedC	907
Elementary	Iden	197
	Croo	412
	Houn	670
	Blan	1006
Eloquent, I am not often	Illu	992
Emotion likely to bias judgment	Sign	157
Emotional qualities are antagonistic to clear reasoning	Sign	96
Engine, My mind is like a racing	Wist	870
Evidence, It is a capital mistake to theorize before you have all the	Stud	27
Evidence, Nothing like firsthand	Stud	32
Evil is the man whom no woman mourns	Houn	748
Except Mr. Sherlock Holmes	Gold	610
Exceptions, I never make	Sign	196
Fact appears to be opposed to a long train of deductions	Stud	49
Fact, There is nothing more deceptive than an obvious	Bosc	204
Facts, I cannot change	Thor	1056
Facts, Capital mistake to theorize in advance of	Seco	657
Facts, Let us get down to the	Thor	1058
Faculties become refined when you starve them	Maza	1014
Faculty of deduction is contagious	Thor	1055
Faith, Because I always keep	Vall	775
Faith, I should have more	Stud	49

Holmes, Sherlock, quotations (*see also* Biblical Quotations/Allusions and Literary references, Shakespearean Quotations/Allusions) (cont'd)

Foil as quick and supple as my own	Houn	697
Followed me so far, Have you	Twis	234
Fool I have been, What a	Cree	1080
Fool that I was	Soli	534
	Houn	743
Game for the game's own sake, I play the	Bruc	917
Game is afoot	Abbe	636
Genius is an infinite capacity for taking pains	Stud	31
Ghosts need apply, No	Suss	1034
Good old Index	Suss	1034
Good old Watson	Last	980
	Illu	994
Grace of God goes Sherlock Holmes, There but for the	Bosc	217
Grotesque, one more specimen of the tragic and	RedC	913
Grotesque, they are singular not to say	SixN	584
Grotesque to the horrible, one step from the	Wist	888
Guess, I never	Sign	93
Heads I win	Stud	42
Hidden fires indeed! These were	Houn	745
Honor, You do me too much	Stud	43
Hounds like us, two old	Prio	543
Human nature is a strange mixture	Stoc	373
Human to err, It is	3Stu	605
Humanity, it is certainly beyond me, If the matter is beyond	Devi	958

Holmes, Sherlock, quotations (*see also* Biblical Quotations/Allusions and Literary references, Shakespearean Quotations/Allusions) (cont'd)

Humour me a little, I must ask you to	Reig	405
Idiot that I was	Stoc	372
Imagination the mother of truth	Vall	802
Imagine, I cannot	Spec	264
Imbecility, incredible	Five	223
Importance, You have missed everything of	Iden	197
	Reti	1116
Impossible, elimination of	Sign	92
	Sign	97
	Sign	111
	Bery	315
	Soli	529
	Bruc	926
	Blan	1011
Impressions, Never trust to general	Iden	197
Improbable as it is, all other explanations are more improbable still	Silv	339
Improve all the time, You	3Gar	1051
Index, Good old	Suss	1034
Inexcusable, Your conduct seems	Shos	1112
Inference, one true . . . invariably suggests others	Silv	349
Infinite variety, I trust that age doth not . . . my	Empt	489
Instinct that I have cries against it, Every	Abbe	642
Iron is hot, We must strike while the	Card	894
Irregulars are sometimes useful, you know	Reti	1119
Irregulars, We are the	Lady	949

Holmes, Sherlock, quotations (*see also* Biblical Quotations/Allusions and Literary references, Shakespearean Quotations/Allusions) (cont'd)

Jealousy is a strange reformer of characters		Nobl	294
Jove, By		Scan	201
		Prio	548
		Chas	582
		3Stu	603
	(2)	Miss	634
		Houn	671
		Houn	760
		Wist	880
		RedC	907
		Bruc	914
		Bruc	919
Journeys end in lovers' meetings		Empt	492
		RedC	908
Judge, It is not for me to		Bosc	217
Jupiter is descending		Bruc	915
Knowlege comes useful to the detective, All		Vall	776
Law, My business . . . to uphold the		Shos	1111
Law, You don't mind breaking the		Scan	169
Life is full of whimsical happenings		Maza	1014
Life is infinitely stranger than		Iden	190
Life is not your own, Your		Veil	1101
Little things are infinitely . . . important		Iden	194
Long shot, A		Silv	346
Lord Harry, By the		Illu	994
Love is an emotional thing		Sign	157
Loved, I have never		Devi	970
Meddle, I don't intend to		Reig	400
Method in these cases, This is my		Lion	1091

Holmes, Sherlock, quotations (*see also* Biblical Quotations/Allusions and Literary references, Shakespearean Quotations/Allusions) (cont'd)

Methodical man, I a	SixN	594
Methods, You know my	Sign	112
	Bosc	214
	Blue	246
	Stoc	363
	Houn	670
Mind, To a great . . . nothing is little	Stud	43
Misdeeds, There is a strong family resemblance about	Stud	24
Missed it for a good deal, I would not have	Bery	312
Missed the case for worlds, I would not have	Yell	359
Modesty among the virtues, I cannot agree with those who rank	Gree	435
Money in this case	Scan	163
Moonshine is a brighter thing than fog	Bosc	211
Mysteries, I have no desire to make	Danc	521
Mystery, Mistake to confound strangeness with	Stud	50
Mystery stimulates imagination	Stud	37
Nettle, Grasp the	Maza	1015
Never trust to general impressions	Iden	197
New under the sun, There is nothing	Stud	29
Notice, I see no more but I	Blan	1000
Nous verrons	Bosc	213
Novel, This is certainly very	SixN	584
Observation and deduction, I have a turn for both	Stud	23

Holmes, Sherlock, quotations (*see also* Biblical Quotations/Allusions and Literary references, Shakespearean Quotations/Allusions) (cont'd)

Observation with me is second nature	Stud	24
Observe, You see but you do not	Scan	162
Obvious, It was	Scan	162
It is	Bosc	214
Odd Watson, very odd	Soli	530
Oscillation on the pavement	Iden	192
Outre	Stud	50
	Iden	191
	Bosc	207
	Stoc	364
	Houn	764
Overconfidence, We must not err on the side of	Sign	110
Parlour game, Quite a little	3Stu	603
Patience, my friend, patience	Stud	49
	3Gar	1045
Patient suffering . . . the most precious of all	Veil	1101
Play tricks and I'll crush you	Abbe	648
Plot thickens, The	Stud	38
	Stud	46
Poetry, Watson, Cut out the	Reti	1114
Point not clear to you, Is any	Wist	887
Point which I can make clear, any other	Nava	468
Points in it which please me, There are	Stoc	369
Poor man, I am a	Prio	558
Power and design, I am conscious always of	Houn	690
Powers, You know my	Fina	471
Precisely	ubiq	

Holmes, Sherlock, quotations (*see also* Biblical Quotations/Allusions and Literary references, Shakespearean Quotations/Allusions) (cont'd)

Prejudices, I make a point of never having any	Reig	407
Press is a most remarkable institution	SixN	590
Presume nothing, I	Houn	745
Pretext, We can find a	Lion	1087
Pride, That hurts my	Five	228
Problem		
It is a curious little	3Gar	1047
It is quite a pretty little	Scan	166
It is quite a three pipe	RedH	184
It is a very sweet little	Bery	312
Progress, my dear Watson, We	Miss	628
Puzzles you, Is there anything else that	Stud	33
Quick, Watson, quick	Miss	634
	Seco	661
Quick, man, quick	Lady	953
Quite so	ubiq	
Read nothing except . . . I	Nobl	288
Reader, I am an omnivorous	Lion	1094
Reason backwards, grand thing to be able to	Stud	83
Reason from what you see, You fail to	Blue	246
Reasoner, Ideal, would deduce	Five	224
Recherché	Musg	387
Remarkable	Vall	774
	Vall	785
	Wist	875
	Bruc	920
	Devi	958
	Devi	959

Holmes, Sherlock, quotations (*see also* Biblical Quotations/Allusions and Literary references, Shakespearean Quotations/Allusions), Remarkable (cont'd)

	Suss	1039
	Veil	1096
	Reti	1115
Reward, The work is its own	Norw	509
Rose is, What a lovely thing a	Nava	455
Rubbish, Watson	Suss	1034
Scintillate, You	Illu	995
Scintillating, You are	Miss	631
Score everytime, We cannot expect to	Nava	465
Silence, You have a grand gift of	Twis	233
Simple as it was, it was instructive	Stud	83
Simple but instructive	Gold	621
Simple often difficult	Bosc	202
	Twis	237
Simple things are easily overlooked	Sign	136
Simplicity itself, it is	Sign	91
	Sign	119
	Scan	162
	Glor	376
	Gold	612
Singularity is almost invariably a clue	Bosc	202
Slow, culpably slow, I was	Lion	1094
Small, To a great mind nothing is	Stud	43
Solved it, I have	Nobl	294
	3Stu	604
	Gold	618
Sorrow, Schoolroom of	Thor	1070
Sorrow, work best antidote for	Empt	488
	Reti	1116
Speculation, It opens a pleasing field for intelligent	RedC	903
Spies in an enemy's country, We are	RedH	184

Holmes, Sherlock, quotations (*see also* Biblical Quotations/Allusions and Literary references, Shakespearean Quotations/Allusions) (cont'd)

Stagnation, My mind rebels at	Sign	89
Standards, To accept such praise was to lower one's own	Lion	1094
Steel, never a foeman more worthy of our	Houn	747
Story against myself, I don't mind telling a	Stud	40
Strong language, Mr. Bates	Thor	1057
Study, Quite an interesting	Iden	196
Successful, It is true that I have been generally	Five	219
Suggestive, some small point which might be	Vall	787
Sun, There is nothing new under the	Stud	29
Superficial	Reig	408
	Croo	422
	Resi	424
	Card	889
Surmise, It is all	Yell	359
Sufficient for tomorrow is the evil thereof	Houn	747
Temptation to form premature theories	Vall	779
Theatrical, I don't wish to be	Sign	119
Thought of that, I had not	Sign	157
Thrice is he armed who has his quarrel just	Lady	950
Touch, a distinct	Vall	769
Touch, Watson, an undeniable touch	Houn	697
Trick, but exceedingly effective, It was a simple	Sign	157

Holmes, Sherlock, quotations (*see also* Biblical Quotations/Allusions and Literary references, Shakespearean Quotations/Allusions) (cont'd)

Tricks and I will crush you, play	Abbe	648
Tricks, Why does fate play such	Bosc	217
Trifles, It is not a time to stick at	Bruc	926
Trifles, Observation of	Bosc	214
Trifles, There is nothing so important as	Twis	238
Truth is better than indefinite doubt, Any	Yell	360
Truth, It is usually wise to tell the	Veil	1099
Try, We can but	Thor	1069
Ugly business, It's an	Houn	698
Ugly, Watson, very ugly	Thor	1057
Unconvincing, interesting but just a little	Vall	789
Unusual, The case is refreshingly	RedH	182
Up-to-date, We pay the price for being too	Vall	773
Violence does, in truth, recoil upon the violent	Spec	272
Walks, So much for afternoon	Yell	351
Watson, My dear	ubiq	
Watson, My good	Vall	773
Wisdom, It is better to learn . . . late than	Twis	241
Wise after the event, It is easy to be	Thor	1070
Witness, You are certainly an admirable	Cree	1073
Wits, I have taken to living by my	Musg	388
Woman be damned, Old	Stud	40
Woman, A most complete and remarkable	Lion	1088
Women are naturally secretive	Scan	171

Holmes, Sherlock, quotations (*see also* Biblical Quotations/Allusions and Literary references, Shakespearean Quotations/Allusions) (cont'd)

Women are never to be entirely trusted	Sign	129
Women have seldom been an attraction to me	Lion	1088
Women, motives of, are so inscrutable	Seco	657
Work is its own reward	Norw	509
Work is the best antidote to sorrow	Empt	488
Work itself is my highest reward	Sign	90
Wrong side, I never used my powers on the	Fina	477
Zero-point, This note . . . marks my	Copp	317
reader, omnivorous	Lion	1094
reading of		
Carlyle	Stud	21
	Sign	121
Petrarch	Bosc	207
Reade	Sign	97
	Sign	137
Richter	Sign	121
Voodooism	Wist	887
Woode, J. G.	Lion	1093
reads Watson's thoughts	Resi	423
	Danc	511
	Card	888
reasoner, ideal, as	Five	224
reasoning machine, not	SixN	594
reasoning simple	Stoc	363
reasoning, synthetic vs. analytic	Stud	83
records		
attempts to destroy	Veil	1095
extent of	Veil	1095

Holmes, Sherlock (cont'd)

records in box at 221B	Musg	386
red-Indian composure	Croo	412
red Indian countenance	Nava	460
reference books (*see* Commonplace books)	Nobl	288
	Empt	493
	Prio	539
	Vall	772
	Vall	776
	Bruc	913
refuges in London	Blac	559
Reichenbach, his account of	Empt	486
relatives of	Gree	435
	Norw	496
reliance on Watson	Sign	115
	Sign	131
	Bosc	202
	Nava	463
	Norw	505
	Soli	530
	Prio	549
	Houn	741
	Lady	944
	Illu	996
	Maza	1015
	Reti	1114
religion and logic	Nava	455
reluctance at having stories told	Seco	650
remarkable man	Empt	483
	Card	888
reminisces with Watson	Last	980
rent paid by	Stud	20
	Dyin	932
reproves Watson	Copp	319
	Soli	531
	Lady	946
	Reti	1116

Holmes, Sherlock (cont'd)
   reputation
      need not enhance   Thor   1058
      stakes on solution   Abbe   645
   rescued by Watson   Devi   965
   rescues Watson   Lady   946
                                     Illu   997
                                     3Gar   1053
   resources, boasts of   Sign   125
   respects Watson's judgment   Vall   800
   rest, ordered by Dr. Agar   Devi   955
   retirement of   Seco   650
                                     Last   978
                                   Lion   1083
   revered by Watson above all   Thor   1055
   revived by problem   Reig   401
                                   Devi   957
   revolver (*see* Weapons)
   revolver practice, indoor   Musg   386
                                   Dyin   932
   rewards received by
      amethyst box   Iden   191
      checks   Bery   313
                                   Prio   558
      cocaine bottle   Sign   158
      disdain for   RedC   907
      emerald tie pin   Bruc   939
      knighthood refused   3Gar   1044
      Legion of Honor   Gold   607
      none   RedH   189
      photograph   Scan   175
      princely offer, promise of   Prio   540
      profession its own   Spec   259
      ring   Iden   191
      seldom large   Blac   559
      uniform or none   Thor   1058
   rheumatism of   (Pref)   Last   869

Holmes, Sherlock (cont'd)

rich men, opinions of	Thor	1061
ring, receives	Iden	191
rising habits		
early as a rule	Stud	20
	Scan	167
	3Gar	1051
	Reti	1116
invariably before Watson	Stud	20
	Houn	750
late as a rule	Spec	258
	Houn	669
six is unseemly	3Stu	604
saved by Watson	Devi	965
schools as beacons of the future	Nava	456
scientific experiment of	Dyin	932
scores on Lestrade	Norw	509
Scotland Yard, Holmes's opinion of	Stud	25
	Stud	26
	Stud	50
	3Gar	1051
Scotland Yard admires Holmes	SixN	595
Scotland Yard Jack-in-office, called	Spec	265
scrapbooks (*see* Commonplace books)	Empt	493
	3Stu	596
	RedC	901
	RedC	904
scrutiny of client	Iden	192
	Copp	318
	Soli	527
sea did not attract	Resi	423
seclusion needed for thought	Houn	683
second highest expert, considered	Houn	672
secret writings, knowledge of	Danc	522
secretive streak in	Illu	994
see in the dark, ability to	Chas	578
self defense	Fina	473

312 ◼ Good Old Index

Holmes, Sherlock (cont'd)
  sense of humor (*see* Mannerisms)

limited		Maza	1014
perverted		Maza	1022
strange and occasionally offensive		Lady	945
senses abnormally acute		Blan	1007
services inestimable		Blac	559
seven separate explanations		Copp	323
seventy-odd cases		Spec	257
shadows suspect		Stud	40
		Devi	967
shakes Watson's hand		Wist	883
		Bruc	926
Sherlock, called			
by Mycroft		Gree	437
		Bruc	916
by old Sherman		Sign	117
referred to by Watson		Gree	437
signs self as		Bruc	920
shortcomings of		Stud	19
singlestick expert		Stud	22
		Illu	993
sits cross-legged		Twis	240
skill exceeded reputation		Bery	316
skull coveted		Houn	672
sleuth-hound		RedH	185
smokes out a culprit		Norw	508
smoking by			
smokes cigar		Sign	133
		Sign	140
		Nobl	294
	(?)	Silv	350
		Glor	376
		Empt	493
		Gold	608
		Vall	812

Holmes, Sherlock, smoking by, smokes cigar (cont'd)

	Card	895
	Bruc	925
	Last	975

    smokes cigarettes

	Scan	162
	Iden	192
	Bosc	207
	Musg	388
	Fina	470
	Empt	486
	Norw	505
	Soli	537
	Gold	615
	Houn	669
	Dyin	940

    smokes pipe

	Stud	19
	Sign	90
	Sign	96
	Sign	117
	Sign	127
	Sign	129
	Scan	168
	RedH	184
	Iden	196
	Five	224
	Twis	233
	Twis	240
	Blue	257
	Spec	270
	Engr	276
	Copp	317
	Silv	335
	Glor	374
	Croo	411
	Resi	425
	Nava	466
	Soli	530
	Prio	545

Holmes, Sherlock, smoking by, smokes pipe (cont'd)

	Blac	571
	Chas	575
	Miss	630
	Abbe	647
	Seco	654
	Houn	683
	Vall	771
	Vall	800
	Wist	869
	Wist	887
	Bruc	915
(?)	Lady	953
	Devi	956
	Devi	960
	Devi	970
	Illu	985
	Illu	994
	Blan	1001
	Maza	1014
	3Gab	1023
	3Gar	1047
	Thor	1056
	Thor	1059
	Thor	1069
	Cree	1071
	Shos	1106
	Reti	1111

smoking equipment
  pipes
    amber stem
    briar

    cherry-wood
    clay

	Prio	545
	Sign	90
	Twis	240
	Copp	317
	Iden	196
	RedH	184
	Blue	257
	Copp	317

Holmes, Sherlock, smoking equipment,
    pipes, clay (cont'd)
        clay, usually
            old black
        tobacco
            black
            shag

            Watson's arcadia mixture
        other
            cigar case
            cigarette case
            tobacco pouch

    smoking habits of
        all night

        as an aid to thought

        asks permission to
        before breakfast
        blows smoke rings

        cigar and cigarette

Chas	575
Houn	683
Copp	317
Cree	1071
Silv	335
Scan	168
Twis	240
Houn	682
Cree	1071
Croo	411
Scan	162
Bosc	207
Dyin	934
Devi	970
Twis	240
Norw	505
Lady	953
RedH	184
Twis	240
Croo	415
Norw	505
Houn	696
Vall	771
Lady	953
RedC	901
Engr	276
Five	224
Nobl	295
Houn	671
Empt	486
Empt	493
Gold	608
Gold	615

Holmes, Sherlock, smoking habits of (cont'd)

cigar and pipe	Sign	90
	Sign	133
	Glor	374
	Glor	376
	Vall	771
	Vall	812
	Bruc	915
	Bruc	925
cigar only	Nobl	294
	Card	895
	Last	975
cigarette and pipe	Scan	162
	Scan	168
	Iden	192
	Iden	196
	Soli	530
	Soli	537
	Houn	669
	Houn	683
cigarettes only	Bosc	207
	Musg	388
	Fina	470
	Norw	505
	Dyin	940
not specific	Lady	953
	Veil	1095
nothing at all	Bery	
	Yell	
	Stoc	
	Reig	
	Gree	
	Danc	
	SixN	
	3Stu	
	RedC	

Holmes, Sherlock, smoking habits of,
  nothing at all (cont'd)

pipe only	Suss	
	Lion	
	Stud	19
	RedH	184
	Five	224
	Twis	233
	Twis	240
	Blue	257
	Spec	270
	Engr	276
	Copp	317
	Silv	336
	Croo	411
	Resi	425
	Nava	466
	Prio	545
	Blac	571
	Chas	575
	Miss	630
	Abbe	647
	Seco	654
	Wist	869
	Devi	956
	Illu	985
	Blan	1001
	Maza	1014
	3Gab	1023
	3Gar	1047
	Thor	1056
	Cree	1071
	Shos	1106
	Reti	1114
several pipes	Scan	168
	Croo	415
	Houn	683
three pipe problem	RedH	184
tobacco, refers to as a filthy habit	Veil	1095

318 ◼ *Good Old Index*

Holmes, Sherlock, smoking habits of (cont'd)

two pipes in a row	Thor	1056
whole ounce of shag	Twis	240
smoking, jokes about	Veil	1095
snuff box, gold with amethyst	Iden	191
sociable fellow, never	Glor	374
social summons, demands of	Nobl	287
softer passions	Scan	161
solar system, views on	Stud	21
	Gree	435
	Houn	713
solutions, three	Blan	1011
souvenir of Adler case	Scan	175
	Iden	191
spartan habits	Houn	739
specialist, consults	Dyin	935
	Blan	1007
specialist in crime	Houn	671
special powers	Abbe	642
speed of train estimated	Silv	336
spies, requires list of	Bruc	925
spirit of inquiry of	Stud	17
sports		
billiards	Danc	511
boxing	Stud	22
	Sign	106
	Five	225
	Yell	351
	Glor	374
	Empt	494
	Soli	532
duck shooting	Glor	374
fencing	Five	225
	Glor	374
	Illu	993

Holmes, Sherlock, sports (cont'd)

fishing	Glor	374
	Shos	1109
revolver practice	Musg	386
	Dyin	932
self-defense	Fina	473
single-stick	Stud	22
	Five	225
	Illu	993
swimming	Lion	1084
swordsman	Stud	22
	Five	225
	Illu	993
wrestling	Empt	486
sports, amateur, ignorance of	Miss	623
spry fellow	Stud	27
	Sign	157
staghound	Stud	51
stagnation, effects of	Sign	89
stamps feet on ground	Houn	743
	Houn	756
starvation, effect of, upon	Maza	1014
stick of	RedH	184
	Empt	486
	Miss	631
stick as weapon	Miss	631
stood alone as detective	Vall	774
stories written by	Blan	1000
	Lion	1083
stormy petrel	Reig	406
Stradivarius, buys for fifty-five shillings	Card	894
strangest case of	Devi	955
stratgems	Nava	569
advertisement	SixN	591
	Bruc	928
aniseed	Miss	633

Holmes, Sherlock, stratgems (cont'd)

ankle injury	Prio	550
apparent accident	Reig	405
appointment mistaken	Cree	1077
architect	Spec	266
architecture, interest in	3Stu	602
betting	Blue	252
boat name wrong	Card	893
boots reversed	Empt	487
botanical study	Wist	879
bust	Empt	489
	Maza	1019
candle message	RedC	909
catalepsy	Resi	430
cigarettes	Gold	621
cigarettes spilled	Gold	617
cipher note	Danc	521
death at Reichenbach	Fina	480
dog	Shos	1109
dress clothes	Chas	577
dummy, takes place of	Maza	1021
engaged	Chas	575
failure, apparent	Houn	746
falsehood to trap liar	3Gar	1047
fire	Scan	172
	Norw	508
fisherman	Shos	1102
foreign secretary	Seco	666
goose fancier	Blue	251
gramaphone	Maza	1021
hat knocked off table	Blan	1007
hotel register	Houn	692
illness feigned	Reig	403
	Dyin	932
injuries exaggerated	Illu	994
injury	Scan	171
	Prio	550

Holmes, Sherlock, stratgems (cont'd)

kidnapping, threat of	3Stu	627
knocks over table	Reig	405
mistake in note	Reig	404
moat, threatens to drain	Vall	808
note to Oberstein	Bruc	911
opium den	Twis	231
pencil, breaks	3Stu	602
phony departure	Houn	751
questioning, trick	Sign	124
	Silv	342
	3Stu	605
	Gold	617
	Miss	628
	Abbe	650
	Seco	661
	Card	893
	3Gab	1026
	3Gar	1047
portmanteau	Stud	51
remembers seeing someone	Silv	342
ring substitution	Stud	37
room kept used	Nava	463
safe	Last	975
smoking	Gold	617
street fight	Scan	171
telegram	Houn	694
	Houn	752
	Reti	1117
telegram lost	Houn	691
telegraph office	Miss	628
third cab	Fina	474
train, leaves early	Fina	476
train trip faked	Nava	463
	Houn	751
violin	Maza	1019
washing	Twis	242

Holmes, Sherlock, stratgems (cont'd)

watering pot	Devi	959
whaling expedition	Blac	571
whereabouts faked	Houn	741
wounds exaggerated	Illu	994
writing	Reig	404
yawning	Seco	661
strong box of	Blue	250
stupidity, cites own	Cree	1080
successes, early cases not all	Musg	387
suggest case for Watson's chronicles	SixN	593
	Lady	954
Sunday, Holmes works on	RedH	185
	Last	970
	Cree	1071
supernatural, impatient with	Houn	682
	Devi	958
	Suss	1034
supreme moment of	Illu	984
surgeon, likened to	Thor	1060
suspects himself	Nava	456
swimmer	Lion	1084
swordsman	Stud	22
	Five	225
	Illu	993
talks at random for purpose	Dyin	936
talks to himself	Bosc	212
tape line in use by	Stud	31
	Sign	112
	Musg	394
target practice indoors, takes	Musg	386
	Dyin	932
tattoo marks, studies of	RedH	177
telegraph, uses	Stud	32
	Stud	85
	Sign	125
	Sign	132

Holmes, Sherlock, telegraph, uses (cont'd)

Bosc	202
Bosc	214
Silv	337
Gree	442
Nava	448
Nava	457
Nava	458
Nava	467
Fina	476
Danc	516
Danc	523
Soli	538
Prio	553
Blac	567
Blac	568
Miss	631
Abbe	646
Houn	694
Houn	752
Wist	869
Wist	875
Card	891
Card	894
Bruc	920
Lady	944
Lady	945
Devi	955
Last	973
Last	978
Suss	1036
Cree	1078

telegraphs rather than writes Devi 955
telephone, uses

Sign	134
Illu	984
3Gar	1047
Reti	1116

Holmes, Sherlock (cont'd)

tells tale to Watson	Glor	374
	Musg	387
textbook on detection, plans	Abbe	636
thanked by police	Danc	523
theories, half a dozen	Norw	502
Theorist, Mr., called	Sign	114
theory of heredity of	Empt	494
theory of brain capacity	Stud	21
	Blue	247
	Lion	1090
theory opposed to facts	Blan	1011
third case	Musg	387
thought-reading,	Resi	423
remarks on	Card	888
thousand cases of	Fina	477
threads of a case	Croo	412
three continents, activities range over	Iden	191
tin box, records in	Musg	386
tobaccos, identifies	Stud	32
	Sign	91
	Bosc	213
	Twis	240
	Yell	352
	Croo	411
	Resi	432
	Houn	682
tokay wine, drinks	Last	974
too busy to take a case	Soli	527
	Prio	539
	RedC	901
	Lady	943
	Reti	1114
too late	Five	227
	Danc	518
	Soli	534
	Houn	743

Holmes, Sherlock (cont'd)

tooth-brush of	Spec	265
tooth knocked out	Empt	494
touch, delicacy of	Stud	20
training, always in	Soli	534
trains of thought intersect	Lady	950
translation of works into French	Sign	91
trap, drives	Twis	232
	Soli	534
travels to Norway	Blac	572
trespasser	Chas	577
	Lady	951
tribute to Watson	Blan	1000
trick, plays on Watson	Houn	741
trifles, looks for	Stud	26
	Sign	91
	Iden	194
	Bosc	214
	Twis	238
	Lion	1094
trifles, no time for	Stud	26
trigonometry, uses	Musg	394
truth better than doubt	Yell	360
truth, imagination is mother of	Vall	802
truth, insists upon	Resi	430
	Abbe	645
	Abbe	648
	Seco	652
	Thor	1059
truth is stranger	RedH	176
than fiction	Iden	191
uncomfortable away from 221B	3Stu	596
uncommon phase of crime	Stud	83
underworld, is aided from	Vall	769
	Illu	989
ungracious acceptance of case	3Stu	596
unique experience	Chas	572

326 ◼ *Good Old Index*

Holmes, Sherlock (cont'd)

university of	Musg	387
unofficial status of	Stud	27
	Iden	199
	Bosc	215
	Silv	345
	Abbe	647
unsolved cases indicated	Yell	351
	Thor	1054
untired by all day work	Prio	553
variety, pride in his	Empt	489
varying moods of	Stud	20
vices, has none other than cocaine	Yell	351
violin, discussion of	Stud	27
	Card	894
violin, purchased at bargain	Card	894
violin, allusions to	Stud	19
	Stud	22
	Stud	27
	Stud	38
	Stud	40
	Sign	128
	Sign	134
	RedH	185
	Five	225
	Five	227
	Nobl	301
	Musg	386
	Norw	502
	Seco	657
	Houn	685
	Card	894
	Illu	987
	Maza	1019
	Cree	1071
violin land, off to	RedH	185

Holmes, Sherlock (cont'd)
  visited
    by Moriarty   Fina   472
    by Mycroft   Gree   443
                                 Bruc   916
    by Watson   Scan   161
                                 Iden   190
                                 Blue   244
                                 Engr   274
                                 Maza   1012
                                 3Gab   1023
  visits
    Khartoum, etc.   Empt   488
    Scotland Yard   Gree   444
    Watson   Engr   274
                                 Stoc   362
                                 Croo   411
                                 Fina   469
                                 Empt   485
  visitors, not encouraged by   Five   218
  voice, does not recognize   Scan   173
  wakes Watson early   Twis   240
                                 Spec   258
                                 Resi   431
  walks
    in Surrey   Wist   879
    on moor   Silv   344
                                 Houn   726
                                 Devi   955
    through London   Yell   351
                                 Resi   424
                                 Gree   436
                                 Chas   572
                                 Seco   659
    through Switzerland   Fina   477

Holmes, Sherlock (cont'd)

watch of		
	Stud	49
	Sign	135
	Silv	336
	Gree	435
	Abbe	647
	Seco	663
	Wist	870
	Thor	1062
	Shos	1102
watch, deductions from	Sign	92
watch, winds as clue	Five	218
watch-chain of	Scan	169
Watson		
Holmes admires	RedH	190
Holmes has not seen for years	Last	978
Watson's aid insisted on	Bery	308
Watson's aid refused	Bery	311
	Dyin	933
	Maza	1014
Watson's aid requested	Scan	169
	RedH	185
	Bosc	202
	Spec	258
	Spec	270
	Copp	322
	Silv	336
	Croo	412
	Croo	419
	Empt	486
	Gold	598
	Illu	984
	3Gab	1024
	Cree	1079
	Veil	1095
	Reti	1114

Holmes, Sherlock (cont'd)

wax figure of	Empt	489
	Maza	1013
weapon, favorite (hunting crop)	SixN	591
welcomes anything when idle	Miss	622
whip, threatens with	Iden	201
whiskers, false	Scan	167
whistle, police, threatens to blow	Abbe	648
will of	Fina	480
witness, puts at ease	Miss	624
wits, lives by his	Musg	388
wizard, called a	Blan	1000
	Reti	1116
woman, beaten by a	Scan	175
	Five	219
women, attitude toward		
aversion to	Gree	435
courteous to	Dyin	932
disliked	Dyin	932
gentle with	Iden	192
	Spec	258
	Dyin	932
	Veil	1101
in need of help	Chas	576
ingratiating with	Gold	617
intuition of, opinion on	Bosc	208
	Twis	239
	Lion	1088
not an admirer of	Vall	801
not to be trusted	Sign	129
opinions on	Spec	258
	Illu	999
seldom an attraction	Lion	1088
workhouse cough as part of disguise	Sign	133
works fifteen hours daily	Reig	398
works for love of art	Spec	257
worst tenant in London	Dyin	932

Holmes, Sherlock (cont'd)

wounded	Illu	993
on hand	Nava	465
in mouth	Empt	494
	Soli	532
writing harder than he thought	Blan	1000
writings of		
"Blanched Soldier"	Blan	1000
"Book of Life"	Stud	23
Chaldean roots in the Cornish language	Devi	955
charters, early English	3Stu	596
ciphers	Danc	522
documents, ancient	Houn	673
ears (2)	Card	896
footsteps, tracing of	Sign	91
hands, effects of trades upon	Sign	91
"Lion's Mane"	Lion	1083
miscellaneous	Sign	91
	Card	896
observation and deduction	Stud	23
polyphonic motets of Lassus	Bruc	929
Practical Handbook of Bee Culture	Last	977
tattoo marks	RedH	177
tobacco ashes	Stud	33
	Sign	91
	Bosc	214
translated into French	Sign	91
writings promised by		
dogs, use of in detection	Cree	1071
malingering	Dyin	941
textbook, whole art of detection	Abbe	636
typewriter and crime	Iden	199
wrong side, never on	Fina	477
write, never, if could telegraph	Devi	955
Holy Four	Stud	64
Holy Land	Lady	944

H □ 331

Holy Peters	Lady	947
Holy War, The (book)	Empt	485
Holy Writ (*see* Bible)	Houn	675
Home Secretary	Maza	1013
Homer (Alexander) Pope's	Reig	399
Hones, Johnny	Stud	54
Honeydew tobacco	Card	890
Honeysuckle	Yell	354
Honour's list	Bruc	917
Hood, General (John)	Five	219
Hookah	Sign	100
Hooliganism	SixN	583
Hope, Jefferson	Stud	51
Hope, Jefferson, Sr.	Stud	60
Hope, Hilda Trelawney	Seco	656
Hope, Rt. Hon. Trelawney	Seco	650
Hope Town (Andamans)	Sign	152
Hopkins, Ezekiah	RedH	178
Hopkins, Stanley	Blac	559
	Gold	608
	Miss	622
	Abbe	636
seven cases with Holmes	Abbe	636
Horace	Stud	86
	Iden	201
	Prio	540
Horner, John	Blue	248
Horse (*see* animal)		
Horse racing	Bosc	203
	Blue	253
	Bery	304
	Silv	347
	3Stu	600
	Miss	628
	Shos	1103

Horseshoes

Horsham

Horsom, Dr.
Hospital
    Bart's (St. Bartholomew's)
    base, Peshawur
    Cape Town
    Charing Cross

    Indian
    King's College
    Leper
    Pretoria
Hotel (*see also* **Boarding Houses, Inns**)
    Anerley Arms
    Bentley's Private
    in Birmingham
    Brambletye Hotel
    Carlton
    Charing Cross
    Claridge's

    Cosmopolitan
    Dacre
    du Louvre (Paris)
    Dulong (Lyons)
    Eagle Commercial (Tunbridge Wells)
    Englischer Hof
        Meiringen
        Baden
    Escurial (Madrid)
    Grand

Stud	32	
Silv	343	
Prio	552	
Five	218	
Suss	1035	
Lady	952	
Stud	17	
Stud	15	
Blan	1001	
Houn	670	
Illu	993	
Sign	145	
Resi	425	
Blan	1010	
Blan	1010	
Norw	500	
Miss	623	
Stoc	367	
Blac	567	
Gree	436	
Bruc	931	
Last	978	
Thor	1056	
Blue	248	
SixN	594	
Bruc	931	
Reig	398	
Vall	803	
Fina	477	
Lady	944	
Wist	887	
Illu	993	

Hotel (*see also* Boarding Houses, Inns)
(cont'd)
Greater London Hotels	Stud	78
	Card	894
	Cree	1075
Grosvenor	Fina	478
Halliday's Private	Stud	46
Hereford Arms (Ross)	Bosc	207
Langham	Sign	94
	Scan	166
	Lady	947
Mexborough Private	Houn	763
National (Lausanne)	Lady	943
Northumberland	Houn	685
Northumberland Avenue hotels	Nobl	296
	Gree	438
Private hotels	Stud	15
	Stud	46
	Miss	623
	Houn	763
in Plymouth	Devi	962
Railway Arms (Little Purlington)	Reti	1118
St. Pancras	Iden	195
Westville Arms (Birlstone)	Vall	785
Hotel bill, as clue	Nobl	296
Hotel Cosmopolitan	Blue	248
Hotel Directory	Houn	691
Hotel du Louvre	Bruc	931
Hotel Dulong	Reig	398
Hotel Escurial	Wist	887
Hotel National	Lady	943
***Hotspur* (ship)**	Glor	385
Hottentot	Houn	678
Hound	Sign	112
	Houn	674
	3Gab	1032

334 ◘ Good Old Index

Hound of the Baskervilles			
(1647)		Houn	673
(1889)		Houn	757
Houndsditch		Stud	39
Household word, Holmes's name a		Bery	302
Housekeeper (*see also* servants)		Stud	23
		Spec	263
		Seco	655
		Lion	1083
Mrs. Allen		Vall	781
Mrs. Barrymore		Houn	676
Eliza		Houn	722
Mrs. Bernstone		Sign	107
Mrs. Dixon		Soli	528
Mrs. Hudson (which see)			
Mrs. King		Danc	518
Mrs. Lexington		Norw	504
Mrs. Marker		Gold	609
Mrs. Porter		Devi	957
Mrs. Saunders		3Gar	1050
Mrs. Turner	(?)	Scan	170
House of Commons		Houn	749
House plans (*see* Chart of house)			
House, the (Stock Exchange)		Blac	563
Houses (*see* Residences)			
Houses of Parliament		Seco	655
		Lady	949
House-surgeon		Houn	671
Howells, Rachel		Musg	389
Howe Street		RedC	905
Hudson (klansman)		Five	223
Hudson (sailor)		Glor	377
Hudson, Morse		SixN	583
Hudson, Mrs.		Sign	126
		Blue	250
		Spec	258
		Nava	465

H ◻ 335

Hudson, Mrs. (cont'd)

				Empt	488
				Danc	517
				Blac	568
				Seco	656
				Vall	865
				Wist	871
				Dyin	932
				Lady	947
				Last	974
				Maza	1022
				3Gar	1045

	(?)	Lion	1083
cuisine of		Nava	465
Holmes' payments to		Dyin	932
hysterics, thrown into		Empt	488
in awe of Holmes		Dyin	932
Turner, Mrs.		Scan	170
visits Watson		Dyin	932
Holmes wires to		Lady	947
Hudson Street (Aldershot)		Croo	417
Huguenot		Nava	455
Huguenots, Les **(Meyerbeer)**		Houn	766
Human bones, as clue		Shos	1106
Human nature,		Sign	137
predictability of		Scan	173
Hung-wu (Chinese emperor)		Illu	995
Hungarian police		Gree	446
Hungary		Gree	446
		Suss	1034
Hunt (policeman)		Vall	853
Hunter, Ned		Silv	337
Hunter, Violet		Copp	318
Hunting (*see* Shooting)			
Hunting crop (*see* Weapons)			
Huret, the Boulevard assassin		Gold	607
Hurlingham (club)		Illu	987
Hurlstone, Manor house of		Musg	388

Hurricane	Gold	611
Huxtable, Thorneycroft	Prio	538
Huxtable's Sidelights on Horace	Prio	540
Hyam (victim)	Vall	822
Hyam's (tailor)	Norw	503
Hyde Park	Nobl	293
"The Park"	RedH	186
	Nobl	294
	Yell	351
	Empt	485
	Bruc	931
Hydraulic engineer	Engr	276
Hydrocarbons	Empt	488
Hydrochloric acid	Iden	198
Hynes, Mr. Hynes	Wist	876
Hypnotism	Illu	989
suggested	Gree	446
Hypochondriac	Sign	105
Hypodermic syringe	Sign	89
	Miss	633
	Dyin	934
	Illu	998
	Cree	1082
Hysterics	Engr	275
	Empt	488

Ice on frozen pond	Abbe	645
Ichneumon (mongoose)	Croo	421
Ichthyosis (pseudo-leprosy)	Blan	1012
Idee fixe	SixN	584
Illinois	Stud	54
Illnesses (*see* Ailments)		
Illustrious client	Bery	303
	Illu	985
"I'm Sitting on the Style, Mary"	Vall	837
Imperial Envoy	Last	979
Imperial Opera of Warsaw	Scan	165
Imperial police of Peking	Illu	995
Imperial Theatre	Soli	527
Imperial Yeomanry	Blan	1000
Impossible, elimination of the	Sign	92
	Sign	97
	Sign	111
	Bery	315
	Soli	529
	Bruc	926
	Blan	1011
Income, single lady's	Iden	193
Income tax	Seco	654
Indelible pencil	Reti	1121
Index, Good Old	Suss	1034

Indexes (*see* Sherlock Holmes—
  Commonplace books)
India

	Stud	15
	Sign	111
	Five	229
	Spec	260
	Croo	419
	Resi	423
	Gree	437
	Vall	772
	Card	888
	Bruc	914
Indian Army	Empt	492
	Thor	1054
Indian file	Cree	1093
Indian lunkah	Sign	91
Indian Mutiny	Sign	145
	Croo	412
Indian peninsula	Sign	127
Indian Pete	Stud	54
Indian regiment	Sign	94
Indian rupee	Croo	418
Indian tapestry	Sign	108
Indians, American	Stud	56
	Stud	60
	Stud	63
	Stud	73
Apache	Nobl	298
Blackfeet	Stud	52
Digger	Sign	127
Pawnee	Stud	52
red-Indian	Croo	412
	Nava	460
Washoe	Stud	68

India-rubber	Engr	282
	Danc	520
Indigo planter	Sign	145
Ineffable twaddle	Stud	23
Infernal couple	Last	947
Initials		
EB (Eustace Brackenstall)	Abbe	636
EJC (clerk)	Suss	1034
EJD (Enoch J. Drebber)	Stud	39
FHM (Francis Hay Moulton)	Nobl	296
HB (Henry Baker)	Blue	245
JA (James Armitage)	Glor	375
JH		
(Jefferson Hope)	Stud	48
(Joseph Harrison)	Nava	449
JHN (John Hopley Neligan)	Blac	562
LL (Laura Lyons)	Houn	729
PC (Peter Carey, Patrick Cairns)	Blac	562
PT (Percy Trevelyan)	Resi	431
Initials, coincidence of	Nobl	296
	Blac	571
Inner Deacon	Vall	853
Inner Temple	Scan	168
Inn (*see also* Boarding House, Hotel, Public House)	Spec	265
	Yell	353
	Nava	466
	Danc	521
	Prio	544
	Gold	613
	Miss	630
	Houn	705
	Blan	1006
	Thor	1069
Alpha (London)	Blue	251
Black Swan (Winchester)	Copp	322
Blue Anchor	Reti	1116
Bull (Esher)	Wist	877

340 ◾ *Good Old Index*

Inn (*see also* Boarding House, Hotel, Public House) (cont'd)
  Chequers
      Lamberley — Suss — 1039
      Camford — Cree — 1076
  Crown (Stoke Moran) — Spec — 263
  "Dangling Prussian" — Last — 980
  Fighting Cock (Hallamshire) — Prio — 552
  Green Dragon (Shoscombe) — Shos — 1103
  Red Bull (Hallamshire) — Prio — 546

Inquisition of Seville — Stud — 62

Insane asylums
  Broadmoor — Reti — 1120
  Helston — Devi — 959

Insects
  bees — Seco — 650
         Last — 978
         Lion — 1083
  beetles — Sign — 117
  bug-hunter (N. Garrideb) — 3Gar — 1054
  butterflies and moths — 3Gar — 1048
    collection — Houn — 758
    Cyclopides — Houn — 709
    lepidoptera — Houn — 711
    Vandeleur moth — Houn — 762
  centipedes — Sign — 146
  cockroaches — Copp — 319
  flies and bluebottles — Blac — 561
  mosquitoes — Sign — 144
  scorpions — Sign — 146
  various insects — Copp — 324

Interlaken (Switzerland) — Fina — 477

International (Rugby) — Miss — 623

International strife avoided — Nava — 460
         Seco — 662
         Bruc — 916

Interpreter — Gree — 440

Iodoform	Scan	162
Ionides (cigarette-maker)	Gold	615
Ireland	Card	890
	Last	973
County Monaghan	Vall	821
Irish-American (Altamont)	Last	973
Iris (racehorse)	Silv	347
Iron Dike Company	Vall	851
Ironhill (U.S.A.)	Vall	849
Isle of Dogs	Sign	138
Isle of Wight	Five	229
Italian code	RedC	907
Italian music	RedH	184
Italian Quarter, of London	SixN	590
Italy	Nava	450
	Fina	474
	RedC	911
	3Gab	1027
Ivernian race	Houn	700
Ivory	Silv	342
	Reig	399
	Gold	610
	Seco	651
	Dyin	934
miniature	Nobl	292
Ivy	Prio	540
	Abbe	637
	Houn	702
	Cree	1081
Ivy Lane	Nava	452
Ivy Plant (pub)	Seco	661

J pen	Gree	443
	Card	891
Jack-in-a-box	Vall	812
Jack-knife, and correspondence	Musg	386
Jackal	Sign	145
Jackson (doctor)	Croo	412
Jackson, General ("Stonewall")	Five	219
Jackson Prize	Houn	671
Jacobean times	Vall	779
Jacobs (butler)	Seco	665
Jacobson's Yard (shipyard)	Sign	135
Jail (*see* gaol)		
James (Watson)	Twis	230
James I (King)	Vall	807
Jacobean	Vall	779
James (postmaster's son)	Houn	705
James, Billy	Vall	822
James, Jack	Last	975
Japan	Glor	375
Japanese armour	Gree	440
Japanese cabinet	Glor	379
Japanese vase	3Gar	1048
Japanese wrestling, baritsu	Empt	486
Jarvey (cab driver)	Stud	85

344 ◼ *Good Old Index*

Jaundice	Glor	383
Jem (nickname)	Blue	256
Jemmy (burglary tool)	Chas	577
	Bruc	925
	3Gar	1053
	Shos	1110
Jimmy	Nava	464
Jenkins (victims)	Vall	853
Jessamine, white (perfume)	Houn	765
"Jeune Fille a l'Agneau, La" (painting)	Vall	776
Jew broker	Card	894
Jew peddler	Stud	22
Jewels and jewelry		
agate	Sign	151
Agra treasure	Sign	151
Albert chain	Stud	30
	RedH	177
	Iden	197
amethyst	Iden	191
beryl	Sign	151
	Scan	164
	Bery	303
breast pin, arc and compass	RedH	177
brilliant	Iden	191
	Lady	948
brooch, beryl	Scan	164
cameo	Houn	677
carbuncle	Blue	248
crown	Bery	303
	Musg	397
diamond	Sign	151
	Iden	191
	Blue	248
	Chas	574
	Chas	582
	Vall	860

Jewels and jewelry, diamond (cont'd)

	Card	893
	Lady	943
	Maza	1013
diamond tiara	Chas	582
diamond earrings, gilt	Card	893
emerald	Sign	151
	Scan	175
	Bruc	931
gold earrings	Iden	197
ivory miniature	Nobl	292
locket	Nobl	292
	Yell	361
	Nava	449
opal tiara	Spec	259
ornaments, black jet	Iden	196
pearl	Sign	95
	SixN	594
	Illu	985
pearl tie pin	Illu	985
pendant	Lady	948
pin, bull dog head	Stud	30
ring	Stud	29
	Stud	30
	Scan	175
	Iden	191
	Twis	238
	Nobl	295
	Vall	784
	Maza	1015
ruby	Stud	30
seal, watch chain	Seco	651
Spanish silver jewelry	Lady	943
tie pin	Maza	1015
	Reti	1116
watch (*which see*)		

Jewels and jewelry (cont'd)
    watch chain (*see also* Albert chain)

RedH	177
Silv	341
Prio	543
Gold	614
Seco	651
Bruc	917
Last	973
Cree	1080

    watch charm   Norw   497
Jews   Shos   1104
Jew's-harp   Empt   490
Jezail bullet
    in shoulder   Stud   15
    in leg   Sign   90

Nobl	287

Jiddah (Arabia)   Sign   155
Jimmy (in agony column)   RedC   904
Jingo, by the living   Soli   535
Jockey   Silv   337

Shos	1106

Johannesburg (South Africa)   Soli   528
John (butler)   Miss   630
John (coachman)   Scan   175
John (coachman)   Twis   233
John Bull   Last   972
John o' Groats (Scotland)   Miss   633
Johnson (athlete)   Miss   623
Johnson, Shinwell   Illu   987
Johnson, Sidney   Bruc   917
Johnson, Theophilus   Houn   692
Johnston (Mormon elder)   Stud   59
Joint, The (bar—Chicago)   Danc   525
Jones, Athelney   Sign   90
Jones, Peter   RedH   186
Jose (servant)   Wist   886
Journal, Watson's   Stud   76

Journal de Geneve (newspaper)	Fina	469
Journal of Psychology	Houn	671
Journalist	Twis	243
	SixN	585
	Vall	837
Jowaki campaign	Empt	494
Jubilee	Danc	512
Judge, jury and executioner	Stud	78
Judge Lynch	Vall	838
Jumping pit	3Stu	606
Junker	Last	973
Jupiter descending	Bruc	915
Jury	Stud	78
	Bosc	213
	Five	221
	Five	222
	Five	226
	Gree	436
	Norw	503
	Norw	504
	Blac	568
	Abbe	650
	Devi	969
Watson as	Abbe	649
Justice, god of	Thor	1068
Justice, leniency of	Soli	538
	Illu	999
Justice of the Peace	Glor	374
	Reig	399
	Wist	876

K

Kabul (Afghanistan)		Empt	494
Kaiser		Last	971
Kansas		3Gar	1045
Kemball (Mormon elder)		Stud	59
Kemp, Wilson		Gree	446
Kennington		SixN	588
Kennington Lane		Sign	121
Kennington Park Gate		Stud	32
Kennington Road		SixN	583
		Lady	948
Kensington		RedH	186
		Gree	438
		Empt	485
		Norw	496
		SixN	585
		Wist	871
	(2)	Bruc	925
		Dyin	936
Kent		Sign	145
		Twis	233
		Fina	476
		Gold	608
		Abbe	636

350 ◼ *Good Old Index*

Kent (cont'd)

Kent (doctor)
Keswick (paperhanger)
Key
   brass
   Chubb's

   forced by wire
   latch
   lost

   scratches from, on watch case
   skeketon
Keyhole, maid listens at
Keyhole, Watson peers through
K.G. (Knight of the Garter)
Khalifa
Khan, Abdullah
Khartoum (Sudan)
Khitmutgar (native butler)

Khyber (Pass)
Kid
Kidnapping (abduction)

Kilburn
Kimberley (South Africa)

Vall	779	
Lion	1093	
Blan	1008	
Stud	40	
Musg	387	
Scan	168	
Gold	614	
Resi	433	
Stud	40	
Sign	141	
Croo	414	
Sign	93	
Chas	578	
3Gab	1025	
Sign	108	
Prio	539	
Empt	488	
Sign	98	
Empt	488	
Sign	100	
Spec	260	
Illu	986	
Wist	879	
Nobl	294	
Gree	446	
Soli	538	
Prio	539	
Miss	627	
Houn	674	
Wist	884	
Lady	947	
Last	980	
Blue	256	
Soli	536	

King
  of Bohemia   Scan   165
  Charles I (England)   Stud   38
                                                 Musg   396
                                                 Vall   807
  Charles II (England)   Musg   397
  David (Israel)   Croo   415
  George II (England)   Vall   807
  Holland, reigning family of   Scan   161
                                                 Iden   191
  James I (England)   Vall   807
  Kaiser (Germany)   Last   971
  "of Proosia" (Prussia)   Blue   254
  of Scandinavia   Scan   166
                                                 Fina   470
  Shomu, (emperor of Japan)   Illu   997
  Solomon (Israel)   Vall   857
  Turkey, Sultan of   Blan   1007
King, Mrs. (cook)   Danc   518
King Edward Street   RedH   182
King's College Hospital   Resi   425
King's Cross   Iden   195
King's Cross Station   Miss   628
King's Pyland (stable)   Silv   336
Kingston   Illu   982
Kirwan, Mrs.   Reig   400
Kirwan, William   Reig   399
K.K.K.   Five   220
Klein (sugar king)   3Gab   1031
Klein, Isadora   3Gab   1031
Klopman (Nihilist)   Last   979
Knee-cap factory   RedH   182
Knees of trousers, as a clue   RedH   184
Kneller (Godfrey)   Houn   749
Knife (*see* **Weapons**)
Knight errant   Sign   129

Knighthood (see also Baronet)
    Appledore, Sir Charles   Prio   539
    Burnwell, Sir George   Bery   304
    Chandos, Sir Charles   Vall   786
    Colin (Campbell), Sir   Sign   151
    Damery, Colonel Sir James   Illu   984
    Falder, Sir Dennis   Shos   1110
    Falder, Sir James   Shos   1103
    Falder, Sir William   Shos   1110
    Ffolliot, Sir George   Wist   876
    Gilchrist, Sir Jabez   3Stu   600
    Hardy, Sir Charles   Seco   666
    Hardy, Sir John   Empt   484
    Holdernesse, Duke of, K.G.   Prio   539
    Holly, Sir Edward   Glor   375
    Lewis, Sir George   Illu   984
    Meek, Sir Jasper   Dyin   933
    Moran, Sir Augustus, C.B.   Empt   494
    Morland, Sir John   Houn   736
    Musgrave, Sir Ralph   Musg   397
    Oakshott, Sir Leslie   Illu   993
    Saunders, Sir James   Blan   1010
    Soames, Sir Cathcart   Prio   540
    Walter, Sir James   Bruc   917
Knighthood, Holmes refuses   3Gar   1044
Knight's Place   Sign   122
Knot, as a clue   Card   891
Knox, Jack   Vall   849
Knuckles, as a clue   Cree   1080
Kramm, Von, Count   Scan   164
Kratides, Paul   Gree   440
Kratides, Sophy   Gree   441
Ku Klux Klan   Five   226

L

Laboratory, chemical		
Bart's	Stud	17
Bartholomew Sholto's	Sign	109
Laburnum Lodge (house)		
Villa (house)	SixN	590
Laburnum Vale	SixN	590
Lachine (house)	Croo	413
Ladder	Stud	47
	Copp	330
Lady Day (March 25)	Resi	426
March quarter day	Wist	873
Lafter Hall (house)	Houn	678
Lag	Maza	1019
"La Jeune Fille a l'Agneau" (painting)	Vall	776
Lake Saloon (Chicago)	Vall	828
Lal Chowdar	Sign	103
Lal Rao	Sign	120
Lama, Head	Empt	488
Lamb	Wist	879
Lamberley	Suss	1035
Lambeth	Sign	115
Lamp (*see also* Lantern)	Sign	100
	Sign	106
	Sign	141

Lamp (*see also* Lantern) (cont'd)

	Scan	172
	Five	218
	Twis	231
	Twis	237
	Twis	240
	Blue	253
	Spec	262
	Spec	269
	Spec	271
	Engr	280
	Bery	314
	Yell	360
	Glor	379
	Musg	389
(2)	Reig	403
	Croo	414
	Resi	424
	Resi	429
(2)	Gree	439
	Fina	469
	Prio	545
	Prio	552
	Prio	553
	Blac	561
	Chas	572
	Chas	573
	Chas	575
	SixN	587
	SixN	591
	Gold	608
	Gold	613
	Miss	631
	Houn	683
	Houn	702
	Houn	703
	Houn	749
	Houn	756

Lamp (*see also* Lantern) (cont'd)

	Houn	759
	Vall	775
	Vall	782
	Vall	809
	Vall	815
	Bruc	929
	Dyin	935
	Devi	963
	Devi	964
	Last	974
	Illu	996
	Blan	1003
	Blan	1005
	Cree	1080
as a signal	Spec	269
	Dyin	978
gate	Gree	444
hand	Vall	872
naval (code)	Last	974
night light	Nava	461
oil	Twis	231
	Engr	286
	Vall	810
	Vall	815
	Vall	818
	Devi	964
railroad	Vall	815
red (doctor's)	SixN	587
red, signal (railway)	Gree	441
side (carriage)	Sign	106
	Resi	424
	Prio	552
	Chas	573
silver dove	Sign	100
spirit	Nava	450
	Gold	613

356 ◼ *Good Old Index*

Lancashire		Prio	539
Lancaster, James		Blac	569
Lancaster Gate		Nobl	289
Lancet		Houn	671
		Blan	1011
Landau (carriage)		Scan	168
		Silv	340
Lander (Scowrer)		Vall	857
Landladies (*see also* Housekeepers)			
Madame Charpentier		Stud	41
Mrs. Hudson (*which see*)			
Widow MacNamara		Vall	830
Mrs. Merrilow		Veil	1095
Mrs. Turner	(?)	Scan	170
Mrs. Warren		RedC	901
of 221B		Stud	23
Landlady's daughter		Stud	44
		Miss	635
Langham Hotel		Sign	94
		Scan	166
		Lady	947
Langmere		Glor	374
Langur (monkey)		Cree	1082
Lanner, Inspector		Resi	431
Lantern (*see also* Lamp)		Stud	35
		Sign	99
		Sign	106
		Sign	108
		Sign	117
		Sign	137
		Sign	153
		RedH	187
		Iden	188
		Twis	233
		Spec	271
		Engr	279
		Engr	283

Lantern (*see also* Lamp) (cont'd)	Silv	337
	Musg	395
	Gree	445
	Empt	492
	Prio	545
	Chas	577
	SixN	592
	Houn	677
	Vall	775
	Wist	878
	RedC	909
	Bruc	925
	Veil	1097
	Shos	1110
bull's eye	Sign	117
dark	Sign	106
	Sign	117
	RedH	187
	Spec	271
	Empt	492
	Chas	577
	SixN	592
	Wist	878
	Bruc	925
	Shos	1110
pocket	Sign	99
	Wist	878
reflector	Vall	775
safety	Vall	815
Larbey, Mrs. (victim)	Vall	853
Larch (tree)	Stud	71
Lark Hall Lane	Sign	99
La Rothiere, Louis	Seco	654
	Bruc	925
La Scala (opera house)	Scan	165
Lascar	Twis	232
Lassus (Orlandus)	Bruc	929

358 ◻ *Good Old Index*

Last offices	Houn	745
Latchkey	Stud	40
Latimer, Harold	Gree	438
Latimer's (shoemaker)	Lady	942
Latin book	Stud	38
Latin characters, in printing	Stud	33
Latin quotations	Stud	86
	RedH	177
	Blue	251
	Abbe	650
Latter-Day Saints	Stud	59
Laudanum	Twis	229
Lauder (Scotland)	Empt	494
Laurel	RedH	184
	Spec	271
	Norw	503
	Soli	535
	Chas	577
	Vall	804
	Bruc	924
	Illu	998
	Blan	1005
Lauriston Gardens	Stud	26
Lausanne (Switzerland)	Lady	942
Law, British, elastic	Illu	999
Law Court	Gree	438
Law, manorial	Houn	715
Law, none to touch the scoundrel	Iden	198
Lawler (Scowrer)	Vall	848
Lawyer (*see also* Barrister, Solicitor)	Five	220
	Yell	353
	Vall	843
	RedC	911
	3Gar	1045
Le Brun (inquiry agent)	Illu	989
Le Villard, Francois	Sign	90
Lead foil	RedH	187

Leadenhall Street	Iden	194
Leases	Norw	500
Leatherhead	Spec	259
Lebanon (Pennsylvania)	RedH	178
Lecoq (character)	Stud	25
Lee (Kent)	Twis	233
	Wist	871
Lee (mine-owner)	Vall	836
Lee, General (Robert E.)	Five	219
Leech, red	Gold	607
Leeds Mercury (newspaper)	Houn	687
Lefevre (criminal)	Stud	18
Legion of Honour	Gold	607
Leicester	Vall	806
Lens, use of (*see* Sherlock Holmes)		
Leonardo (strong man)	Veil	1097
Leper hospital	Blan	1010
Lepidoptera	Houn	711
Leprosy	Blan	1012
Les Huguenots (Meyerbeer)	Houn	766
Lestrade, G.	Stud	22
	Sign	90
	Bosc	204
	Nobl	288
	Empt	491
	Norw	498
	Chas	581
	SixN	582
	Seco	658
	Houn	752
	Card	890
	Bruc	916
	Lady	948
	3Gar	1051
beady eyes of	Stud	50
best of professionals	Houn	752
bull-dog features	Seco	659

Lestrade, G. (cont'd)
    bull-dog tenacity — Card 895
    cock-a-doodle victory cry — Norw 505
    devoid of reason — Card 895
    ferret-like — Stud 29
        Bosc 207
        Card 891
    furtiveness of — Bosc 207
    G., first initial — Card 898
    sallow, rat-faced — Stud 22
    small, wiry bulldog — Houn 754

Lesurier, Madame — Silv 342
Letter-weight, ivory — Reig 399
Leturier of Montpellier — Stud 84
Leuk (Switzerland) — Fina 477
Leverstoke, Lord — Prio 541
Leverton (detective) — RedC 908
Lewes — Lion 1086
Lewis, Sir George — Illu 984
Lewisham — Reti 1113
Lewisham gang — Abbe 637
Lexington, Mrs. (housekeeper) — Norw 504
Lhassa (Tibet) — Empt 488
Liberal administration — Stud 41
Liberal candidate — Houn 676
Library, London — Illu 994
Library, rector's — Vall 811
License, marriage — Scan 169
    Copp 332

Lieder, **Mendelssohn's** — Stud 22
Liege — Stud 38
Life preserver — Bery 316
    Gree 445
    Bruc 930

Light Blues (Cambridge Varsity) — Miss 633
Lighthouses — Nava 456
    Veil 1095

Lighting (*see* candles, gas, electric, lamps, lanterns)

Lightning	Musg	393
	Chas	576
Lime (tree)	Glor	374
Lime-cream	Blue	246
Lime Street	Maza	1020
Lincoln, Abraham	Thor	1058
Linder, Max and Co.	Vall	836
Linoleum	Five	230
	Croo	411
	Nava	453
Lion	Seco	652
	Devi	961
	Maza	1016
Sahara King	Veil	1097
Liquor (*see* Alcohol)		
List slippers	Nava	453
Literary references and allusions (*see also* Sherlock Holmes)		
Anthropological Journal	Card	896
Arabian Nights	Nobl	296
Balzac	Iden	197
Baxter (for Bradford)	Bosc	217
Bible (*see also* Biblical Quotations/Allusions	Sign	140
	Iden	195
	Croo	422
	Houn	675
	Vall	772
Boswell	Scan	164
Bradford (Baxter)	Bosc	217
Bradshaw	Copp	322
	Vall	772
British Birds	Empt	485
British Medical Journal	Stoc	362
	Blan	1011

Literary references and allusions (see also Sherlock Holmes) (cont'd)

Carlyle	Stud	21
	Sign	121
Catullus	Empt	485
Clarendon, Lord	Houn	674
Continental Gazetteer	Scan	163
Crockford	Reti	1117
Cuvier	Five	225
Darwin	Stud	37
	Stud	41
Decameron	Stud	30
De Jure inter Gentes	Stud	38
De Quincy	Twis	229
Don Juan (Byron)	Musg	389
Dynamics of an Asteroid	Vall	770
Encyclopedia, American	Five	225
Encyclopedia Britannica	RedH	181
Eckermann (*Voodooism and the Negroid Religion*)	Wist	887
Flaubert, Gustave	RedH	190
Gaboriau	Stud	25
Goethe	Sign	115
	Sign	157
Grimm (brothers)	Suss	1034
Hafiz	Iden	201
Heavy Game of the Western Himalayas (Moran)	Empt	494
Holy War, The	Empt	485
Homer, Pope's	Reig	399
Horace	Stud	86
	Iden	201
Horace, Huxtable's Sidelights on	Prio	540
Lancet	Houn	671
	Blan	1011
Les Huguenots (Meyerbeer)	Houn	766
Martyrdom of Man	Sign	97

Literary references and allusions (see also Sherlock Holmes) (cont'd)

Meredith, George	Bosc	210
Murger (*Vie de Boheme*)	Stud	39
Origin of Tree Worship	Empt	485
Out of Doors	Lion	1093
Petrarch	Bosc	207
Pickwick (Dickens)	Chas	573
Poe	Stud	24
	Resi	423
	Card	888
Pope	Reig	399
prayerbook	Soli	535
Richter, Jean Paul	Sign	121
Reade, Winwood	Sign	97
	Sign	137
Russell, Clark	Five	218
Sand, George	RedH	190
Shakespeare, First Folio	3Gab	1027
Shakespearean Quotations/Allusions		
The game is afoot. (H)	Abbe	636
the game was afoot. (W)	Wist	879

        "The game's afoot!"
            Henry V
                Act III Scene 1
                Line 32
      "the game is afoot"
        Henry IV Part 1
            Act I Scene 3
            Line 278

Literary references and allusions (*see also* **Sherlock Holmes**),
  Shakespearean Quotations/Allusions (cont'd)

Journeys end in lovers' meetings, (H)	Empt	492
Journeys end with lovers' meetings. (H)	RedC	908

      "Journeys end in lovers meeting,"
      Twelfth Night
        Act II Scene 3
        Line 43

A touch, Watson-an undeniable touch! (H)	Houn	697
A touch! A distinct touch! (H)	Vall	769

      "[A touch, a touch,] I do confess't."
      Hamlet
        Act V Scene 2
        Line 286

it would make all fiction most stale and unprofitable. (H)	Iden	191

      "How [weary], stale, flat, and unprofitable seem to me"
      Hamlet
        Act I Scene 2
        Line 133

Literary references and allusions (*see also* Sherlock Holmes),
Shakespearean Quotations/Allusions (cont'd)

Thrice is he armed who hath his quarrel just. (H) *"Thrice is he arm'd that hath his quarrel just;"* **Henry VI Part 2** Act III Scene 2 Line 233	Lady	950
I trust that age doth not wither nor custom stale my infinite variety, (H) *"Age cannot wither her, nor custom stale her infinite variety."* **Antony and Cleopatra** Act II Scene 2 Line 234–5	Empt	489
the landlady babbled of green peas at seven-thirty. (H) *"'a babbl'd of green fields."* **Henry V** Act II Scene 3 Line 17	3Stu	603
All is well that ends well, (H) **All's Well That Ends Well**	Sign	141

Literary references and allusions (*see also* Sherlock Holmes),
Shakespearean Quotations/Allusions (cont'd)

    Grasp the nettle, Watson! (H)   Maza   1015
        "out of this nettle, danger, we pluck this flower, safety."
        Henry IV Part I
          Act II Scene 3
          Line 9

    You can write me down an ass this time, Watson, (H)   Bruc   929
        "O that he were here to write me down an ass!"
        Much Ado About Nothing
          Act IV Scene 2
          Lines 75–6

    A strange enigma is man! (H)   Sign   137
        "What [a] piece of work is a man,"
        Hamlet
          Act II Scene 2
          Lines 303–4

    Violence does, in truth, recoil upon the violent, (H)   Spec   272
        "These violent delights have violent ends,"
        Romeo and Juliet
          Act II Scene 6
          Line 9

Literary references and allusions (*see also* Sherlock Holmes),
  Shakespearean Quotations/Allusions (cont'd)
    Who is Cadogan West, and what is he to Mycroft? (H)   Bruc   915
      "What's Hecuba to him, or he to [Hecuba],"
      Hamlet
        Act II Scene 2
        Line 559

    Ah, thereby hangs a rather painful tale. (H)   Bosc   210
      "and thereby hangs a tale."
      The Taming of the Shrew
        Acts IV Scene 1
        Line 58
      As You Like It
        Act II Scene 7
        Line 28
      "Well, thereby hangs a tale"
      The Merry Wives of Windsor
        Act I Scene 4
        Line 149
      "O, thereby hangs a tail."
      Othello
        Act III Scene 1
        Line 8

Literary references and allusions (*see also* Sherlock Holmes),
  Shakespearean Quotations/Allusions (cont'd)

he can't be quite in the sere and yellow. (H) *"my way of life is fall'n into the sear, the yellow leaf,"* **Macbeth** Act V Scene 3 Lines 22–3	Stud	33
Alone, I did it. Behold the fruit of . . . (H) *"Alone I did it."* **Coriolanus** Act V Scene 3 Line 116	Last	978
This man's occupation is gone. (H) *"Othello's occupation's gone."* **Othello** Act III Scene 3 Line 357	Fina	477
It's not an airy nothing, you see, (H) *"The poet's pen turns them to shapes, and gives to aery nothing a local habitation"* **A Midsummer-Night's Dream** Act V Scene 1 Line 15–7	Fina	470

Literary references and allusions (*see also* Sherlock Holmes),
    Shakespearean Quotations/Allusions (cont'd)

there was method in his madness. (W)	Reig	402
there was madness in his method, (Ins. Forrester)	Reig	402

        "Though this be madness yet there is method in't."
          Hamlet
            Act II Scene 2
            Line 205

And yet the course of true love does not run quite as smoothly as one would under the circumstances expect. (W)	Houn	717

        "The course of true love never did run smooth;"
          A Midsummer-Night's Dream
            Act I Scene 1
            Line 134

But her mind was pure as snow. (Green)	Lady	947

        "be thou as chaste as ice, as pure as snow, thou shalt not escape calumny. Get thee to a nunn'ry,"
          Hamlet
            Act III Scene 1
            Lines 135–7

Literary references and allusions (*see also* Sherlock Holmes),
  Shakespearean Quotations/Allusions (cont'd)

I will go no further in this matter. (Porlock) *"We will proceed no further in this business;"* **Macbeth** Act I Scene 7 Line 31	Vall	771
as one who did not wish to have greatness thrust upon him. (McMurdo) *"Some are [born] great, some [achieve] greatness, and some have greatness thrust upon 'em."* **Twelfth Night** Act II Scene 5 Lines 145–6	Vall	832
a dark, lack-lustre eye turned upon the newcomer. *"And looking on it, with lack-lustre eye,"* **As You Like It** Act II Scene 7 Line 21	Twis	231

L ◼ 371

Literary references and allusions (*see also* Sherlock Holmes),
  Shakespearean Quotations/Allusions (cont'd)
    Holmes (dummy/statue) suddenly come to life in order to confound an enemy of the crown.   Maza   1020
      The Winter's Tale
        Act V Scene 3
        Line 103
    Croker told to go away for a year.   Abbe   650
      Love's Labour's Lost
        Act V Scene 2
        Line 821

Spectator	Blan	1005
Thoreau	Nobl	294
Three Months in the Jungle (Moran)	Empt	494
Thucydides	3Stu	597
Vie de Boheme	Stud	39
Voodooism . . .	Wist	887
Whitaker's Almanac	Vall	772
Wood, J.G.	Lion	1093
Yellow-backed novel	Bosc	209
	Copp	325
Lithotypes, of hands	Sign	91
Litmus-paper	Nava	448
Little George Street	Stud	47
Little Purlington	Reti	1117
Little Russia	Houn	754
Little Ryder Street	3Gar	1045
Liverpool	Stud	30
	Prio	541
	Vall	806
	Card	893

372 ◼ Good Old Index

Liverpool (cont'd)	Illu	994
	Maza	1020
Liverpool, Dublin and London Steam Packet Company	Card	897
Liverpool express	Stud	41
Liverpool Street Station	Danc	514
	Reti	1117
Lloyd's registers	Five	228
Locked room	Sign	109
	Croo	414
	Empt	484
Locales of case (*see* Scenes of Investigations)		
Locket	Nobl	292
	Yell	361
	Nava	449
Locus standi	Copp	332
Lodes, silver	Stud	61
Lodger, mysterious	RedC	902
	Veil	1096
Lodgekeeper (*see also* Servants)	Bosc	203
	Abbe	637
keeper	Shos	1109
McMurdo (gatekeeper)	Sign	126
Logic, rarity of	Copp	317
Lomax (sublibrarian)	Illu	994
Lombard Street	Stoc	364
Lomond, Duke of	3Gab	1031
London, bridges of		
Hammersmith	SixN	591
London	Twis	230
	Twis	233
	Gree	444
	Norw	497
	Bruc	918
	Reti	1116
Vauxhall	Sign	99

London, bridges of (cont'd)
    Waterloo

	Stud	79
	Five	227
	Twis	241
Westminster	Lady	949

London, districts and environs of

Aldersgate	RedH	184
Barking Level	Sign	138
Beckenham	Gree	443
Bermondsey	Stoc	369
Blackheath	Norw	499
	Miss	623
	Suss	1036
Blackwall	Sign	138
Bloomsbury	Blue	251
Borough, The (Southwark)	Houn	697
Brixton	Sign	121
	Nava	456
	Blac	568
	Lady	949
	3Gar	1054
Camberwell	Stud	41
	Sign	115
	Sign	121
	Iden	196
	Five	218
	Vall	775
	Lady	943
Chiswick	SixN	590
City (of London), The	Sign	137
	RedH	184
	Iden	198
	Five	227
	Twis	230
	Twis	234
	Bery	302

London, districts and environs of, City
(of London), The (cont'd)

	Yell	356
	Stoc	364
Covent Garden	Blue	251
	RedC	913
East London	Five	225
East Ham	Vall	806
Esher	Wist	871
Greenwich	Sign	124
	Engr	276
Hammersmith	Seco	655
Hampstead	Stoc	365
	Chas	572
	Vall	781
	RedC	905
Harrow	Spec	260
	3Gab	1023
Houndsditch	Stud	39
Hyde Park	Nobl	293
"The Park"	RedH	186
	Nobl	294
	Yell	351
	Empt	485
Isle of Dogs	Sign	138
Kennington	SixN	588
Kensington	RedH	186
	Gree	438
	Empt	485
	Norw	496
	SixN	585
	Wist	871
	Bruc	925
	Dyin	936
Kilburn	Blue	256
Kingston	Illu	982
Lambeth	Sign	115
Lee	Twis	233
	Wist	871

London, districts and environs of
(cont'd)

Lewisham	Abbe	637
	Reti	1113
Lower Brixton	Gree	444
Lower Camberwell	Sign	115
Lower Norwood	Norw	497
Norbury	Yell	353
Norwood	Sign	95
Nottinghill	Houn	701
	RedC	910
	Bruc	925
	Dyin	936
Oxshott	Wist	872
Paddington	Bosc	202
	Engr	274
	Stoc	362
Peckham	Stud	39
Penge	Card	890
Pinner	Yell	353
Plumstead Marshes	Sign	138
Poplar	Sign	132
Richmond	Sign	130
Rotherhithe	Dyin	932
Saffron Hill	SixN	590
St. John's Wood	Scan	167
South Brixton	Veil	1095
South London	Sign	100
Stepney	SixN	588
	Cree	1082
Streatham	Sign	121
	Bery	304
Sydenham	Norw	498
	Abbe	637
Upper Norwood	Sign	95
Wallington	Card	894
Wandsworth Common	Gree	442

London, districts and environs of (cont'd)

Willesden	Bruc	915
Wimbledon	Veil	1097
Woolwich	Sign	123
	Bruc	915

London, Streets, Squares, Places, etc. of

Admiralty Place	Bruc	916
Audley Court	Stud	32
Baker Street (*which see*)		
Barclay Square	Bruc	917
Belmont Place	Sign	123
Bentinck Street	Fina	473
Berkeley Square	Illu	991
Blandford Street	Empt	489
Bond Street		
Kennington	Sign	122
Westminster	Silv	342
	Houn	692
Bow Street	Twis	241
Brixton Road	Stud	26
	Blue	253
	Lady	953
Broad Street	Sign	123
Brook Street	Resi	425
Camberwell Road	Stud	43
Campden House Road	SixN	586
Campden Mansions	Bruc	925
Cannon Street	Twis	233
Carlton House Terrace	Prio	539
Carlton Terrace	Last	973
Caulfield Gardens	Bruc	925
Cavendish Square	Resi	425
	Empt	489

London, Streets, Squares, Places, etc.
  of (cont'd)
    Charing Cross

	Twis	240
	Gree	438
	Wist	870
	Thor	1054
Charles Street	Nava	451
Church Row	Chas	577
Church Street	Empt	485
	SixN	588
Coburg Square	RedH	178
Cold Harbour Lane	Sign	99
Commercial Road	Cree	1078
Conduit Street	Empt	494
Craven Street	Houn	763
Cross Street (Croydon)	Card	890
Curzon Square	Wist	887
Curzon Street	Shos	1102
Downing Street	Nava	459
Draper Gardens	Stoc	364
Duncan Street	Stud	39
Edgeware Road	Scan	168
	3Gar	1047
Edmonton Street	Wist	887
Endell Street	Blue	252
Farrington (don) Street	RedH	187
Fenchurch Street	Iden	196
Firbank Villas	Lady	952
Fleet Street	RedH	178
	Resi	424
Fresno Street	Twis	234
Fulham Road	Houn	762
Glasshouse Street	Illu	993
Gloucester Road	Bruc	925
Godolphin Street	Seco	655
Goodge Street	Blue	245
Gordon Square	Nobl	299

London, Streets, Squares, Places, etc.
of (cont'd)

Gray's Inn Road	Miss	628
Great George Street	Bruc	925
Great Orme Street	RedC	905
Great Peter Street	Sign	125
Gresham Buildings	Norw	498
Grosvenor Square	3Gab	1031
Half Moon Street	Illu	995
Hanover Square	Nobl	289
Harley Street	Blue	251
	Resi	430
	Devi	955
	Shos	1103
Henrietta Street	Stud	34
High Holborn	Wist	878
High Street	SixN	588
Holborn	Blue	251
Holland Grove	Stud	34
Howe Street	RedC	905
Ivy Lane	Nava	450
Kennington Lane	Sign	121
Kennington Park Gate	Stud	32
Kennington Road	SixN	583
	Lady	948
King Edward Street	RedH	182
King's Cross	Iden	195
Knight's Place	Sign	122
Lancaster Gate	Nobl	289
Lark Hall Lane	Sign	99
Lauriston Gardens	Stud	26
Leadenhall Street	Iden	194
Lime Street	Maza	1020
Little George Street	Stud	47
Little Ryder Street	3Gar	1045
Lombard Street	Stoc	364
London Road	Twis	240

L ◻ 379

London, Streets, Squares, Places, etc.
  of (cont'd)

Lowther Arcade	Fina	474
Lower Brixton Road	SixN	583
Lower Burke Street	Dyin	935
Lord Street	Blac	568
Lyon Place	Iden	196
Manchester Street	Empt	489
Marylebone Lane	Fina	473
Mayfield Place	Stud	39
Miles Street	Sign	122
Mincing Lane	Suss	1034
Minories, The	Maza	1014
Montague Place	Copp	318
Montague Street	Musg	387
Moorside Gardens	Maza	1014
Mortimer Street	Fina	474
Nine Elms (Lane)	Sign	122
Northumberland Avenue	Nobl	300
	Gree	438
	Illu	984
Old Jewry	Suss	1034
Oxford Street	RedH	186
	Blue	251
	Resi	430
	Gree	438
	Fina	473
	Empt	485
	Prio	554
	Chas	577
	Gold	608
	Houn	690
	Houn	740
	Lady	942
Pall Mall	Gree	436
	Fina	473
	Bruc	914

380 ◘ *Good Old Index*

London, Streets, Squares, Places, etc.
  of (cont'd)

Park Lane	Empt	483
Pinchin Lane	Sign	115
Pitt Street	SixN	585
Pope's Court	RedH	178
Potter's Terrace	Stoc	365
Poultney Square	Lady	949
Prince's Street	Sign	123
Priory Road	Sign	99
Queen Anne Street	Illu	984
Ratcliffe Highway	Stud	41
	Blac	567
Regent Circus	Gree	436
	Chas	582
Regent Street	Scan	168
	Bosc	216
	Houn	690
	Illu	993
Robert Street	Sign	99
Rochester Row	Sign	99
Russell Square	Danc	512
St. James's Square	Gree	436
	Illu	994
St. James's Street	3Gab	1028
Saxe-Coburg Square	RedH	183
Serpentine Avenue	Scan	167
Serpentine Mews	Scan	168
Shaftesbury Avenue	Gree	438
Stockwell Place	Sign	99
Strand, The	Stud	15
	Stud	30
	Sign	98
	RedH	184
	Resi	424
	Fina	474

London, Streets, Squares, Places, etc. of, Strand, The (cont'd)

	Miss	624
	Houn	688
	Illu	988
Swandam Lane	Twis	234
Sydenham Road	Norw	498
Threadneedle Street	Twis	235
	Bery	302
Throgmorton Street	Blan	1000
Torquay Terrace	Stud	41
Tottenham Court Road	Iden	193
	Blue	245
	Card	894
	RedC	905
Trafalgar Square	Nobl	295
	Houn	697
Turpey Street	Houn	697
Upper Swandam Lane	Twis	230
Vauxhall Bridge Road	Sign	99
Vere Street	Fina	473
Victoria Street	Engr	274
Vincent Square	Sign	99
Waterloo Bridge Road	Twis	241
Waterloo Road	3Gar	1052
Welbeck Street	Fina	473
Wellington Street	Twis	241
Westminster Road	Lady	948
Whitehall Terrace	Seco	651
	Bruc	914
	Maza	1018
Wigmore Street	Blue	251
Wimpole Street	Blue	251
Wordsworth Road	Sign	99
London Bridge	Twis	230
	Twis	233
	Gree	444
	Norw	497

382 ◘ Good Old Index

London Bridge (cont'd)	Bruc	918
	Reti	1116
London dangers	RedC	909
London Library	Illu	994
London Road	Twis	240
London University	Stud	15
	Resi	425
Lone Star (ship)	Five	228
Long Down	Houn	714
Long Island cave mystery	RedC	908
Long vacation	Glor	374
Lopez (secretary)	Wist	886
Lord Street	Blac	568
Lothario	Reti	1116
Louisiana	Five	226
Lowenstein, H.	Cree	1082
Lower Brixton	Gree	444
Lower Brixton Road	SixN	583
Lower Burke Street	Dyin	935
Lower Camberwell	Sign	115
Lower Gill Moor	Prio	545
Lower Grove Road (Reading)	SixN	590
Lower Norwood	Norw	497
Lowther Arcade	Fina	474
Lucas (alias)	Wist	882
Lucas, Eduardo	Seco	654
Lucca, Emilia	RedC	910
Lucca, Gennaro	RedC	910
Lucerne (Switzerland)	Fina	478
	3Gab	1027
Lucknow (India)	Sign	146
Lumbago	Cree	1074
Lumber-room	Stud	21
	Five	225
at Baker street	SixN	591
box room	Bery	305
	Lion	1090

Lunkah	Sign	91
Lurcher (dog)	Sign	117
Luxembourg	Fina	476
Lyceum Theater	Sign	95
Lynch, Victor	Suss	1034
Lynch law (Judge Lynch)	Vall	838
Lynx	Stud	69
Lyon Place	Iden	196
Lyons (France)	Reig	398
Lyons, Laura	Houn	730

Maberley, Douglas	3Gab	1025
Maberley, Mary	3Gab	1024
Maberley, Mortimer	3Gab	1024
Machiavellian intellect, Watson's	Vall	771
Mackintosh (coat)	Silv	338
Mackleton	Prio	539
Macphail (coachman)	Cree	1080
Madeira	3Gab	1030
Madras (India)	Sign	152
Madrid (Spain)	Seco	666
	Wist	885
Mafia	SixN	590
Magnifying glass, use of (*see* Sherlock Holmes—lens)		
Mahratta (Indian people)	Vall	772
Maid (*see also* servants)	Stud	40
	Scan	168
	Bosc	202
	Bosc	211
(3)	Bery	304
	Yell	357
	Glor	377

386 ◘ *Good Old Index*

Maid (*see also* servants) (cont'd)			
	(8)	Seco	651
	(2)	Musg	388
		Croo	413
		Resi	431
		Seco	651
		Houn	692
		Houn	704
		Houn	733
		Card	891
		Bruc	914
		3Gar	1027
Agatha		Chas	577
Alice		Nobl	293
Carrie Evans		Shos	1105
Catherine Cusack		Blue	248
Dolores		Suss	1037
Edith Baxter		Silv	337
Jane Stewart		Croo	414
Lucretia Venucci		SixN	594
Lucy Parr		Bery	304
Marie Devine		Lady	943
Mary		Five	220
Mary		3Gab	1029
Mary Jane		Scan	162
Rachel Howells		Musg	389
Saunders		Danc	518
Susan Stockdale		3Gab	1026
Susan Tarlton		Gold	609
Theresa Wright		Abbe	638
Maids, Watson's		Scan	162
		Bosc	202
		Engr	274
		Empt	485
Mail-boats		Sign	155
Mail delivery		Scan	163
		Iden	194
		Twis	238

Mail delivery (cont'd)	Reig	402
	Resi	423
	Danc	512
	Soli	533
	Prio	542
	Blac	567
	Houn	685
	Vall	770
	Card	888
	3Gab	1026
	Suss	1033
	Cree	1079
	Veil	1102
	Shos	1103
Maiwand, Battle of	Stud	15
Malay	Twis	231
Malay pilgrims	Sign	155
Malingering, as an art	Dyin	941
Malplaquet, date of (1709)	Reig	403
Malthus, principles of	Stud	41
Manaos (Brazil)	Thor	1060
Manchester Street	Empt	489
Manders (Scowrer)	Vall	851
Mangrove (tree)	Sign	144
Manor House case	Gree	437
Manorial law	Houn	715
Mansel (Scowrer)	Vall	838
Manson (iron-works owner)	Vall	836
Man upon the tor	Houn	726
Manuscript, identification of	Musg	392
	Houn	673
Map	Stud	54
	Stud	58
	Stud	78
	Sign	98
	Sign	151
	Sign	154

Map (cont'd)   Bosc   214
                                                         Glor   383
                                                         Musg   389
                                                         Nava   451
                                                         Blac   561
                                                         SixN   586
                                                         Gold   610
                                                         Vall   804
                                                         Bruc   925
                                                         Lady   944
    Ordnance map   Engr   285
                                                         Prio   545
                                                         Houn   683
Map-dealer (Stamford's)   Houn   683
Mapleton   Silv   336
Marcini's Restaurant   Houn   766
Marconi (wireless codes)   Last   975
Mare's-tail   Houn   709
Marengo (battle)   Abbe   644
Margate   Seco   657
                                                         Veil   1101
Marines   Glor   381
    Major   Spec   260
    Royal Marine Light Infantry   Stud   25
Marker, Mrs. (housekeeper)   Gold   609
Market Square (Vermissa)   Vall   841
Market Street (Chicago)   Vall   828
Marley Creek (Vermissa)   Vall   836
Marriage, forced   Soli   536
Marriage license   Scan   169
                                                         Copp   332
                                                         Soli   536
Marseilles (France)   Iden   192
Marsham   Abbe   636
Martha (servant)   Last   974
Martin, Inspector   Danc   517
Martin, Lieutenant   Glor   383

Martini bullet	Sign	118
Martyrdom of Man	Sign	97
Marvin, Captain Teddy	Vall	831
Marx and Co. (clothiers)	Wist	878
Mary (servant)	Five	220
Mary (maid)	3Gab	1029
Mary Jane (servant)	Scan	162
Marylebone Lane	Fina	473
Mask	Scan	164
	Yell	361
	Chas	577
Mason (platelayer)	Bruc	915
Mason (criminal)	Stud	18
Mason, John	Shos	1103
Mason, Mrs. (nurse)	Suss	1037
Mason, White	Vall	778
Mason (*see* Freemason)		
Masonic devices	Stud	30
	RedH	177
	Reti	1116
Mastiff	Copp	326
	Houn	671
	Houn	757
Matches, burnt, deductions from	Silv	343
	RedC	903
Mathews (adversary)	Empt	494
Matilda Briggs (ship)	Suss	1031
Maudsley (ex-convict)	Blue	256
Maupertuis, Baron	Reig	398
Mauritius	Copp	332
Mawson & Williams (stockbrokers)	Stoc	364
Maxillary curve	Houn	686
May Day (steam packet)	Card	893
Mayfield Place	Stud	39
Maynooth, Earl of	Empt	483
Maynooth, Lady	Empt	483
Mazarin Stone	Maza	1014

390 ◻ Good Old Index

MacDonald, Inspector Alec	Vall	773
MacKinnon, Inspector	Reti	1119
MacNamara, widow	Vall	830
MacPherson, Constable	Seco	661
McCarthy, Charles	Bosc	203
McCarthy, James	Bosc	203
McCauley (victim)	Five	223
McFarlane, John Hector	Norw	497
McFarlane, Mr. & Mrs.	Norw	499
McFarlane's carriage building depot	RedH	185
McGinty, Bodymaster John	Vall	797
McGregor, Mrs.	Stud	54
McLaren, Miles	3Stu	601
McMurdo (prizefighter)	Sign	106
McMurdo, John	Vall	817
McPherson, Fitzroy	Lion	1084
McQuire's camp	Nobl	298
Mecca (Arabia)	Empt	488
Medical Directory	Houn	671
Medieval (*see* Middle Ages)		
Mediterranean (Sea)	Nava	450
	Illu	986
Meek, Sir Jasper	Dyin	933
Meiringen (Switzerland)	Fina	477
Melas (Greek interpreter)	Gree	438
Melbourne (Australia)	Bosc	216
Melville (retired brewer)	Wist	871
Member (of Parliament)	Musg	388
Mendelssohn's *Lieder*	Stud	22
Meningitis, spinal, suspected	Suss	1039
Menzies (victim)	Vall	850
Mercer (Holmes's agent)	Cree	1078
Meredith, George	Bosc	210
Mereer (ship's officer)	Glor	382
Merivale, Inspector	Shos	1102
Merridew, of abominable memory	Empt	494
Merrilow, Mrs. (landlady)	Veil	1095

Merripit House	Houn	706
Merrow, Lord	Seco	666
Merryweather (banker)	RedH	186
Merton, Sam	Maza	1014
Merton County (USA)	Vall	815
Mesmerism	Gree	446
Message, cut from newspaper	Houn	687
Messenger	SixN	585
	Bruc	925
Cartwright	Houn	691
district	Illu	996
express	SixN	592
government	Bruc	925
Metropolitan (underground line)	Bruc	915
Metropolitan Station	Bery	301
Meunier, Oscar	Empt	489
Mews	Stud	47
	Empt	489
Serpentine Mews	Scan	168
Mexborough Private Hotel	Houn	763
Meyer, Adolph	Bruc	925
Meyers (bootmaker) Toronto	Houn	760
Mica	Stud	54
Michael (stablehand)	Suss	1037
Michaelmas	Houn	674
Michigan	Vall	821
Microscope (*see also* Sherlock Holmes—lens)	Stud	18
	3Gar	1048
	Shos	1102
high-powered lens	Scan	161
Mid-Devon (parliamentary division)	Houn	676
Middle Ages	Sign	134
	Prio	558
	3Stu	602
	Bruc	913
	Last	972
	Illu	991

392 ◼ *Good Old Index*

Middle Ages (cont'd)	Suss	1033
	Reti	1120
Middlesex	Twis	237
	Yell	353
Middlesex Corps	Blan	1000
Middleton (landowner)	Houn	736
Midianites	Lady	944
Midland Electric Company	Soli	529
Midlands	Stoc	372
Milano (Italy)	3Gab	1027
Miles, Hon. Miss	Chas	574
Miles Street	Sign	122
Military (*see* Army and Navy)		
Milk	Stud	49
	Spec	268
	Nobl	294
	Prio	539
	Veil	1096
Milkboy	Stud	47
Milkman	Veil	1096
Millar, Flora	Nobl	290
Millbank Penitentiary	Sign	125
Miller Hill (Vermissa)	Vall	840
Milliner's bill, as a clue	Silv	350
Milman (victim)	Vall	822
Milner, Godfrey	Empt	484
Milverton, Charles Augustus	Chas	572
Mincing Lane	Suss	1034
Mind, capacity, and size of brain	Stud	21
	Blue	247
Mine, mining		
gold	Bosc	208
	Nobl	292
	Vall	792
	Thor	1055
salt	Gold	620

Mine, mining (cont'd)
   tin

Ming dynasty
Minories
Minstrel's gallery
Miracle plays
Mirror

	Houn	759
	Devi	958
	Illu	995
	Maza	1014
	Houn	703
	Sign	134
	Stud	66
	Sign	134
	Bery	310
	Bery	311
	Copp	325
	Seco	651
	Vall	826
	RedC	905
	Dyin	937
	Lady	953
	Veil	1101

Mirror, coffee pot as   Houn   669
Miser   Stud   86
    Sign   102
    Sign   104
    Miss   624
    Reti   1116

Mississippi River   Stud   58
Missouri River   Stud   54
Mitral valve   Sign   100
Mitton, John   Seco   655
Moat   Vall   779
Mob cap   Lady   946
Moffat (murderer)   Resi   434
Mohammedans   Sign   120
Monaghan, County (Ireland)   Vall   821
Money (*see* coins and currency)
Money lenders   Shos   1108
Mongoose   Croo   421
Monocle   Silv   340

Monocle case	Bery	303
Monographs (*see also* Sherlock Holmes, Writings)		
Armstrong, Leslie (medical treatise)	Miss	629
Gruner, Baron (Chinese pottery)	Illu	987
Moran, Sebastian		
(*Heavy Game of the Western Himalayas*)	Empt	494
(*Three Months in the Jungle*)	Empt	494
Mortimer, James (medical essays)	Houn	671
Shlessinger, Dr. (the kingdom of the Midianites)	Lady	944
Staff-Commander (deep-sea fishes)	Scan	165
Trevelyan, Percy (obscure nervous lesions)	Resi	425
Monomania	Engr	281
	SixN	594
Montague Place	Copp	318
Montague Street	Musg	387
Montalva, Marquess of	Wist	887
Montana	Nobl	298
Montgomery, Inspector	Card	898
Montmarte (Paris)	Illu	989
Montpellier (France)	Stud	18
	Empt	488
	Lady	943
Montpensier, Madame	Houn	761
Montrachet (wine)	Veil	1098
Moon, in cases	Stud	72
	Sign	106
	Sign	139
	Engr	283
	Copp	326
	Musg	397
	Nava	467
	Danc	515
	Prio	546

Moon, in cases (cont'd)	Abbe	639
	Houn	674
	Houn	703
	Houn	724
	Houn	744
	Houn	755
	Vall	838
	Vall	852
	Last	980
	Blan	1003
	Cree	1075
	Cree	1080
	Shos	1105
half-moon	Sign	106
	Houn	703
	Houn	756
	Vall	838
	Blan	1003
	Cree	1080
Moonlight, identification by	Sign	109
	Cree	1075
Moor	Silv	336
	Prio	544
	Houn	700
	Houn	724
	Devi	955
	Thor	1069
Moor farmers	Prio	546
Moor-gate	Houn	679
	Houn	714
Moorhouse (rugby player)	Miss	622
Moorside Gardens	Maza	1014
Moorville (Kansas)	3Gar	1045
Moosmoor-cum-Little-Purlington	Reti	1117
Moran (lodge-keeper)	Bosc	212
Moran, Sir Augustus	Empt	494

Moran, Colonel Sebastian	Empt	484
	Last	979
	Illu	985
6000 per year	Vall	777
second most dangerous man in London	Empt	494
Moran. Patience	Bosc	203
Morcar, Countess of	Blue	248
Morecroft (alias)	3Gar	1051
Morgan (poisoner)	Empt	494
Moriarty, Colonel James	Fina	469
Moriarty, Professor	Fina	470
	Empt	486
	Norw	496
	Miss	630
	Vall	769
	Last	979
	Illu	985
appearance	Fina	472
as army coach	Fina	471
and binomial theorem	Fina	470
brain of the first order	Fina	471
brother James	Fina	469
	Empt	494
brother a stationmaster	Vall	776
calls on Holmes	Fina	472
evidence of wealth of	Vall	776
eyes, gray	Empt	486
first brains of Europe, one of	Vall	771
first mention of	Fina	469
gang, two remaining	Empt	486
genius of	Fina	471
	Empt	494
	Vall	770
as greatest schemer of all time	Vall	769
and Greuze painting	Vall	775
and mathematical chair	Fina	470

Moriarty, Professor (cont'd)
    as most dangerous criminal   Fina   477
    as Napoleon of Crime   Fina   471
    as Napoleon-gone wrong   Vall   777
    spider-like   Norw   496
    the late   Norw   496
        Miss   630
        Illu   985
    Watson had heard of   Vall   769
    Watson had not heard of   Fina   470
        Empt   494
Morland, Sir John   Houn   736
Mormons   Stud   57
Morning Chronicle (newspaper)   RedH   178
Morning Post (newspaper)   Nobl   288
        Chas   574
        Illu   999
Morocco leather   Sign   89
        Blue   248
        Bery   303
Moroni, Angel   Stud   57
Morphine (morphia)   Sign   89
        Illu   993
        Illu   998
        Cree   1081
        Lion   1092
Morphy, Alice   Cree   1072
Morphy, Professor   Cree   1072
Morris (Scowrer)   Vall   836
Morris, Fred   Vall   842
Morris, William (alias)   RedH   182
Morrison, Annie   Reig   411
Morrison, Miss   Croo   414
Morrison, Morrison and Dodd   Suss   1034
Morstan, Captain Arthur   Sign   93
Morstan, Mary   Sign   93

398 ◻ Good Old Index

Mortgage	Spec	259
	Norw	500
Mortimer (gardener)	Gold	609
Mortimer, James	Houn	669
Mortimer Street	Fina	474
Mortimer's (tobacconist)	RedH	185
Morton (rugby player)	Miss	623
Morton, Cyril	Soli	528
Morton, Inspector	Dyin	936
Morton & Kennedy	Soli	538
Morton and Waylight	RedC	905
Mortuary (undertakers)	Stud	29
	SixN	586
	Lady	949
Moser (hotel manager)	Lady	944
Moss rose	Nava	455
Most accomplished swindler in Europe	Reig	398
Most dangerous man in England, one of the	Bery	313
Most dangerous man in Europe	Illu	985
Most dangerous man in London	Chas	582
Most dangerous man in London, second	Empt	494
Most daring man in London, third	RedH	184
Most interesting object in the North	Prio	558
Most lovely lady in London	Seco	656
Most unscrupulous rascal	Lady	947
Motets of Lassus	Bruc	929
Motto, Holmes's	Cree	1076
Moulton, Francis Hay	Nobl	297
Moulton, Mrs. Francis Hay (Hatty Doran)	Nobl	297
Mount Harriet (Andamans)	Sign	152
Mount-James, Lord	Miss	624
Mounts Bay	Devi	955

Mouse

Mousseline de soie
Moustache
    Anderson, Constable (ginger)
    Baldwin (grayish)
    Barker (dark)
    Crocker (golden)
    Douglas
        grizzling
        brown
    Gruner (black)
    Hope
    Leonardo
    Lucca
    Martin, Inspector
    Moran, Colonel (grizzled)
    Neligan (black)
    Norberton
    Norton
    Pycroft (yellow)
    Sylvius (dark)
    Watson

        modest
        gray
    Woodley (red)
Moustache, false
    Angel (black)
Moustache, waxed
M.R.C.S.
Mulatto cook
Muller (criminal)
Mummy

Munich (Germany)

Copp	324	
Nava	641	
Illu	988	
Twis	237	
Lion	1085	
Vall	804	
Reti	1114	
Abbe	647	
Vall	780	
Vall	827	
Illu	988	
Seco	651	
Veil	1099	
RedC	903	
Danc	518	
Empt	491	
Blac	565	
Shos	1110	
Scan	168	
Stoc	364	
Maza	1015	
Nava	449	
Chas	582	
RedC	903	
Last	974	
Soli	528	
Iden	197	
Illu	996	
Houn	669	
Wist	872	
Stud	18	
Wist	878	
Shos	1106	
Nobl	293	

Munro, Colonel Spence	Copp	318
Munro, Effie	Yell	353
Munro, Grant	Yell	353
Munsters, Royal (regiment)	Croo	412
Murcher, Constable Harry	Stud	34
Murdoch, Ian	Lion	1084
Murdoch, James	Vall	853
Murger, Henri	Stud	39
Mule	Stud	59
	Stud	68
Murillo, Don Juan	Wist	884
Murillo, papers of ex-President	Norw	496
Murphy (gypsy)	Houn	677
Murphy (Chicagoan)	Vall	820
Murphy, Major	Croo	413
Murray, *The Gallant* (orderly)	Stud	15
Murray (card-player)	Empt	484
Museum		
British	Blue	251
	Musg	387
	Houn	762
	Wist	879
	RedC	905
College of Surgeons	Houn	699
Duke of Holdernesse's	Prio	558
Garrideb's	3Gar	1048
Scotland Yard	Empt	496
Tussaud's, Madame	Maza	1019
Musgrave, Reginald	Musg	388
Musgrave, Sir Ralph	Musg	397
Musgrave Ritual	Musg	387
Musicians, composers		
Chopin	Stud	36
DeReszkes	Houn	766
Hoffman	Maza	1019
Lassus	Bruc	929
Mendelssohn	Stud	22

Musicians, composers (cont'd)

Norman-Neruda	Stud	34
Paganini	Card	894
Sarasate	RedH	184
Wagner	RedC	913
Mustang	Stud	60
Mutiny, Indian	Sign	145
	Croo	412
Muttra (India)	Sign	145
Myrtles, The (house)	Gree	443

Nail scissors, as a clue	Houn	687
Nails, brass-headed	Vall	783
Names, Personal—Given Names		
Abdullah Achmet	Sign	140
Abdullah Khan	Sign	98
Abe Slaney	Danc	521
Abel White	Sign	145
Adelbert Gruner	Illu	985
Adolph Meyer	Bruc	925
Agatha (maid)	Chas	577
Alec Cunningham	Reig	399
Alec Fairbairn	Card	899
Alec MacDonald	Vall	773
Alexander H. Garrideb	3Gar	1046
Alexander Holder	Bery	302
Alexis (nihilist)	Gold	620
Alicia Whittington, Lady	Nobl	290
Alice (maid)	Nobl	293
Alice Charpentier	Stud	44
Alice Morphy	Cree	1072
Alice Rucastle	Copp	321
Alice Turner	Bosc	215
Aloysius Doran	Nobl	289
Aloysius Garcia	Wist	870

Names, Personal—Given Names
(cont'd)

Andrew Rae	Vall	834
Anna Coram	Gold	619
Annie Fraser	Lady	947
Annie Harrison	Nava	449
Annie Morrison	Reig	411
Anthony (servant)	Houn	764
Archie (Morris)	RedH	189
Archie Stamford	Soli	527
Archie Swindon	Vall	836
Arthur, Lord Saltire	Prio	539
Arthur Cadogan West	Bruc	914
Arthur Charpentier	Stud	42
Arthur Holder	Bery	304
Arthur Morstan	Sign	94
Arthur Pinner	Stoc	365
Arthur H. Staunton	Miss	623
Arthur Willaby	Vall	838
Athelney Jones	Sign	90
Augusto Barelli	RedC	911
Augustus Moran, Sir	Empt	494
Barney Stockdale	3Gab	1024
Bartholomew Sholto	Sign	101
Bartholomew Wilson	Vall	827
Beatrice Falder, Lady	Shos	1103
Beppo	SixN	588
Bert Stevens	Norw	504
Beryl Stapleton	Houn	708
Bill (helper)	Blue	253
Billy James	Vall	822
Billy (page)	Vall	770
	Maza	1012
	Thor	1057
Birdy Edwards	Vall	835
Bob Carruthers	Soli	528
Bob Ferguson	Suss	1034

Names, Personal—Given Names
(cont'd)

Bob (Ferrier?)	Stud	54
Brenda Tregennis	Devi	956
Bromley Brown	Sign	152
Carrie Evans	Shos	1105
Cathcart Soames, Sir	Prio	540
Catherine Cusack	Blue	248
Cecil Barker	Vall	781
Cecil Forrester, Mrs.	Sign	94
Charles Appledore, Sir	Prio	539
Charles Baskerville, Sir	Houn	673
Charles Chandos, Sir	Vall	786
Charles Gorot	Nava	450
Charles Hardy, Sir	Seco	666
Charles McCarthy	Bosc	203
Charles Augustus Milverton	Chas	572
Charles Williams	Vall	849
Chester Wilcox	Vall	836
Clara St. Simon, Lady	Nobl	290
Clothilde von Saxe-Meningen	Scan	166
Culverton Smith	Dyin	935
Cyril Morton	Soli	528
Cyril Overton	Miss	622
Daulat Ras	3Stu	598
Denis Falder, Sir	Shos	1110
Dolores (maid)	Suss	1037
Dost Akbar	Sign	98
Douglas Maberley	3Gab	1025
Duncan Ross	RedH	178
Edith Appledore (Duchess of Holdernesse)	Prio	539
Edith Baxter	Silv	337
Edith Presbury	Cree	1072
Edith Woodley	Empt	483
Eduardo Lucas	Seco	654
Edward Holly, Sir	Glor	375

Names, Personal—Given Names
(cont'd)

Edward Rucastle	Copp	325
Effie Hebron (Munro)	Yell	353
Elias Openshaw	Five	219
Elias Whitney	Twis	229
Elise	Engr	283
Eliza Barrymore	Houn	722
Elizabeth Baskerville	Houn	676
Elsie Cubitt (Patrick)	Danc	512
Emilia Lucca	RedC	910
Enoch Drebber	Stud	26
Ettie Shafter	Vall	820
Eugenia Ronder	Veil	1101
Eustace Brackenstall, Sir	Abbe	637
Eustace St. Simon, Lord	Nobl	290
Eva Blackwell, Lady	Chas	573
Evans Pott	Vall	848
Ezekiah Hopkins	RedH	178
Fairdale Hobbs	RedC	901
Fitzroy McPherson	Lion	1084
Fitzroy Simpson	Silv	336
Flora Millar	Nobl	290
Frances Carfax, Lady	Lady	943
Francis Hay Moulton	Nobl	297
Francis Prosper	Bery	310
Francois Le Villard	Sign	90
Frank Moulton	Nobl	297
Fred Morris	Vall	842
Fred Porlock	Vall	769
Fritz von Waldbaum	Nava	447
Fritz	Engr	283
Gennaro Lucca	RedC	910
George Burnwell, Sir	Bery	304
George Ffolliot, Sir	Wist	876
George Lewis, Sir	Illu	984
George Tregennis	Devi	956

Names, Personal—Given Names
(cont'd)

Giuseppe Gorgiano	RedC	908
Gloria Scott (ship)	Glor	374
Godfrey Emsworth	Blan	1001
Godfrey Milner	Empt	484
Godfrey Norton	Scan	168
Godfrey Staunton	Miss	623
Grace Dunbar	Thor	1056
Grant Munro	Yell	353
Grimesby Roylott, Dr.	Spec	258
Hall Pycroft	Stoc	364
Harold Latimer	Gree	438
Harold Stackhurst	Lion	1083
Harry Murcher	Stud	34
Harry Pinner	Stoc	366
Harry Wood	Croo	421
Harvey (groom)	Shos	1106
Hatty Doran	Nobl	289
Heath Newton	Silv	347
Heinrich	Last	979
Helen Stoner	Spec	259
Henri Fournaye	Seco	659
Henry Baker	Blue	245
Henry Baskerville, Sir	Houn	677
Henry Peters (Holy)	Lady	947
Henry Staunton	Miss	623
Henry Wood	Croo	418
Herman Strauss	Vall	849
Hilda Adair	Empt	483
Hilda Trelawney Hope, Lady	Seco	656
Hill Barton	Illu	995
Hilton Cubitt	Danc	512
Hilton Soames	3Stu	596
Honoria Westphail	Spec	260
Horace Harker	SixN	585
Hosmer Angel	Iden	192

Names, Personal—Given Names
(cont'd)

Howard Garrideb	3Gar	1050
Hugh Boone	Twis	235
Hugh Pattins	Blac	569
Hugo Baskerville, c. 1640	Houn	673
Hugo Baskerville, 1742	Houn	676
Hugo de Capus	Vall	779
Hugo Oberstein	Seco	654
	Bruc	925
Hynes Hynes	Wist	876
Ian Murdoch	Lion	1084
Ikey Sanders	Maza	1018
Irene Adler	Scan	161
Isa Whitney	Twis	229
Isadora Klein	3Gab	1031
Isadora Persano	Thor	1055
Ivy Douglas	Vall	774
Jabez Gilchrist, Sir	3Stu	600
Jabez Wilson	RedH	176
Jack (Trevor) Bennett	Cree	1075
Jack, Black, of Ballarat	Bosc	216
Jack Crocker, Captain	Abbe	646
Jack Douglas	Vall	774
Jack Ferguson	Suss	1037
Jack James	Last	975
Jack Knox	Vall	849
Jack McMurdo	Vall	817
Jack Munro	Yell	354
Jack Prendergast	Glor	382
Jack Smith	Sign	123
Jack Stapleton	Houn	678
Jack Woodley	Soli	528
Jacob Shafter	Vall	818
James Armitage	Glor	381
James Barclay	Croo	412
James Cecil Barker	Vall	781

Names, Personal—Given Names
(cont'd)

James Browner	Card	893
James Calhoun, Captain	Five	228
James Carnaway	Vall	835
James Damery, Sir	Illu	984
James Desmond	Houn	695
James Dodd	Blan	1000
James Falder, Sir	Shos	1103
James Griggs	Veil	1097
James Lancaster	Prio	569
James McCarthy	Bosc	203
James Moriarty, Colonel	Fina	469
James Mortimer, Dr.	Houn	669
James Murdoch	Vall	853
James Phillimore	Thor	1055
James Ryder (Jem)	Blue	245
James Saunders, Sir Dr.	Blan	1010
James Scott	Vall	817
James Smith	Sign	124
	Soli	527
James Stanger	Vall	837
James Walter, Sir	Bruc	917
James Watson	Twis	230
James Wilder	Prio	540
James Baker Williams	Wist	876
James Windibank	Iden	192
James Winter	3Gar	1051
James (postmaster's son)	Houn	705
Jane Stewart	Croo	414
Janet Tregellis	Musg	389
Jasper Meek, Sir	Dyin	933
Jefferson Hope	Stud	51
Jefferson Hope, Sr.	Stud	60
Jem Ryder	Blue	256
Jephro Rucastle	Copp	321
Jeremiah Hayling	Engr	284

Names, Personal—Given Names
(cont'd)

Jeremy Dixon	Miss	632
Jimmy	RedC	904
John Barrymore	Houn	676
John Baskerville	Houn	676
John Clay	RedH	186
John Clayton	Houn	697
John Cobb	Bosc	205
John Scott Eccles	Wist	869
John Ferrier	Stud	57
John Garrideb	3Gar	1045
John Vincent Harden	Soli	527
John Hardy, Sir	Empt	484
John Hare	Scan	170
John Hebron	Yell	361
John Holder	Sign	144
John Hones	Stud	54
John Horner	Blue	248
John Mason	Shos	1103
John Hector McFarlane	Norw	497
John McGinty	Vall	797
John Mitton	Seco	655
John Morland, Sir	Houn	736
John Hopley Neligan	Blac	566
John Openshaw	Five	219
John Rance	Stud	32
John Robinson	Blue	254
John Sholto	Sign	95
John Straker	Silv	336
John Swain	Five	223
John Turner	Bosc	203
John Underwood	Stud	43
John Warner	Wist	882
John H. Watson (*which see*)		
John (butler)	Miss	630
John (coachman)	Scan	169

Names, Personal—Given Names
(cont'd)

John (coachman)	Twis	233
Johnny Hones	Stud	54
Jonas Oldacre	Norw	497
Jonas Pinto	Vall	828
Jonathan Small	Sign	98
Jose (butler)	Wist	886
Joseph Harrison	Nava	449
Joseph Openshaw	Five	219
Joseph Stangerson	Stud	30
Joshua Stone, Reverend	Wist	876
Josiah Amberley	Reti	1113
Josiah Barnes	Shos	1104
Josiah Brown	SixN	590
Josiah H. Dunn	Vall	849
Joyce Cummings	Thor	1065
Juan Murillo	Wist	884
Jules Vibart	Lady	944
Julia Stoner	Spec	260
Kate Whitney	Twis	230
Kitty Winter	Illu	989
Lal Chowdar	Sign	103
Lal Rao	Sign	120
Langdale Pike	3Gab	1028
Laura Lyons	Houn	730
Leon Sterndale, Dr.	Devi	961
Leonardo (strongman)	Veil	1097
Leslie Armstrong, Dr.	Miss	629
Leslie Oakshot, Sir	Illu	993
Louis LaRothiere	Seco	654
	Bruc	925
Lucy Ferrier	Stud	57
Lucy Hebron	Yell	361
Lucy Parr	Bery	304
Lucretia Venucci	SixN	594
Lysander Stark	Engr	277

Names, Personal—Given Names
(cont'd)

Lysander Starr	3Gar	1047
Maggie Oakshott	Blue	253
Mahomet Singh	Sign	98
Maria Pinto (Gibson)	Thor	1060
Marie Devine	Lady	943
Marlow Bates	Thor	1057
Martha	Last	974
Mary Brackenstall	Abbe	637
Mary Cushing	Card	893
Mary Fraser	Abbe	639
Mary Holder	Bery	304
Mary Maberley	3Gab	1024
Mary Morstan	Sign	93
Mary Sutherland	RedH	176
	Iden	192
Mary (maid)	Five	220
	3Gab	1029
Mary Jane (maid)	Scan	162
Matilda Briggs (ship)	Suss	1034
Maud Bellamy	Lion	1086
Michael (stablehand)	Suss	1037
Mike Scanlan	Vall	817
Miles McLaren	3Stu	601
Minnie Warrender	Maza	1017
Moore Agar, Dr.	Devi	955
Mordecai Smith	Sign	123
Morse Hudson	SixN	583
Mortimer Maberley	3Gab	1024
Mortimer Tregennis	Devi	956
Mycroft Holmes (*which see*)		
Nancy Devoy Barclay	Croo	413
Nathan Garrideb	3Gar	1045
Ned Hunter	Silv	337
Ned, Uncle	Iden	193
Negretto Sylvius, Count	Maza	1014

Names, Personal—Given Names
(cont'd)

Neil Gibson	Thor	1055
Neville St. Clair	Twis	232
Norah Creina (ship)	Resi	434
Oscar Meunier	Empt	489
Owen Tregennis	Devi	956
Patience Moran	Bosc	203
Patrick Cairns	Blac	569
Paul Kratides	Gree	440
Penrose Fisher	Dyin	933
Percy Armitage	Spec	263
Percy Phelps	Nava	447
Percy Trevelyan	Resi	425
Pete, Indian	Stud	54
Peter Carey	Blac	559
Peter Jones	RedH	186
Peter Steiler	Fina	477
Peter (groom)	Soli	534
Philip Green, Hon.	Lady	946
Phillipe de Croy	Stud	38
Pierrot	Bruc	928
Pietro Venucci	SixN	590
Rachel Howells	Musg	389
Ralph Musgrave, Sir	Musg	397
Ralph (butler)	Blan	1002
Ralph Smith	Soli	527
Ray Ernest, Dr.	Reti	1113
Reginald Musgrave	Musg	388
Reuben Hayes	Prio	550
Richard Brunton	Musg	398
Robert Carruthers	Soli	528
Robert Ferguson	Suss	1034
Robert Norberton, Sir	Shos	1102
Robert St. Simon, Lord	Nobl	287
Rodger Baskerville	Houn	676
	Houn	681

414 ◼ *Good Old Index*

Names, Personal—Given Names
(cont'd)

Rodger Prescott	3Gar	1052
Ronald Adair, Hon.	Empt	483
Rose Spender	Lady	951
Sally Dennis	Stud	39
Sam Brewer	Shos	1102
Sam Brown	Sign	143
Sam Merton	Maza	1014
Sandy Bain	Shos	1106
Sarah Cushing	Card	893
Sebastian Moran, Colonel	Empt	484
	Vall	777
	Last	979
	Illu	985
Sergius	Gold	619
Sherlock Holmes (*which see*)		
Shinwell Johnson	Illu	987
Sidney Johnson	Bruc	917
Silas Brown	Silv	337
Simon Bird	Vall	849
Sophy Anderson (ship)	Five	218
Sophy Kratides	Gree	441
Spence Munro, Colonel	Copp	318
Spencer John	3Gab	1024
Stanley Hopkins	Blac	559
	Gold	608
	Miss	622
	Abbe	636
Steve Dixie	3Gab	1023
Steve Wilson	Vall	858
Susan Cushing	Card	890
Susan Dobney	Lady	943
Susan Stockdale	3Gab	1026
Susan Tarlton	Gold	609
Tadpole Phelps	Nava	447
Ted Baldwin	Vall	813

Names, Personal—Given Names
(cont'd)

Teddy Marvin	Vall	831
Thaddeus Sholto	Sign	100
Theophilus Johnson	Houn	692
Theresa Wright	Abbe	638
Thorneycroft Huxtable	Prio	538
Tiger Cormac	Vall	834
Tito Castalotte	RedC	911
Tobias Gregson	Stud	26
	Sign	90
	Gree	444
	Wist	871
	RedC	908
Tom Bellamy	Lion	1087
Tom Dennis	Stud	39
Tonga	Sign	140
Trelawney Hope	Seco	650
Trevor Bennett	Cree	1075
Valentine Walter, Colonel	Bruc	917
Vincent Spaulding	RedH	178
Victor Durando	Wist	885
Victor Hatherley	Engr	274
Victor Lynch	Suss	1034
Victor Savage	Dyin	939
Victor Trevor	Glor	374
Vigor	Suss	1034
Violet de Merville	Illu	986
Violet Hunter	Copp	318
Violet Smith	Soli	526
Violet Westbury	Bruc	915
Vittoria	Suss	1034
White Mason	Vall	778
Wilhelm von Ormstein	Scan	165
William Baskerville, Sir	Houn	749
William Bellamy	Lion	1087
William Crowder	Bosc	203

Names, Personal—Given Names
(cont'd)

William Derbyshire	Silv	342
William Falder, Sir	Shos	1110
William Hales	Vall	850
William James	Vall	822
William Kirwan	Reig	399
William Morris	RedH	182
William Whyte	Stud	38
Willoughby Smith	Gold	607
Wilson Hargreave	Danc	523
Wilson Kemp	Gree	446

Names, Personal—Nicknames

Baldy Simpson	Blan	1009
Birdy Edwards	Vall	855
Holy Peters	Lady	947
Ikey Sanders	Maza	1018
Indian Pete	Stud	54
Killer Evans	3Gar	1051
Jem Ryder	Blue	256
Porky Shinwell Johnson	Illu	989
Roaring Jack Woodley	Soli	536
Tadpole Phelps	Nava	447
Tiger Cormac	Vall	834

Names, Personal—Surnames (for Nobility *see* Peerage)

Abernetty	SixN	584
Abrahams, old	Lady	943
Achmet, Abdullah	Sign	140
Acton, old	Reig	398
Adair, Hilda	Empt	483
Adair, Ronald	Empt	483
Adams	Gree	437
Adler, Irene	Scan	161
Agar, Dr. Moore	Devi	955
Ainstree, Dr.	Dyin	934
Akbar, Dost	Sign	98

Names, Personal—Surnames (for Nobility *see* **Peerage) (cont'd)**

Aldridge	Card	897
Algar	Card	897
Alison	Sign	106
Allan Bros.	Wist	873
Allardyce	Blac	559
Allen, Mrs.	Vall	781
Altamont	Last	973
Amberley, Brickfall &	Reti	1113
Amberley, Josiah	Reti	1113
Amberley, Mrs.	Reti	1113
Ames	Vall	781
Anderson, Sophy (ship)	Five	218
Anderson (victim)	Houn	754
Anderson (soldier)	Blan	1009
Anderson (constable)	Lion	1085
Andrews	Vall	848
Angel, Hosmer	Iden	192
Anstruther, (Dr.)	Bosc	202
Appledore, Sir Charles	Prio	539
Appledore, Edith	Prio	539
Armitage, James	Glor	381
Armitage, Percy	Spec	263
Armitage, Mr.	Spec	263
Armstrong, Dr. Leslie	Miss	629
Atkinson Bros.	Scan	161
Atwood	Vall	836
Aveling	Prio	547
Bain, Sandy	Shos	1106
Baker, Henry	Blue	245
Baker, Mrs.	Blue	245
Baldwin, Ted	Vall	813
Bannister	3Stu	597
Barclay, Colonel	Croo	412
Barclay, Nancy	Croo	413
Bardle, Inspector	Lion	1090

Names, Personal—Surnames (for Nobility see Peerage) (cont'd)

Barelli, Augusto	RedC	911
Barker, Cecil James	Vall	781
Barker, Mr.	Reti	1118
Barnes, Josiah	Shos	1104
Barnicot, Dr.	SixN	583
Barraud	Stud	30
Barrett	Seco	655
Barrymore, John	Houn	676
Barrymore, Eliza	Houn	676
Barton, Dr. Hill	Illu	995
Barton, Inspector	Twis	236
Basil, Captain	Blac	559
Baskerville, Beryl (Stapleton)	Houn	709
Baskerville, Sir Charles	Houn	673
Baskerville, Elizabeth	Houn	676
Baskerville, Sir Henry	Houn	677
Baskerville, Hugo, c. 1640	Houn	673
Baskerville, Hugo, 1742	Houn	676
Baskerville, John	Houn	676
Baskerville, Rear Admiral	Houn	749
Baskerville, Rodger	Houn	676
Baskerville, Rodger	Houn	681
Baskerville, Sir William	Houn	749
Baskerville	Houn	681
Bates, Marlow	Thor	1057
Baxter, Edith	Silv	337
Baynes, Inspector	Wist	871
Becher, Dr.	Engr	286
Beddington	Stoc	373
Beddoes	Glor	377
Bellamy, Maud	Lion	1086
Bellamy, Tom	Lion	1087
Bellamy, William	Lion	1087
Bender	Stud	54
Bennett, Trevor	Cree	1072

Names, Personal—Surnames (for
  Nobility *see* Peerage) (cont'd)

Bernstone, Mrs.	Sign	107
Biddle	Resi	434
Bird, Simon	Vall	849
Blackwell, Lady Eva	Chas	573
Blaker	Vall	835
Blessington	Resi	425
Blount	Lion	1090
Blymer	Maza	1017
Boone, Hugh	Twis	235
Bovington	Lady	948
Brackenstall, Sir Eustace	Abbe	637
Brackenstall, Lady Mary	Abbe	637
Bradley	Houn	740
Bradstreet, Inspector	Twis	241
	Blue	248
	Engr	284
Breckenridge	Blue	251
Brewer, Sam	Shos	1102
Brickfall & Amberley	Reti	1113
Briggs, Matilda (ship)	Suss	1034
Broderick & Nelson	Sign	122
Brooks	Bruc	914
Brown, Lieutenant Bromley	Sign	152
Brown, Josiah	SixN	590
Brown, Sam	Sign	143
Brown, Silas	Silv	337
Browner, Jim	Card	893
Bruce-Partington	Bruc	916
Brunton, Richard	Musg	388
Burnett, Miss	Wist	882
Burnwell, Sir George	Bery	304
Cairns, Patrick	Blac	569
Calhoun, Captain James	Five	228
Carere, Mlle.	Houn	761
Carey, Captain Peter	Blac	559

Names, Personal—Surnames (for Nobility *see* Peerage) (cont'd)

Carey, Miss	Blac	560
Carey, Mrs.	Blac	563
Carfax, Lady Frances	Lady	943
Carina	Reti	1116
Carnaway, James	Vall	835
Carriton	Suss	1035
Carruthers, Robert	Soli	528
Carruthers, Colonel	Wist	870
Carter	Vall	858
Cartwright	Resi	434
Cartwright	Houn	691
Cassel-Felstein	Scan	165
Castalotte, Tito	RedC	911
Castalotte & Zamba	RedC	911
Caunter	Prio	540
Chandos, Sir Charles	Vall	786
Charpentier, Alice	Stud	44
Charpentier, Arthur	Stud	42
Charpentier, Mme.	Stud	41
Cheeseman	Suss	1035
Chowdar, Lal	Sign	103
Clay, John	RedH	186
Clayton, John	Houn	697
Cobb, John	Bosc	205
Conk-Singleton	SixN	596
Cook	Five	227
Coram, Professor	Gold	608
Cormac, Tiger	Vall	834
Cornelius, Mr.	Norw	505
Coventry, Sergeant	Thor	1062
Cowper	Stud	73
Cox & Co.	Thor	1054
Coxon	Stoc	364
Coxon & Woodhouse	Stoc	364
Crabbe	Vall	857

Names, Personal—Surnames (for Nobility *see* Peerage) (cont'd)

Creina, Norah (ship)	Resi	434
Crocker, Captain Jack	Abbe	646
Crosby	Gold	607
Crowder, William	Bosc	203
Cubitt, Hilton	Danc	512
Cubitt, Elsie	Danc	512
Cummings, Joyce	Thor	1065
Cunningham, Alec	Reig	399
Cunningham, old	Reig	399
Cusack, Catherine	Blue	248
Cushing, Mary	Card	893
Cushing, Sarah	Card	893
Cushing, Susan	Card	890
d'Albert, Countess	Chas	580
Damery, Sir James	Illu	984
Darlington	Scan	173
Davenport, J.	Gree	443
Dawson	Sign	145
Dawson	Silv	344
Dawson & Neligan	Blac	566
de Brinvilliers, Marchioness	Stud	41
de Capus, Hugo	Vall	779
de Croy, Philippe	Stud	38
de Merville, General	Illu	986
de Merville, Violet	Illu	986
de Vere	Nobl	288
Dennis, Sally	Stud	39
Dennis, Tom	Stud	39
Derbyshire, William	Silv	342
Desmond, James	Houn	695
Devine	SixN	584
Devine, Marie	Lady	943
Devoy, Nancy (Barclay)	Croo	413
Dixie, Steve	3Gab	1023
Dixon, Jeremy	Miss	632

Names, Personal—Surnames (for Nobility *see* **Peerage)** (cont'd)

Dixon, Mrs.	Soli	528
Dobney, Susan	Lady	943
Dodd, James M.	Blan	1000
Dodd, Morrison, Morrison & Dolsky	Suss	1034
	Stud	84
Dorak, A.	Cree	1078
Doran, Aloysius	Nobl	289
Doran, Hatty	Nobl	289
Dorking, Colonel	Chas	574
Douglas, Jack	Vall	774
Douglas, Ivy	Vall	774
Downing, Constable	Wist	880
Dowson, Baron	Maza	1016
Drebber, Enoch J.	Stud	26
Drebber, Elder	Stud	26
Dubugue, M.	Nava	447
Dunbar, Grace	Thor	1056
Dundas	Iden	191
Dunn, Josiah H.	Vall	849
Durando, Victor	Wist	885
Durando, Signora	Wist	885
Eccles, John Scott	Wist	869
Eckermann	Wist	887
Edmunds, Constable	Veil	1098
Edwards, Birdy	Vall	855
Egan	Vall	857
Elman, J. C.	Reti	1117
Elrige	Danc	521
Emsworth, Colonel	Blan	1001
Emsworth, Godfrey	Blan	1001
Emsworth, Mrs.	Blan	1001
Ernest, Dr. Ray	Reti	1113
Escott	Chas	576
Etherege, Mrs.	Iden	192
Evans, Carrie	Shos	1105

Names, Personal—Surnames (for
Nobility *see* Peerage) (cont'd)

Evans, Killer	3Gar	1051
Evans	Glor	382
Evans	Vall	853
Evans	Shos	1111
Fairbairn, Alec	Card	899
Falder, Lady Beatrice	Shos	1103
Falder, Sir Denis	Shos	1110
Falder, Sir James	Shos	1103
Falder, Sir William	Shos	1110
Farintosh, Mrs.	Spec	259
Farquhar, Mr.	Stoc	362
Ferguson, Captain	3Gab	1026
Ferguson, Jack	Suss	1037
Ferguson, Robert	Suss	1034
Ferguson, Mrs.	Suss	1034
Ferguson & Muirhead	Suss	1034
Ferguson	Engr	281
Ferguson	Thor	1057
Ferrers	Prio	539
Ferrier, Dr.	Nava	454
Ferrier, John	Stud	57
Ferrier, Lucy	Stud	57
Ffolliot, Sir George	Wist	876
Fisher, Penrose	Dyin	933
Forbes	Nava	453
Fordham, Dr.	Glor	379
Fordham	Five	220
Forrester, Mrs. Cecil	Sign	94
Forrester, Inspector	Reig	400
Fournaye, Henri	Seco	659
Fournaye, Mme. Henri	Seco	658
Fowler, Mr.	Copp	331
Frankland, Mr.	Houn	678
Fraser, Annie	Lady	947
Fraser, Mary	Abbe	639

Names, Personal—Surnames (for Nobility *see* **Peerage) (cont'd)**

Fraser	Houn	762
Freebody, Major	Five	222
Garcia, Aloysius	Wist	870
Garcia, Beryl (Stapleton)	Houn	761
Garrideb, Alexander Hamilton	3Gar	1046
Garrideb, Howard	3Gar	1050
Garrideb, John	3Gar	1045
Garrideb, Nathan	3Gar	1045
Gelder & Co.	SixN	588
Gibson, J. Neil	Thor	1055
Gibson, Maria (Pinto)	Thor	1060
Gilchrist, Sir Jabez	3Stu	600
Gilchrist	3Stu	600
Goldini	Bruc	925
Gorgiano, Giuseppe	RedC	908
Gorot, Charles	Nava	450
Gower	Vall	850
Graham & McFarlane	Norw	498
Green, Admiral	Lady	948
Green, Hon. Philip	Lady	946
Gregory, Inspector	Silv	337
Gregson, Tobias	Stud	26
	Sign	90
	Gree	444
	Wist	871
	RedC	908
Grice Paterson	Five	218
Griggs, Jimmy	Veil	1097
Gross & Hankey	Scan	168
Gruner, Baron Adelbert	Illu	985
Haines-Johnson	3Gab	1027
Hales, William	Vall	850
Halliday	Stud	46
Hammerford	Illu	984
Hankey, Gross &	Scan	168

Names, Personal—Surnames (for Nobility *see* Peerage) (cont'd)

Harden, John Vincent	Soli	527
Harding, Mr.	SixN	593
Harding Bros.	SixN	585
Hardy, Sir Charles	Seco	666
Hardy, Sir John	Empt	484
Hardy, Mr.	Iden	193
Hargrave	Vall	803
Hargreave, Wilson	Danc	523
Harker, Horace	SixN	585
Harold, Mrs.	Maza	1017
Harraway	Vall	835
Harris	Stoc	369
Harrison, Annie	Nava	449
Harrison, Joseph	Nava	449
Harvey	Suss	1035
Hatherley, Victor	Engr	274
Hayes, Reuben	Prio	550
Hayes, Mrs.	Prio	556
Hayling, Jeremiah	Engr	284
Hayter, Colonel	Reig	398
Hayward	Resi	434
Hebron, John	Yell	361
Hebron, Lucy	Yell	353
Heidegger	Prio	541
Henderson	Wist	876
Higgins	Vall	834
Hill, Inspector	SixN	590
Hobbs, Fairdale	RedC	901
Holder, Alexander	Bery	302
Holder, Arthur	Bery	304
Holder, Sergeant John	Sign	144
Holder, Mary	Bery	304
Holder & Stevenson	Bery	302
Hollis	Last	976
Holloway & Steele	3Gar	1051

Names, Personal—Surnames (for Nobility *see* Peerage) (cont'd)

Holly, Sir Edward	Glor	375
Holmes, Mycroft (*which see*)		
Holmes, Sherlock (*which see*)		
Hones, Johnny	Stud	54
Hope, Lady Hilda	Seco	656
Hope, Trelawney	Seco	650
Hope, Jefferson	Stud	51
Hope, Jefferson, Senior	Stud	60
Hopkins, Ezekiah	RedH	178
Hopkins, Stanley	Blac	559
	Gold	608
	Miss	622
	Abbe	636
Horner, John	Blue	248
Horsom, Dr.	Lady	952
Howells, Rachel	Musg	389
Hudson (seaman)	Glor	377
Hudson	Five	223
Hudson, Mrs. (*which see*)		
Hudson, Morse	SixN	583
Hunt	Vall	853
Hunter, Ned	Silv	337
Hunter, Violet	Copp	318
Huret	Gold	607
Huxtable, Thorneycroft	Prio	538
Hyam	Vall	822
Hyams	Norw	503
Hynes, Hynes	Wist	876
Ionides	Gold	615
Jackson, Dr.	Croo	412
Jacobs	Seco	665
Jacobson	Sign	135
James, Billy	Vall	822
James, Jack	Last	975
Jenkins	Vall	853

Names, Personal—Surnames (for Nobility *see* Peerage) (cont'd)

John, Spencer	3Gab	1024
Johnson (athlete)	Miss	623
Johnson, Haines-	3Gab	1027
Johnson, Shinwell	Illu	987
Johnson, Sidney	Bruc	917
Johnson, Theophilus	Houn	692
Johnston (elder)	Stud	59
Jones, Athelney	Sign	90
Jones, Peter	RedH	186
Kemp, Wilson	Gree	446
Kennedy, Morton &	Soli	538
Kent	Blan	1008
Keswick	Stud	40
Khan, Abdullah	Sign	98
King, Mrs.	Danc	518
Kirwan, William	Reig	399
Kirwan, Mrs.	Reig	400
Klein, Isadora	3Gab	1031
Klein	3Gab	1031
Klopman	Last	979
Knox, Jack	Vall	849
Kratides, Paul	Gree	440
Kratides, Sophy	Gree	441
Lancaster, James	Blac	569
Landers	Vall	857
Lanner, Inspector	Resi	431
Larbey, Mrs.	Vall	853
La Rothiere, Louis	Seco	654
	Bruc	925
Latimer, Harold	Gree	438
Latimer	Lady	942
Lawler	Vall	848
Le Brun	Illu	989
Le Villard, Francois	Sign	90
Lee	Vall	836

Names, Personal—Surnames (for Nobility *see* Peerage) (cont'd)

Lefevre	Stud	18
Lestrade (*which see*)		
Lesurier, Mme.	Silv	342
Leturier	Stud	84
Leverton	RedC	908
Lexington, Mrs.	Norw	504
Linder, Max, & Co.	Vall	836
Lomax	Illu	994
Lopez	Wist	886
Lowenstein	Cree	1082
Lucas, Eduardo	Seco	654
Lucca, Emilia	RedC	910
Lucca, Gennaro	RedC	910
Lynch, Victor	Suss	1034
Lyons, Laura	Houn	730
Maberley, Douglas	3Gab	1025
Maberley, Mary	3Gab	1024
Maberley, Mortimer	3Gab	1024
Macphail (coachman)	Cree	1080
Manders	Vall	851
Mangles, Ross &	Houn	762
Mansel	Vall	838
Manson	Vall	836
Marbank, Westhouse &	Iden	196
Marcini	Houn	766
Marker, Mrs.	Gold	609
Martin, Inspector	Danc	517
Martin, Lieutenant	Glor	383
Marvin, Captain Teddy	Vall	831
Marx & Co.	Wist	877
Mason, John	Shos	1103
Mason, White	Vall	778
Mason, Mrs.	Suss	1037
Mason (platelayer)	Bruc	915
Mason (criminal)	Stud	18

Names, Personal—Surnames (for Nobility *see* **Peerage)** (cont'd)

Matheson, Venner &	Engr	276
Mathews	Empt	494
Maudsley	Blue	256
Mawson & Williams	Stoc	364
MacDonald, Alec	Vall	773
MacKinnon, Inspector	Reti	1119
MacNamara, widow	Vall	830
MacPherson	Seco	661
McCarthy, Charles	Bosc	203
McCarthy, James	Bosc	203
McCauley	Five	223
McFarlane, Graham &	Norw	498
McFarlane	RedH	185
McFarlane, Mr. & Mrs.	Norw	499
McFarlane, John Hector	Norw	497
McGinty, John	Vall	797
McGregor, Mrs.	Stud	54
McLaren, Miles	3Stu	601
McMurdo, Jack	Vall	817
McMurdo	Sign	106
McPherson, Fitzroy	Lion	1084
McQuire	Nobl	298
Meek, Sir Jasper	Dyin	933
Melas, Mr.	Gree	438
Melville	Wist	871
Menzies	Vall	850
Mercer	Cree	1078
Mereer	Glor	382
Merivale, Inspector	Shos	1102
Merridew	Empt	494
Merrilow, Mrs.	Veil	1095
Merryweather	RedH	186
Merton, Sam	Maza	1014
Meunier, Oscar	Empt	489
Meyer, Adolph	Bruc	925

Names, Personal—Surnames (for Nobility *see* **Peerage) (cont'd)**

Meyers (Toronto)	Houn	760
Middleton	Houn	736
Miles, Hon. Miss	Chas	574
Millar, Flora	Nobl	290
Milman	Vall	822
Milner, Godfrey	Empt	484
Milverton, Charles Augustus	Chas	572
Mitton, John	Seco	655
Moffat	Resi	434
Montgomery, Inspector	Card	898
Montpensier, Mme.	Houn	761
Moorhouse	Miss	622
Moran, Sir Augustus	Empt	494
Moran, Colonel Sebastian	Empt	484
	Vall	777
	Last	979
	Illu	985
Moran, Patience	Bosc	203
Moran (lodgekeeper)	Bosc	212
Morecroft	3Gar	1051
Morgan	Empt	494
Moriarty, Professor (*which see*)		
Moriarty, Colonel James	Fina	469
Morland, Sir John	Houn	736
Morphy, Alice	Cree	1072
Morphy, Professor	Cree	1072
Morris, Brother	Vall	836
Morris, Fred	Vall	842
Morris, William	RedH	182
Morrison, Annie	Reig	411
Morrison, Morrison & Dodd	Suss	1034
Morrison, Miss	Croo	414
Morstan, Captain Arthur	Sign	94
Morstan, Mary	Sign	93
Mortimer, Dr. James	Houn	669

Names, Personal—Surnames (for Nobility see Peerage) (cont'd)

Mortimer, Smith-	Gold	607
Mortimer (tobacconist)	RedH	185
Mortimer (gardener)	Gold	609
Morton, Cyril	Soli	528
Morton, Inspector	Dyin	936
Morton & Kennedy	Soli	538
Morton and Waylight	RedC	905
Morton	Miss	623
Moser, M.	Lady	944
Moulton, Francis Hay	Nobl	297
Moulton, Mrs. Francis Hay	Nobl	297
Muirhead, Ferguson &	Suss	1034
Muller	Stud	18
Munro, Effie	Yell	353
Munro, Grant	Yell	353
Munro, Colonel Spence	Copp	318
Murcher, Harry	Stud	34
Murdoch, Ian	Lion	1084
Murdoch, James	Vall	853
Murillo, Don Juan	Wist	884
Murillo (ex-President)	Norw	496
Murphy, Major	Croo	413
Murphy (gypsy)	Houn	677
Murphy (Chicagoan)	Vall	820
Murray (orderly)	Stud	15
Murray (cardplayer)	Empt	484
Musgrave, Sir Ralph	Musg	397
Musgrave, Reginald	Musg	388
Neal	Vall	811
Neligan, John Hopley	Blac	566
Neligan, Dawson &	Blac	566
Nelson, Broderick &	Sign	122
Newton, Heath	Silv	347
Nicholson	Vall	822
Norberton, Sir Robert	Shos	1102

Names, Personal—Surnames (for Nobility _see_ Peerage) (cont'd)

Norlett, Mr.	Shos	1111
Norlett, Mrs.	Shos	1111
Norton, Godfrey	Scan	168
Oakshott, Sir Leslie	Illu	993
Oakshott, Maggie	Blue	253
Oberstein, Hugo	Seco	654
	Bruc	925
Odley	Suss	1035
Oldacre, Jonas	Norw	497
Oldmore, Mrs.	Houn	692
Openshaw, Colonel Elias	Five	219
Openshaw, John	Five	219
Openshaw, Joseph	Five	219
Overton, Cyril	Miss	622
Paramore	Five	223
Parker	Stoc	365
Parker	Empt	490
Parker	Danc	512
Parr, Lucy	Bery	304
Partington, Bruce-	Bruc	916
Paterson, Grice	Five	218
Patrick, Elsie	Danc	512
Patrick, Mr.	Danc	525
Patterson, Inspector	Fina	480
Pattins, Hugh	Blac	569
Paul (wharf owner)	Twis	232
Perkins	Houn	679
Perkins	3Gab	1023
Persano, Isadora	Thor	1055
Peters, Henry	Lady	947
Peterson	Blue	245
Phelps, Mrs.	Nava	454
Phelps, Percy	Nava	447
Phillimore, James	Thor	1055
Pike, Langdale	3Gab	1028

Names, Personal—Surnames (for Nobility *see* **Peerage)** (cont'd)

Pinner, Arthur	Stoc	365
Pinner, Harry	Stoc	366
Pinto, Jonas	Vall	828
Pinto, Maria (Gibson)	Thor	1060
Pollock, Constable	Stoc	373
Porlock, Fred	Vall	769
Porter, Mrs.	Devi	957
Pott, Evans	Vall	848
Prendergast, Jack	Glor	382
Prendergast, Major	Five	219
Presbury, Edith	Cree	1072
Presbury, Professor	Cree	1070
Prescott, Rodger	3Gar	1052
Price	Stoc	369
Pringle, Mrs.	Seco	655
Prosper, Francis	Bery	310
Pycroft, Hall	Stoc	364
Rae, Andrew	Vall	834
Rae & Sturmash	Vall	834
Rance, John	Stud	32
Randall	Abbe	637
Rao, Lal	Sign	120
Ras, Daulat	3Stu	598
Reilly	Vall	845
Reilly	Vall	851
Richards, Dr.	Devi	957
Ricoletti	Musg	387
Robinson, John	Blue	254
Ronder, Eugenia	Veil	1095
Ronder	Veil	1096
Ross, Colonel	Silv	336
Ross, Duncan	RedH	178
Ross & Mangles	Houn	762
Roundhay (vicar)	Devi	956
Roylott, Dr. Grimesby	Spec	258

Names, Personal—Surnames (for Nobility see Peerage) (cont'd)

Roylott, Mrs.	Spec	260
Rucastle, Alice	Copp	321
Rucastle, Edward	Copp	325
Rucastle, Jephro	Copp	321
Rucastle, Mrs.	Copp	324
Rulli	Wist	887
Ryder, James	Blue	248
St. Clair, Neville	Twis	232
St. Clair, Mrs.	Twis	234
St. Simon, Lady Clara	Nobl	290
St. Simon, Lord Eustace	Nobl	290
St. Simon, Lord Robert	Nobl	287
Samson	Stud	18
Sandeford	SixN	590
Sanders, Ikey	Maza	1018
Saunders, Sir James	Blan	1010
Saunders, Mrs.	3Gar	1050
Saunders (maid)	Danc	518
Savage, Victor	Dyin	939
Sawyer, Mrs.	Stud	39
Scanlan, Mike	Vall	817
Scott, James H.	Vall	817
Scott Eccles, John	Wist	869
Selden	Houn	701
Shafter, Ettie	Vall	820
Shafter, Jacob	Vall	818
Sherman	Sign	115
Shipley	Houn	697
Shlessinger, Reverend	Lady	944
Shlessinger, Mrs.	Lady	944
Sholto, Bartholomew	Sign	101
Sholto, Major John	Sign	95
Sholto, Thaddeus	Sign	100
Shuman	Vall	836
Sigerson	Empt	488

Names, Personal—Surnames (for Nobility *see* Peerage) (cont'd)

Simpson, Baldy	Blan	1009
Simpson, Fitzroy	Silv	336
Simpson (BSI)	Croo	419
Sinclair, Admiral	Bruc	917
Singh, Mahomet	Sign	98
Singleton, Conk-	SixN	596
Slaney, Abe	Danc	521
Slater	Blac	561
Small, Jonathan	Sign	98
Smith, Culverton	Dyin	935
Smith, Jack	Sign	123
Smith, James	Soli	527
Smith, Jim	Sign	124
Smith, Mordecai	Sign	123
Smith, Mrs. Mordecai	Sign	123
Smith, Ralph	Soli	527
Smith, Violet	Soli	526
Smith, Willoughby	Gold	607
Smith-Mortimer	Gold	607
Soames, Sir Cathcart	Prio	540
Soames, Hilton	3Stu	596
Somerton, Dr.	Sign	152
Spaulding, Vincent	RedH	178
Spencer John	3Gab	1024
Spender, Rose	Lady	951
Stackhurst, Harold	Lion	1083
Stamford, Archie	Soli	527
Stamford, Young	Stud	16
Stamford	Houn	683
Stanger, James	Vall	837
Stangerson, Joseph	Stud	30
Stangerson (elder)	Stud	30
Staphouse	Vall	853
Staples	Dyin	936
Stapleton, Jack	Houn	678

Names, Personal—Surnames (for Nobility *see* **Peerage) (cont'd)**

Stapleton, Beryl	Houn	709
Stark, Colonel Lysander	Engr	277
Starr, Dr. Lysander	3Gar	1047
Staunton, Arthur H.	Miss	623
Staunton, Godfrey	Miss	622
Staunton, Henry	Miss	623
Staunton, Mrs.	Miss	634
Steele, Holloway &	3Gar	1051
Steiler, Peter	Fina	477
Steiner	Last	976
Stendal	Vall	853
Stephens	Shos	1104
Sterndale, Dr. Leon	Devi	961
Stevens, Bert	Norw	504
Stevenson	Miss	623
Stevenson, Holder &	Bery	302
Stewart, Jane	Croo	414
Stewart, Mrs.	Empt	494
Stimson & Co.	Lady	952
Stockdale, Barney	3Gab	1024
Stockdale, Susan	3Gab	1026
Stone, Reverend Joshua	Wist	876
Stoner, Helen	Spec	259
Stoner, Julia	Spec	260
Stoner, Major General	Spec	260
Stoner, Mrs.	Spec	260
Stoper, Miss	Copp	318
Straker, John	Silv	336
Straker, Mrs.	Silv	338
Straubenzee	Maza	1014
Strauss, Herman	Vall	849
Sturmash, Rae &	Vall	834
Sudbury	Lion	1090
Sumner	Blac	567

Names, Personal—Surnames (for Nobility *see* Peerage) (cont'd)

Sutherland, Mary	RedH	176
	Iden	192
Sutro	3Gar	1025
Sutton	Resi	434
Swain, John	Five	223
Swindon, Archie	Vall	836
Sylvius, Count Negretto	Maza	1014
Tangey	Nava	450
Tangey, Miss	Nava	453
Tangey, Mrs.	Nava	453
Tarleton	Musg	387
Tarlton, Susan	Gold	609
Tavernier	Maza	1016
Thurston	Danc	511
Tobin	Resi	434
Todman	Vall	836
Toller	Copp	324
Toller, Mrs.	Copp	324
Tosca, Cardinal	Blac	559
Tregellis, Janet	Musg	389
Tregennis, Brenda	Devi	956
Tregennis, George	Devi	956
Tregennis, Mortimer	Devi	956
Tregennis, Owen	Devi	956
Trepoff	Scan	161
Trevelyan, Dr. Percy	Resi	425
Trevor, Victor	Glor	374
Trevor	Glor	374
Turner, Alice	Bosc	215
Turner, John	Bosc	203
Turner, Mrs. (Hudson)	Scan	170
Tuson, Sergeant	Stoc	373
Underwood, John	Stud	43
Underwood & Sons	Stud	43
Upwood, Colonel	Houn	761

Names, Personal—Surnames (for Nobility *see* **Peerage) (cont'd)**

Vamberry	Musg	387
Van Deher	Vall	836
Van Jansen	Stud	29
Van Seddar	Maza	1020
Van Shorst	Vall	822
Vandeleur	Houn	753
Vanderbilt	Suss	1034
Venner & Matheson	Engr	276
Venucci, Lucretia	SixN	594
Venucci, Pietro	SixN	590
Verner, Dr.	Norw	496
Vibart, Jules	Lady	944
von Bischoff	Stud	18
von Bork	Last	974
von Herder	Empt	493
von Herling	Last	971
von Kramm	Scan	164
von Ormstein, Wilhelm	Scan	165
von Saxe-Meningen, Clothilde	Scan	166
von Waldbaum, Fritz	Nava	447
Wainwright	Illu	987
Waldron	3Gar	1052
Walker Bros.	Vall	836
Wallenstein	Scan	163
Walsingham	Nobl	288
Walter, Colonel Valentine	Bruc	917
Walter, James	Bruc	917
Walters	Wist	877
Warburton, Colonel	Engr	274
Wardlaw, Colonel	Silv	347
Warner, John	Wist	882
Warren	RedC	902
Warren, Mrs.	RedC	901
Warrender, Minnie	Maza	1017
Watson, John H. (*which see*)		

Names, Personal—Surnames (for Nobility *see* Peerage) (cont'd)

Watson, H.	Sign	92
Waylight, Morton &	RedC	905
Weiss & Co.	Silv	342
West, Arthur Cadogan	Bruc	914
West, Mrs.	Bruc	915
Westaway	Copp	318
Westbury, Violet	Bruc	915
Westhouse & Marbank	Iden	196
Westphail, Honoria	Spec	260
White, Abel	Sign	145
Whitney, Elisa	Twis	229
Whitney, Isa	Twis	229
Whitney, Kate	Twis	230
Whittington, Lady Alicia	Nobl	290
Whitworth, Rudge-	Vall	791
Whyte, William	Stud	38
Wiggins (BSI)	Stud	42
Wilcox, Chester	Vall	836
Wilder, James	Prio	540
Willaby, Arthur	Vall	838
Willaby	Vall	838
Williams, Charlie	Vall	849
Williams, James Baker	Wist	876
Williams, Mawson &	Stoc	364
Williams	Sign	101
Williamson	Soli	531
Willows, Dr.	Bosc	208
Wilson (canary trainer)	Blac	559
Wilson (chaplain)	Glor	383
Wilson (constable)	Gold	613
Wilson (messenger)	Houn	691
Wilson (sergeant)	Vall	781
Wilson (Scowrer)	Vall	834
Wilson, Bartholomew	Vall	827
Wilson, Jabez	RedH	176

Names, Personal—Surnames (for Nobility see Peerage) (cont'd)

Wilson, Steve	Vall	858
Windibank, James	Iden	192
Windigate	Blue	251
Windle, J. W.	Vall	834
Winter, James	3Gar	1051
Winter, Kitty	Illu	989
Wood, Dr.	Vall	781
Wood, Henry	Croo	418
Woodhouse	Stoc	364
Woodhouse	Bruc	914
Woodhouse, Coxon &	Stoc	364
Woodley, Edith	Empt	483
Woodley, Jack	Soli	528
Worthington	Resi	434
Wright, Theresa	Abbe	638
Youghal, Inspector	Maza	1015
Zamba, Castalotte &	RedC	911
Zamba, Tito	RedC	911

Names, Personal—Real Persons

Balzac (Honore de)	Iden	197
Bathsheba	Gree	422
Beecher, Henry Ward	Resi	423
	Card	889
	Last	971
Bertillon (Alphonse)	Nava	460
	Houn	672
Boccaccio (Giovanni)	Stud	30
Boswell (James)	Scan	164
Bouguereau (Adolphe)	Sign	101
Bradshaw	Copp	322
	Vall	772
Carlyle (Thomas)	Stud	21
	Sign	121
Catullus	Empt	485

Names, Personal—Real Persons
(cont'd)

Charles I	Stud	38
	Musg	396
	Vall	807
Charles II	Musg	397
Chopin (Frederic)	Stud	36
Christie's	Illu	995
	3Gar	1048
Chubb	Scan	168
	Gold	614
Claridge's	Last	978
	Thor	1056
Colin, (Campbell) Sir	Sign	151
Copernicus (Nicholas)	Stud	21
Corot (Jean Baptiste)	Sign	101
Crockford	Reti	1117
Cunard	Illu	994
Cuvier (Baron)	Five	225
Danton (George Jacques)	Vall	848
Darwin (Charles)	Stud	37
David (King)	Croo	415
De Quincey (Thomas)	Twis	229
De Reszke (Jean and Edouard)	Houn	766
Edison, Swan and	Houn	702
Eley's	Spec	265
Faber, Johann	3Stu	599
Flaubert, Gustave	RedH	190
Ford	Last	974
Franz Josef	Last	977
Gaboriau (Emile)	Stud	25
George II	Vall	807
Gladstone	Twis	240
Goethe (Johann Wolfgang von)	Sign	115
	Sign	157
Gordon, General (Charles George)	Resi	423
	Card	889

Names, Personal—Real Persons
(cont'd)

Greathed, Colonel (Edward Harris)	Sign	151
Greuze, Jean Baptiste	Vall	775
Grimm (Jakob and Wilhelm)	Suss	1034
Guion	Stud	30
Hafiz	Iden	201
Halle (Charles)	Stud	34
Hare, John	Scan	170
Hoffman	Maza	1019
Homer	Reig	399
Hood, General (John Bell)	Five	219
Horace	Stud	86
	Iden	201
Jackson, General ("Stonewall")	Five	219
James I	Vall	807
Kemball (Kimball), Heber C.	Stud	59
Kneller (Godfrey)	Houn	749
Lassus (Orlandus)	Bruc	929
Lee, General (Robert E.)	Five	219
Lewis, Sir George	Illu	984
Lincoln, Abraham	Thor	1058
Malthus (Thomas Robert)	Stud	41
Marconi (Guglielmo)	Last	975
Martini	Sign	118
Mendelssohn (Bartholdy, Felix)	Stud	22
Meredith, George	Bosc	210
Murger (Henri)	Stud	39
Nana Sahib	Sign	151
Neill, General (James George)	Croo	420
Napoleon	RedH	187
	SixN	583
Norman Neruda (Wilhelmine)	Stud	34
Paganini (Niccolo)	Card	894
Palladio (Andrea)	Abbe	637
Palmer (William)	Spec	270
Peace, Charlie	Illu	987

Names, Personal—Real Persons
(cont'd)

Petrarch (Francesco Petrarca)	Bosc	207
Pinkerton	Vall	854
	RedC	908
Poe (Edgar Allan)	Stud	24
	Resi	423
	Card	888
Pope (Alexander)	Reig	399
Pritchard (Edward William)	Spec	270
Raphael (Santi)	3Gab	1027
Reade (Winwood)	Sign	97
	Sign	137
Remington (Frederick)	Houn	733
Reynolds (Joshua)	Houn	749
Richter, Johann Paul	Sign	121
Roberts, Lord	Blan	1011
Robespierre (Maximilien)	Vall	848
Rodney, Admiral	Houn	749
Rosa, Salvator	Sign	101
Russell, Clark	Five	218
Samuel	Croo	422
Sand, George	RedH	190
Sanger (John)	Veil	1097
Sarasate (Pablo)	RedH	184
Shakespeare (William)	3Gab	1027
Shomu, Emperor	Illu	997
Simpson's	Dyin	941
	Illu	988
Sloane, Hans	3Gar	1049
Smith, Joseph	Stud	57
Smith & Wesson	Vall	861
Solomon (King)	Vall	857
Sotheby's	Illu	995
	3Gar	1048
Stuart (Kings)	Musg	397
Swan and Edison	Houn	702

Names, Personal—Real Persons
(cont'd)

Thoreau (Henry David)	Nobl	294
Thucydides	3Stu	597
Tussaud (Madame)	Maza	1019
Uriah	Croo	422
Vernet (Horace)	Gree	435
Wagner (Richard)	RedC	913
Wallenstein (Albrecht)	Scan	163
Wesson, Smith &	Vall	861
Whittaker	Vall	772
Wild, Jonathan	Vall	777
Wilhelm, Kaiser	Last	971
Wilson (Archdale)	Sign	151
Wombwell (George)	Veil	1097
Wood, J. G.	Lion	1093
Young, Brigham	Stud	58
Zeppelin, Count	Last	974

Nana Sahib — Sign 151
Naples (Italy) — SixN 590
 — RedC 911
Napoleon (I) — SixN 583
Napoleon (coin) — RedH 187
Napoleon of crime — Fina 471
Napoleon-gone-wrong — Vall 777
Nara (Japan) — Illu 997
Narbonne (France) — Fina 469
Narcotics
    Bang

	Sign	147
Cocaine	Sign	89
	Sign	158
	Scan	161
	Five	225
	Twis	232
	Yell	351
	Miss	622
	Dyin	934

Narcotics, Cocaine (cont'd)
possible illusion	Devi	955
	Cree	1071
Laudanum	Twis	229
Morphine (morphia)	Sign	89
	Illu	993
	Illu	998
	Cree	1081
Opium	Lion	1092
	Stud	21
	Sign	147
	Twis	229
	Silv	338
	Wist	884

Nark (informer)   Illu   987

Narration
four years after events	Nobl	287
ten years after events	Empt	483
thirteen years after events	Devi	956
twenty (?) years after events	Vall	815

Nature   Gold   607
Nauvoo (Illinois)   Stud   57
Navy, Royal   Stud   42
     Nava   450
     Bruc   914

Navy, Royal, personnel (*see also* **Army personnel**)
Baskerville, Rear-Admiral	Houn	749
Charpentier, Sub-lieutenant Arthur	Stud	42
Green, Admiral	Lady	948
Sinclair, Admiral	Bruc	917

Neal (outfitter)   Vall   811
Neanderthal (early man)   3Gar   1048
Neapolitan society   RedC   911
Nebraska   Stud   52
Necromancer   Stud   23
Ned, Uncle   Iden   193

446 ◼ *Good Old Index*

Negro, The (horse)	Silv	347
Negro (race)	Five	219
	Yell	361
	Houn	686
	Wist	872
	3Gab	1023
Neill, General (James)	Croo	420
Neligan, John Hopley	Blac	566
Neolithic man	Houn	709
	Devi	961
Nepal	Croo	420
Neruda (*see* Norman Neruda)		
Nether Walsling (house)	Wist	876
Netherland-Sumatra Company	Reig	398
Netley (hospital)	Stud	15
Nevada	Stud	61
Nevada Mountains	Stud	61
New Brighton	Card	900
New device in crime, a	Lady	954
New England	Vall	849
New Forest	Resi	423
	Card	888
New Jersey	Scan	165
New Mexico	Nobl	298
New Orleans (Louisiana)	Stud	18
New Street, Birmingham	Stoc	367
New Street, Wallington	Card	894
New York	Stud	30
	Abbe	647
	Houn	761
	Vall	836
	RedC	908
	Last	976
New York Police Bureau	Danc	523
New Zealand	Iden	193
	Glor	375
New Zealand Consolidated (stock)	Stoc	365

Newcastle   Houn   692
Newfoundland dog   Sign   138
                                                 Cree   1081
Newgate Calendar   3Gar   1051
Newhaven   Fina   476
Newmarket Heath   Shos   1102
Newspaper (*see also* Press)
   Chronicle (*see also Daily Chronicle*)   Iden   196
                                                 Silv   336
   Daily Chronicle (*see also Chronicle*)   Card   890
   Daily Gazette   RedC   902
   Daily News   Stud   41
                                                 Gree   442
   Daily Telegraph (*see also Telegraph*)   Stud   41
                                                 Copp   316
                                                 Norw   497
                                                 Seco   658
                                                 Bruc   928
   Devon County Chronicle   Houn   676
   Echo   Stud   86
                                                 Blue   249
   Evening News   Blue   249
   Evening Standard (*see also Standard*)   Stoc   372
   Family Herald   Thor   1055
   Globe   Blue   249
                                                 Prio   539
   Herald   Vall   837
   Journal de Geneve   Fina   469
   Leeds Mercury   Houn   687
   Morning Chronicle   RedH   178
                                                 Silv   335
   Morning Post   Nobl   288
                                                 Chas   574
                                                 Illu   999
   North Surrey Observor   Reti   1122
   Pall Mall (*Gazette*)   Blue   249
   St. James's (*Gazette*)   Blue   249

Newspaper (*see also* Press) (cont'd)

society papers		Nobl	289
Standard (*see also Evening Standard*)		Stud	41
		Sign	125
		Sign	131
		Blue	249
Star		Blue	249
Telegraph (*see also Daily Telegraph*)		Silv	335
Times, The		Sign	95
		Sign	97
		Blue	248
		Engr	276
		Soli	527
		Miss	622
		Houn	686
		Last	972
Western Morning News		Houn	687

Newspaper Headlines

"Brixton Myster"	Stud	41
"Mysterious Business at Upper Norwood"	Sign	125
"A Husband's Cruelty to His Wife"	Iden	191
"Tragedy Near Waterloo Bridge"	Five	227
"Singular Occurrence at a Fashionable Wedding"	Nobl	290
"Crime in the City"	Stoc	372
"Mysterious Affair at Lower Norwood"	Norw	497
"Kensington Outrage: Murder by a Madman"	SixN	589
"Murder in Westminster"	Seco	655
"Law and Order!"	Vall	837
"Outrage at the Herald Office"	Vall	840
"The Oxshott Mystery"	Wist	880
"A Gruesome Packet"	Card	890
"Mysterious Attack upon Sherlock Holmes"	Illu	993

Newspaper Headlines (cont'd)		
"The Haven Horror"	Reti	1122
"Brilliant Police Investigation"	Reti	1122
Newspaper type	Houn	687
Newspapers, fresh editions	Silv	335
News-vendor	Illu	993
Newton, Heath	Silv	347
Niagara (Falls)	Stud	23
	Card	900
Nicholson (victims)	Vall	822
Night-club	Last	972
	Illu	987
	3Gar	1052
Night-glasses	Sign	137
Nihilists	SixN	588
	Gold	619
	Wist	887
	Last	979
Nimes (France)	Fina	469
Nine Elms (Lane)	Sign	122
Nitrate of silver	Scan	162
Nitrates	Suss	1035
Nitrite of amyl	Resi	428
Nitsky (slang)	Last	976
Nobility (*see* **Peerage, Royalty**)		
Nom-de-plume	Vall	769
Nonconformist clergyman	Scan	170
Nonpareil Club	Houn	761
Norah Creina (ship)	Resi	434
Norberton, Sir Robert	Shos	1102
Norbury	Yell	353
Norfolk	Glor	374
	Danc	512
Norfolk Constabulary	Danc	518
Norfolk jacket	Blac	565
Norlett (servant)	Shos	1111
Norlett, Mrs.	Shos	1111

Norman Conquest	Musg	393
Norman Neruda (Wilhelmine)	Stud	34
North Africa	Veil	1097
North American Continent	Stud	52
North camp (Aldershot)	Croo	413
North Carolina	Houn	754
North Devon line	Houn	762
North Surrey Observer (newspaper)	Reti	1122
North Walsham	Danc	517
Northumberland	Nava	457
Northumberland Avenue	Nobl	300
	Gree	438
	Illu	984
Northumberland Avenue hotels	Nobl	300
	Gree	438
Northumberland Hotel	Houn	685
Northwest Provinces (India)	Sign	145
Norton, Godfrey	Scan	168
Norway	Blac	566
Norwegian (Sigerson)	Empt	488
Norwich	Danc	517
Norwood	Sign	95
Norwood police station	Sign	126
Nosebleed	Stud	81
Note in bouquet	Nobl	298
Note on shirt-cuff	Nava	452
	Houn	682
Note-paper, pink tinted	Scan	163
Nottingham	Vall	806
Notting Hill	Houn	701
	Bruc	925
	Dyin	936
Notting Hill hooligan	RedC	910
Notting Hill murderer (Selden)	Houn	701
Nova Scotia	Copp	318
Nurse	Nava	454
	Suss	1035

O

Oak	Five	226
	Musg	392
	Reig	403
	Soli	533
	Houn	700
	Vall	787
Oakington	Miss	632
Oakshott, Maggie	Blue	253
Oakshott, Sir Leslie	Illu	993
Oberstein, Hugo	Seco	654
	Bruc	925
Obliquity of the ecliptic	Gree	435
Oceans		
Arctic	Blac	566
Atlantic	Stud	23
	Stud	59
German	Danc	517
Pacific	Stud	59
	Nobl	292
Odessa (Russia)	Stud	84
	Scan	161
Odley's (house)	Suss	1035
Office, temporary	RedH	180
	Stoc	366

Official Pass (jail)	Thor	1062
Official Registry (cabs)	Houn	696
Official warning	RedC	910
Ohio	Stud	26
Oilcan	Vall	791
Ointment box	Stud	48
Oldacre, Jonas	Norw	497
Old Deer Park (Richmond)	Suss	1037
Old Jewry (street)	Suss	1034
Oldmore, Mrs.	Houn	692
Olympia (race course?)	Last	972
"On the Banks of Allan Water"	Vall	837
One Hundred and Seventeenth (regiment)	Croo	413
One-legged man	Sign	102
	Sign	110
	Bery	310
	Illu	993
	Reti	1114
Onyx	Sign	151
Opal tiara	Spec	259
Openshaw, Colonel Elias	Five	219
Openshaw, John	Five	219
Openshaw, Joseph	Five	219
Opera, Imperial, of Warsaw	Scan	165
Operas		
Les Huguenots	Houn	766
Wagner	RedC	913
Opium (*see also* Narcotics)	Stud	21
	Sign	147
	Twis	229
	Silv	338
	Wist	884
Opium den	Twis	230
Opium pipe	Twis	231
Oporto (Portugal)	Resi	434
Orange barrow	RedH	179

Orchid	Houn	709
Order, The (secret society)	Gold	607
Ordnance maps (*see also* Maps)	Engr	285
	Prio	545
	Houn	683
Oriental vase	Sign	100
Origin of Tree Worship (book)	Empt	485
Ormstein, House of	Scan	165
Ormstein, Wilhelm von	Scan	165
Orontes (troopship)	Stud	15
Orphan, Hatherley	Engr	276
Orphanage	RedH	186
Oscillation on pavement	Iden	192
Ostlers	Scan	168
Ostrich feather	Silv	342
"Our own colours, green and white"	Wist	874
Out of Doors (Wood)	Lion	1093
	Sign	122
Outhouse	Blac	561
Oval, The	Sign	122
Overton, Cyril	Miss	622
Owl	Stud	69
Oxford (University)	RedH	186
	Empt	494
	Miss	623
Oxford Street	RedH	186
	Blue	251
	Resi	430
	Gree	438
	Fina	473
	Empt	485
	Prio	554
	Chas	577
	Gold	608
	Houn	690
	Houn	740
	Lady	942

Oxfordshire	Engr	278
Oxshott	Wist	872
Oxshott Common	Wist	874
Oxshott Towers (house)	Wist	876
Oysters	Sign	134
	Dyin	936

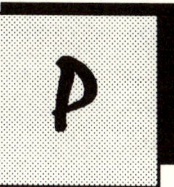

Pacific Ocean	Stud	59
	Nobl	292
Paddington	Stoc	362
Paddington Station	Bosc	202
	Engr	274
	Engr	278
	Silv	336
	Houn	696
Paganini (Niccolo)	Card	894
Page boy	Bery	304
	Copp	320
	Resi	427
	Houn	764
at Baker Street	Sign	93
	Iden	192
	Nobl	291
	Yell	351
	Gree	444
	Nava	448
	Wist	875
	Shos	1103
Billy	Vall	770
	Maza	1012
	Thor	1057

Page boy (cont'd)
  boots
  boy in buttons
Pail

Paint, green
Paint, red
Painting, as a clue

  paint odor
Paisley shawl
Palace clock
Palimpsest
Palladio (Andrea)
Pall Mall

Pall Mall (Gazette—newspaper)
Palmer (William)
Palmer (tyres)
Palmyra (New York)
Palmyra (ship)
Panama hat
Pandies
Pannikin
Paperhanger
Papers on sundial

Parade, The (New Brighton)
Paradol Chamber
Paramore (victim)
Parasol (*see* Umbrella)
Paregoric
Parietal bone fissure

Card	890	
Iden	192	
Wist	879	
Veil	1100	
Reti	1114	
Scan	172	
Houn	740	
Vall	775	
Reti	1120	
Nava	452	
Sign	117	
Gold	607	
Abbe	637	
Gree	436	
Fina	473	
Soli	531	
Abbe	645	
Bruc	914	
Blue	249	
Spec	270	
Prio	547	
Stud	57	
Vall	865	
Danc	524	
Sign	151	
Houn	739	
Stud	40	
Five	222	
Danc	513	
Card	900	
Five	218	
Five	223	
3Gab	1026	
Bosc	209	
Houn	672	

Paris (France)	Stud	76
	Nobl	299
	Stoc	367
	Nava	447
	Fina	475
	Seco	658
	Wist	885
	Bruc	931
Parish, civil	Engr	286
	Reig	400
	Houn	671
	Illu	990
	Veil	1095
Parish, ecclesiastical	Danc	512
	Houn	682
	Devi	956
Park, The (Hyde Park)	RedH	186
	Nobl	294
	Yell	351
	Empt	485
	Bruc	931
Parker (manager)	Stoc	365
Parker (garroter)	Empt	490
Parker (vicar)	Danc	512
Parkhurst (prison)	Illu	987
Park Lane	Empt	483
Park Lane Mystery	Empt	484
Parliament	Resi	423
	Card	888
Parliament Houses of (*see also* Commons, House of)	Seco	655
	Houn	749
	Lady	949
Parliament, Member of	Musg	388
Parr, Lucy	Bery	304
Parsley, sunk into butter	SixN	585
Parsonage	Spec	272
Parthian shot	Stud	32

Partie carrée | RedH | 188
Partnerships (*see also* Businesses)
   Allan Brothers' | Wist | 873
   Brickfall & Amberley | Reti | 1113
   Broderick and Nelson's | Sign | 122
   Castalotte & Zamba | RedC | 911
   Coxon & Woodhouse | Stoc | 364
   Dawson & Neligan | Blue | 566
   Ferguson & Muirhead | Suss | 1034
   Graham & McFarlane | Norw | 498
   Gross and Hankey | Scan | 168
   Harding Brothers | SixN | 585
   Holder & Stevenson | Bery | 302
   Holloway and Steele | 3Gar | 1051
   Mawson & Williams | Stoc | 364
   Morrison, Morrison and Dodd | Suss | 1034
   Morton and Kennedy | Soli | 538
   Morton & Waylight | RedC | 905
   Rae and Sturmash | Vall | 834
   Ross and Mangles | Houn | 762
   Underwood and Sons | Stud | 43
   Venner & Matheson | Engr | 276
   Walker Brothers | Vall | 836
   Westhouse & Marbank | Iden | 196
Partridge | Veil | 1098
Password | Stud | 69
  | Vall | 817
  | Vall | 833
Pate de fois gras pie | Nobl | 296
Patent leather | Stud | 33
  | Nobl | 291
  | Stoc | 363
  | Houn | 693
Paterson, Grice | Five | 218
Pathan | Sign | 155
Patience, sea air, sunshine and | Devi | 960
Patrick (Chicago boss) | Danc | 525

Patrick, Elsie	Danc	512
Patterson, Inspector	Fina	480
Pattins, Hugh	Blac	569
Paul's Wharf	Twis	232
Pawnbroker	Sign	93
	RedH	178
	Lady	948
Pawnees	Stud	52
P. C. (Privy Councilor)	Prio	539
Peace, Charlie	Illu	987
Peak country	Prio	543
Pearl	Sign	95
	SixN	594
	Illu	985
Peat	Prio	547
	Houn	759
Peckham	Stud	39
Peerage (*see also* Baronet, Knighthood, Royalty)		
Backwater, Lord	Nobl	288
	Silv	337
Balmoral, Duke of	Nobl	290
	Silv	347
Balmoral, Lord	Empt	484
Bellinger, Lord	Seco	650
Belminster, Duke of	Seco	656
Beverley, Baron (Holdernesse)	Prio	539
Blackwater, Earl of	Prio	540
Cantlemere, Lord	Maza	1013
Carston, Earl of (Holdernesse)	Prio	539
Clarendon, Lord	Houn	674
Colonna, Prince and Princess of	SixN	594
Dovercourt, Earl of	Chas	573
Dowson, Baron	Maza	1016
Flowers, Lord	Seco	666
Grafenstein, Count	Last	979
Greyminster, Duke of	Blan	1007

Peerage (*see also* Baronet, Knighthood, Royalty) (cont'd)

Gruner, Baron Adelbert	Illu	985
Harringby, Lord	Wist	876
Holdernesse, Duke and Duchess of	Prio	539
Holdhurst, Lord	Nava	447
Leverstoke, Lord	Prio	540
Lomond, Duke of	3Gab	1031
Maupertuis, Baron	Reig	398
Maynooth, Earl of	Empt	483
Merrow, Lord	Seco	666
Montalva, Marquess of	Wist	887
Morcar, Countess of	Blue	248
Mount-James, Lord	Miss	624
Roberts, Lord	Blan	1011
Rufton, Earl of	Lady	943
Singleford, Lord	Silv	347
Southerton, Lord	Copp	324
Sylvius, Count Negretto	Maza	1014
von Herling, Baron	Last	971
von Kramm, Count	Scan	164
von Saxe-Meningen, Clothilde	Scan	166
Zeppelin, Count	Last	974

Peine forte et dure — Vall — 811
Peking (China) — Illu — 995
Pen — Iden — 197
    "J" — Gree — 443
            — Card — 891
    quill — RedH — 181
            — Nobl — 288
            — Miss — 625
    sharp-pointed — Wist — 874
Penang lawyer (stick) — Silv — 339
            — Houn — 669
Pencil — Stud — 23
Pencil, as a clue — 3Stu — 599
            — Reti — 1121

Pencil, as a clue (cont'd)		
indelible	Reti	1121
violet	RedC	903
Pencil case, aluminum	Silv	341
Penge	Card	890
Penitentiary	Sign	125
	3Gar	1052
Penitentiary job	Vall	817
Pennsylvania	RedH	178
	Vall	785
Pennsylvania Small Arms Company	Vall	785
Pension	Nava	458
	Vall	770
	Veil	1102
Pentonville (prison)	Blue	256
Perfume	Houn	765
Pericolo, Attenta	RedC	907
Perkins (groom)	Houn	679
Perkins (victim)	3Gab	1023
Pernambuco (Brazil)	3Gab	1031
Persano, Isadora	Thor	1055
Pershore	Sign	144
Persia	Empt	488
British Minister to	Empt	494
Persian adage	Iden	201
Persian slipper (*see* Baker Street, 221)		
Personal column (*see* Agony column)		
Peru	Suss	1035
Peshawar (India)	Stud	15
Peter (groom)	Soli	534
Peters, Henry ("Holy")	Lady	947
Petersfield	Nobl	289
Peterson (commissionaire)	Blue	245
Petrarch	Bosc	207
Petrel, stormy	Reig	406
	Nava	448
Petroleum	Abbe	640

Pheasant
  hen
    in preserve
    months
Phelps, Percy
Philadelphia mint

Phillimore, James
Philosophical instruments
Phoenician traders in tin
Phonograph (gramaphone)
Phosphorus, cunning preparation of
Photograph

Nobl	296	
Glor	374	
Thor	1063	
Musg	388	
Nava	447	
Copp	321	
Vall	836	
Vall	828	
Thor	1055	
Stud	20	
Devi	955	
Maza	1021	
Houn	757	
Scan	171	
Scan	174	
Twis	242	
Silv	346	
Yell	358	
Resi	433	
Norw	503	
Chas	582	
SixN	586	
Seco	656	
Seco	659	
Seco	663	
Houn	753	
Card	893	
Devi	968	
Illu	990	
Lion	1091	
Veil	1097	
Veil	1099	
Veil	1100	
Reti	1113	
Reti	1116	

Photography		
as a hobby	RedH	178
	Copp	327
as an investigative method	Lion	1091
Physician (*see* Doctor)		
Piano	Bruc	927
Pickwick	Chas	573
Picture-frame maker (suspect)	Shos	1102
Pierced ears	RedH	183
	Card	892
Pierrot (alias)	Bruc	928
Pig	Blac	559
Pigeon	Last	976
Pigs'-bristles	Vall	773
Pike (fish)	Houn	752
	Shos	1107
Pike, Langdale	3Gab	1028
Pills, poison	Stud	48
	Reti	1117
Pince-nez	Iden	197
	Five	218
	Nobl	291
	Copp	318
	Gold	612
Pinchin Lane	Sign	115
Pine	Stud	71
	3Gab	1024
Pinkerton (American agency)	Vall	854
	RedC	908
Pinkerton, Bruce, prize and medal	Resi	425
"Pink 'un" (sporting paper)	Blue	253
Pinner (village)	Yell	353
Pinner, Arthur (alias)	Stoc	365
Pinner, Harry (alias)	Stoc	366
Pinto, Jonas	Vall	828
Pinto, Maria	Thor	1060

Pipes (*see also* **Holmes and Watson**)

A. D. P.		Silv	341
amber stem		Yell	351
		Prio	545
briar (brier)		Sign	90
		Twis	240
		Silv	341
		Yell	351
cherrywood		Copp	317
clay		RedH	184
		Iden	196
		Blue	257
		Copp	317
		Chas	575
		Houn	683
	black clay	Iden	198
		Houn	683
metal		Twis	231
old black		Cree	1071
	coal scuttle, in	Maza	1012

Pipette

	Stud	18
	Nava	448

Pitt (William) — Houn 749

Pitt Street — SixN 585

Plan, of building

Nava	451
Gold	610

Plane tree — Thor 1055

Plants (*see also* flowers & trees)

bracken	Houn	700
bramble	Silv	343
	Fina	479
	Houn	700
	Devi	966
catkins	Wist	879
cotton grass	Houn	713
	Houn	760

Plants (*see also* **flowers & trees**) (cont'd)

fern	Silv	343
	Fina	479
	Houn	700
	Houn	707
	Thor	1063
gourd	Sign	155
lichen	Bosc	211
	Spec	266
	Houn	701
	Vall	787
	Suss	1039
	Reti	1114
moss	Bosc	212
	Nava	455
	Empt	487
	Prio	547
	Houn	700
	Devi	956
	Reti	1114
privet	Norw	503
reed	Houn	759
	Thor	1063
Plantagenet	Nobl	288
Plaster of Paris	Sign	91
	SixN	589
Plaster bust	SixN	583
	SixN	584
	SixN	585
	SixN	586
	SixN	594
Plaster skulls	3Gar	1048
Plough	Vall	815
	3Gar	1051
Plover	Copp	318
	Prio	546

466 ◼ *Good Old Index*

Plumber
                                                Scan   170
                                                Iden   193
                                                Blue   248
                                                Nava   467
                                                Chas   576
    gas workman   Croo   411
    gasfitter   Iden   193
Plumber's smoke rocket   Scan   170
Plumstead Marshes   Sign   138
Plymouth   Silv   342
                                                Houn   717
                                                Devi   961
Pneumonia   3Gab   1025
Poaching   Glor   375
                                                Houn   737
Poe (Edgar Allan)   Stud   24
                                                Resi   423
                                                Card   888
Points (railway junctions)   Fina   476
                                                Norw   501
                                                Bruc   919
Poison   Sign   96
                                                Spec   262
    Camberwell poisoning case   Five   218
    darts   Sign   109
    forcible administration of   Stud   84
    in Holmes's work   Stud   18
    Morgan   Empt   494
    pills   Stud   80
                                                Reti   1119
    vial of   Gold   621
Poison, types of
    alkaloids   Stud   17
                                                Sign   113
    aqua tofana   Stud   41
    bang   Sign   147
    belladona   Dyin   941

Poison, types of (cont'd)
    charcoal fumes

charcoal fumes	Gree	445
chloroform	Lady	953
	Last	977
	3Gab	1029
cocaine	Sign	89
	Sign	158
	Scan	161
	Five	225
	Twis	232
	Yell	351
	Miss	622
	Dyin	934
possible allusions	Devi	955
	Cree	1071
curare	Suss	1043
Cyanea capillata	Lion	1093
devil's-foot root	Devi	964
gas	Reti	1120
morphine (morphia)	Sign	89
	Illu	993
	Illu	998
	Cree	1081
	Lion	1092
opium	Sign	147
	Twis	229
	Silv	338
	Wist	884
Oriental disease culture	Dyin	939
prussic acid	Veil	1102
serum of anthropoid	Cree	1082
snake venom	Spec	272
strychnine	Sign	105
	Sign	113
vitriol	Blue	249
	Illu	998
Poker (card game)	Vall	844

Poker (fireplace)		Spec	265
		Stoc	373
		SixN	586
		Abbe	638
		3Gab	1023
Poldhu Bay		Devi	955
Poldhu Cottage		Devi	960
Police (for Metropolitan police, see Scotland Yard)			
English constabularies			
Berkshire			
Inspector Edmunds		Engr	284
		Veil	1098
Cornwall		Devi	963
Devonshire		Houn	736
Inspector Gregory		Silv	337
Hallamshire constable		Prio	546
Hampshire		Glor	385
		Croo	414
Sergeant Coventry		Thor	1062
Hereford			
Inspector		Bosc	204
Constable Wilson		Gold	613
Norfolk			
constables		Danc	518
		Danc	519
		Danc	526
Inspector Martin		Danc	517
Surrey			
constables		Reig	406
	(3)	Norw	507
		Soli	538
Constable Downing		Wist	880
Constable Walters		Wist	877
Inspector Forrester		Reig	400
Inspector Baynes		Wist	871

Police (for Metropolitan police, *see* Scotland Yard), English constabularies (cont'd)

Sussex			
inspector		Five	223
constable		Musg	395
		Vall	816
White Mason		Vall	778
Inspector Bardle		Lion	1090
Constable Anderson		Lion	1085
Constable Wilson		Vall	781
Liverpool force		Stud	47
Algar		Card	897
City (of London)		Stoc	373
Constable Pollock		Stoc	373
Sergeant Tuson		Stoc	373
Rhodesian Police		3Stu	606
Skibbareen (Ireland) Constabulary		Last	978
European forces		Reig	398
Dantzig			
Fritz von Waldbaum		Nava	447
Hungarian		Gree	446
Paris		Seco	658
M. Dubugue		Nava	447
Francois le Villard		Sign	90
Le Brun		Illu	989
Russia		Gold	619
United States police			
Chicago			
Captain Marvin		Vall	831
Cleveland		Stud	30
		Stud	85
Coal and Iron Police (Vermissa)		Vall	818
Evans		Vall	853
Hunt		Vall	853
New York			
Wilson Hargreave		Danc	523

470 ■ *Good Old Index*

Police, chief of	Stud	76
Police, river	Sign	135
	Five	227
	Card	897
Police-court	Bosc	204
	Blue	249
	Spec	260
	Copp	331
	Nava	467
	Vall	865
	Bruc	916
	Illu	999
	Thor	1056
Bow Street	Twis	241
platitudes of the magistrate	Iden	191
Police launch	Sign	135
"Police News of the Past"	Stud	18
Police station, Norwood	Sign	126
Police whistle	Stud	35
	Reig	406
	Empt	491
	SixN	586
	Card	897
Politician, the Lighthouse and the trained cormorant, the	Veil	1095
Pollock, Constable	Stoc	373
Polo	Last	971
	Illu	987
Polyphonic Motets of Lassus	Bruc	931
Pompey (draghound)	Miss	632
Poncho (horse)	Stud	59
Pond, frozen	Abbe	645
Pondicherry (India) postmark	Five	220
Pondicherry Lodge	Sign	102
Pony, lost in Grimpen Mire	Houn	707
Pool (Thames River)	Sign	138

Pope, The
   (Cardinal Tosca)   Blac   559
   (Vatican Cameos)   Houn   677
Pope's Court   RedH   178
Pope's (Alexander) *Homer*   Reig   399
Popham House   Wist   871
Poplar (borough)   Sign   132
Porky Shinwell (Johnson)   Illu   989
Porlock, Fred   Vall   769
Port (wine)   Sign   135
    Glor   375
    Cree   1076
Portalis sale   Vall   776
Port Blair (Andamans)   Sign   127
Porter, Mrs. (housekeeper)   Devi   957
Portland (prison)   Last   975
Portsdown Hill   Five   222
Portsmouth   Stud   15
    Nava   456
    Last   973
Portsmouth jail   Last   976
Portuguese coast   Resi   434
Posilippo (Italy)   RedC   911
Post-hypnotic suggestion   Illu   989
Post Office
   Great Peter Street   Sign   125
   Leadenhall Street   Iden   194
   mail delivery   Scan   163
    Iden   194
    Twis   238
    Reig   402
    Resi   423
    Danc   512
    Soli   533
    Prio   542
    Blac   567
    Houn   685

472 ◼ *Good Old Index*

Post Office, mail delivery (cont'd)		Vall	770
		Card	888
		3Gab	1026
		Suss	1033
		Cree	1079
		Veil	1102
		Shos	1103
	post, registered	Houn	752
	postage stamp	Sign	92
		Five	220
		Stoc	364
	postage stamp, American	Danc	513
	postage stamp, Austrian	Cree	1082
	postal cards	Sign	92
	postmaster	Houn	694
	post-office bank	3Gab	1027
	second post	Vall	770
	telegrams, for	Sign	191
		Houn	694
		Cree	1078
	Wigmore Street	Sign	91
Pott, Evans		Vall	848
Potter's Terrace		Stoc	365
Pottery, Chinese		Illu	987
Poultney Square		Lady	949
Powder stains		Danc	519
Practical Handbook of Bee Culture		Last	977
Prague (Austria)		Scan	165
		Illu	985
		Cree	1073
Prayer		Stud	55
Prehistoric dwellings		Houn	709
		Devi	955
Prehistoric skull		Houn	714
	plaster skull	3Gar	1048
Premier (*see also* **Prime Minister**)		Seco	650
Prendergast, Jack		Glor	382

Prendergast, Major	Five	219
Presbury, Edith	Cree	1072
Presbury, Professor	Cree	1070
Prescott, Rodger	3Gar	1052
Preserves, game	Copp	325
	Glor	374
	Musg	388
	Thor	1063
warren	Bosc	205
	Houn	736
Press a valuable institution (*see also* Newspapers)	SixN	590
Pretoria (South Africa)	Blac	1001
Price (alias)	Stoc	369
Prime Minister	Seco	650
	Seco	666
	Bruc	916
	Last	978
	Maza	1013
Prince of Colonna	SixN	594
Princess of Colonna	SixN	594
Prince's Skating Club	RedC	904
Prince's Street	Sign	123
Princetown (prison)	Houn	684
Dartmoor	Sign	140
Pringle, Mrs. (housekeeper)	Seco	655
Printing and detection	Houn	687
Priory Road	Sign	99
Priory School	Prio	540
Prisons and jails		
Andaman Islands	Sign	95
Dartmoor (Princetown)	Sign	140
Hereford (jail)	Blac	208
Millbank Penitentiary	Sign	125
Parkhurst	Illu	987
Pentonville	Blue	256
Portland	Last	975

Prisons and jails (cont'd)
    Portsmouth (jail)
    Princetown (Dartmoor)
Pritchard (Edward)
Prizefighter

Probabilities balanced

Profanity

		Last	976
		Houn	684
		Spec	270
		Stud	22
		Sign	102
		Sign	106
		Glor	375
		Maza	1014
		3Gab	1023
		Shos	1103
		Sign	135
		Houn	687
	(2)	Stud	40
		Stud	44
		Stud	74
		Sign	103
		Sign	106
		Five	220
		Five	226
		Twis	231
		Twis	242
		Twis	244
		Blue	248
		Blue	255
		Spec	262
		Spec	271
		Bery	307
		Bery	311
		Bery	314
		Copp	331
		Yell	352
		Yell	356
		Yell	360
		Yell	361
		Stoc	370
	(2)	Stoc	372

Profanity (cont'd)

	Glor	379
(2)	Glor	382
	Glor	383
	Musg	390
	Croo	418
	Croo	419
	Resi	431
	Nava	467
	Soli	534
	Soli	535
	Soli	536
	Blac	562
	Houn	708
	Houn	709
(2)	Houn	724
	Houn	728
	Houn	743
	Houn	744
	Houn	757
	Vall	791
	Vall	818
	Vall	821
	Vall	823
	Vall	825
	Vall	829
	Wist	871
	Card	898
	Card	900
	RedC	910
	Bruc	922
	Dyin	932
	Lady	947
	Illu	997
	Illu	998
	Blan	1008
	Maza	1017
	Maza	1019

476 ◘ *Good Old Index*

Profanity (cont'd)		3Gab	1024
		3Gab	1026
		Suss	1037
		Suss.	1039
		Suss	1043
		3Gar	1050
	(2)	3Gar	1053
		Thor	1056
		Cree	1081
		Lion	1092
		Veil	1096
Professor Coram		Gold	608
Professor Moriarty (*which see*)			
Professor Morphy		Cree	1072
Professor Presbury		Cree	1070
Prophet, Mormon		Stud	57
Prosper, Francis		Bery	310
Prussic acid		Veil	1102
Pseudo-leprosy		Blue	1012
Public-house (*see also* **Businesses and Inns**)		Sign	121
		Copp	330
		Soli	532
		Blac	561
		Shos	1107
alehouse		Sign	136
gin palace		Stud	80
gin-shop		Twis	230
Publican		Prio	551
Pugilist (horse)		Silv	347
Pullman car		Silv	348
Punjab (India)		Croo	421
Punjabees (Sikhs)		Sign	147
Punts		Sign	123
Puppets		Soli	536
Purdey Place (house)		Wist	876
Puritan		Blac	560
Pycroft, Hall		Stoc	364

Quarter Day	Wist	873
Lady Day	Resi	426
Quarter-mile posts (railway)	Silv	335
Quarter Sessions	Vall	865
Queen		
arrest made in name of	Sign	114
a certain gracious lady	Bruc	931
Queen Anne (architecture)	Resi	403
	3Gar	1051
Queen Anne Street	Illu	984
Queen's Bench, court of	Houn	736
Queen's horses and men	Bruc	925
Queen's shilling	Sign	144
Queer grammar as clue	3Gab	1030
Queer Street (fig.)	Seco	662
	Shos	1103
Quid	Maza	1019
Quill pen	RedH	181
	Nobl	288
	Miss	625
Quinine bottle	Sign	102
Quinsy	Iden	194

Quotations
    French

Stud	42
Sign	104
Sign	114
RedH	190
Bosc	213

    German

Sign	115
Sign	158

    Latin

Stud	86
RedH	177
Blue	251
Abbe	650

R

Rabbi, Hebrew	Scan	165
Rabbit		
in warren	Bosc	205
stuffed	Sign	115
presumed	Norw	510
Rabbit-skin cap	Sign	105
Race course	Last	972
Winchester	Silv	347
Race horses (*see* horse racing)	Silv	347
	Shos	1103
"**Rache**"	Stud	31
	Stud	47
Rachel (sic)	Stud	31
Radiator	Last	973
Radix pedis diaboli	Devi	968
Rae, Andrew	Vall	834
Rae & Sturmash (coal owners)	Vall	834
Ragbag of singular happenings (agony column)	RedC	904
Ragged shaw	Prio	545
Railway		
accident	Spec	260
bonds	Stoc	373
special	Fina	476

480 ◻ *Good Old Index*

Railway (cont'd)
  speed of train
  station-master

	Silv	336
	Engr	286
	Danc	517
	Houn	700
	Vall	776
	Blan	1006

  timetable

	Copp	322
	Danc	517
	Vall	772

  uniform, velveteen   Stud   22
Railway Arms (inn)   Reti   1118
Railway companies
  Ayrshires (stock of Glasgow and South-Western Railway)   Stoc   365
  Canadian Pacific Railway   Blac   562
  Eastern railway line (South Africa)   Blan   1009
  North Devon line   Houn   762
  State and Merton County Railroad   Vall   836
Railway journeys—Traveller(s) (Destination)
  Adler, Norton (Continent)   Scan   174
  Amberley, Watson (Frinton)   Reti   1117
  Amberley, Watson (London)   Reti   1118
  Baskerville (London)   Houn   681
  Baskerville, Watson (London)   Houn   699
  Bradford, Holmes, Watson, Hatherley
    (Eyford)   Engr   284
    (London)   Engr   287
  Browner, Mrs. Browner, Fairbairn (New Brighton)   Card   900
  Cubitt (London)

	Danc	512
	Danc	514

  Dodd
    (Tuxbury)   Blan   1002
    (London)   Blan   1006
  Dodd, Holmes, Saunders (Tuxbury)   Blan   1007

Railway journeys—Traveller(s) (Destination) (cont'd)

Edwards (Vermissa)	Vall	815
Fairbairn, Browner, Mrs. Browner (New Brighton)	Card	900
Ferguson, Holmes, Watson (Lamberley)	Suss	1038
Ferrier, Phelps (Woking)	Nava	454
Garrideb		
(Birmingham)	3Gar	1050
(London)	3Gar	1050
Gregson, Holmes, Watson (Beckenham)	Gree	444
Harrison (Woking)	Nava	468
Hatherley		
(London)	Engr	274
(Eyford)	Engr	279
Hatherley, Holmes, Watson, Bradford		
(Eyford)	Engr	284
(London)	Engr	287
Holmes		
(Donnithorpe)	Glor	377
(Farnham)	Soli	532
(Hereford)	Bosc	209
(London)	Nava	463
	Soli	532
(Ross)	Bosc	209
Holmes, Dodd, Saunders (Tuxbury)	Blan	1007
Holmes, Musgrave (Hurlstone)	Musg	393
Holmes, Watson		
(Aldershot)	Croo	412
(Cambridge)	Miss	628
(Camford)	Cree	1076
(Canterbury)	Fina	474
(Chiselhurst)	Abbe	636
	Abbe	643
(Croydon)	Card	890

Railway journeys—Traveller(s) (Destination), Holmes, Watson (cont'd)

(Farnham)	Soli	533
(Harrow Weald)	3Gab	1024
(Leatherhead)	Spec	265
(London)	Spec	272
	Silv	346
	Croo	422
	Nava	456
	Danc	526
	Blac	567
	Lady	946
	Cree	1083
(toward London)	Abbe	642
(Newhaven)	Fina	476
(Norbury)	Yell	360
(North Walsham)	Danc	517
(Ross)	Bosc	202
(Shoscombe)	Shos	1107
(Tavistock)	Silv	335
(Thor Place)	Thor	1068
(Winchester)	Copp	322
	Silv	347
	Thor	1062
(Woking)	Nava	449
	Nava	460
(Woolwich)	Bruc	920
Holmes, Watson, Colonel Ross (London)	Silv	348
Holmes, Watson, Ferguson (Lamberley)	Suss	1038
Holmes, Watson, Gregson, Mycroft (Beckenham)	Gree	444
Holmes, Watson, Hatherley, Bradford (Eyford)	Engr	284
(London)	Engr	287

Railway journeys—Traveller(s)
(Destination) (cont'd)

Holmes, Watson, Helen Stoner (Harrow)	Spec	272
Holmes, Watson, Hopkins		
(Chatham)	Gold	613
(Forest Row)	Blac	563
(London)	Gold	621
Holmes, Watson, Huxtable (Mackleton)	Prio	543
Holmes, Watson, MacDonald (Birlstone)	Vall	778
Holmes, Watson, Mycroft, Gregson (Beckenham)	Gree	444
Holmes, Watson, Pycroft (Birmingham)	Stoc	364
Hopkins		
(Chatham)	Gold	608
(London)	Gold	608
Hopkins, Holmes, Watson		
(Chatham)	Gold	613
(Forest Row)	Blac	563
(London)	Gold	621
Hunter (Farnham)	Soli	528
Huxtable (London)	Prio	539
Huxtable, Holmes, Watson (Mackleton)	Prio	543
Lestrade (Devonshire)	Houn	752
MacDonald, Holmes, Watson (Birlstone)	Vall	778
McFarlane (London)	Norw	497
McMurdo (Hobson's Patch)	Vall	858
Melas (London)	Gree	442
Moriarty (Dover-Special)	Fina	476
Mortimer, Watson, Baskerville (Dartmoor)	Houn	699

Railway journeys—Traveller(s) (Destination) (cont'd)

Munro		
(London)	Yell	357
(Norbury)	Yell	357
Overton (London)	Miss	623
Phelps, Ferrier (Woking)	Nava	454
Phelps, Watson (London)	Nava	463
Pycroft		
(Birmingham)	Stoc	367
(London)	Stoc	368
Pycroft, Holmes, Watson (Birmingham)	Stoc	364
Ross, Colonel, Holmes, Watson (London)	Silv	348
St. Clair (London)	Twis	234
St. Clair, Mrs. (London)	Twis	234
Sandeford (London)	SixN	593
Staunton (Cambridge)	Miss	624
Stoner		
(London)	Spec	258
(Leatherhead)	Spec	263
Stoner, Holmes, Watson (Harrow)	Spec	272
Stapleton (Dartmoor)	Houn	762
Watson		
(Farnham)	Soli	530
(Lewisham)	Reti	1114
(London)	Soli	531
	Reti	1116
Watson, Amberley		
(Frinton)	Reti	1117
(London)	Reti	1118
Watson, Baskerville, Mortimer (Dartmoor)	Houn	699
Watson, Phelps (London)	Nava	463

Railway journeys—Traveller(s) (Destination) (cont'd)
  Watson, Holmes (*see* Holmes, Watson above)
  West (London) | Bruc | 915

Railway journeys—method
  Pullman | Silv | 348
  train deluxe | Maza | 1018
  third class | Reti | 1117
   | Reti | 1118
  Underground(*see* Underground railway)

Railway porter | Stud | 22
  | Engr | 279

Railway station (halt-on-demand) | Shos | 1107

Railway stations—London
  Aldersgate | RedH | 184
  Aldgate | Bruc | 915
  Blackheath | Reti | 1116
  Cannon Street | Twis | 233
  Chiselhurst | Abbe | 637
  Charing Cross | Scan | 174
  | Empt | 494
  | Gold | 608
  | Abbe | 636
  | Seco | 659
  | Illu | 993
  Euston | Stud | 41
  | Prio | 543
  | Blan | 1007
  Gloucester Road | Bruc | 926
  High Street | SixN | 585
  King's Cross | Miss | 628
  Liverpool Street | Danc | 514
  | Reti | 1117
  London Bridge | Gree | 444
  | Norw | 497

486 ◻ *Good Old Index*

Railway stations—London, London Bridge (cont'd)
    Metropolitan (Baker Street)
    Paddington

	Bruc	918
	Reti	1116
	Bery	301
	Bosc	202
	Engr	274
	Engr	278
	Silv	335
	Houn	696
Victoria	Silv	350
	Gree	442
	Fina	474
	Vall	776
	Suss	1038
Waterloo	Five	224
	Spec	259
	Spec	265
	Croo	411
	Nava	449
	Nava	454
	Nava	463
	Soli	530
	Houn	681
	Houn	697
Weald	3Gab	1024
Woolwich	Bruc	924
Rain	Stud	27
	Stud	80
	Five	218
	Spec	261
	Silv	338
	Yell	360
	Stoc	363
	Resi	422
	Nava	452
	Soli	533
	Blac	565
	Gold	607

Rain (cont'd)	Houn	677
	Houn	683
	Houn	724
	Houn	727
	Wist	875
	Wist	877
	Card	890
	Devi	961
	Illu	998
	Shos	1104
Raj	Sign	148
Rajah	Sign	148
Rajpootana (India)	Sign	149
Rake	Bosc	212
Ralph (butler)	Blan	1002
Rance, Constable John	Stud	32
Randalls, The (burglars)	Abbe	637
Rao, Lal	Sign	120
Raphael (Santi)	3Gab	1027
Ras, Daulat	3Stu	598
Rashers, of bacon	Engr	276
Rasper (horse)	Silv	347
Rat, as a clue	Bosc	206
Rat, giant, of Sumatra	Suss	1034
Ratcliff Highway	Blac	567
Ratcliff Highway Murders	Stud	41
Rates and taxes	SixN	588
Rattle (toy)	Gree	437
Raven	Houn	708
	Houn	745
Razor	Seco	658
Reade, Winwood	Sign	97
	Sign	137
Reading	Bosc	202
	Spec	263
	Engr	278

488 ◼ *Good Old Index*

Reading (cont'd)	Silv	336
	SixN	590
Rebus, on tile	Suss	1039
Red Bull (inn)	Prio	546
Red Circle (secret society)	RedC	908
Red-headed men	Sign	100
	Sign	109
	RedH	176
	RedH	180
	Soli	528
	Prio	543
	Lion	1087
false	RedH	180
	Twis	235
Red King (William Rufus)	Vall	779
Red lamp	SixN	587
Red leech	Gold	607
Red republican	SixN	588
Red tape	Miss	626
Redruth	Devi	958
Redskins	Stud	54
Regency	Spec	259
	Shos	1103
Regency bucks	Houn	703
	Shos	1103
Regent (Regent's) Circus	Gree	436
	Chas	582
Regent Street	Scan	168
	Bosc	216
	Houn	690
	Illu	993
Registry, marriage at	Danc	512
Registry office	Bosc	210
Reichenbach Falls (Switzerland)	Fina	478
	Empt	487
Reigate	Reig	398

Reigning family of Holland	Scan	161
	Iden	191
Reilly (lawyer)	Vall	845
Reilly (Scowrer)	Vall	851
Reincarnation	Houn	750
Rejuvenation	Cree	1082
Religion, alien	Suss	1035
Religious organization	Croo	413
Remand	Twis	241
	Wist	880
Remarkable book	Sign	97
Remarkable worm	Thor	1055
Remington typewriter	Houn	733
Rendezvous, in railway carriage	Fina	474
Reported cases referred to		
Abbe	Seco	650
Blue	Copp	318
Bosc (indirect)	Blue	245
Chas (?)	Houn	695
	Houn	730
Copp	Cree	1071
Empt	Maza	1013
Fina	Empt	495
Five	Wist	869
(indirect)	Blue	245
Glor	Musg	387
	Resi	422
	Suss	1034
Gree	Bruc	914
Iden	Blue	245
	Copp	317
(in advance)	RedH	176
Musg	Yell	351
Nava	Fina	469
Nobl	Copp	317
Prio	Blac	559

Reported cases referred to (cont'd)

RedH	Wist	869
(indirect)	Blue	245
Scan	Iden	191
	Iden	198
	Blue	245
	Copp	317
	Last	979
Seco (in advance)	Nava	447
Sign	Scan	161
	Scan	167
	RedH	186
	Iden	198
	Five	224
	Stoc	362
	Gold	613
	Card	895
Spec	Nava	467
Stud	Sign	90
	Sign	119
	Scan	161
	Scan	167
	RedH	186
	Iden	198
	Bosc	204
	Musg	387
	Resi	422
	Fina	469
	Card	895
Twis	Blue	245
	Copp	317
Republican (Party)	Five	219
Republican lady	Nobl	289
Republicans, red	SixN	588

Residences (Occupants)

Abbey Grange (Brackenstall)	Abbe	636
Albemarle Mansion (Melville)	Wist	871

Residences (Occupants) (cont'd)

Appledore Tower (Milverton)	Chas	572
Arnsworth Castle	Scan	173
Baskerville Hall (Baskerville)	Houn	674
Birchmoor (St. Simon)	Nobl	289
Birlstone Manor House (Douglas)	Vall	774
Briarbrae (Phelps)	Nava	447
Briony Lodge (Irene Adler)	Scan	167
Campden Mansions (La Rothiere)	Bruc	925
Carriton's	Suss	1035
Carston Castle (Holdernesse)	Prio	539
Cedars, The (St. Clair)	Twis	233
Charlington Hall (Williamson)	Soli	528
Cheeseman's (Ferguson)	Suss	1035
Chiltern Grange (Carruthers)	Soli	528
Copper Beeches (Rucastle)	Copp	319
Crane Water (Armitage)	Spec	263
Deep Dene House (Oldacre)	Norw	498
Dingle, The (Harringby)	Wist	876
Fairbank (Holder)	Bery	308
Folkestone Court	Houn	764
Forton Old Hall (Williams)	Wist	876
Grosvenor Mansions (St. Simon)	Nobl	288
Hales Lodge (Barker)	Vall	781
Harvey's	Suss	1035
Hatherley Farm (Turner)	Bosc	203
Haven, The (Amberley)	Reti	1114
Haven, The (Bellamy)	Lion	1087
High Gable (Henderson-Murillo)	Wist	876
High Lodge (Oldmore)	Houn	692
Holdernesse Hall (Holdernesse)	Prio	539
Hurlstone Manor House (Musgrave)	Musg	388
King's Pyland (Ross)	Silv	336
Laburnum Lodge (Brown)	SixN	590
Lachine (Barclay)	Croo	413
Lafter Hall (Frankland)	Houn	678
Manor House	Gree	437

Residences (Occupants) (cont'd)

Mapleton (Backwater)	Silv	336
Merripit House (Stapleton)	Houn	706
Myrtles, The (Kratides)	Gree	443
Nether Walsling (Stone)	Wist	876
Odley's	Suss	1035
Oxshott Towers (Ffolliot)	Wist	876
Poldhu Cottage (Holmes and Watson)	Devi	960
Pondicherry Lodge (Sholto)	Sign	102
Popham House (Eccles)	Wist	871
Purdey Place (Hynes)	Wist	876
Riding Thorp Manor (Cubitt)	Danc	512
Shoscombe Old Place (Falder)	Shos	1102
Stoke Moran (Roylott)	Spec	257
Thor Place (Gibson)	Thor	1062
Three Gables (Maberley)	3Gab	1024
Torrington Lodge (McFarlane)	Norw	499
Tredannick Wartha (Tregennis)	Devi	956
Tuxbury Old Park (Emsworth)	Blan	1000
Vicarage, The (Elman	Reti	1117
Vernon Lodge (Gruner)	Illu	987
Wisteria Lodge (Garcia)	Wist	870
Woodman's Lee (Carey)	Blac	559
Yoxley Old Place (Coram)	Gold	607

Restaurants (*see* **Businesses**)

Cafe Royal	Illu	993
Claridge's	Last	978
Criterion	Stud	16
Goldini's	Bruc	925
Holborn	Stud	16
Marcini's	Houn	766
Simpson's	Dyin	941
	Illu	998
in Strasbourg	Fina	477
vegetarian	RedH	185

Restoratives
    ammonia and brandy   Gree   445
    biscuit and claret   Dyin   941
    brandy   Sign   140
         Blue   255
         Glor   376
         Nava   466
         Empt   485
         Prio   539
         3Stu   597
         Seco   661
         Houn   757
         Houn   758
         Vall   774
         Lion   1092
    brandy and soda   Wist   871
    brandy and water   Engr   275
         Engr   276
    coffee   Wist   884
    ether, injected   Lady   953
    fresh air   Devi   959
         Devi   965
    milk and biscuit   Prio   539
    water   Stud   79
         Sign   104
         Sign   132
         Engr   275
         Stoc   371
         Glor   375
         Miss   623
    water and lemon   Gold   608
    whisky and soda   Sign   132
         RedH   189
         Nobl   294
    whisky and water   Stud   42
         Sign   150

Retort (chemical)		Stud	17
		Sign	109
		Copp	322
		Nava	448
Reuter's		Fina	469
Revolver practice		Musg	386
		Dyin	932
Revolvers (*see* **Weapons**)			
Reynolds, Sir Joshua		Houn	749
Rheumatic fever		Lion	1084
Rheumatism	(Pref)	Last	869
		Lady	942
Rhodesia		3Stu	607
Rhodesian police		3Stu	606
Rhododendrons		Nava	466
Rhone, valley of the		Fina	477
Ribston pippin		Blac	569
Richards, Dr.		Devi	957
Richest men in England, one of the		Miss	624
Richmond		Sign	130
		Vall	806
		Suss	1036
Richter (Jean Paul)		Sign	121
Rickets		Dyin	937
Ricoletti (club-foot)		Musg	387
Riding Thorp Manor		Danc	512
Riga (Russia)		Sign	90
Rigor mortis		Sign	112
Ring, as a clue		Stud	29
		Twis	238
		Nobl	295
		Vall	784
Rio Grande		Stud	56
Ripley		Nava	466
Risus sardonicus		Sign	112

Ritual	Musg	392
	Vall	829
	Vall	832
River police	Card	897
water-police	Five	227
police launch	Sign	135
Rivers		
Amazon	Thor	1060
Amoy	Blue	249
Arkansas	3Gar	1046
Cam	Miss	633
Colorado	Stud	52
Ganges	Sign	144
Mississippi	Stud	58
Missouri	Stud	54
Rhone	Fina	477
Rio Grande	Stud	56
Severn	Bosc	207
Thames	Sign	99
	Twis	244
	SixN	583
	Gold	613
	Card	897
	Bruc	921
Yellowstone	Stud	52
Riviera	Maza	1018
	3Gab	1030
Roaring Jack Woodley	Soli	536
Robbery, faked	Reig	409
	Abbe	649
Robert Street	Sign	99
Roberts, Lord	Blan	1011
Robespierre (Maximilien)	Vall	848
Robinson, John (alias)	Blue	254
Rochester Row	Sign	99
Rock of Gibraltar (ship)	Abbe	646
Rocking chair	Stoc	362

496 ◼ *Good Old Index*

Rocky Mountains	Stud	58
	Nobl	298
Rodney (admiral)	Houn	749
Rogue's portrait gallery (Scotland Yard)	3Gar	1051
Roman Catholic Church	Croo	413
	SixN	590
	Vall	842
alien religion	Suss	1035
Pope	Blac	559
	Houn	677
Rome (Italy)	Stoc	367
	Wist	885
	3Gab	1025
Ronder (circus-owner)	Veil	1096
Ronder, Eugenia	Veil	1095
Roof tops, fly over in fancy	Iden	191
Rosa, Salvator	Sign	101
Rose, moss	Nava	455
Rose, plaster	Reti	1120
Rose, sulphur	Houn	733
Rose-bushes	Engr	284
Rose-water, in hookah	Sign	101
Rosenlaui (Switzerland)	Fina	478
Ross (town)	Bosc	203
Ross, Colonel	Silv	336
Ross, Duncan	RedH	178
Ross and Mangles (animal dealers)	Houn	762
Rosythe (naval base, Scotland)	Last	973
Rotherhithe	Dyin	932
Rothiere, La, Louis	Seco	654
	Bruc	925
Rotterdam (Holland)	Bosc	214
	Last	976
Rouge	Dyin	941
Roundhay (vicar)	Devi	956
Roy (dog)	Cree	1072

Royal Artillery	Gree	437
Royal Marine Light Infantry	Stud	25
Royal Munsters	Croo	412
Royal relic	Musg	397
Royalty (*see also* **Peerage**)		
Bohemia, King of	Scan	165
Charles I	Stud	38
	Musg	396
	Vall	807
Charles II	Musg	397
Colonna, Prince and Princess of	SixN	594
David, King	Croo	415
George II	Vall	807
Holland, reigning family of	Scan	161
	Iden	191
James I	Vall	807
Kaiser	Last	971
"King of Proosia"	Blue	254
Scandinavia, royal family of	Scan	166
	Fina	470
King of	Nobl	291
Shomu, Emperor	Illu	997
Soloman, King	Vall	857
Sultan of Turkey	Blan	1007
von Saxe-Meningen, Clothilde	Scan	166
Roylott, Dr. Grimesby	Spec	258
Roylott, Mrs.	Spec	260
Rubber, of cards	RedH	186
Rubber band	Danc	520
Rubies	Stud	30
	Sign	151
Rucastle, Alice	Copp	321
Rucastle, Edward	Copp	325
Rucastle, Jephro	Copp	321
Rucastle, Mrs.	Copp	324
Rudge-Whitworth (bicycle)	Vall	791
Rue Austerlitz (Paris)	Seco	658

498 ◼ *Good Old Index*

Rue de Trajan (Montpellier)	Lady	944
Rugby	3Stu	600
	Miss	623
	Suss	1036
Ruined chapel	Shos	1104
Rufton, Earl of	Lady	943
Rule of three	Sign	112
Rulli (alias)	Wist	887
Rum	Blac	562
Rupee	Sign	143
	Croo	418
Ruritania (ship)	Illu	994
Russell, Clark	Five	218
Russell Square	Danc	512
Russia	Gold	619
	Houn	754
	Vall	844
Russian Embassy	Gold	621
Russian Foreign Office	Nava	450
Russian leather card case	Stud	30
Russian nobleman	Resi	427
Russian woman, old	Musg	387
Russo-German grain taxes	Seco	666
Rutland Island (Andaman Islands)	Sign	127
	Sign	154
Ryder, James	Blue	248

S

"S. H. for J. O."	Five	228
Sacred Council of Four	Stud	64
Safe	Spec	268
	Bery	304
	Norw	498
	Chas	577
	SixN	595
	Seco	651
	Bruc	916
	Last	972
Saffron Hill	SixN	590
Sahara King (lion)	Veil	1097
Sailor	Twis	244
Sailors, hands of	Sign	91
St. Augustine (Florida)	Five	223
St. Batholomew's Hospital (*see* Bart's)		
St. Clair, Neville	Twis	232
St. Clair, Mrs.	Twis	234
St. George, Guild of	Croo	413
St. George's (church)	Nobl	289
St. George's Theological College	Twis	229
St. Helena (island)	Vall	865
St. Ives	Devi	959
St. James's Gazette	Blue	249

"St. James's (street) end" of Pall Mall	Gree	436
St. James's Hall	RedH	184
St. James's Square	Illu	994
St. James's Street	Gree	436
	3Gab	1028
St. John's Wood	Scan	167
St. Louis (Missouri)	Stud	60
	Sign	90
St. Luke's, College of	3Stu	596
St. Monica, Church of	Scan	168
St. Oliver's (school)	Houn	753
St. Pancras case	Shos	1102
St. Pancras Hotel	Iden	195
St. Paul's (cathedral)	Sign	137
	RedH	182
St. Petersburg (Russia)	Stud	76
St. Saviour's (church)	Iden	195
St. Simon, Lady Clara	Nobl	290
St. Simon, Lord Eustace	Nobl	290
St. Simon, Lord Robert	Nobl	287
St. Vitus's dance	Stoc	362
	Gree	441
Salad oil	Lion	1092
Salt, as a preservative	Card	891
Salt, those who have been true to their	Sign	148
Salt Lake City	Stud	59
Salt Lake Mountains	Stud	77
Saltire, Lord	Prio	539
Samson, of New Orleans	Stud	18
Samuel, first or second (book) of	Croo	422
Sand, George	RedH	190
Sandeford	SixN	590
Sanders, Ikey	Maza	1018
San Francisco (California)	Nobl	289
Sanger (John)	Veil	1097
San Paulo (Sao Paulo, Brazil)	Blac	562
San Pedro	Wist	884

San Remo (Italy)	Stoc	366
Sandwich	RedH	185
	Bery	311
	Seco	657
	Nava	466
Sapphire	Sign	151
Sarasate (Pablo)	RedH	184
Sarcophagus	Shos	1110
Satan	Devi	963
devil	Blue	249
	Spec	264
	Glor	377
	Houn	684
	Wist	883
	Devi	963
evil one	Chas	573
father of evil	Houn	681
Saunders (maid)	Danc	518
Saunders, Mrs. (housekeeper)	3Gar	1050
Saunders, Sir James	Blan	1010
Savage, Victor	Dyin	939
Savannah (Georgia)	Five	228
Sawyer, Mrs.	Stud	39
Saxe-Coburg Square	RedH	183
Saxe-Meningen, Clothilde von	Scan	166
Saxons	Spec	259
	Blac	564
	Suss	1041
	Shos	1110
Anglo-saxon tenacity	Stud	58
Scandinavia, royal family of	Scan	166
	Fina	470
King of	Nobl	291
Scanlan, Mike	Vall	817
Scarlet thread of murder	Stud	36

Scenes of Investigations

Bedfordshire	Blan	1007
Berkshire	Engr	278
	Shos	1106
Birmingham	Stoc	363
Cambridgeshire (?)	3Stu	596
	Miss	622
Camford	Cree	1072
Cornwall	Devi	955
Devonshire	Silv	340
	Houn	699
Essex	Last	974
France	Lady	945
Hallamshire	Prio	539
Hampshire	Copp	319
	Silv	347
	Croo	412
	Thor	1055
Herefordshire	Bosc	203
Kent	Twis	233
	Gold	608
	Abbe	636
London	Stud	26
	Sign	94
	Scan	166
	RedH	178
	Iden	193
	Five	218
	Twis	229
	Blue	245
	Nobl	288
	Bery	304
	Yell	353
	Resi	425
	Gree	442
	Nava	458
	Fina	469

Scenes of Investigations, London		Empt	483
(cont'd)		Chas	572
		SixN	583
		Seco	651
		Houn	669
		RedC	905
		Bruc	915
		Dyin	932
		Lady	947
		Illu	987
		Maza	1012
		3Gar	1045
		Veil	1095
		Reti	1113
	Middlesex	3Gab	1024
	Norfolk	Glor	374
		Danc	512
	Surrey	Spec	257
		Reig	398
		Nava	449
		Norw	497
		Soli	527
		Wist	871
		Card	890
	Sussex	Musg	388
		Blac	560
		Vall	778
		Suss	1035
		Lion	1083
	Switzerland	Fina	477
		Lady	944
	United States	Last	978
Scheming mind		Wist	887
		Reti	1120
Schoenbrunn Palace (Austria)		Last	977
Scholarship, Fortesque		3Stu	596
School, best preparatory, in England		Prio	540

Good Old Index

School, failure of	Houn	710
School, summer term begins	Prio	540
Schoolmaster	Prio	540
	Houn	742
	Lion	1083
Schools, colleges and universities		
Abbey School	Blan	1007
Board schools	Nava	456
Boarding establishment	Sign	94
Cambridge University	Nava	447
	Gold	609
	Miss	622
Camford University	Cree	1072
College of St. Luke's	3Stu	596
Eton	RedH	186
	Empt	494
Gables, The	Lion	1083
London University	Stud	15
	Resi	425
Oxford University	RedH	186
	Empt	494
	Miss	623
Priory School	Prio	540
Private school	Copp	332
St. Oliver's	Houn	753
Theological College of St. George's	Twis	229
Trinity College (Cambridge)	Miss	622
Uppingham	Gold	609
York College (US)	Stud	80
Science of Deduction and Analysis	Stud	23
Scissors	Card	891
nail	Houn	687
	Wist	874
Scissors-grinder	Scan	171
Scorbutic symptoms	Illu	989
Scotch accent	Vall	798
Scotchwoman's breakfast	Nava	465

Scotland			RedH	186
			Blac	570
Scotland Yard			Stud	25
			Stud	40
			Spec	265
			SixN	595
			Thor	1062
			Lion	1095
	Inspectors		Stud	77
			Sign	113
		(2)	Sign	135
			Sign	141
			RedH	188
			Bery	302
			Illu	998
			3Gab	1029
	Barton		Twis	236
	Bradstreet		Twis	241
			Blue	248
			Engr	284
	Brown		Sign	143
	Forbes		Nava	453
	Gregory		Silv	337
	Gregson		Stud	26
			Sign	90
			Gree	444
			Wist	871
			RedC	908
	Hill		SixN	590
	Hopkins		Blac	559
			Gold	608
			Miss	622
			Abbe	636
	Jones, Athelney		Sign	90
	Jones, Peter		RedH	186
	Lanner		Resi	431
	Lestrade (*which see*)			

Scotland Yard, inspectors (cont'd)

MacDonald		Vall	773
MacKinnon		Reti	1119
Merivale		Shos	1102
Montgomery		Card	898
Morton		Dyin	936
Patterson		Fina	480
Youghal		Maza	1015
Sergeants		Sign	117
		Lady	952
Constables		Stud	27
	(4)	Stud	29
	(2)	Stud	35
	(2)	Stud	45
	(2)	Sign	117
	(2)	Twis	234
	(2)	Twis	241
		Bery	306
		Nava	452
	(2)	Empt	491
	(2)	Norw	499
		Norw	506
	(3)	Norw	507
		SixN	583
		Lady	952
		3Gab	1029
		Reti	1119
Barrett		Seco	655
Cook		Five	227
MacPherson		Seco	661
Murcher		Stud	34
Rance, John		Stud	32
Other			
officers	(2)	RedH	188
police	(2)	Nobl	293
police		Bruc	927

Scotland Yard, other (cont'd)

police		Maza	1021
		Nava	458
police launch		Sign	135
police woman		Nava	454
		Nava	458
river police		Card	897
water-police		Five	227
Scotland Yard Museum		Empt	496
Scott, James H.		Vall	817
Scott Eccles, John		Wist	869
Scowrers		Vall	815
password of		Vall	817
		Vall	833
Scrap of paper, as a clue		Nobl	296
		Glor	374
		Musg	389
		Reig	401
		Miss	625
		Wist	873
		3Gab	1029
Screw-driver		Resi	432
		Lady	953
Scripture (*see* Biblical Quotations/Allusions)			
Scrub oak		Houn	700
Scrum		Miss	622
Sculptor (Devine)		SixN	584
Scylla and Charybdis		Resi	422
Sea air, sunshine and patience		Devi	960
Sea of Azov fleet		Lady	948
Sea Unicorn **(ship)**		Blac	560
Sea-faring, evidence of		Stud	39
		Five	225
		Glor	381
		Blac	560
		Card	895

Sea-stories of Clark Russell
Seal
    Sealskin pouch
Seal, on letter
Sealing wax knife

Searchlight
Seasons of cases, probable
    Autumn

    Winter

    Spring

Five	218
Blac	560
Silv	341
Nobl	287
Wist	873
Gold	610
Sign	138
Sign	98
RedH	176
Five	218
Nobl	287
Glor	377
Resi	422
Gold	607
Seco	650
Houn	700
Houn	707
Bruc	913
Dyin	932
Lady	944
Suss	1034
Thor	1055
Veil	1095
Blue	244
Bery	301
Chas	572
3Stu	598
Miss	622
Abbe	635
Vall	773
RedC	907
Blan	1000
Stud	15
Scan	162
Spec	258
Copp	317

Seasons of cases, probable, Spring (cont'd)	Yell	351
	Reig	398
	Fina	469
	Empt	483
	Soli	527
	Prio	540
	Wist	869
	Devi	955
	3Gar	1047
	Shos	1103
Summer	Iden	192
	Bosc	203
	Twis	229
	Engr	274
	Silv	337
	Stoc	362
	Musg	394
	Croo	411
	Gree	435
	Nava	447
	Norw	504
	Danc	513
	Blac	559
	SixN	589
	Card	888
	Last	970
	Illu	984
	Maza	1012
	3Gab	1029
	Cree	1071
	Lion	1083
	Reti	1114
Second Afghan War	Stud	15
Second cab	Fina	474
Second most dangerous man in London (Moran)	Empt	494

Second most interesting object in the North	Prio	558
Second post	Vall	770
Second Stain, story of, promised	Nava	447
Secrecy delays narration	Spec	258
	Empt	483
	Chas	572
	Seco	650
	Devi	956
	Illu	984
Secrecy requested	Scan	164
	Engr	277
Secret societies	Stud	33
Brotherhood	Gold	620
Carbonari	Stud	41
	RedC	911
Danite band	Stud	63
Irish, Buffalo	Last	978
Italian	Stud	62
Ku Klux Klan	Five	226
Mafia	SixN	590
Red Circle	RedC	908
Scowrers	Vall	815
Vehmgericht	Stud	41
	Stud	62
Secretary	Chas	577
	Gold	609
	Gold	620
Bennett, Trevor	Cree	1075
Ferguson	Engr	281
	Thor	1057
Lucas	Wist	882
Phelps, Percy	Nava	447
Smith, Willoughby	Gold	607
Stangerson, Joseph	Stud	41
Wilder, James	Prio	540
Secretary for European Affairs	Seco	650

Secretary for Foreign Affairs	Nobl	288
Secretary of State, Chief	Prio	539
Securities		
American Railway bonds	Stoc	373
Ayrshires	Stoc	365
British Broken Hills	Stoc	365
Canadian Pacific Railway	Blac	562
Mining scrip	Stoc	373
New Zealand Consolidated	Stoc	365
New Zealand stock (bond)	Iden	193
Scrip	Norw	500
South African gold shares	Soli	530
South African gold stocks	Danc	511
South African speculation	Houn	676
Stocks	Nava	467
Venezuelan loan	Stoc	364
Securities, losses from dabbling in	Nava	467
Sedative, Strychnine as	Sign	105
Selden (convict)	Houn	701
Semaphore	Last	975
Senator (US)	Thor	1055
Senegambia	Sign	111
Sepoys	Sign	145
Sergeant of marines, retired	Stud	25
Sergius	Gold	619
Serpentine (lake)	Nobl	295
Serpentine Avenue	Scan	167
Serpentine-mews	Scan	168
Serpents, in the Zoo	Chas	572
Serum of anthropoid	Cree	1082
Servants (*see also* **Baker Street, butlers, coachmen, governesses, housekeepers and maids**)		
boy	Musg	388
cook	Musg	388
	Croo	414

Servants (see also Baker Street, butlers, coachmen, governesses, housekeepers and maids), cook (cont'd)
    (Mrs. Porter)
  footman

		Resi	433
		Wist	872
		Devi	957
		Nobl	290
(2)		Musg	388
		Prio	557
(2)		Chas	573
		Wist	872
		Wist	882
		Illu	991
		3Gab	1031

    several
  game-keeper

	Illu	998
	Musg	389
	Thor	1056

  gardener

	Glor	378
	Musg	388
	Gold	609

    (Warner)
    under-gardener
  gatekeeper (McMurdo)
  girl

	Wist	882
	Chas	582
	Sign	126
	RedH	178
	RedC	902
	Devi	959

  groom

	Bery	304
	Danc	519
	Soli	535
	Houn	699
	Vall	790

    (Cobb)
    (Toller)
  house-maid
  lad

	Bosc	205
	Copp	324
	Seco	651
	Spec	268
	Prio	551

Servants (*see also* Baker Street, butlers, coachmen, governesses, housekeepers and maids) (cont'd)

lodge-keeper		Bosc	203
		Abbe	637
keeper		Shos	1109
maidservant	(3)	Bery	304
		Wist	882
man		Bosc	203
manservant		Houn	713
		Wist	882
page		Bery	304
		Resi	428
porters		Sign	102
servant		Sign	119
		Blac	560
	(8)	Abbe	641
	(6)	Vall	781
		Vall	792
	(2)	Suss	1037
half-dozen		Bosc	203
native		Sign	102
(Mrs. Toller)		Copp	324
Watson's		Croo	411
slavey		Scan	162
stable-boy		Danc	513
stable-hand		Musg	388
		Suss	1037
stable-lads	(3)	Silv	336
staff, small		Soli	532
valet		Seco	651
		Bruc	926
(Mitton)		Seco	655
waiting-maid		Blue	255
(Parr)		Bery	304
Severn (river)		Bosc	207
Seville (Spain)		Stud	62

514 ◼ *Good Old Index*

Shadwell Police Station		Card	898
Shafter, Ettie		Vall	820
Shafter, Jacob		Vall	818
Shaftesbury Avenue		Gree	438
Shag (tobacco)		Scan	168
		Twis	240
		Houn	682
		Cree	1071
Shahgunge (India)		Sign	146
Shakespeare, First Folio		3Gab	1027
Shakespearean Quotations/Allusions (*see* Literary references)			
Shape, at window		Wist	877
Shark		Sign	127
Sheeny		Stoc	365
Sheep		Stud	60
		Silv	346
bighorn		Stud	72
moor		Prio	546
Sheep dog		Houn	679
Sheridan Street (Vermissa)		Vall	818
Sherman (bird-stuffer)		Sign	115
Sherpur (Afghanistan)		Empt	494
Sherry	(2)	Nobl	296
		Glor	383
Shetland Lights (lighthouse)		Blac	570
Shikari (hunter)		Empt	492
Shipley's Yard (cabyard)		Houn	697
Shipping office		Twis	234
		Abbe	645
		Houn	672
Shipping agent		Blac	567
Ships and Boats			
Alicia (cutter)		Thor	1055
Aurora (steam launch)		Sign	124
Bass Rock (liner)		Abbe	646
Conqueror (steam packet)		Card	893

Ships and Boats (cont'd)
Esmeralda	Sign	141
Friesland (steamship)	Norw	496
Gloria Scott (bark)	Glor	380
Hotspur (brig)	Glor	385
Lone Star (bark)	Five	228
Matilda Briggs	Suss	1034
May Day (steam packet)	Card	893
Norah Creina (steamer)	Resi	434
Orontes (troopship)	Stud	15
Palmyra (liner)	Vall	865
Rock of Gibraltar (liner)	Abbe	646
Ruritania (liner)	Illu	994
Sea Unicorn (steam sealer)	Blac	560
Sophy Anderson (bark)	Five	218
yacht	Blac	566
Ship's tobacco	Stud	19
Shirt cuff, notes on	Nava	452
	Houn	682
Shlessinger, Dr. (alias)	Lady	944
Shlessinger, Mrs. (alias)	Lady	944
Shoes, significance of	Stud	33
	Sign	91
	Scan	162
	Iden	197
	Five	219
	Houn	760
	Reti	1114
Sholto, Bartholomew	Sign	101
Sholto, Major John	Sign	95
Sholto, Thaddeus	Sign	100
Shomu, Emperor	Illu	997
Shooting and hunting (*see also* Sports)	Stud	60
	Stud	68
	Stud	72
	Bosc	205
	Glor	374

516 ■ *Good Old Index*

Shooting and hunting (*see also* Sports) (cont'd)	Empt	492
	Houn	736
	Devi	961
	Last	971
	Maza	1015
	Thor	1063
Shop window, murderer's picture in	Chas	582
Shorthand	Stud	45
	Card	898
Shoscombe	Shos	1107
Shoscombe Old Place	Shos	1102
Shoscombe Park	Shos	1103
Shoscombe Prince (horse)	Shos	1103
Shoscombe spaniels	Shos	1103
Shoso-in	Illu	997
Shuman (ironworks owner)	Vall	836
Siam	Bruc	916
Siberia (Russia)	Gold	620
Sidelights on Horace, Huxtable's	Prio	540
Sierra Blanco (US)	Stud	52
Sierra Leone	Glor	384
Sierra Nevada	Stud	52
Siesta	3Gar	1052
Sigerson (alias)	Empt	488
Sign of Four, described	Sign	98
	Sign	151
Sikhs	Sign	146
	Croo	420
Silver	Stud	61
	Engr	285
prospectors	Stud	61
Silver Blaze (horse)	Silv	336
Silvester's (bank)	Lady	943
Simpson (BSI)	Croo	419
Simpson, Baldy	Blan	1009
Simpson, Fitzroy	Silv	336

Simpson's (restaurant)	Dyin	941
	Illu	988
	Illu	991
Sinclair, Admiral	Bruc	917
Singapore	Sign	155
Singh, Mahomet	Sign	98
Singleford, Lord	Silv	347
Singlestick	Stud	22
	Illu	993
Singularity, as a clue	Bosc	202
Skating Club, Prince's	RedC	904
Skein, tangled	Cree	1071
Skibbareen (Ireland)	Last	978
Skiffs	Sign	123
Skirts, frou-frou of	Seco	657
Skull, capacity of	Blue	247
	Dyin	937
Skull, Holmes's, client's interest in	Houn	672
Skull, prehistoric	Houn	714
Skulls, plaster	3Gar	1048
Slaney, Abe	Danc	521
Slate	Gree	440
Slater (stonemason)	Blac	561
Slaters, lands of	Sign	91
Slavey (maid)	Scan	162
Sleepy Hollows	Miss	632
Sleeves, importance of	RedH	177
	Iden	196
	Spec	259
Sleuth-hound	RedH	185
	Cree	1071
Slips, common to all mortals	Lady	954
Sloane, Hans	3Gar	1049
Slop shop	Twis	230
Slowworm	Sign	117
Small, Jonathan	Sign	98
Smith, Culverton	Dyin	935

Smith, Jack	Sign	123
Smith, James	Soli	527
Smith (Jim)	Sign	124
Smith, Joseph	Stud	57
Smith, Mordecai	Sign	123
Smith, Mrs. Mordecai	Sign	123
Smith, Ralph	Soli	527
Smith, Violet	Soli	526
Smith, Willoughby	Gold	607
Smith and Wesson revolver	Vall	861
Smith-Mortimer succession case	Gold	607
Smoke rocket, plumber's	Scan	170
Smoking (*see* tobacco)		
Snake		
cobra	Croo	421
serpents, in the Zoo	Chas	572
swamp adder	Spec	272
viper	Dyin	941
	Suss	1034
Snorter, case a	Vall	778
Snuff	RedH	180
	Gree	437
snuff-box, tortise shell	Gree	437
Soames, Sir Cathcart	Prio	540
Soames, Hilton	Miss	596
Sobbing of wind in chimney	Five	218
	Houn	704
Socialists	Stud	33
	Stud	41
Solar system	Stud	21
Soldering of grate	Blue	248
Solent	Last	978
Solicitor (*see also* Barrister, Lawyer)	Reig	408
	Soli	527
	Houn	692
Fordham	Five	220
McFarlane, John Hector	Norw	497

Solicitor (*see also* Barrister, Lawyer)
  (cont'd)
    Morris (imposter)   RedH   182
    Morrison, Morrison and Dodd   Suss   1034
    Sutro   3Gab   1025
    Whyte, William   Stud   38
Solomon   Vall   857
Somerton (doctor)   Sign   152
Somomy stock (racehorse)   Silv   337
Songs   Vall   837
Sophy Anderson (ship)   Five   218
Sorrow as a teacher   Thor   1070
Sotheby's (auction rooms)   Illu   995
     3Gar   1048
"Souls I have ruined" (Baron Gruner's diary)   Illu   990
South Africa   Soli   528
     3Stu   606
     Houn   678
     Vall   865
     Lady   946
     Illu   996
     Blan   1000
South African War   3Gar   1044
  Boer War   Blan   1000
South America   Stud   80
     Sign   127
     Blac   563
     Houn   728
     Card   893
     Lady   944
     Suss   1039
South Australia   Abbe   638
South Brixton   Veil   1095
South coast (of England)   Houn   700

South Downs
    Sussex Downs

South London

    Surrey side

Southampton

Southampton Highroad
Southerton, Lord
Southsea

Spaniel

  Carlo
  Shoscombe spaniels
Spanish Embassy
Spanner
Sparking plugs (code word)
Spatulate fingers, meaning of
Spaulding, Vincent (alias)
Special (train)
Speckled band
Spectacles

Last	978
Seco	650
Lion	1083
Sign	100
SixN	583
Twis	241
Reti	1119
Copp	324
Copp	332
Abbe	646
Houn	681
Vall	806
Blan	1001
Copp	324
Copp	324
Resi	423
Card	888
Sign	117
Houn	671
Suss	1039
Shos	1103
Wist	872
Vall	791
Last	973
Soli	527
RedH	178
Fina	476
Spec	262
Iden	197
Silv	340
Gree	444
Prio	548
Vall	784
Vall	816
Vall	839
Bruc	922

Spectacles (cont'd)	Devi	956
	3Gar	1048
blue-tinted	Sign	117
coloured	Empt	485
field	Silv	336
gold rimmed	Five	218
	Nobl	291
	Chas	573
	Gold	612
	Houn	671
	Wist	870
gray-tinted	Reti	1116
horn	Cree	1076
night	Sign	137
pince-nez	Iden	197
	Five	218
	Nobl	291
	Copp	318
	Gold	612
sunglasses	Reti	1116
tinted	Iden	194
as a clue	Gold	612
Spectator (newspaper)	Blan	1005
Spencer John gang	3Gab	1024
Spender, Rose	Lady	951
Sphinx	Blan	1012
Spies	Seco	654
	Bruc	925
	Last	971
Spinal meningitis, suspected	Suss	1039
Spine, twisted	Suss	1037
Spirit-case	Scan	162
Splashes, on sleeve	Spec	259
	Lady	942
Splay foot	Vall	790
Spleen, enlarged	Sign	102
Splugen Pass (Switzerland-Austria)	Illu	985

Sponge

	Sign	123
	Twis	242
	Blan	1009

Sports and Games

archery	RedH	182
backgammon	Five	220
bicycling	Five	219
	Soli	527
	Prio	541
	Prio	547
	Miss	631
	Vall	790
billiards	Glor	376
	Musg	389
	Gree	437
	Danc	511
	Miss	624
	Abbe	638
	Houn	703
blue, Light Blue (sports award)	3Stu	600
	Miss	633
	Lion	1083
boating	Card	900
bowling	Soli	535
boxing	Stud	22
	Sign	102
	Sign	106
	Five	225
	Yell	351
	Glor	374
	Soli	532
	Last	972
	Maza	1014
	3Gab	1023
	Shos	1103
cards	Sign	152
	RedH	188

Sports and Games, cards (cont'd)

	Bery	304
	Empt	484
	Soli	537
	3Stu	601
	Vall	844
	Devi	957
chess	Reti	1113
cricket	Nava	447
	3Stu	600
croquet	Devi	963
dancing	Iden	193
draughts	Five	220
fishing	Glor	374
	Musg	394
	Shos	1109
four-in-hand	Last	971
fox hunting	Vall	787
golf	Gree	435
	Blac	568
horse racing	Bosc	203
	Blue	253
	Bery	304
	Silv	347
	3Stu	600
	Miss	628
	Shos	1103
polo	Last	971
	Illu	987
revolver practice	Musg	386
	Dyin	932
rugby	3Stu	600
	Miss	623
	Suss	1036
self-defense	Fina	473
shooting and hunting	Stud	60
	Stud	68
	Stud	72

524 ◾ *Good Old Index*

Sports and Games, shooting and hunting (cont'd)

	Bosc	205
	Glor	374
	Empt	492
	Houn	736
	Devi	961
	Last	971
	Maza	1015
	Thor	1063
bearskin	Prio	539
deer's heads	Abbe	639
gunroom	Musg	389
	Abbe	638
	Shos	1111
stag's heads	Houn	702
tiger skin	Sign	100
	Abbe	640
single stick	Stud	22
	Illu	993
skating	RedC	904
swimming	Lion	1084
swordsmanship	Stud	22
	Five	225
	Glor	374
tennis, lawn	Danc	517
tennis shoes	Chas	577
	Devi	968
canvas shoes	Lion	1084
track and field	3Stu	600
wrestling	Empt	486
yachting	Last	971
Square-toes	Stud	33
	Bosc	212
	Silv	345
	Resi	430
Squire	Spec	259
	Musg	393
	Danc	513

Squire (cont'd)	Chas	573
	Last	973
Stackhurst, Harold	Lion	1083
Staff-commander	Scan	165
Stag's heads	Houn	702
Staghound	Stud	51
Stagnant days	Miss	622
	Vall	778
Stagville (US)	Vall	815
Stained glass	Sign	116
	Houn	702
Stair-rods	Sign	116
Stake Royal (mine)	Vall	850
Stamford (dresser)	Stud	16
Stamford, Archie	Soli	527
Stamford's (map-dealer)	Houn	683
Stamp, American	Danc	513
Stamp, Austrian	Cree	1082
Stamps, postage (*see* Post Office)		
Stamps and postcards	Sign	92
Standard (newspaper; *see also Evening Standard*)	Stud	41
	Sign	125
	Sign	131
	Blue	249
Stanger, James	Vall	837
Stangerson (Mormon elder)	Stud	30
Stangerson, Joseph	Stud	30
Staphouse (victim)	Vall	853
Staples (butler)	Dyin	936
Stapleton, Beryl	Houn	708
Stapleton, Jack (Baskerville)	Houn	678
Star (newspaper)	Blue	249
Starr, Dr. Lysander	3Gar	1047
Starr, Colonel Lysander	Engr	277
Stars and Stripes	Nobl	300
State and Merton County Railroad Company	Vall	836

526 ◼ *Good Old Index*

States, U. S.
    Arizona   Nobl   298
    California   Stud   60
                               Nobl   289
                               Vall   780
    Carolinas   Five   226
    Florida   Five   219
                               Five   226
    Georgia   Five   226
                               Five   228
    Illinois   Stud   54
    Kansas   3Gar   1045
    Louisiana   Five   226
    Michigan   Vall   821
    Montana   Nobl   298
    Nebraska   Stud   52
    Nevada   Stud   61
    New Jersey   Scan   165
    New Mexico   Nobl   298
    North Carolina   Houn   754
    Ohio   Stud   26
    Pennsylvania   RedH   178
                               Vall   785
    Tennessee   Five   226
    Texas   Five   229
    Utah   Stud   58
Station-master   Engr   286
                               Danc   517
                               Houn   700
                               Blan   1006
    younger Moriarty   Vall   776
Staunton, Arthur H.   Miss   623
Staunton, Godfrey   Miss   622
Staunton, Henry   Miss   623
Staunton, Mrs.   Miss   634
Steiler, Peter, the elder   Fina   477
Steiner (spy)   Last   976

Stendal (victims)	Vall	853
Stepfather	Iden	193
	Spec	259
Stephens (butler)	Shos	1104
Stepney	SixN	588
Sterndale, Dr. Leon	Devi	961
Stethoscope	Sign	100
	Scan	162
Stevens, Bert	Norw	504
Stevenson (rugby player)	Miss	623
Stewart, Jane	Croo	414
Stewart, Mrs.	Empt	494
Sticking plaster	Gree	440
Sticks, deductions from	Glor	375
	Norw	498
	Houn	670
Stile	Spec	266
Stimson and Co. (undertakers)	Lady	952
Stimulants (*see* Restoratives)		
Stoat	Sign	117
	Croo	416
Stock Exchange	Blac	562
	Bruc	930
Stockdale, Barney	3Gab	1024
Stockdale, Susan	3Gab	1026
Stocks (*see* Securities)		
Stockwell Place	Sign	99
Stoke Moran	Spec	257
Stone hammer	Sign	109
Stone huts, on moor	Houn	709
Stone, leave none unturned	Silv	340
	Miss	627
	Bruc	919
Stone, Rev. Joshua	Wist	876
Stoner, Helen	Spec	259
Stoner, Julia	Spec	260
Stoner, Major-General	Spec	260

528 ◻ *Good Old Index*

Stoner, Mrs.	Spec	260
Stoper, Miss	Copp	318
Stormy petrel, of crime	Reig	406
	Nava	448
Stradivarius (violin)	Stud	27
	Sign	134
	Card	894
Straight-jacket	Houn	719
Straker, John	Silv	336
Straker, Mrs.	Silv	338
Strand	Stud	15
	Stud	30
	Sign	98
	RedH	184
	Resi	424
	Fina	474
	Miss	624
	Houn	688
	Illu	988
Strand-end, of Lowther Arcade	Fina	474
Stranger's Room (Diogenes Club)	Gree	436
Strasbourg (Germany)	Fina	476
Straubenzee	Maza	1014
Strauss, Herman	Vall	849
Straw	Norw	507
Streatham	Sign	121
	Bery	304
Street Arabs	Stud	42
	Sign	99
	Sign	126
Streets, gaslit	Sign	98
	Sign	116
	Scan	171
	RedH	187
	Blue	245
	Croo	417
	Resi	430

S ◼ 529

Streets, gaslit (cont'd)		Empt	488
	(?)	Gold	607
		Miss	631
		Seco	662
		Vall	819
		RedC	907
Streets (*see* London Streets)			
Stretcher		Stud	29
Stride, animal's		Croo	416
Stride and age, of man		Stud	33
String, ball of		Musg	387
String, tarred, as a clue		Card	891
Stroke		Glor	379
apoplexy		Glor	377
		Croo	422
Strong-room (*see* safe)		Reti	1115
Stroud Valley		Bosc	207
Strychnine, as a sedative		Sign	105
Strychnine-like substance		Sign	113
Stuart (royal house)		Musg	397
Study in Scarlet		Stud	86
Stuffiness, of room, as a clue		Devi	964
Stylestown (U.S.A.)		Vall	857
Subclavian artery		Stud	15
Subjects of the Crown, one of the greatest		Prio	540
Submarine		Bruc	916
		Last	972
Sudbury (student)		Lion	1090
Suez Canal (Egypt)		Abbe	646
Sugar, for dog		Sign	117
Sugar King		3Gab	1031
Sugar-tongs		Dyin	935
Suicide		Gold	621
attempted		Danc	525
		Reti	1119
favorite time for		Resi	432

Suicide (cont'd)
    presumed

	Five	221
	Five	222
	Five	227

    prevented

	Stoc	361
	Veil	1101

    suspected   Gold   616
Sultan of Turkey   Blan   1007
Sulphur rose   Houn   733
Sumatra

	Sign	127
	Dyin	933

Sumatra, giant rat of   Suss   1034
Summer term (school)   Prio   540
Sumner (shipping agent)   Blac   567
Sun

	Sign	121
	Sign	137
	Spec	265
	Copp	322
	Silv	343
	Glor	378
	Musg	394
	Norw	507
	Soli	530
	Gold	613
	Miss	635
	Abbe	639
	Houn	701
	Houn	704
	Houn	738
	Houn	743
	Bruc	921
	3Gar	1047
	Thor	1069

    sunrise

	Sign	119
	Twis	240

Sundial	Five	222
	Danc	513
	Vall	798
	Thor	1066
Sung (Chinese dynasty)	Illu	995
Sunglasses (*see also* Spectacles)	Reti	1116
Sunshine and patience, sea air	Devi	960
Supernatural, suspected	Houn	681
Superstition, popular	Houn	678
Supper, follows dinner	Blue	251
	Houn	748
Surrey	Sign	99
	Sign	137
	Twis	237
	Spec	257
	Reig	398
	Nava	465
	Soli	527
	Wist	871
Surrey Constabulary	Wist	871
Surrey side (of London)	Twis	241
	Reti	1119
South London	Sign	100
	SixN	583
Sussex	Five	219
	Musg	388
	Blac	560
	Vall	778
	Suss	1035
	Lion	1083
Sussex Constabulary	Vall	781
Sussex Downs	Seco	650
	Lion	1083
South Downs	Last	978
Sutherland, Mary	Iden	192
	RedH	176
Sutro (lawyer)	3Gab	1025

532 ◼ *Good Old Index*

Sutton (Blessington)	Resi	434
Swain, John	Five	223
Swamp adder	Spec	272
Swan	Abbe	645
Swan and Edison (lighting manufacturers)	Houn	702
Swandam Lane	Twis	234
Sweating	Copp	319
Swedish Pathological Society	Houn	671
Swimming	Lion	1084
Swindler, most accomplished, in Europe	Reig	398
Swindon	Bosc	207
Swindon, Archie	Vall	836
Swiss youth	Fina	478
Switzerland	Fina	476
	Empt	495
	Lady	942
Swordsmanship	Stud	22
	Five	225
	Glor	374
Sydenham	Norw	498
	Abbe	637
Sydenham Road	Norw	498
Sydney (Australia)	Glor	385
Sylvius, Count Negretto	Maza	1014
Syracusan coin	3Gar	1048
Syria (Turkey)	Gold	615
Syringe		
horrifies Watson	Miss	633
hypodermic	Sign	89
	Dyin	934

T

Tallow stains, inferences from	Blue	247
Tang (Chinese dynasty)	Illu	995
Tangey (commissionaire)	Nava	450
Tangey, Mrs.	Nava	453
Tangey, Miss	Nava	453
Tang-ying	Illu	995
Tankerville Club	Empt	494
Tankerville Club scandal	Five	219
Tantalus	Blac	562
spirit-case	Scan	162
Tapanuli fever	Dyin	934
Tape measure	Stud	31
	Sign	112
Tapping at door, queer	Stoc	370
Tarleton murders	Musg	387
Tarlton, Susan	Gold	609
Tarred string, as a clue	Card	891
Tattoo marks	Stud	26
	RedH	177
	Glor	376
	Vall	784
Tavern (*see also* Inn, Public House)	Shos	1107
Tavernier (modeller)	Maza	1016
Tavistock	Silv	337

534 ◼ *Good Old Index*

Taxes		SixN	588
		Seco	654
		Last	972
Taxidermist		Sign	115
Tea		Sign	97
		Bosc	207
		Bery	311
		Yell	360
		Croo	414
		Gree	431
		Gree	435
		Nava	465
		Nava	466
		3Stu	597
		Abbe	636
		Vall	783
		Vall	799
		Card	900
		Devi	956
		Suss	1040
		Cree	1083
		Lion	1090
Teddy (mongoose)		Croo	421
Teeth, false		Iden	191
Telegram (wire)		Stud	30
		Stud	32
		Stud	47
		Stud	48
		Stud	85
		Sign	91
		Sign	94
		Sign	125
		Sign	132
	(2)	Bosc	202
		Bosc	214
		Five	222
		Twis	234

Telegram (wire) (cont'd)

	Copp	322
(2)	Silv	336
	Silv	337
	Yell	360
	Glor	377
(2)?	Reig	398
	Gree	442
	Nava	448
	Nava	455
	Nava	457
	Nava	458
	Nava	467
(2)	Fina	476
	Norw	500
	Norw	505
	Danc	514
	Danc	516
	Danc	517
	Danc	521
(2)	Danc	523
	Soli	536
	Soli	538
	Prio	553
	Prio	555
	Prio	557
	Blac	559
	Blac	567
	Blac	568
	SixN	585
	Miss	622
(2)	Miss	624
	Miss	625
	Miss	631
	Miss	632
	Miss	635
	Abbe	646
	Seco	653

Telegram (wire) (cont'd)

	Seco	658
	Houn	681
	Houn	692
	Houn	694
(3)	Houn	696
	Houn	712
(2)	Houn	752
	Vall	806
(2)	Wist	869
	Wist	874
	Wist	875
	Wist	876
	Wist	878
	Card	890
	Card	891
	Card	894
	Card	895
	Card	897
	Bruc	914
	Bruc	920
(2)	Lady	944
(2)	Lady	945
(2)	Lady	947
	Devi	955
(2)	Devi	962
	Last	973
	Last	978
	Illu	991
	3Gab	1024
	3Gab	1028
	Suss	1036
	Cree	1071
(2)	Cree	1078
	Reti	1117
(2)	Reti	1118

Telegram (wire) (cont'd)
   American | Stud | 38
   cipher | Seco | 653
   counterfoils | Miss | 627
Telegraph **(newspaper)** | Silv | 336
   Daily Telegraph | Stud | 41
| Copp | 316
| Norw | 497
| Seco | 658
| Bruc | 928
Telegraph, electro- | Stud | 64
Telegraph office | Stud | 32
| Copp | 329
| Gree | 442
| Miss | 627
| Abbe | 646
| Card | 894
| Reti | 1118
   in grocery | Houn | 705
Telegraph-poles, counted | Silv | 336
Telephone
   across from 221B | Sign | 134
   at 221B | Illu | 984
| 3Gar | 1047
| Reti | 1116
   in the country | Blan | 1008
| Reti | 1118
   at police station | Twis | 241
   private number | Illu | 987
Telephone directory | 3Gar | 1045
Telescope | Houn | 715
Temporary offices | RedH | 180
| Stoc | 366
Tendo Achillis | Sign | 121
Tennessee | Five | 226
Tennis, lawn | Danc | 517

Tennis shoes

    canvas shoes

Tenor

Terai (India)
Terra del Fuegians
Terrier

    bull terrier
    Airedale

Test-tube

Tetanus
Teutonic
Texas
Thames

Theatres
    Albert Hall
    Allegro
    Covent Garden
    Day's Music Hall (Birmingham)
    Haymarket
    Imperial
    Lyceum
    St. James's Hall
    Woolwich

"The Woman"

Chas	577	
Devi	968	
Lion	1084	
Seco	655	
Vall	780	
Glor	385	
Sign	127	
Stud	48	
Houn	671	
Glor	374	
Lion	1090	
Stud	17	
Sign	109	
Iden	198	
Copp	322	
Nava	448	
Danc	511	
Sign	113	
SixN	589	
Five	229	
Sign	99	
Twis	244	
SixN	583	
Gold	613	
Card	897	
Bruc	921	
Reti	1116	
Nobl	290	
RedC	913	
Stoc	368	
Reti	1115	
Soli	527	
Sign	95	
RedH	184	
Bruc	916	
Scan	161	

Theological College of St. George's	Twis	229
Theorist, Mr., Holmes called	Sign	114
Third Bengal Fusiliers (regiment)	Sign	146
Third Buffs (regiment)	Sign	144
Third shot, mystery of the	Danc	520
Thirty-fourth Bombay Infantry (regiment)	Sign	95
Thor Bridge	Thor	1057
Thor Mere	Thor	1057
Thor Place	Thor	1062
Thoreau (Henry David)	Nobl	294
Thorn	Sign	109
Thorsley (parish)	Houn	671
Threadneedle Street	Twis	235
	Bery	302
Three Gables (house)	3Gab	1024
Three Months in the Jungle (Moran)	Empt	494
Three pipe problem	RedH	184
Three-fold oath	Sign	147
Three-quarter (Rugby position)	Miss	622
	Suss	1036
Throgmorton Street	Blan	1000
Throwback	Houn	750
Thucydides	3Stu	597
Thumb-prints	Sign	95
	Twis	239
	Norw	506
	Card	891
Thurston	Danc	511
Thyme	Lion	1097
Tibet	Empt	488
Ticket, on train without	Bruc	915
Tide, significance of	Twis	235
Tidewaiter	Nobl	287

Tiger
   man-eating
   cub

   tiger-skin
     rug
Tiger of San Pedro
Timber-toe (wooden leg)
Times, The

Time (date) of story concealed
Tin

   tin mine
Tin Box
   Holmes's
   Stapleton's
   dispatch-box, at Cox and Co.

Tinker's curse
Tinted glasses
Tire change
Tire impressions
Tire, unbreakable
"Tired Captain, The Adventure of the"
Title—deeds
Tobacco (*see also* **Cigar, Cigarette, Pipe, Holmes and Watson**)
   Arcadia
   Bird's-eye

Empt	494	
Sign	99	
Iden	201	
Sign	100	
Abbe	640	
Wist	884	
Sign	100	
Sign	95	
Sign	97	
Blue	248	
Engr	276	
Soli	527	
Miss	622	
Houn	686	
Last	972	
Seco	650	
Engr	286	
Devi	955	
Houn	759	
Silv	341	
Musg	386	
Houn	706	
Thor	1054	
Cree	1070	
Illu	992	
Iden	194	
Prio	548	
Prio	547	
Five	219	
Nava	447	
Norw	500	
Croo	411	
Sign	91	

Tobacco (*see also* Cigar, Cigarette, Pipe, Holmes and Watson) (cont'd)

black	Silv	335
Cavendish	Silv	341
chewing	Twis	239
coat scuttle	Maza	1012
Eastern, odour of	Sign	101
Grosvenor mixture	Yell	352
honeydew	Card	890
shag	Scan	168
	Twis	240
	Houn	682
	Cree	1071
ship's	Stud	19
	Blac	562
snuff	RedH	180
	Gree	437
monograph upon	Stud	33
	Sign	91
	Bosc	214
millionaire (Harden)	Soli	527
Persian slipper	Musg	386
	Nava	448
	Empt	493
	Illu	994
poisoning, Holmes's	Five	225
	Devi	960
pouch		
Holmes's	Dyin	934
Watson's	Croo	411
pouch, as clue	Scan	168
	Blac	560
Tobacconist		
Bradley	Houn	682
Ionides	Gold	615
Mortimer	RedH	185
Tobin (caretaker)	Resi	434

542 ◼ *Good Old Index*

Toby (dog)	Sign	115
Todman (mine-owner)	Vall	836
Tokay (wine)	Sign	101
	Last	974
Toller (servant)	Copp	324
Toller, Mrs.	Copp	324
Tomboy	Nobl	292
Tonga (Andaman Islander)	Sign	140
	Gold	613
Tooth, gold	Stoc	368
Topeka (Kansas)	3Gar	1046
Tor, man on the	Houn	726
Toronto (Canada)	Houn	760
Torquay Terrace	Stud	41
Torrington Lodge	Norw	499
Tortise-shell snuff box	Gree	437
Tosca, Cardinal	Blac	559
Tottenham Court Road	Iden	193
	Blue	245
	Card	894
	RedC	905
Tower (of London)	Sign	135
Track and field	3Stu	600
Trade, influence of, upon the form of the hand	Sign	91
	RedH	177
	Iden	192
	Copp	317
	Soli	527
	Cree	1080
Trafalgar Square	Houn	697
Trafalgar Square fountain	Nobl	295
Train deluxe	Maza	1018
Trajan, Rue de (Montpellier)	Lady	944
"Tra-la-la-lira-lira-lay"	Stud	36
Tram-car	Bruc	918
Transylvania (Austria)	Suss	1034

T ◻ 543

Trap (*see also* Cart)	Bosc	205
	Twis	240
	Spec	265
	Copp	330
	Reig	403
	Soli	529
	Prio	552
	Gold	613
	Houn	751
	Wist	872
	Blan	1006
	Thor	1069
Treasure chest	Sign	105
Treaty, Naval	Nava	450
Tredannick Wartha	Devi	956
Tredannick Wollas	Devi	956
Tree Worship, Origin of	Empt	485
Trees		
beech	Sign	119
	Bosc	212
	Copp	319
	Musg	393
	Vall	779
chestnut	Yell	351
	Wist	877
cottonwoods	Sign	127
elm	Yell	351
	Musg	392
	Abbe	637
	Vall	787
evergreens	Vall	791
	Vall	840
	Wist	872
firs	Yell	359
	Nava	449
	Houn	700
firs, Scotch	Yell	354

544 ◻ *Good Old Index*

Trees (cont'd)		
fruit, stunted	Houn	710
hazel	Wist	879
holly	Shos	1109
larch	Stud	71
lime	Glor	374
mangrove	Sign	144
oak	Five	226
	Musg	392
	Reig	403
	Soli	533
	Vall	787
scrub oak	Houn	700
pine	Stud	71
	3Gab	1024
plane	Thor	1055
yew	Prio	553
	Houn	677
	Vall	787
Trees and humans, development of	Empt	494
Tregellis, Janet	Musg	389
Tregennis, Brenda	Devi	956
Tregennis, George	Devi	956
Tregennis, Mortimer	Devi	956
Tregennis, Owen	Devi	956
Trelawney Hope, Lady Hilda	Seco	656
Trelawney Hope, Rt. Hon.	Seco	656
Trepoff murder	Scan	161
Trespasser, on own land	Houn	736
Trevelyan, Dr. Percy	Resi	425
Trevor, Victor	Glor	374
Trevor Senior	Glor	374
Trichinopoly cigar	Stud	32
	Sign	91
Triggers, shotgun, wired together	Vall	782
Trigonometry	Musg	393
Trincomalee (Ceylon)	Scan	161

Trinity College (Cambridge)	Miss	622
Trip around world	Houn	759
	3Gab	1030
Triple Alliance	Nava	450
Tropical diseases	Dyin	934
Trouser buttons	Norw	503
Trouser(s), knee of, as clue	RedH	184
	Iden	197
Trout	Shos	1109
in milk	Nobl	294
Trumpington	Miss	624
Trustee	Houn	681
Tudor (royal House)	Nobl	288
Tudor architecture	Soli	531
	Suss	1039
	Thor	1063
Elizabethan	Prio	553
	Blan	1002
Tugboat	Sign	138
Tunbridge Wells	Blac	571
	Vall	779
Turkey, Sultan of	Blan	1007
Turkish bath	Lady	942
	Illu	984
Turkish slipper	Spec	272
Turner, Alice	Bosc	215
Turner, John	Bosc	203
Turner, Mrs.	Scan	170
Turpey Street	Houn	697
Turquoise	Sign	151
Tuson, Sergeant	Stoc	373
Tussaud, Madame	Maza	1019
Tuxbury Old Park	Blan	1000
Twaddle, ineffable	Stud	23
Tweed	Silv	337
	Soli	535
	Blac	559

546 ◼ *Good Old Index*

Tweed (cont'd)

    Harris tweed
    Heather tweed

Twine, ball of

Twins

Two Twenty One B (*see* Baker Street)

Tyburn tree

Type, newspaper

Typewriter

    rates of payment for typing

Typhoid

Tyre (*see* Tire)

Vall	785	
Dyin	936	
Shos	1102	
Iden	197	
Engr	274	
Thor	1069	
Sign	102	
Spec	260	
3Gar	1047	
Houn	687	
Iden	192	
Houn	733	
Card	898	
Iden	193	
Stud	34	
Vall	793	

Ubanghi country	Devi	969
Uffa (island)	Five	218
Ugly business	Houn	698
Ugly sound	Yell	359
Ululation, feminine	Vall	801
Umbrella	Five	218
	Seco	651
	Vall	803
	Maza	1013
	Thor	1054
Uncle Sam	Last	975
Underground railway	Stud	23
	RedH	184
	Bery	302
	Bery	308
	Bery	311
	Bruc	915
Under-Secretary for the colonies	Nobl	288
Undertaker	Stud	29
	Lady	949
Undertaker's mute	Miss	626
Underwood, John and Sons	Stud	43
Unexpected visitor	Five	218
	Thor	1057

548 ◻ *Good Old Index*

Uniform		Stud	22
		Stud	25
		Blue	245
Union boat		Stud	39
Union House (saloon)		Vall	818
Union Jack		Nobl	300
United States (*see* American backgrounds; Cities, U.S.; States, U.S.)			
University scene		3Stu	596
		Miss	629
		Cree	1076
Unnamed cases	(5)	Stud	22
	(3)	Nava	464
		Houn	695
		Houn	730
Unreported cases of Holmes			
Abbey School		Blan	1007
Abergavenny murder		Prio	539
Abernetty family		SixN	584
Abrahams, Old		Lady	943
Adams (Manor House case)		Gree	437
Addleton tragedy		Gold	607
Agar, Dr. Moore		Devi	955
Aldridge (bogus laundry affair)		Card	897
Alicia (cutter)		Thor	1055
Aluminum crutch		Musg	387
Amateur Mendicant Society		Five	218
Ancient British barrow		Gold	607
Arnsworth Castle business		Scan	173
Atkinson brothers at Trincomalee		Scan	161
Backwater, Lord		Nobl	288
Bishopgate jewel case		Sign	113
Blackmailing case		Houn	695
		Houn	730
Bogus laundry affair		Card	897
Brooks		Bruc	914

Unreported cases of Holmes (cont'd)

Camberwell poisoning case	Five	218
Cardinal Tosca, death of	Blac	559
Carruthers, Colonel	Wist	870
Clay, John, one or two turns with	RedH	186
Coiner, case of the	Shos	1102
Conk-Singleton forgery case	SixN	596
Coptic Patriarchs, two	Reti	1114
Crosby the banker	Gold	607
Darlington substitution scandal	Scan	173
Dowson, Baron	Maza	1016
Dundas separation case	Iden	191
Etherege, Mrs.	Iden	192
Europe, Royal House of	Scan	163
Farintosh, Mrs. (Opal tiara)	Spec	259
Ferrers Documents	Prio	539
Fishmonger	Nobl	287
Forgery case, Lestrade's	Stud	24
Forrester, Mrs. Cecil	Sign	94
French government	Fina	469
French will case	Sign	90
Friesland, Dutch steamship	Norw	469
Gentleman, old	Stud	22
Girl, young	Stud	22
Grafenstein, Count (Klopman)	Last	979
Grice Patersons in the island of Uffa	Five	218
Grosvenor Square furniture van	Nobl	288
Harden, John Vincent	Soli	527
Hobbs, Fairdale	RedC	901
Holland, Reigning family of	Scan	161
	Iden	191
Huret, the Boulevard assassin	Gold	607
Jew peddler	Stud	22
Klopman, Nihilist	Last	979
Litmus-test murder	Nava	448
Maberley affair	3Gab	1024
MacDonald, Inspector (two cases)	Vall	773

Unreported cases of Holmes (cont'd)

Manor House case	Gree	437
Margate, woman at	Seco	657
Marseilles, case from	Iden	192
Mathews	Empt	494
Matilda Briggs	Suss	1034
Maupertuis, Baron	Reig	398
Merridew	Empt	494
Molesey Mystery	Empt	492
Montpensier, Mme.	Houn	761
Morgan, poisoner	Empt	494
Murillo, papers of ex-President	Norw	496
Netherlands-Sumatra Company	Reig	398
Nonpareil Club	Houn	761
Opal tiara	Spec	259
Paradol Chamber	Five	218
Parsley in butter (Abernetty case)	SixN	585
Perkins, killing of	3Gab	1023
Persano, Isadora, and the remarkable worm	Thor	1055
Phillimore, James	Thor	1055
Politician, Lighthouse and Trained Cormorant	Veil	1095
Pope, cases	Blac	559
undertaken for	Houn	677
Prendergast, Major	Five	219
Railway porter	Stud	22
Rat, giant, of Sumatra	Suss	1034
Red leech	Gold	607
Remarkable worm, unknown to science	Thor	1055
Ricoletti of the club-foot and his abominable wife	Musg	387
Riviera robbery	Maza	1018
Royal House of Europe, one of the	Scan	163
Russian woman, old	Musg	387
St. Pancras case	Shos	1102

Unreported cases of Holmes (cont'd)

Saunders, Dr. James	Blan	1010
Savage, Victor	Dyin	939
Scandinavia, King of	Nobl	291
	Fina	470
Smith-Mortimer succession case	Gold	607
Sophy Anderson	Five	218
Spencer John gang	3Gab	1024
Stamford, Archie	Soli	527
Staunton, Henry	Miss	623
Stevens, Bert	Norw	504
Sultan of Turkey	Blan	1007
Tankerville Club scandal	Five	219
Tarleton murders	Musg	387
Tidewaiter	Nobl	287
Tired Captain	Nava	447
Tosca, Cardinal	Blac	559
Trepoff murder	Scan	161
Uffa, Grice Patersons in	Five	218
Upwood, Colonel	Houn	761
Vamberry	Musg	387
Vatican cameos	Houn	677
Warburton, Colonel, madness of	Engr	274
Wilson, the notorious canary trainer	Blac	559
Wilson, district messenger	Houn	691
Woman, elderly	Stud	22
Woodhouse	Bruc	914

Unreported cases, other than Holmes's

Aberdeen	Nobl	295
Anderson murders	Houn	754
Andover	Iden	196
Brewer, Sam	Shos	1102
Folkestone Court	Houn	764
Godno	Houn	754
Hague, The	Iden	196
Hammerford Will case	Illu	984

Unreported cases, other than Holmes's (cont'd)

Harold, Mrs.	Maza	1017
Hayling, Jeremiah	Engr	284
Lefevre	Stud	18
Lewisham gang	Abbe	637
Little Russia (Godno)	Houn	754
Long Island Cave mystery	RedC	908
Lowenstein of Prague	Cree	1082
Lynch, Victor	Suss	1034
Mason of Bradford	Stud	18
Muller	Stud	18
Munich, case at	Nobl	293
Ratcliff Highway Murders	Stud	41
Riga	Sign	90
St. Louis	Sign	90
Samson (New Orleans)	Stud	18
Selden	Houn	701
Staunton, Arthur H.	Miss	623
Stewart, Mrs.	Empt	494
Vanderbilt and the Yeggman	Suss	1034
Venomous lizard or gila	Suss	1034
Victor Lynch	Suss	1034
Vigor, the Hammersmith wonder	Suss	1034
Vittoria, the circus belle	Suss	1034
Von Bischoff	Stud	18
Warrender, Minnie	Maza	1017
Worthington Bank gang	Resi	434

Upon the Distinction between the Ashes...

	Sign	91
(without title)	Stud	33
	Bosc	214

Upper Norwood — Sign — 95
Upper Swandam Lane — Twis — 230
Uppingham (school) — Gold — 609

Upwood, Colonel	Houn	761
Uriah	Croo	422
Utah	Stud	58
Utrecht (Holland)	Stud	29

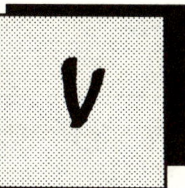

V.C. (Victoria Cross)	Blan	1000
V.R. (Victoria Regina)	Musg	386
VV 341 (lodge)	Vall	783
Vacation, long	Glor	374
Valetudinarian	Sign	105
Valise	Bosc	202
Valley of Fear	Vall	796
Vamberry (wine merchant)	Musg	387
Vampires	Suss	1034
Van	Yell	354
	Fina	473
	Lady	949
Van Deher (ironworks owner)	Vall	836
Van Jansen (victim)	Stud	29
Van Seddar	Maza	1020
Van Shorst (victim)	Vall	822
Vandeleur (alias)	Houn	753
Vanderbilt and the Yeggman	Suss	1034
Varsity	Miss	623
Vase, oriental	Sign	100
Vaseline	Dyin	941
Vatican cameos	Houn	677
Vauxhall Bridge	Sign	99
Vauxhall Bridge Road	Sign	99

Vegetable alkaloid | Stud | 17
 | Sign | 113
Vegetarian restaurant | RedH | 185
Vehicle (*see* Cab, Carriage, Trap, etc.)
Vehmgericht | Stud | 41
 | Stud | 62
Veil, lady's | Twis | 230
 | Spec | 258
 | Veil | 1096
Velveteen (fabric) | Stud | 22
 | Stud | 56
Venetian carafe | Sign | 104
Venezuelan loan | Stoc | 364
Venner & Matheson | Engr | 276
Venomous lizard or gila | Suss | 1034
Venucci, Lucretia | SixN | 594
Venucci, Pietro | SixN | 590
Verbs, Germans uncourteous to their | Scan | 163
Vere Street | Fina | 473
Vermissa (U.S.A.) | Vall | 811
Vermissa Herald | Vall | 839
Vermissa Valley | Vall | 811
Verner (doctor) | Norw | 496
Vernet (Horace) | Gree | 435
Vernon Lodge (house) | Illu | 987
Vestas, wax | Twis | 235
 | Silv | 343
Vibart, Jules | Lady | 944
Vicar | Blac | 560
 | Danc | 512
 | Devi | 956
 | Reti | 1117
Vicarage, The | Reti | 1117
Victoria (Australia) | Bosc | 208
Victoria Station | Silv | 350
 | Gree | 442
 | Fina | 474

Victoria Station (cont'd)	Vall	776
	Suss	1038
Victoria Street	Engr	274
Vie de Boheme (Murger)	Stud	40
View-halloa	Chas	581
	Devi	956
Vigor, the Hammersmith wonder	Suss	1034
Villard, Francois le	Sign	90
Vincent Square	Sign	99
Vinegar and water	Abbe	637
Violins (*see* Holmes)		
Viper	Dyin	941
	Suss	1034
Wiper	Sign	116
Vitriol	Blue	249
	Illu	998
Vittoria (circus belle)	Suss	1034
Vixen Tor	Houn	738
Vizard mask	Scan	164
Vocabulary, nervous and terse	Vall	772
Von Bischoff (murderer)	Stud	18
Von Bork (spymaster)	Last	971
Von Herder (airgun maker)	Empt	493
Von Herling, Baron	Last	971
Von Kramm, Count	Scan	164
Von Ormstein, Wilhelm	Scan	165
Von Saxe-Meningen, Clothilde	Scan	166
Von und zu Grafenstein, Count	Last	979
Von Waldbaum, Fritz	Nava	447
Voodoo	Wist	887
Voodooism and the Negroid Religions (Eckermann)	Wist	887
Vox populi, vox Dei	Abbe	650

Wagner night	RedC	913
Wagon	Stud	55
	Bosc	216
Wagonette	Houn	700
	Houn	754
Wainwright (Wainewright)	Illu	987
Waldbaum, Fritz Von	Nava	447
Waldron (alias)	3Gar	1052
Wales	Musg	389
	Prio	539
	Miss	623
Walker Brothers	Vall	836
Walking calendar of crime	Stud	18
Wall, message on	Stud	31
	Stud	47
	Reti	1121
Wallenstein (Albrecht)	Scan	163
Wallington	Card	894
Walsall	Copp	332
Walter, Sir James	Bruc	917
Walter, Colonel Valentine	Bruc	917
Walters, Constable	Wist	877
Wandsworth Common	Gree	442
Warburton, Colonel	Engr	274
Wardlaw, Colonel	Silv	347

Warner, John
Warning, official, by police

War-path
Warrant
  not needed
  too late
Warren (timekeeper)
Warren, Mrs.
Warrender, Minnie
Warsaw (Russia)
Warships of the future
Wasatch Mountains
Washington (D.C.)
Washoe hunter
Watch

Wist	882	
Stud	76	
Sign	114	
Norw	499	
Danc	525	
Wist	871	
Dyin	940	
Reti	1119	
Sign	133	
RedC	909	
Lady	949	
RedC	902	
RedC	901	
Maza	1017	
Scan	165	
Sign	134	
Stud	59	
Vall	864	
Stud	68	
Stud	30	
Scan	172	
Five	218	
Twis	235	
Silv	341	
Yell	355	
Musg	391	
Norw	499	
Chas	579	
Houn	681	
Vall	776	
Wist	872	
Bruc	929	
Last	973	
3Gar	1050	

Watch (cont'd)
    as clue to character

    fifty-guinea
    gold
    Holmes's

    silver
    Watson's

    winding of, as evidence
Water-police
    river police
    police launch
Waterbeach
Waterford (Ireland)
Waterloo (battle)
Waterloo Bridge

Waterloo Bridge Road
Waterloo Road
Waterloo Station

Sign	92	
Yell	352	
Sign	93	
Scan	168	
Stud	49	
Sign	135	
Silv	336	
Gree	435	
Abbe	647	
Seco	663	
Wist	870	
Thor	1062	
Shos	1102	
Silv	341	
Sign	92	
Twis	240	
Five	218	
Five	227	
Card	897	
Sign	135	
Miss	632	
Card	896	
Abbe	644	
Stud	79	
Five	227	
Twis	241	
3Gar	1052	
Five	224	
Spec	259	
Spec	265	
Croo	411	
Nava	449	
Nava	463	
Soli	530	
Houn	681	
Houn	697	

Watson, H. | Sign | 92
Watson, John H.
  adventure, love for | Houn | 695
  Afghan campaign | Stud | 15
 | Sign | 89
 | Musg | 386
 | Resi | 423
  age of | Bosc | 204
 | Stoc | 362
 | Last | 974
  agent of Holmes | Houn | 727
  aliases
    Dr. Hill Barton | Illu | 995
    Price | Stoc | 369
  alone on case | Soli | 530
 | Miss | 632
 | Houn | 695
 | Lady | 943
 | Reti | 1114
  amazed | Stud | 27
 | Stud | 40
 | Reig | 409
 | Resi | 423
 | Empt | 483
 | Empt | 485
 | Empt | 486
 | Empt | 489
 | Danc | 511
 | Gold | 618
 | Card | 888
 | Dyin | 940
 | Maza | 1013
 | 3Gar | 1045
 | Reti | 1118
  annoyed by Holmes | Sign | 90
 | Vall | 769

Watson, John H. (cont'd)
   apology, receives
      from Holmes
   appearance inspired confidence
   archives referred to
   army career
   asked to go on cases

	Dyin	941
	Devi	965
	Lady	950
	Reti	1122
	Stud	15
	Stud	27
	Sign	95
	Bosc	202
	Twis	232
	Spec	263
	Bery	308
	Copp	322
	Stoc	363
	Croo	412
	Resi	431
	Nava	460
	Fina	470
	Empt	486
	Norw	505
	Blac	563
	Houn	695
	Card	890
	3Gab	1024
	3Gab	1031
	Suss	1038
	Veil	1095
asked to go on case by patient	Twis	230
asked whether he has time to accompany Holmes	Houn	695
	3Gab	1024
asks to accompany Holmes	Spec	269
	Silv	335
	Chas	576
astonished	Stud	18
	Spec	269
	Fina	475

Watson, John H., astonished (cont'd)

    bank account of

    bereavement
    betting of
    bewildered
    billiards, plays
    bitter reply to Holmes

    books of
    blunders by

    bohemianism of
    Boswell to Holmes
    breakfast, comes down to

    British jury, fitted to be
    brother of
    brown study by

    bull pup, kept by
    bull's-eye for
    burglary, engages in

    busybody, fears himself a
    called upon by Mrs. Hudson
    called upon by Holmes
    cane of
    card of

Abbe	643
Houn	740
Sign	97
Resi	423
Card	888
Empt	488
Shos	1102
Houn	683
Danc	511
Abbe	636
Lady	946
Resi	423
Soli	531
Lady	946
Musg	386
Scan	164
Sign	125
Five	227
Spec	258
Illu	998
Bery	312
Norw	505
Thor	1055
Abbe	650
Sign	92
Resi	423
Card	888
Stud	19
Reti	1120
Chas	577
Bruc	927
Stud	20
Dyin	932
Cree	1071
Shos	1109
Nava	449
Dyin	936

Watson, John H., card of (cont'd)	Illu	998
	3Gab	1031
	Cree	1076
case, brings to Holmes	Engr	274
cases, how chosen, for publication	Resi	422
	Soli	526
	Card	888
ceramics, studies	Illu	994
challenges Holmes to write story	Abbe	636
chauffeur, a	Last	974
check book of	Danc	511
club of	Houn	683
common sense, claim to	Houn	727
compares self to Holmes	RedH	185
	Cree	1071
complimented by Holmes	Reig	398
	Houn	695
	Houn	741
	3Gar	1051
conductor of light	Houn	669
confidence in Holmes	Silv	336
convenience of, consulted	Houn	689
	3Gab	1024
craniology, uses as a diversion	Houn	731
crime, interest in	Empt	483
curiosity of	Stud	20
	Danc	516
danger, exults in	Chas	578
dangerous ruffian, called by Holmes	Lady	951
deductions of	Iden	197
	Houn	669
defends Holmes		
with chair	Chas	575
with poker	3Gab	1023
depressed	Sign	105
	Houn	738
description of	Chas	582

Watson, John H. (cont'd)

deserts Holmes for a wife	Blan	1000
detachment, no power of	Bruc	929
diabetes not recognized by	Bosc	215
diary of	Houn	726
journal of	Stud	76
	Stud	86
discretion, the soul of	Cree	1072
dispatch—box (tin)	Thor	1054
dispatch—cases	Veil	1095
tin box	Cree	1070
dissimulation, no talent for	Dyin	941
doctor, addressed as by Holmes	RedH	176
	RedH	178
	RedH	185
	RedH	187
	Iden	191
	Five	227
	Blue	257
Doctor of Medicine	Stud	15
doctors without fee	RedC	907
dress of		
boots	Houn	683
	Houn	690
	RedC	906
dress-clothes	Chas	577
hat	Sign	98
	Chas	582
	Houn	683
	Houn	690
	Houn	709
	Vall	799
top hat	Scan	162
tennis shoes	Chas	577
waterproof	Houn	730
duty to old friend	Dyin	933
duty to tell unpleasant tale	Fina	469

Watson, John H. (cont'd)

ear, neglects query about	Lady	945
eating habits, irregular	Gold	603
effects on, of life with Holmes	Houn	731
embellished the tales	RedH	176
	Copp	316
end justifies means	Chas	576
excitement enough in Afghanistan	Stud	17
eyes, gives himself away through	Resi	423
	Card	889
fails	Soli	531
	Lady	946
faints	Empt	485
fair sex his department	Seco	657
faith in Holmes	Bosc	209
features easy to read	Resi	423
	Card	889
	Dyin	941
felon in eyes of the law	Chas	576
field glasses of	Silv	336
finances of	Stud	16
	Sign	97
	Resi	423
	Card	888
first asked into Holmes's cases	Stud	27
first meeting with Holmes	Stud	17
fleet of foot	Houn	757
followed	Houn	739
fooled by Holmes	Dyin	941
forgets a case	Veil	1097
fortune seeker, fears he may be thought	Sign	116
four-mile walk	Houn	714
friend Watson, called by Holmes	Danc	511
	Seco	662
	Vall	803
friends, few	Houn	683

Watson, John H. (cont'd)

friends, none	Stud	20
generosity of	Twis	231
gift of silence, possesses	Twis	233
glad to see Holmes	Empt	486
	Houn	741
Stamford	Stud	16
glorifies Holmes	Musg	386
handkerchief in sleeve, carries	Croo	411
"Handy Guide to the Turf," as	Shos	1102
hat, carries stethoscope in	Scan	162
health of	Stud	15
	Sign	89
heat, stands, better than cold	Resi	423
	Card	888
hides behind bed	Dyin	938
historian of this bunch	Vall	812
Holmes, partnership with, function in	Houn	669
	Cree	1071
length of	Veil	1095
Holmes's methods, uses	Houn	669
home life of	Bosc	202
	Five	218
	Twis	230
	Engr	276
	Croo	411
	Fina	470
honour, word of	Chas	576
humor, pawky, vein of	Vall	769
hunter	Sign	138
hurt by Holmes	Houn	741
	Dyin	933
	Lady	946
ideas limited	Blan	1000
identified by cigarette	Houn	740
illness of	Stoc	363

Watson, John H. (cont'd)

income of (pension)	Stud	15
	Shos	1102
Indian service of	Resi	423
	Card	888
injured	3Gar	1053
injustice to, by Holmes	3Stu	599
insight into Holmes's feelings	3Gar	1053
introduces two cases to Holmes	Engr	274
invaluable to Holmes	Blan	1000
	Lion	1083
	Reti	1120
Italian not good	Fina	475
irritated by Holmes	Sign	90
James, called by wife	Twis	230
jangled nerves of	Vall	798
jemmy on person	Bruc	925
jokes with Holmes	Vall	769
journal of	Stud	76
	Stud	86
diary of	Houn	726
keeps us flat-footed on the ground	Cree	1074
Kensington	RedH	186
	Empt	485
	Norw	496
known at Scotland Yard	Illu	998
Ku Klux Klan, never heard of	Five	226
laughs	Stud	19
	Sign	125
	Sign	157
	Scan	162
	RedH	182
	Five	225
	Blue	247
	Engr	276
	Yell	361
	Gree	437

Watson, John H., laughs (cont'd)

		Houn	671
		Houn	698
		Shos	1102
learns of Holmes's regard		3Gar	1053
letters to Holmes		Houn	712
		Houn	716
light, a conductor of		Houn	669
light sleeper		Houn	715
limps		Sign	92
lived			
	Kensington	RedH	186
		Empt	485
		Norw	496
	Paddington	Engr	274
		Stoc	362
	private hotel in the Strand	Stud	15
	Queen Anne Street	Illu	984
	221B (*which see*)		
long-suffering		Vall	769
		Reti	1120
loses blood		3Gar	1053
love discussed by		Sign	107
love professed by		Sign	143
Machiavellian intellect of		Vall	771
maid of		Scan	162
		Bosc	202
		Engr	274
		Empt	485
man of action		Houn	747
man of letters		Wist	869
marriage, alludes to		Sign	99
		Scan	161
		RedH	176
		Iden	190
		Bosc	202
		Five	218
		Twis	230

Watson, John H., marriage, alludes to (cont'd)	Blue	247
	Engr	274
	Nobl	287
	Stoc	362
	Croo	411
	Nava	447
	Fina	469
	Empt	488
	Dyin	932
first indication of	Sign	99
second	Blan	1000
Mary Morstan, first meeting with	Sign	94
masked	Chas	577
mass of records	Soli	526
	Thor	1054
master of own establishment	Scan	161
medical knowledge and skill	Sign	89
	Twis	230
	Stoc	371
	Reig	398
	Resi	424
	Gree	445
	Prio	539
	SixN	583
	Dyin	941
	Lady	953
	Illu	998
	Suss	1040
	Suss	1041
diabetes	Bosc	215
exhaustion	Prio	539
heart	Stud	77
	Sign	100
aneurism	Stud	77
Holmes appreciates	Dyin	941

Watson, John H. (cont'd)
   medical practice, engages in

	Scan	161
	RedH	184
	Iden	198
	Bosc	202
	Five	228
	Twis	230
	Blue	250
	Engr	274
	Stoc	362
	Croo	411
	Nava	457
	Fina	469
	Empt	483
	Norw	496
	Illu	987
	Maza	1014
	Cree	1071
busy	Bosc	202
	Twis	230
	Croo	411
	Empt	483
	Maza	1014
	Cree	1076
buys	Scan	162
cared for in absence by		
Anstruther	Bosc	202
Jackson	Croo	412
neighbor	Stoc	363
	Fina	474
important case	Iden	198
increases by 1889	Engr	274
never absorbing	RedH	184
place of		
Kensington	RedH	186
	Empt	485
	Norw	496

Watson, John H., medical practice,
  engages in, place of (cont'd)

	Paddington	Engr	274
		Stoc	362
	Queen Anne Street	Illu	984
quiet		Fina	474
remarks upon		RedH	184
		Nava	457
returns to		Scan	161
		Engr	274
sells		Norw	496
slack in July		Nava	457
small, in Kensington		Norw	496
summoned from by Holmes		Bosc	202
		Cree	1076
memoirs, incoherent		Musg	386
memoirs to end with "The Final Problem"		Fina	477
memory of Holmes thrills		Empt	483
mess, makes, of a case		Soli	531
		Lady	946
messengers, best of		Dyin	938
middle-aged		Bosc	204
missed by Holmes		Blan	1011
		Lion	1083
misses vital points		Reti	1116
modest, says Holmes		Blan	1000
monomania, thoughts on		SixN	584
moral sense of		Chas	576
Moriarty			
known to		Vall	769
not known to		Fina	470
		Empt	494
moustache of		Nava	449
		Chas	582
		RedC	903
		Last	974

Watson, John H. (cont'd)
    music, put to sleep by   Sign   128
    name James   Twis   230
    name John   Stud   15
          Thor   1054
    natural turn for burglary   Chas   577
    neatness of   Bosc   204
    neighbours of   Stoc   363
    nerves
        hardened   Stud   37
          Engr   275
        jangled   Vall   798
        shaken   Sign   115
    notebooks and notes   Five   217
          Blue   245
          Spec   257
          Stoc   363
          Nava   447
          Norw   496
          Danc   516
          Soli   527
          Gold   607
          Seco   650
          Houn   727
          Wist   869
          Card   888
          Devi   955
          Veil   1095
    notes
        uses Holmes's   Musg   387
        uses Lestrade's   Stud   78
    observation, powers of   Soli   531
          Lady   944
    objects to rows   Stud   19
    offended by Holmes   Sign   90
          Dyin   933
          Lady   946

Watson, John H. (cont'd)

offers to accompany Holmes	Silv	335
	Chas	576
	Maza	1014
one fixed point in a changing age	Last	980
only unselfish act	Blan	1000
orderly (Murray)	Stud	15
Paddington practice	Engr	274
	Stoc	362
partnership with Holmes, years of	Veil	1095
function in	Houn	669
	Cree	1071
patients from railway	Engr	274
pawky humour of	Vall	769
pistol, holds to man's head	Soli	535
	Blac	569
pleased by praise	Houn	741
pleasure		
in admiring Holmes	Spec	258
in working with Holmes	Croo	419
poetic description cut off	Reti	1114
poker, aids Holmes with	3Gab	1023
pottery expert, poses as	Illu	995
powers of selection praised	Abbe	636
practical as usual	RedC	906
practice of (*see* Medical practice)		
produces effects by concealment	Blan	1008
promises to publish study	Stud	86
puzzled (special instances)	Sign	97
	Nava	465
questions witnesses	Houn	733
	Vall	801
	Lady	944
quick preparation for journey	Bosc	202
	Abbe	636

Watson, John H. (cont'd)
quotations

Benefactor of the race, You are a	RedH	190
Child has done this horrid thing, A	Sign	112
Come with pleasure, I will	Houn	695
Country, I know that	Suss	1035
Dark, I am still in the	Scan	172
Delighted, I should be	Croo	412
Deserved better at your hands Holmes, I have	Houn	741
Dock, My friend has not yet stood in the	Illu	999
Fail to see how you could have done more, I	Houn	691
Game, But what is his	3Gar	1052
Help, I only wish to	Dyin	933
Honored, I shall be	Illu	984
Hungry, You are	Five	228
Ineffable twaddle	Stud	23
Jove, By	Stud	16
Judgment, I trust your	Abbe	647
Lived for years with Sherlock Holmes for nothing, I have not	Houn	731
Longing for something to do, I was	Card	888
Man, Then I am your	Scan	170
Miss it for anything, I wouldn't	Spec	258
My dear Holmes	Blue	246
	Spec	270
	Nobl	294
	Resi	433
	Fina	470
	Gold	616
	Houn	683
	Houn	712
	Houn	716
	Houn	721
	Houn	726

Watson, John H., quotations, My dear Holmes (cont'd)	Bruc	914
	Dyin	938
	Thor	1068
	Shos	1108
Mystery is it, Oh! a	Stud	19
Proper study of mankind is man	Stud	19
Try, We can but	Cree	1076
Word of honor, I give you my	Chas	576
indicating puzzlement		
Ass I have been, What an	Reig	409
Dark, I am still rather in the	Stud	36
	Scan	172
	Twis	233
Depths, I am out of my	Stoc	371
Escaped me, Has anything	Houn	670
Head is in a whirl, My	Stud	33
Head or tail of it, I can make neither	3Gar	1051
Missed, What have I	Reti	1116
Mystery, This is all an insoluble	Sign	109
Obtuse, I may be very	Sign	97
Point, I am afraid I miss the	Stoc	371
Point, Then I do not see the	Five	226
Reasoning certainly is plausible, Your	Blue	247
Reasoning, I cannot see all the steps of your	Iden	201
railway officials as patients	Engr	274
reader interest not waning	Seco	650
reading of		
"Book of Life"	Stud	23
British Medical Journal	Stoc	362
Martyrdom of Man (Reade)	Sign	97
novel	Bosc	209
	Croo	411
pathology	Sign	97
sea story (Russell)	Five	218

Watson, John H., reading of (cont'd)

treatise on nervous lesions	Resi	425
surgery	Gold	607
Vie de Bohème (Murger)	Stud	40
yellow-backed novel	Bosc	209
reads aloud to Holmes	Stud	26
records at Cox & Co.	Thor	1054
regular in habits	Spec	258
relatives in England, none	Stud	15
remonstrates with Holmes over drugs	Sign	89
report to Holmes	Soli	531
	Houn	712
	Houn	716
	Lady	944
	Lady	945
reputation, jealous of his own	Chas	577
rescued by Holmes	Lady	946
	Illu	997
	3Gar	1053
rescues Holmes	Devi	965
respect for Holmes	Fina	480
	Dyin	933
responsibility too much	Houn	741
restless nights, spends	Nava	465
	Houn	704
resuscitates suspect	Stoc	371
returns to 221B	Norw	496
returns to civil practice	Scan	161
	Engr	274
reveres Holmes	Thor	1055
revolver of (*see* Revolver under weapons)		
rheumatic and old, feels	Lady	942
rising habits	Stud	19
	Stud	22
	Spec	258

Watson, John H. (cont'd)

role of, in partnership	Houn	669
	Cree	1071
rubber shoes of	Chas	577
rubbing his hands	Stud	19
satisfied to help Holmes	Wist	879
school days, refers to	Nava	447
	Suss	1036
scintillating	Miss	631
scores on Holmes	Silv	344
	Vall	769
scrapbook of	Stud	41
selection of cases for publications	Resi	422
	Soli	526
	Gold	607
	Card	888
selfish act, only	Blan	1000
sent for by Holmes	Bosc	202
	Cree	1071
	Veil	1095
separated from Holmes	Scan	161
	Cree	1071
servants of	Scan	162
	Bosc	202
	Engr	274
	Croo	411
	Empt	485
shaving habits of	Bosc	204
shock of life, greatest	Dyin	934
silence, gift of	Twis	233
simulated anger	Illu	997
six-mile limp of	Sign	121
skeptical	Vall	799
slippers of	Stoc	363
smiles	Stud	21
	Stud	24
	Sign	133

Watson, John H., smiles (cont'd)

    smokes
        eternally
        cigar

        cigarette

        pipe

    tobacco
        Arcadia mixture
        ship's
  snuff, takes
  spare room at home after marriage
  speaks without facts
  speculates about case

    spots figure in doorway
    startled

Iden	191
Twis	240
Bery	301
Copp	317
Resi	424
Gold	603
Bosc	213
Silv	337
Card	895
Prio	548
Houn	703
Houn	721
Houn	738
Stud	39
Croo	411
Nava	448
Chas	581
Devi	970
Thor	1069
Croo	411
Stud	19
Iden	191
Croo	411
Houn	737
Stud	37
Bosc	209
Gree	442
Nava	465
Houn	684
Houn	714
Houn	727
Houn	735
Vall	801
Empt	490
Stud	25

Watson, John H. (cont'd)

stethoscope, carries in hat	Scan	162
stick, uses as weapon	Sign	98
	Sign	121
	Lady	950
stories, tells wrong end foremost	Wist	870
stormy petrel of crime	Nava	448
stupid, others are as	3Stu	599
stupidity of	RedH	185
	Lady	946
summer cold of	Stoc	363
summer quarters near Shoscombe	Shos	1102
surgeon-assistant	Stud	15
surprised	Stud	21
surprised at request to investigate alone	Houn	695
	Lady	943
surprised by visit from Holmes	Croo	411
	Fina	469
	Empt	485
swift runner	Houn	725
	Houn	757
taken in	Lady	946
thunderstruck	Silv	346
tiger cub, double-barreled	Sign	99
time on hands of	Maza	1014
timid in inferences	Blue	246
tin dispatch—box of	Cree	1070
tin box	Thor	1054
tobacco pouch of	Croo	411
top hat of	Scan	162
touched by appeal	Nava	448
for help	Fina	478
tout and ally of (railway guard)	Engr	274
transparency of	Resi	423
	Card	889
	Dyin	941
tricked by Holmes	Houn	741

Watson, John H. (cont'd)
    tries Holmes's methods

	Fina	479
	Empt	483
	Soli	531
	Houn	669
	Lady	944
trusts Homes completely	Abbe	647
umbrella	Vall	810
value to Holmes	Twis	233
	Houn	741
vices of	Stud	19
views on human mind	Stud	21
violin, put to sleep by	Sign	128
visited by Holmes	Stoc	362
	Croo	411
	Fina	469
	Empt	485
wager by	Stud	23
walks with Holmes	Yell	351
	Resi	424
	Chas	572
war of 1914, joins	Last	980
watch of	Sign	92
	Twis	240
waterproof (coat) of	Houn	730
weans Holmes from cocaine	Miss	622
whetstone to Holmes's mind	Cree	1071
wife	Sign	158
alludes to	Scan	161
	RedH	176
	Bosc	202
	Five	218
	Twis	230
	Blue	247
	Engr	274
	Silv	337
	Stoc	362

Watson, John H., wife, alludes to	Croo	411
(cont'd)	Nava	448
	Fina	470
	Empt	488
	Blan	1000
attitude toward Holmes's cases	Bosc	202
away on visit	Five	218
	Fina	470
loss of	Empt	488
relatives, has none in England	Sign	94
second	Blan	1000
visiting mother	Five	218
wine and	Sign	135
	Houn	736
women		
fair sex his department	Seco	657
is attractive to	Reti	1116
wide experience with	Sign	94
wound		
forgotten in excitement	Houn	705
	Houn	757
in leg	Sign	90
in limb	Nobl	287
in shoulder (or arm?)	Stud	24
mentions (leg?)	Sign	118
	Resi	424
	Card	889
by Holmes	Stud	24
	Sign	118
pension for	Shos	1102
wounded while with Holmes	3Gar	1053
writings of	Sign	90
	Sign	119
	Scan	161
	RedH	176
	Iden	191

Watson, John H., writings of (cont'd)

Five	217
Twis	233
Blue	245
Copp	316
Silv	337
Stoc	363
Glor	385
Musg	387
Croo	412
Resi	422
Fina	477
Norw	504
Norw	509
Danc	516
Soli	526
Soli	538
Blac	559
SixN	593
3Stu	596
Gold	607
Abbe	636
Seco	650
Houn	669
Houn	706
Vall	787
Wist	869
Card	888
Card	895
RedC	913
Bruc	925
Lady	954
Devi	954
Devi	961
Blan	1000
3Gab	1023
Suss	1034
Thor	1054

Watson, John H., writings of (cont'd)	Cree	1071
	Lion	1090
	Veil	1095
embellishes cases	RedH	176
	Copp	316
proceed backwards	Thor	1056
reduced by Holmes's diffidence	Devi	955
undesirable to Holmes	Seco	650
wrong side of law, on	Chas	576
	Houn	728
	Bruc	927
yearbooks of	Veil	1095
yellow-backed novel read by	Bosc	209
Watson, Mary (Morstan)	Sign	158
Watt Street Chapel (Aldershot)	Croo	413
Wax, purple sealing	Wist	873
Wax bust of Holmes	Empt	489
	Maza	1013
Wax matches	Twis	235
	Silv	343
Weald (forest)	Blac	564
	Vall	779
Weald Station	3Gab	1024
Wealthiest subjects of the crown, one of the	Prio	540
Weapons		
air gun	Fina	470
	Empt	493
	Maza	1014
arrows, poisoned	Suss	1043
artillery	Sign	146
	Croo	420
bayonet	Glor	383
battle-axe	Musg	389
blasting powder	Vall	852
gunpowder	Glor	385

Weapons (cont'd)

bludgeon		Gree	438
		Fina	473
boulder		Fina	477
		Lion	1093
	rock	Empt	487
		Houn	725
	stone	Bosc	212
brick		Fina	473
cane		Silv	337
	Holmes's	Spec	271
carbine		Sign	155
	short rifle	Houn	700
chair		Chas	575
		Seco	655
cleaver		Engr	283
club			
	bludgeon	Gree	438
		Fina	473
	carved wooden	Croo	415
	claw-like	Veil	1100
	cudget	Stud	45
		Sign	133
		Lady	946
	life-preserver	Bery	316
		Gree	445
		Bruc	930
	stone	Sign	109
collections		Musg	389
		Croo	415
		Abbe	639
	gunroom	Musg	389
		Reig	398
		Abbe	635
		Shos	1111
	Oriental arms	Seco	655
	Peruvian weapons	Suss	1039

Weapons (cont'd)
cudgel	Stud	45
	Sign	133
	Lady	946
dagger	Seco	655
	RedC	909
dart, poisoned	Sign	109
decanter	Abbe	644
dog-whip	Spec	272
	Wist	883
dynamite	RedC	912
elephant gun	Blan	1001
Eley's No. 2 (cartridges)	Spec	265
firearms	Bosc	216
	Vall	828
	Vall	836
	Vall	850
	Vall	852
	Vall	853
	Wist	885
	Thor	1063
flintlock pistol	Houn	674
gunroom	Musg	389
	Reig	398
	Abbe	635
	Shos	1111
pistol	Bosc	216
	Glor	383
	Reig	398
	Resi	429
	Houn	764
	Danc	515
	Danc	518
	Soli	534
	Soli	535

Weapons, firearms, pistol (cont'd)	Chas	581
	Vall	835
	Vall	851
	Vall	863
brace	Thor	1056
	Thor	1069
flintlock	Houn	674
hair-trigger	Musg	386
revolver	Stud	69
	Sign	102
	Sign	145
	RedH	189
	Five	221
	Reig	406
	Houn	754
	Chas	575
	Vall	793
	Vall	816
	Vall	827
	Devi	970
	Maza	1016
	3Gar	1053
	Thor	1064
Holmes's	Sign	98
	Bery	316
	Gree	444
	Fina	472
	Danc	524
	Soli	533
	Houn	756
	Dyin	932
	Lady	951
	Maza	1020
	3Gar	1052
McGinty's	Vall	844
pinfire	Wist	878
six-shooter	Vall	844

Weapons, firearms, revolver (cont'd)

	Watson's	Stud	18
		Sign	135
		RedH	185
		Copp	330
		Empt	488
		Prio	552
		Blac	568
		SixN	591
		Houn	699
		Bruc	925
		3Gar	1052
		Thor	1068
	Eley's No. 2	Spec	265
rifle		Sud	53
		Stud	55
		Stud	60
		Stud	70
		Stud	71
		Sign	146
		Glor	378
		Empt	492
		Houn	700
		Houn	701
		Vall	863
		Blan	1003
carbine		Sign	155
elephant gun		Blan	1001
Jezail		Stud	15
musket		Sign	99
		Sign	144
		Glor	383
		Croo	413
shotgun		Stud	65
		Bosc	203
sawed-off		Vall	779

Weapons, firearms, shotgun (cont'd)
    Winchester

gunpowder
  blasting powder
gunroom

hair-trigger
hammer
harpoon

hatpin
horse whip
hunting crop

    Holmes's

  horse whip
  riding crop
  riding whip

hydraulic press
Jezail (musket)
knife

Vall	840
Vall	844
Glor	385
Vall	852
Musg	389
Reig	398
Abbe	635
Shos	1111
Musg	386
Vall	813
Blac	559
Blac	561
Abbe	645
Shos	1102
Spec	264
Silv	344
Houn	724
RedH	186
Iden	201
SixN	591
Shos	1102
Soli	535
Stud	61
Stud	64
Veil	1100
Engr	282
Stud	15
Stud	48
Sign	145
Sign	147
Sign	150
Glor	375
Glor	385
Gree	446
Nava	461
Norw	503

Weapons, knife (cont'd)

	Blac	563
	Blac	564
	Vall	813
	Vall	852
	Wist	886
	Card	900
	RedC	909
	Lion	1086
cataract	Silv	338
clasp	Blac	571
	SixN	586
dagger	Seco	655
	RedC	909
multiplex	Abbe	642
pen	Blac	564
sealing-wax	Gold	610
sheath	Blac	563
	SixN	592
life-preserver	Bery	316
	Gree	445
	Bruc	930
musket	sign	144
	Glor	383
	Croo	413
oar	Card	900
pinfire revolver	Wist	878
poisoned arrow	Suss	1043
poisoned dart	Sign	109
poker	Stoc	373
	SixN	586
	Abbe	637
	3Gab	1023
pole	Veil	1097
riding crop	Soli	535
riding whip	Stud	66
	Veil	1110
horse whip	Shos	1102

Weapons, riding crop (cont'd)
       hunting crop

Spec	264
Silv	344
Houn	724

     Holmes's

RedH	186
Iden	201
SixN	591

  rock

Empt	487
Houn	725

    boulder

Fina	477
Lion	1093

      stone
sandbag
shotgun

Bosc	212
Wist	874
Stud	65
Bosc	203

     sawed-off
six-shooter
spanner
spear, bamboo
stick

Vall	779
Vall	844
Vall	850
Sign	155
Stud	45
Scan	171
Blue	245
Copp	330
Glor	375
Gree	446
Prio	552
Abbe	638
Vall	839
Illu	993
Maza	1016
Suss	1035
Shos	1110

     Holmes's

Stud	17
Miss	631
Illu	993

Weapons, stick (cont'd)			
Watson's		Sign	98
		Sign	121
		Lady	950
cane		Spec	271
		Silv	337
walking stick		Norw	498
stone		Bosc	212
boulder		Fina	477
		Lion	1093
rock		Empt	487
		Houn	725
van		Fina	473
walking stick		Norw	498
whip		Blac	560
wiper (snake)		Sign	116
wooden leg		Sign	155
Weasel		Sign	115
		Croo	416
Weather (*see* Baker Street)			
Weaver			
hands of		Sign	91
identifiable by tooth		Copp	317
Wedding		Scan	169
		Soli	535
Wei dynasty (China)		Illu	997
Weighing-chair		Silv	336
Weiss & Co.		Silv	342
Welbeck Street		Fina	473
Wellington Street		Twis	241
Wells, artesian		3Gar	1050
Wessex Cup		Silv	336
West Africa		Devi	969
West country		Blac	566
		Houn	764
West End (of London)		Bery	312
		Copp	318

594 ◻ *Good Old Index*

West End (of London) (cont'd)	Resi	427
	Seco	656
	Bruc	926
	3Gab	1031
West Gilmerton General Mining Company	Vall	836
West India Docks	Sign	138
West Indies	Houn	749
West Section Coaling Company	Vall	836
West, Arthur Cadogan	Bruc	914
West, Mrs.	Bruc	915
Westaway's (agency for governesses)	Copp	318
Westbury House festivities	Nobl	289
Westbury, Violet	Bruc	915
Western (Canadian) dialect	Houn	693
Western Morning News (newspaper)	Houn	687
Western Sussex	Musg	388
Westhouse & Marbank	Iden	196
Westminster	Soli	538
	Seco	655
	Bruc	925
Westminster Abbey	Seco	655
Westminster Bridge	Lady	949
Westminster Road	Lady	948
Westminster Stairs	Sign	134
Westminster Wharf	Sign	135
Westmoreland	Houn	695
Westphail, Miss Honoria	Spec	260
Westville Arms (inn)	Vall	785
Whale	Blac	560
Wharfingers	Sign	125
Wheat	Stud	58
Wheat pit	3Gar	1046
Wheel tracks	Stud	32
	Stud	84
	Gree	444
	Prio	547

Wherry	Sign	124
Whimsical happenings	Maza	1014
Whimsical story	3Gar	1044
Whippoorwill	Stud	69
Whiskers (*see* Beards and Whiskers)		
Whisky (*see also* Alcohol)	Stud	42
	Sign	132
	Scan	162
	RedH	189
	Nobl	294
	Blac	562
	Vall	821
	Vall	831
	Vall	837
	Vall	843
	Vall	845
	Vall	854
	Vall	862
whiskey-peg	Sign	145
Whist	Empt	484
	Devi	957
rubber missed	RedH	188
Whistle, in the night	Spec	261
Whitaker's Almanac	Vall	772
White, Abel	Sign	145
White Eagle (tavern)	Sign	122
White Hart (tavern)	Stud	34
White jessamine (perfume)	Houn	765
Whitehall	Gree	436
	Nava	451
	Bruc	914
	Maza	1018
Whitehall Terrace	Seco	651
Whitney, Elias, D.D.	Twis	229
Whitney, Isa	Twis	229
Whitney, Kate	Twis	230
Whittington, Lady Alicia	Nobl	290

Whyte, Gulielmi   Stud   38
Wide-awake (hat)   Yell   352
Wiggins (street Arab)   Stud   42
    Stud   51
    Sign   125
Wigmore Street   Blue   251
Wigmore Street Post Office   Sign   91
Wigwam   Houn   709
Wilcox, Chester   Vall   836
Wild, Jonathan   Vall   777
Wilder, James   Prio   540
Wills
    Baskerville   Houn   681
    deductions from   Norw   501
    French will case   Sign   90
    Garrideb   3Gar   1046
    Hammerford will case   Illu   984
    Holmes's   Fina   480
    Hopkins   RedH   179
    Munro, Effie   Yell   354
    none owing to illiteracy   Soli   537
    Oldacre   Norw   499
    Openshaw   Five   220
    Rucastle   Copp   331
    Stoner, Mrs.   Spec   265
    Uncle Ned   Iden   193
Willaby, Arthur, and brother   Vall   838
Willesden   Bruc   915
Williams (servant)   Sign   101
Williams, Charlie   Vall   849
Williams, James Baker   Wist   876
Williamson (defrocked clergyman)   Soli   531
Will-o'-the-wisp   Bery   311
Willows (doctor)   Bosc   208
Wilson (Archdale)   Sign   151
Wilson (canary trainer)   Blac   559
Wilson (chaplain)   Glor   383

Wilson (constable)	Gold	613
Wilson (district messenger)	Houn	691
Wilson (Scowrer)	Vall	834
Wilson, Batholomew	Vall	827
Wilson, Jabez	RedH	176
Wilson, Sergeant	Vall	781
Wilson, Steve	Vall	858
Wimbledon	Veil	1097
Wimpole Street	Blue	251
Winchester	Copp	319
	Thor	1056
Winchester (race course)	Silv	347
Wind in chimney	Five	218
Windibank, James	Iden	192
Windigate (publican)	Blue	251
Windle, J. W.	Vall	834
Windsor	Bruc	931
Wine (*see* Alcohol)		
Wine cellar	Copp	329
Wine glasses (clue in)	Abbe	641
Winter, James	3Gar	1051
Winter, Kitty	Illu	989
Wiper (viper) (snake)	Sign	116
Wistaria	Cree	1076
Wisteria Lodge	Wist	870
Witchcraft	Vall	774
Woking	Nava	447
Wolfhound	Cree	1072
Woman		
agitated, flown to tea	Croo	417
cleverness of	Scan	175
cunning of	RedC	901
delusion, do not snatch from	Iden	201
drifting and friendless, dangerous class	Lady	942
fascinating and beautiful	Houn	713
impressions of	Twis	239
inscrutable	Seco	657

Woman (cont'd)

insoluble puzzle to the male	Illu	988
instinct of	Scan	173
	Bery	309
	Copp	327
	Vall	847
	3Gab	1032
	Lion	1088
intuition of	Bosc	208
	Twis	239
	Cree	1076
	Lion	1088
motives inscrutable	Seco	657
nose unpowdered, significance	Seco	657
paid reply, never would send	Wist	870
perceptions of	Gree	446
pertinacious	RedC	901
trivial acts, importance of	Seco	657
secretive, naturally	Scan	171
"Woman, The"	Scan	161
Wombwell (George)	Veil	1097
Wood (doctor)	Vall	781
Wood, Henry	Croo	418
Wood, J. G.	Lion	1093
Woodcock	Blue	250
	Nobl	296
Wooden box	Musg	387
Wooden leg	Sign	102
	Sign	110
	Bery	310
	Illu	973
	Reti	1114
Wooden peg	Musg	387
Woodhouse (villain)	Bruc	914
Woodley, Edith	Empt	483
Woodley, Jack	Soli	528
Woodman's Lee	Blac	559

Woolwich	Sign	123
	Bruc	915
Woolwich Arsenal	Bruc	915
Woolwich Station	Bruc	924
Woolwich Theatre	Bruc	916
Worcestershire	Sign	144
Wordsworth Road	Sign	99
Workhouse	Lady	952
Workhouse cough	Sign	133
Workmen, in house, evidence of	Croo	411
World tour	Houn	759
	3Gab	1030
Worm, remarkable, unknown to science	Thor	1055
Worry, effect of	Bery	302
	Bery	307
Worst man in London	Chas	572
Worst tenant in London (Holmes)	Dyin	932
Worthingdon Bank gang	Resi	434
Wreckage, ponderous piece of	Prio	539
Wrestling	Empt	486
Writing, age of man deduced from	Reig	408
Writing, clues from	Sign	96
	Scan	163
	Twis	238
	Reig	408
	Nava	448
	Norw	501
	Vall	769
	Wist	874
	Card	891
	RedC	903
Wright, Theresa	Abbe	638

Other Gasogene Titles Available

0-938501-01-1	*Immortal Sleuth*—Harrison	$24.95
0-938501-00-3	*For the Sake of the Game*—Hammer	$23.95
0-938501-03-8	*The Game is Afoot*—Hammer	$15.95
0-938501-04-6	*London by Gaslight*—Harrison	$24.95
0-938501-05-4	*The Ragged Shaw*—Shaw	$12.95
0-938501-07-0	*Studies in Scarlet*—Monographs	$19.95
0-938501-08-9	*The Twenty-Second Man*—Hammer	$15.95
0-938501-09-7	*Ms. Holmes of Baker Street*—Bradley/Sarjeant	$19.95
0-938501-11-9	*To Play the Game*—Hammer (hard-cover)	$39.95
0-938501-12-7	*To Play the Game*—Hammer (soft-cover)	$19.95
0-938501-13-5	*Doggerel in the Night-Time*—Sage	$10.95
0-938501-14-3	*A Compound of Excelsior*—Rice	$10.95
0-938501-15-1	*Skewed Sherlock*—Hunter/Hammer	$12.95
0-938501-17-8	*The Worth of the Game*—Hammer	$18.95
0-938501-18-6	*The Really Ragged Shaw*—Shaw	$16.95
0-938501-19-4	*The Quest*—Maclaren/Hammer	$15.95

Add $2.75 to each title for shipping and handling, not to exceed $5.50. Iowa residents add 6% sales tax. U.S. Dollars

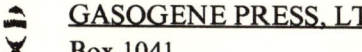

GASOGENE PRESS, LTD.
Box 1041
Dubuque, IA 52001-1041